SURVIVAL
IN THE
CITY

Also by Anthony Greenbank

THE BOOK OF SURVIVAL

MR. TOUGH

Anthony Greenbank

SURVIVAL
IN THE
CITY

HARPER & ROW, PUBLISHERS
NEW YORK, EVANSTON, SAN FRANCISCO, LONDON

SURVIVAL IN THE CITY. Copyright © 1974 by Wolfe Publishing Limited.
All rights reserved. Printed in the United States of America. No part of this
book may be used or reproduced in any manner whatsoever without written
permission except in the case of brief quotations embodied in critical articles
and reviews. For information address Harper & Row, Publishers, Inc.,
10 East 53rd Street, New York, N.Y. 10022.

FIRST U.S. EDITION

Designed by Gwendolyn O. England

Library of Congress Cataloging in Publication Data

Greenbank, Anthony.
   Survival in the city.
   1. Crime prevention.   I. Title.
HV7431.G73 1975   364.4'09173'2   74-1811
ISBN 0-06-011607-2
ISBN 0-06-011612-9 (pbk.)

75 76 77 78 79 10 9 8 7 6 5 4 3 2 1

CONTENTS

PART FIVE: CITY BUSINESSES

Shops, Banks and Offices

PART SIX: CITY LUNGS

Parks and Stadiums

PART SEVEN: CITY BRIGHT LIGHTS

Bars, Diners, Theaters, Clubs

INTRODUCTION

BIG CITY here you come—like a lamb to the slaughter. Everyone is vulnerable in so many ways in the oppressive canyons, gorges and ravines of the concrete jungle. This book tells you how to survive despite yourself.

New York. London. Paris. Rome. Any mighty conurbation poses daily threats which escalate into imminent danger when we, our own worst enemies, leap into the fray and unknowingly side with the forces against us. Yet it is not so much the pressure which cities impose on their victims that causes the damage as the wildly irrational and illogical behavior of the victims in the first place.

We have only to read between the headlines. MAN SHOT (he carried a gun swearing no one would ever rob him). GIRL RAPED (followed from the subway by a suspicious-looking man; she wouldn't talk to him, then thought, "What kind of person am I?"). BUS KILLS (vain, he had been mesmerized by his reflection in a store window during rush hour). WAR HERO SLAIN (his mother said he was tired of life and needed someone else to pull the trigger—which someone did when he set about a robbery). CRIPPLE BURGLARIZED (she had a Doberman pinscher but limped out with it at the same time each evening—when the felon chose to break in).

YOU too can be the architect of your own downfall. We are all vulnerable and easy prey to devils of our own creation.

It is a fact that absolutely anyone in a massive city can all too easily invite and shape the emergencies and disasters which may befall him. When it does happen, we frequently have only ourselves to blame.

Yet only too often we don't know just where we are at our weakest. If we do, we choose to ignore it. For death wishes vary from the mild tempting of fate to the crazy airplane hijacker.

A certain type of person, for example, has been found to seek out jobs and situations which can more easily lead to his becoming the target of criminals. He can then press home his disadvantage by they-asked-for-it behavior and compound the weaknesses which can only draw disaster in the city.

Nor is the gentlest temper of fate ever exempt from sudden and self-inflicted crisis in a savage form. Not when, in America alone, there are nearly a million known crimes a year—15,000 murders, 120,000 aggravated assaults, 17,000 rapes, 90,000 robberies, 40,000 larcenies, 900,000 burglaries. Over 200,000 criminals are in state and federal prisons; more than 600,000 mentally sick persons are locked up in hospitals. Think of the countless millions of psychos, sadists and unbalanced people, some extremely dangerous, roaming the streets each day—many armed with deadly weapons.

Survival in the City covers all forms of personal frailties, whether physical, mental or spiritual. We are all Losers in one way or another even when all seems to be going our way. Here we see how to become Winners in the very areas where we reveal perfectly normal and understandable human weaknesses.

The real Winners are as vulnerable as the rest of us, only they know their weak spots. By reading their Loser instincts correctly they overlay the damage potential of harmful tendencies with a veneer of Winning characteristics. In this way we see the Winner's ultimate urban defense: never to place himself in hostile circumstances if it is possible to avoid them.

You will object that we cannot change our basic characters. The person who is very much a GOOD SAMARITAN (a Loser) will always want to help the old lady lying on the sidewalk—a potentially hostile situation that could have been staged by pickpockets or muggers. However, as the Loser responses flash, "Lift her up," the Winner instincts—in this case the COLD-BLOODED Winner—will urge, "Use the one-handed wallet-clutch when you help her in case she is one of a gang." And so the original Loser is spared in spite of himself.

Books which advise that the non-agile and non-brave can become superheroes in times of city stress are shamefully misleading.

If it is not in a person to defend himself when face to face with calamity, he will have little chance if he tries. If, for example, you are elderly, ailing, failing, sick, partially crippled or pregnant and you come face to face with a brutal mugger, there is every chance your puny resistance will be punished by an even more cruel and vicious assault.

Here, instead, is full and practical advice on how to blend *and* bend. How to fit into the city scene until you are invisible; how to give way and survive, when catastrophe does arise, like the reed which survived a flood (while the log which offered resistance to a force far greater than itself was ripped in half by the waters).

For those who have a heart-of-oak disposition, however—bloody-minded, stubborn and inclined to retaliate—and whom nothing on earth will stop in their urge to fight, here is how to fight right. Be it fire, famine, flood or forays and punchups on the streets, in bars, in elevators, in the rear seats of automobiles or in bedrooms . . . here is how to carry out survival techniques never before packed together between the covers of one book.

It is the REAL mark of the Winner, and the whole message of this volume, that you should avoid last-ditch measures at all costs. It is only by blending with the wallpaper that you can survive in the city.

Just imagine yourself a complete stranger to the big city. Read the book quickly. Then go back through the *odd*-numbered chapters again. These cover our personal weaknesses in different sections of the city from Chapter 1, which deals with airports and bus depots, to Chapter 13, bars, restaurants, theaters and clubs. Tick those vulnerabilities which seem most applicable to you. Follow the cross references from each Loser situation you're likely to be in to the appropriate Winner techniques. These, again, are arranged by parts of the city, from terminals in Chapter 2 to bright lights in Chapter 14.

Here is an example. If you are elderly, fragile, suffering from a disability and in pain at the airport—all these are Losing traits covered in Chapter 1. You will then be referred to Chapter 2 (Terminals) where THE SHEEP, THE CANNY, THE LEERY and THE NERVOUS are the Winner techniques which concern you. Now, by giving yourself and loved ones a repeated dose of the stuff of Winners—wherever it may be applicable—you become much safer in the city.

Unfortunately, we have short memories; we are quick to forget vital truths we may have heard about, but which have not yet concerned us directly.

Survival in the City sets out to overcome this attitude by its arrangement. Here we can prepare for any city zone before we head into it. (You are taking a child to a football game in a crowded stadium: then read Chapters 11 and 12 and those sections of other chapters to which you are referred by the ever backtracking cross-references.) Yes, from Chapter 11 we will be referred to THE LEERY—just one instance—in Chapter 1, where key advice is given on keeping your money safe as well as what to do when the child wants to use the toilet and is of the other sex.

Hundreds of thousands of otherwise sensible and mature people will always attract trouble in an urban society, just as the lamb draws the wolf. Yet by more searching examination of ourselves, we need not number among them. We cannot change our weaknesses, but we can learn to live more safely with them.

The only sure way of avoiding disaster in the city is by not creating crises ourselves. Cut down the number of our vulnerabilities by half and we halve the odds of being killed, maimed, robbed or terrified out of our wits. We can expect to go twice as long without coming to harm.

Survival in the City will show YOU how to slice these weaknesses, not merely by a half, but by a full 99 per cent.

Part One

CITY
TERMINALS

Plane, Boat, Bus and Train

1

CITY TERMINALS

LOSERS

Big city here you are! Shepherded in a flock from baggage claim to customs, stiff and rumpled, grubby and weary, will YOU be an instant victim, fleeced from the start by the waiting wolves?

A suitcase can be stolen, a wallet lifted, a child snatched—or an argument may end in a knifing. Or you may be a runaway teenager picked up by a pimp, possibly even the gray-suited executive taken in a confidence trick. Such things happen when travelers are penned in an airport because of a grounded plane, or when we simply walk through the maw of an immense bus or train station.

How do we avoid calamity? By *expecting* train and bus stations to be in sleazy areas (they often are), and international airports to receive us in our weakest condition (long flights stress our bodies) and everything to go wrong. Winners anticipate the worst, so as to get there one step ahead.

The Shattered (Dog-Tired)

Are the most commonly vulnerable of 200 million people arriving in large cities each year. Three thousand miles by bus or plane will leave anyone feeling weak.

SIGNS AND SYMPTOMS

Thinking of a charter flight across the Atlantic in terms of the image the admen have created . . . the jet journey into a setting sun. Bitterly resenting the elbows sticking into you or the attache case that keeps you from stretching your legs. Hating the neighbor who snores/smokes/talks. Letting rugs, pillows or a magazine lie on the floor where dropped—though you could still do with them. Screwing up eyes in disgust at the fantastic gold sheen of dawn at 30,000 feet.

CAUSES

Many of us cannot sleep at strange times outside our normal nightly schedule. Even if we snatch a quick nap, the constant noise, movement and never-quite-dark conditions of traveling reduce it to such a shallow pitch it gives us little rest.

It is also impossible to sleep when we are afraid of missing a bus or train stop, scared of being interfered with, or terrified of waking to find the plane or train about to crash.

Senior citizens face a harder time because, even though they need less sleep they get tired quicker and have so much less resilience than the young.

We are also vulnerable after taking drugs for travel sickness. *And* after drinking alcohol. Drink plus pills makes for bad judgment and mental confusion—and still keeps us from deep slumber.

It is also a fact that women a day or two before their period often suffer from premenstrual tension; this is aggravated by travel. It is the time of month when (statistically) they are most likely to have an accident or a breakdown.

The strain of a long journey will almost certainly mean one or more of the following reactions: irritation, headaches, jitteriness, vertigo, anxiety, depression, backache, lethargy, belligerence—all aggravated by the lack of satisfactory sleep.

ILLOGICAL BEHAVIOR

Every exhausted person arriving in the city is a victim of his whims, none of which has much reasoning behind it. All are born of fatigue and disorientation.

The very hugeness of a city terminal can quickly confuse and intimidate the old, nervous, sick, very young or plain unready. Upper and lower levels, passageways leading off in all directions, notices showing directions which don't seem clear, and confusing messages over public address systems—all these can hurry us into rash decisions and faulty judgments. Too often we did not anticipate the enormous complexity of a vast terminal, but simply considered it as a stopping-off or stepping-off point en route.

We lacked the energy to go to the rest room on the plane because there was a long line, yet we stampede from the aircraft as soon as it stops.

This kind of inconsistency is typical. We conform when we should branch out and rebel when it is safer and more sensible to conform.

If we use the terminal rest rooms we face more risk than if we had gone on the plane/bus/train—from pickpockets, purse snatchers, homosexuals and panhandlers who aggressively demand money. And suppose you are traveling with a child of the opposite sex? If your little boy, say, does now need to use the bus depot rest room and is too old to go into the ladies' with you, he will have to use the men's without your being there—always a risk in city toilets where degenerates pose as ordinary-looking, harmless citizens.

That urge to rush from the plane was also illogical. After all, the first person into the baggage claim must still stand and wait until his suitcases catch up—so he might as well have been last.

It is also easier for a pickpocket to dip a hand into your pockets in the crush than when you have waited for everyone else to leave. All he has to do is cover his actions with a rug, pillow, magazine or large Kleenex held casually in the other hand. And you never know until too late.

We are as vulnerable in the baggage claim. It is a failing of the tired that they dump their hand luggage—a briefcase, say—on the floor and momentarily forget about it. Suddenly, distraction— a drunk riding noisily round and round the luggage carousel. While your attention is focused elsewhere the briefcase is taken, carried to a distant corner, opened, emptied of blank checks, airline tickets, personal credentials etc. and then replaced while your back is still turned.

While you feel too sleepy to watch closely for a suitcase to appear after 2,000 miles by bus—and so allow the suitcase snatcher to reach it first and hurry it out through the barrier flashing a phony claim ticket—your temper flares when someone accidentally treads on your shoe. Then an equally at-the-end-of-his-tether passenger swings the punch which began with your push.

Any long trip will bring you to the nervous, weary state where you raise, very quickly, the Devil. It aggravates every other weakness you have as you enter the city.

Remedy: The Sheep, p. 28

The Fearful (Scared Stiff)

See threats at every step, vulnerable points inside them by the dozen, and crises to come by the score.

Does your imagination work overtime? Is this feeling of alarm really warranted? It can be as bad to undermine your confidence by imagining unreal dangers as it is to fail to see the real ones.

SIGNS AND SYMPTOMS

Feeling trapped and staying close to the pillars and walls of the reception halls. Taking the most circuitous paths to walk short distances. Constantly moving around shops, telephone booths and rest rooms without using any of them. Plus a racing pulse, throbbing temples, sweaty hands, dry fingertips, parched mouth, squeaky voice and butterflies in the bowels.

CAUSES

The reason you're afraid does not have to be that you are terrified of the abortion you are going to have in the city. Or that you expect the police to seize you at the airport ahead.

It is most probably because you have never been to a huge city before and are suffering from a type of neophobia: the fear of anything new.

We all tend to magnify fear of the unknown. This means that fear can take over and control our behavior; we begin to react to the thoughts and feelings that cause the fear rather than to the actual problems. When fancy distorts moderate danger into a major crisis, behavior can become abnormal.

What do you actually fear?

Being alone, because you have no friends in the city? Suffering at the hands of muggers/rapists/mobs? Discomfort because you have little money and are not sure how to survive? Are you afraid that someone will laugh at you, causing loss of face or ridicule? Or do you dread inconveniencing or worrying others? Do you lack confidence in your personal fortitude and ability?

It should be encouraging to know such fears are usually groundless. Yet the truly frightened person may still be broken despite the best assurances.

We must recognize that basic fears do exist and that under stress we are at the mercy of our minds.

ILLOGICAL BEHAVIOR

The feelings of unreality and panic, the desire to escape, grow as the plane or bus nears the city. It is easy to feel is this really happening to me? But it is at the terminal that your behavior becomes really illogical and you tempt fate.

Suffering from the desperate need to get it over with fast, you may be terrified and find excuses by which you can always claim the city never gave you a chance.

YOU find ways in which, it seems, your destiny is taken from your hands—a direct result of that numbing inner fright which may show itself in a mild or an extreme form.

It may even be that you beg to be found out. You open the suitcase which has gold watches in the lining of its lid in front of the customs officer before he asks, or you tell the immigration official a lie he can easily check up on.

When the worst does happen, the frightened person is unlikely to have allies who will intervene or be a moral support—even though they are among the people who have sat near him or her for hours on a long journey.

The reason is that when you are scared stiff, your irritation with others whose mannerisms annoy you is obvious. Although you never realize it, this just adds to your troubles by increasing hostility. And others in the same boat as yourself—new arrivals to the city—just will not want to know about your problems.

Remedy: The Nervous, p. 52

The Relieved (Euphoric)

Cannot believe their luck in arriving at the airport or the bus station. They are as vulnerable as spring lambs because of this heady joy.

SIGNS AND SYMPTOMS

Floating on cloud nine as you struggle with suitcases. Flying in a seventh heaven during a long delay at the customs barrier. Hugging yourself instead of the stewardess. Grinning massively when the terminal cop snarls, "Waddya think I am, a walking clock?" as you ask him the time.

CAUSES

If you suffer from the phobia that tops the terror league—the fear of flying—the best part of a plane trip is the relief that it's over.

This dread of crashing, pain or death can be so intense that the feeling of elation on arriving safely is like no other you have ever known.

Anything, however, which makes you wildly happy in the city will also make you vulnerable—whether you are meeting someone you love, have successfully run drugs/rings/gems past the customs or have simply waited 50 years to reach this tremendous city and have finally made it.

ILLOGICAL BEHAVIOR

Your guard is down and you fail to see threats which *do* exist in city terminals.

Normally you are more alert, but there is a danger you will say "Sure" once too often when you are very happy. It can be your undoing in various ways.

The euphoric 45-year-old who says "Sure" to the girl who asks for a hand with a heavy suitcase forgets that after 40 you have to be more careful. His sudden and over-enthusiastic effort puts a violent strain on his heart. He collapses with a coronary.

Anyone who is elated will say "Sure" when someone asks him to watch his bags while he goes to the rest room. But there is risk in doing even this favor. That person could be one of a gang of baggage stealers. Shortly after he leaves you with his suitcases, another member of the troupe walks past, picking the bags up as he/she goes. Distracted, you chase after her to explain her mistake. A third colleague now steals your bags.

It is also easy to say "Sure" when the old man asks if you know the way to the rest rooms with facilities for the disabled. As you turn to point the way his accomplice fits his extra-large suitcase over yours. His bag will have a false bottom and powerful springs in the sides which grip your suitcase as he lifts it and walks away. And he will have time, because that old man pretends he is deaf and it takes him time to understand you.

You say "Sure" too when someone in the next rest room toilet drops a pocketful of coins and asks you to hand back the ones that roll into your stall. Your quickness to please blinds you to everything but bending down, scooping up the money and dropping it into the hand reaching under the wall. It certainly does not strike you that he may have an accomplice who is now leaning over the other wall of your toilet—who slips your wallet from the jacket hanging on the door.

It is this "Sure, sure" attitude which will make you a victim of

Thieves often use false-bottomed suitcases which they slip over yours.

the professional burglar who visits airports to check affluent-looking new arrivals.

If YOU fit his bill—if your clothes are beautifully cut and your suitcases expensive—he simply hands you a billfold he says he has found. He is rushing for a plane, he says, and he asks you to do him a favor and hand the billfold in to the terminal police. Oh —and can he have your address in case there is a reward to share?

The contents of the billfold are worthless in comparison to your name and the name of your hotel, or the address of your apartment—which is ransacked later.

Remedy: The Leery, p. 47; The Confused, p. 59

The Bored (Grounded)

Have seen it all before simply because one terminal is the same as any other. And now, because of a delay caused by airport fog or a train connection hours away, they yearn for pastures new.

SIGNS AND SYMPTOMS

Slickly planning to board a plane at the last minute by telephoning the airline from the airport and asking for a *guaranteed* reservation (you agree to pay if you miss the flight) as "my chauffeur is waiting outside and can reach the airport in ten minutes"; then walking to the front of the line waiting for possible standby seats at the ticket counter and saying you have a reservation and collecting your ticket. And then, after this small triumph . . . being grounded en route in a city terminal where the only diversion is trying to spot hijackers from a magazine article which says they are shy, extremely soft-spoken, probably small, unathletic and clumsy and that they will be wearing sports shirts and slacks on a winter flight because they know the plane is going to the sun.

CAUSES

The more well-traveled you are, the more likely you are to become bored during long terminal delays.

Having survived so far in cities without really experiencing a frightening incident breeds a confidence which has nothing to do with logic or probability. Reflexes are developed which you imagine will pilot you through dangerous situations without your having to think.

But you can be caught off balance by the frustration which aggravates boredom into something quite unbearable. And you may, in some way, have encouraged and brought on this frustration because you know your way around too well.

Many seasoned travelers try to create diversions on a trip. It is when these backfire that they leave you feeling more thwarted than ever.

An example is the businessman who regularly picks up girls on planes by always being the last person on board.

This gives him the pick of all unaccompanied women, because men will not normally choose seats next to attractive females sitting on their own. As last passenger, however, breathing hard after his effort to catch the plane in time, he has every excuse. Only on this flight the girl he chooses to sit next to is the supreme bore. Charged high at first, his trip has now fallen flat. The plane is grounded en route in winter murk and there is no relief in sight.

He does not realize that his insistence on seeking frivolous diversion is responsible for his feeling let down—and for a state of mind which may now reach for more harmful distractions.

ILLOGICAL BEHAVIOR

The biggest threat a bored person can face at the terminal is to leave it. Venturing into the city to kill the dragging hours means taking risks in the dangerous areas hard by bus and train stations.

That these are so obviously skid row or red light areas will not for one moment deter the truly bored male seeking entertainment. He will stride past the misfits and vagrants and drinkers, intent on hunting down the most incredibly risk-crammed prey: *any*thing by which he can kill the barren hours of waiting.

Moreover, there is every incentive for a man to stay in these seamy zones. They are so near and he may like the feeling of knowing the station is close at hand.

Backed by this comfort, the bored male quickly sets sail for trouble, drinking in sordid bars and clubs. Even if it is only passing static with prostitutes, perverts, panhandlers, hucksters, swindlers, muggers or drunks, it all makes a stranger—with his polished shoes and pressed suit—more vulnerable and liable to meet the trouble he invites. The denizens of such districts may make you a target of abuse, suspicion, belligerence and possibly violence.

Risk exists too when it is impossible to leave a terminal. The airport is closed down for 24 hours because of a strike, say, and planes are stranded. Limousines, buses and supply trucks can't get in through the pickets; everyone is stuck.

They run out of commodities: food, coffee, booze, Cokes, candy, toilet paper, paper towels and patience. All the benches are taken and the only sleeping space is on the stone floor or balanced on suitcases.

Here it is the hardened traveler who, among a nucleus of other tough nuts, may suggest a game of cards to kill time. Yet the rule is simple: never play friendly games of cards with strangers.

Card cheats, who make over $20,000,000 a year, are always on the move. On bus, boat, plane or train they look for the fast pickup action which you are now proposing. For it is hardly ever they who get the cards out, but . . . YOU, asking if they have any.

Once upon a time card cheats picked your wallet, examined it for indications of your worth, then returned it saying it had been "found"—and gently steered you into a crooked game. Today they simply ask about your family: this is disarming, helps them gauge your probable means and decide whether to maneuver you into proposing a game.

Remedy: The Sheep, p. 28; The Leery, p. 47; The Confused, p. 59

The Algophobiac (Ailing)

Are vulnerable because they will do anything for a quiet life, a most dangerous characteristic in the city.

Algophobia is the fear of pain. It is always present when someone who is new to crutches or a folding wheelchair has to travel. Watch out for it too when you are simply old, arthritic or carrying twins and near your time.

SIGNS AND SYMPTOMS

The pain, of course. But an even greater dread of incurring extra and excruciating pain that can rocket through your system

in a flash . . . so complete resignation when the stewardess brings
you coffee instead of the tea you wanted; inability to concentrate
on filling in the customs declaration form; only half-watching the
midflight film in case enjoying it too much will bring the ache
back.

CAUSES

The stress of jet fatigue (pilots get it) will take up to two weeks
to disappear in someone who is fit and well. So we already begin
with a handicap when broken bones have still to knit, a wound
has yet to heal or our babies are almost ready to appear.

The reason is that the rhythms in our bodies—already under the
strain of pain—are upset even more by the stresses of long journeys. Trips by bus or train are hell for the non-fit; long-distance
flying is even worse.

Long-distance flights cause psychological and chemical changes
in the body which impair our faculties—from blunting romantic
drive to altering the regularity of our bowels. Many such rhythms
are affected—normal resistance to infection, blood pressure, mood,
pulse rate, respiratory rate, blood sugar level, ability to handle
drugs. All these rise and fall over the ordinary 24-hour day.

Flying affects these rhythms because they are fundamental to
our bodies. They shift only gradually to a new time zone. On
eastbound flights, for example, when you are adding hours to
your day, they may take 14 days to resynchronize. Westbound
flights are easier.

Most of us ignore our 24-hour changes. We time our activities
according to the imperatives of society, and slot ourselves into
the schedule.

But, unlike mechanical clocks, our bodies will not adjust instantly—as a lengthy trip shows. Travelers who have crossed time
zones and who are phase-shifting may have an altered response
to their usual medications.

ILLOGICAL BEHAVIOR

Anyone who suffers—even temporarily—from recurrent pain may easily develop a dangerously passive nature.

It shows when we expect people to take pity on us because of a missing leg, a bandaged head or a well-advanced pregnancy. Our attitude, really, is to do *nothing*, to seek the quiet life. By keeping as inert as possible, we think the pain will stay away—and other people will know of our predicament and help us.

But in the city terminal baggage thieves, pickpockets, taxicab touts and other villains immediately spot this passivity.

While our mind is on pain, we cannot pay full attention to the basic elements of city survival. So they hustle, bump, bang and barge into us all the more.

Therefore we get hustled into taking a limousine ride from the airport to the city when we cannot afford it. The ride costs ten times as much as the airport bus, but the driver is so aggressively persuasive we give in.

We cannot handle our luggage and so trust total strangers who offer to carry the bags—not safe in the city!

The man with his left arm in a sling will still keep his wallet in his inner right-hand jacket pocket—as usual—because it hurts too much to try placing it elsewhere. Now, however, it is that much more difficult to reach. As he fumbles for, then with it, he is sure to flash its whereabouts and availability.

A pickpocket bangs into him two minutes later. And all the wallet owner can think about is pain. The thief apologizes profusely, sets the sling straight, sliding out the wallet as he does so, brushes the victim down and sets him on his way once more.

Of course, when you are forewarned you may decide to arm yourself as a compensation for your general disability; you will show them. It is a dangerous idea because of the ways in which pain will trigger temper.

If your path is blocked by a panhandler bumming coins or a taxicab driver touting a hotel, it is not too serious a matter. Yet the pain suddenly produced as they jostle you can make you bring out the tear-gas aerosol and squirt it.

The result is YOU are arrested and charged with assault, violation of the weapons law and violation of an administrative code for possessing a tear-gas weapon. Possible sentence: a jail term of up to two and a half years.

Fear of pain makes us expose ourselves to risk when we try to alleviate it at all costs. We will suffer much more as a result.

Remedy: The Sheep, p. 28; The Canny, p. 40; The Leery, p. 47; The Nervous, p. 52

The Trusting (Sincere)

Can be a grave danger to themselves and their loved ones in the city. Artlessness and ingenuousness will always lose against the artful and ingenious.

SIGNS AND SYMPTOMS

Thinking in terms of "the old one-two" when you see punches being swapped by the terminal newsstand (and not knowing it is "the old one-three"; the opponent usually replies with the "two" punch). Presuming the man with the deep knife scar on his face in the bus depot must be really tough (not so, it is the one who gave him the scar to watch out for).

CAUSES

Honest as they come, you like to believe others are honest too—you are unable and unwilling to believe the harsh reality of life in the city.

This ostrich-with-its-head-in-the-sand attitude is unrealistic. It holds a hidden menace.

It is often the escapist, forever running away from his problems, who puts on a *show* of being utterly trusting, kind and sincere as a kind of compensation for his insecurity.

ILLOGICAL BEHAVIOR

A man who takes everything on trust is lens-clear to villains.

The expectation that city criminals will look spotty, shifty-eyed and mean is not justified. These are the failures—or they may be guilty of nothing more than an inferiority complex caused by their appearance.

The city's worst wolves, on the contrary, wear sheep's clothing. Dressing quietly. Talking softly. Courteous and kind. Possibly silver-haired and distinguished. So diffident—and deadly.

It is they who are likely to rob your briefcase as you wait in the baggage claim (see THE SHATTERED, p. 3). And you will never suspect them. You will be amazed, however, at how they moved in so quickly.

For your faith in baggage locks is also wrong. They are notoriously frail, pickable by an expert in seconds. There are hundreds of thousands of examples of expensive executive-styled briefcases which—so very sleek with heavy metal rim and monogram by the two keyholes—can be opened simply by inserting a paper clip and turning it like a key.

Expecting card sharps to have squinty eyes and pasty complexions—presumably the result of long, hard nights in smoke-filled rooms under glaring lights—will see you into trouble again.

The card game in which you lose your shirt/tie/shoes at the bus depot looks like an ordinary one. Nothing criminal about this soldier, that sales rep, those three college boys.

So you trust the soldier who wins your all, but who then relents and rips up your check—"because it's Thanksgiving." What he has done is palmed the check and torn up some other piece of paper—to prevent your telephoning your bank to stop payment.

Nor do the city wolves have to be male. According to FBI records violence and crime committed by women are rising. Women who split away from their time-hewn woman's-place demesne can be a great deal rougher than men.

The result is that your suitcase is stolen even when you left it in what you thought was the safety of the back of baggage lockers at the bus or train station.

Terminal baggage lockers lock when you insert a coin and twist and then withdraw the key. But it is possible for someone who has previously used the locker to make a duplicate key. She is there now as you arrive in search of an empty locker.

If she thinks your baggage worth robbing she only has to open her locker, pull out a suitcase and say "All yours." She comes back to rob your bag after you have gone.

Remedy: The Canny, p. 40; The Leery, p. 47; The Confused, p. 59

The Peacock (Flashy)

Care about their appearance too much. This attitude can lead to behavior so irrational that it will create crises in the city.

SIGNS AND SYMPTOMS

A rubber band around your passport so that no one can get a peep at your age or non-pinup photo. A $100 bill wrapped around a wad of toilet paper so your billfold looks rich. Costly suitcases holding cheap personal effects. Cheap suitcases with the maker's name taken off and costly baggage manufacturers' name tags stuck back on. Never keeping money in the side pockets of the trousers because it spoils the line of your suit.

CAUSES

Such vanity is based on a very strong desire to make yourself out to be that bit grander than you really are.

We all have, at times, a dread of losing face. We like others to think we can afford the best—even when we cannot. We are all over-self-conscious at times.

You may decide to buy a pair of new shoes for your sojourn in the city, but first you shine the old, cracked ones. Not to impress yourself. You already know the truth. But THEM, the shoe store sales staff.

Arriving in the city bustle, you are determined to make your mark, your presence felt. With all the outward finery you cannot, perhaps, really afford.

ILLOGICAL BEHAVIOR

There is a great tendency to make yourself a victim when you think you know you are looking your best and standing out from all the rest.

You will go to extremes to assert your image. Especially when you are with others who look presentable and affluent. And who may be looked on as competition.

It is *so human* to flash a fake-flush billfold more than necessary. It happens every hour.

It is madness which makes you overlook the fact that criminals take jets the same way cops ride subways. A pickpocket—and he will be a good one; that's how he can afford to fly—has you lined up at his leisure once he sees the wealth you carry. If he decides to steal it, it will simply be a bonus for him as he goes on his way to the more serious business of picking pockets at some big city race track.

The rush on leaving the plane; the crowds milling on a station concourse; a packed ship's deck as an ocean liner churns toward the city skyline. . . . All are ideal setups for the pickpocket and his colleagues.

Think of how suddenly seeing a glob of spit or splash of bird-lime staining your best coat will momentarily stun you . . .

Sneak thieves know just how hypnotized YOU will be. So they contrive such a situation.

One of them builds up a mouthful of saliva and shoots it at you as he passes—accidentally, of course. Two well-dressed strangers instantly rush up, tut-tutting all the while, as they clean away the mess with handy Kleenex. And then, as they move around you, they pick every pocket clean in the process.

In the case of the birdlime, forget the seagulls above. It is shot from a splatter-gun held in the thief's palm: a plastic capsule containing a mixture of starch, milk of magnesia and egg yolk.

We can also hurt ourselves physically by overindulging our vanity.

We may slip a disc or become hernia victims while bending down to lift heavy suitcases. Scared of spoiling the scalpel-sharp trouser creases, we keep our legs straight and bend our backs as we stoop to lift—the most dangerous way of handling an awkward weight.

Then there is the elderly man who helps a pretty girl with her case (see also THE RELIEVED, p. 8) and either permanently damages his lower back or suffers a coronary. The suitcase is far weightier than he imagined, but his vanity will not let him put it down—the vanity of the not-so-young who still pretend they are lamb, not mutton.

The dread of looking middle-aged makes a woman wear brand-new contact lenses instead of her glasses as she arrives in the city. Her eyes now feel as if she has been up all night having the corneas sandpapered. They give her a confused, blurry and painful first view of the city terminal. She has set herself up for the kill.

Remedy: The Canny, p. 40

The Bewildered (Runaways)

Are at once vulnerable because they look it. Any young girl or boy running away from home is likely to fall prey to the very nastiest breed of city wolf.

SIGNS AND SYMPTOMS

Buying dark glasses in the terminal drugstore so people cannot tell how young you are. Loitering in the huge reception areas where anonymity makes you feel safer. But wishing you did not feel so shy, anxious, travel-creased and bewildered. Looking at departure boards for the next train or bus *back*. Fingering the penknife in your pocket with which you are prepared to slash any policeman who spots you and tries to get you into a patrol car—because you just aren't ready to go home yet.

CAUSES

The teenage runaway daughter (or "mystery") is always pulled willy-nilly by the magnet of the big city. Dropping out on Broadway has to be better than dropping out in Cabbageville. Cabbageville being home wherever it may be.

The home life that may have been unhappy, deadly boring or too disciplined; the first love affair that curdled; the job or non-job you hated; that dreaded day-to-day of the home town. . . . Any of these might seem to be a good reason to run away to the city. Or you may have been on the road for some time and have now, too proud to face your folks, drifted to the great metropolis.

Often a distressed father or mother appears in the city, clutching a photograph and going from policeman to policewoman to find if the runaway has been seen.

Yet they get little comfort. For in most countries the police are not obliged—cannot afford—to launch a massive search for a young person unless a serious crime or danger is suspected. Even if the child is under 16.

For police experience shows that most girls, even of only 15, who run away are mature for their age, well aware of what they are doing, and do not want to return.

Well aware of what they are doing up to a point, that is. . . .

ILLOGICAL BEHAVIOR

Lack of knowledge of how the city ticks forces the runaway to hang around the crowds at a terminal or in the areas nearby.

You do not know where to go, nor do you know anyone who can tell you. But the fact you have got here by your own initiative may give you a false confidence that, because you have managed so far, you can make out. But you know nothing, yet, of human nature.

As a newcomer to the city, on the run from home, you will find the metropolis will alienate you even further. No welcome here. Arriving in the labyrinths of the concrete jungle with no money and no place to go means survival by resort to petty crime. To hustling, or pushing drugs, or worse. It is impossible to build up regular relationships in this situation because—all too frequently— you end up conning your acquaintances in petty crime in order to survive.

You are easy prey for the wolves battening on youth and in- experience.

There are the peddlers who must have new flesh for the porno magazine and blue film trade, with its turnover of millions of dollars a year. They are constantly on the lookout for the fresh "meat" by which they make their living . . . the young girl who, in her desperation, can be induced to satisfy the strange appetites of their customers.

The approach is skillful, smooth and well-timed. You know no one in the city? You have nowhere to stay? Or you have some- where to go, but need directions? The friendly procurer or pimp can offer help—from lemon tea in the coffee house to having an aunt who will accommodate you.

Perhaps you expect such an approach from a stranger; and you are prepared to go along.

Or conversely, you may have no choice in the matter. You have loitered in the bus station concourse for hours. And now—sud- denly—two men approach you. One picks up your single suitcase, the other grabs one of your hands, wrests it up high behind your back and propels you between them out into the street and toward the waiting car . . . all before you had time to utter the slightest sound. It has happened so fast.

You fail to spot the far-reaching implications of what a terminal pickup can bring. . . . A hell on earth that starts from the moment you leave the bus, plane, train or ship. Stowaways are included.

Remedy: The Sheep, p. 28; The Leery, p. 47; The Confused, p. 59

The Wise Guy (Grasping)

Will be far more vulnerable than that man-about-town appear- ance suggests—because of his basic dishonesty.

SIGNS AND SYMPTOMS

Always carrying a $100 bill on flights because the stewardess is instructed to give free drinks if the passenger has no smaller bills or change.

Telephoning the airline to book 12 seats under fictitious names when you are eligible for a reduced standby plane fare because you are a student/soldier/senior citizen—and so ensuring that 12 seats will be empty just before takeoff and you will be offered that cheap standby seat.

CAUSES

Someone who is "smart" and wants to show he knows all the ropes automatically gives something else away to the person who is trained to spot it. He gives away a strong desire to get something for nothing, or for considerably less than what it is worth.

Anyone nurturing such a calculating attitude shows that he is ready to cut corners in pursuit of any project that will fetch a fast buck.

Con men know their natural "marks." They recognize what they call "larceny in the heart." That is why the toughest policeman reserves a soft spot for them; he knows that those they fleece most are the greediest and stupidest rogues.

This is the basis of the con trick, which is quite different from the swindle.

The swindle is when you are taken in over something which is misrepresented to you. If, say, you buy a costly souvenir of the city from a well-dressed huckster at the airport and then find on the plane that it is so much rubbish under the wrapper, that is a swindle. You were gullible but not greedy.

A confidence trick, however, is when you fall in with a scheme by which you stand to gain tainted money. Moreover, it can only work in a devious and roundabout way.

YOU won't be caught, though, with your quick-witted appraisal of the *clever* way to make out.

ILLOGICAL BEHAVIOR

First, you feel immune to ever being taken by a con man. You are the con man's "dream"; you invariably feel superior to more slow-brained mortals.

This is so dangerously illogical an attitude that it is worth seeing just how the trickster works.

That he *does* work at terminals is certain. Attracted by the tens of thousands of people coming in here every few hours, how can he miss? With his many ploys, he will always convince the "smartie"—YOU—that the money to be gained in such and such a venture is certain. Yet the fact is that the only easy money he is after is *yours*.

He will feel immensely superior to you; but he never shows it. Instead, he will win your friendship by playing himself down.

Also, as he always reads the *Reader's Digest* (and has done so for years), he has stock conversation gleaned from this source which will fit naturally into your own experiences, occupation and intentions.

Now, by offering you something of the same value as a patch of blue sky, he has the faculty of working on your blind side and making YOU behave like Mr. Tassle from Corntown.

In the most amazing ways. . . .

But always it will be by keeping his own personality invisible. The con man mirrors back at you the attributes you admire. It is yourself you are seeing, and when suddenly asked to hand over money, you do.

So beware the con man's plausibility, shrewdness, agility, acting ability—and the "grift," or sixth sense, which spots the larceny in your heart, no matter how deeply you may think it's hidden.

Remedy: The Confused, p. 59

The Unassuming (Poor)

Need not be poverty-stricken, but a strong inferiority complex makes them feel second-best. When actions are allowed to match these thoughts, behavior can become alarming.

SIGNS AND SYMPTOMS

Asking permission from the person behind to tilt the bus or plane seat back. Not ringing for service on a charter flight because the stewardess may be busy at the far end of the plane. Not collecting your bags first time round in the baggage claim because someone is blocking your way and you balk at pushing past—so you wait for next time around to take your cheap, cracked and battered suitcase.

CAUSES

When we travel we see people with more money than ourselves. This encourages the thought, "I am not rich, nor a celebrity. I have nothing as valuable as theirs."

Nothing that anyone would take the trouble to steal, for instance.

But you may feel, in a completely irrational moment, that it would be flattering if they *did* . . . If that one fairly expensive object wrapped in brown paper were taken. Or if that suitcase which holds something costly-for-you were pinched from the conveyor belt before you could spot the theft.

Such thoughts, of course, may not lead directly to your semiconsciously leaving baggage unattended for a moment. But they can be a contributing factor to any loss you suffer.

Through a mixture of being careless and thinking, "I am not worth anyone's attention," you generally tempt fate and may well find your worst dreams come true.

You will be amazed. For a split second you may experience that flash of perverse pleasure which says, "I did have something after all." But the spark dies in an instant.

And you realize that though you may have thought you were in bad straits before, you are in much more serious waters now.

ILLOGICAL BEHAVIOR

The careless behavior which allows a criminal to steal relatively worthless goods is based on a belief that only the rich are the aim of thieves.

So you, unassuming as you are, can afford to leave your baggage lying about as you pay a call to the rest room or use the telephone.

Not so. There are thieves and criminals to suit everyone in the city. The addicted, debt-ridden and starving will steal the most unprepossessing-looking objects—so long as they are easy to take.

It is their experience that the brown paper parcel, cardboard box, supermarket paper carrier or old airline travel bag will often pay far more than the price of the drink, fix or meal they crave for.

One reason is that people do sometimes hide valuable cargo in disreputable-appearing packages and bags so that there should be less likelihood of their being stolen.

Another is that even the most ordinary- and just-about-solvent-looking traveler will usually carry credit cards, blank checks, various credentials, an airline, bus or train ticket, bottles of duty-free liquor and cartons of cigarettes.

Most of these help to make up a big "package" which undergoes a chain-like processing, sold first to a "connection."

Depending on the prevailing market it might bring $200-$300.

Of course, the poorish person's gas station credit card will fetch far less than an American Express or Carte Blanche credit card; but along with the various other possessions held in that chain-store-bought attache case, the thief will gain enough—especially when he has a connection who can sell the stuff to a ring specializing in such workaday goods.

Any credit or bank account is then raped by the city wolves, to whom changing the photograph printed on a credit card or copying the signature on a traveler's check first time is child's play, his bread and butter, what he knows the way you know *your* livelihood.

But the most important factor is that to tempt snatch thieves brings a real risk of violence.

The defective who is tempted to steal an old suitcase, its

handle held with string, could pull a knife if you attempt to stop him—his need is so great. And there is no reasoning with him.

He is far more likely to go for the old, dilapidated and battered than the smart although mass-produced suitcase that stands out a mile in his grimy fists.

Remedy: The Canny, p. 40; The Leery, p. 47; The Nervous, p. 52

2

CITY TERMINALS

WINNERS

We have seen what characteristics can make us Losers in the great airports, railroad stations and bus depots of the largest cities. But who are classed as the Winners?

Here are the kinds of people most likely to fare best on reaching town. No one is likely to have all these attributes of arrival-survival, but it is important to try to inject as much of their good sense as possible into our own makeups.

The Sheep (Non-Lambs)

Blend with the terminal traffic by staying in the flock streaming from the just-arrived bus/plane/train. But you must work at losing yourself in a terminal crowd all the way along your trip right to the final run—into the terminal. It does not come easily.

NOTE: THE SHEEP are NOT "Lemmings," the airline passengers, for example, who ignore the PLEASE DISREGARD notices placed right across the computerized airport indicator boards which riffle like a pack of cards and then tell you your flight number and takeoff time. For even though the computer has broken down AND *despite* the notices, the majority of people still follow the rogue indicator directions. Not so THE SHEEP. They—like that animal—use their brains when guided and stay with the correctly heading flock no matter how small it may be.

Here are the reasons why the sheep flock so efficiently and thus never draw undue attention to themselves.

SLEEPING SOUNDLY

In a big city, the ability to keep a clear head is an invaluable asset. We are more likely to exercise it if we arrive refreshed.

It is so important to sleep properly on a long journey that we should be prepared to use *any* of the measures which can produce sleep for us. No matter what kind of person you are, there is always *one* way that will work for you.

Since restorative effects of sleep are felt even after catnaps, learning to catch up on sleep by any of the following ways is important.

Practice this yoga cure for insomnia. Place the first three fingers (index nearest the wrist rather than near the forearm) on the wrist pulse. The fingertips should lie on the line of the artery with the thumb supporting the back of heartbeats. The entire exercise should now be carried out at a similar tempo.

While counting from one to six, take in a deep breath. Retain the air for the count of three. Exhale fully at the count of six. Remain deflated for the count of three. Repeat the above sequence seven times.

Or try any of these:

Taking a sleeping pill.

Relaxing your muscles as completely as possible in your seat.

Placing a pillow below your head after reclining your seat and your outstretched legs on the briefcase lying on the floor in front of you (if you are too timid to ask its owner to move it).

Drinking a glass of lukewarm milk with a spoonful of honey stirred into it at a rest stop or on the plane (you carry the honey).

Drinking a little whiskey neat.

Wrapping up warmly in a rug.

Letting the throbbing drone of the plane or the diddly-dum rhythm of a rocking train lull you into dozing.

Reading a newspaper or book.

Knitting.

Any of these can induce a drowsy feeling and bring on quiet and strength-reviving slumber.

However, in the interests of safety:

If you suffer from travel sickness which affects your sleep, do not use a pillow. Just bend your head back against the reclined seat and hold it still.

Pad the window with a sweater where there is a large glass area—as in some buses and trains. The effect of "cold shoulder" is not obvious at first, but quickly takes a numbingly unpleasant effect if you do happen to nap with your shoulder pressed to the glass (chilled by the wind speed outside).

Then there's the problem of being so afraid of flying that you simply *cannot* sleep; the fear has you in a grip that does not allow you to slide into comfortable oblivion.

You are not such a rare bird as you think! There are thousands with the same phobia and, while there are specialist cures for the worst cases, most of us can do a lot to help ourselves before ever taking the trip.

For instance, you can take a course in aerodynamics and learn how a plain flies. Then you could spend time at a local airport near your home watching the planes come and go.

Try to relax about the whole idea of planes.

If you could persuade an aircraft company to let you sit inside a plane on the ground for a while, then take a brief flight with some friends, you should be well on the way to losing your fear of flying. And able to enjoy a good flight's rest as a result.

Remember it takes the body time to get rid of alcohol. Drinks drunk thousands of miles from the city can still be around when you arrive—even though you have slept. The better judgment that would have been produced by that sleep is consequently clouded by booze. It takes three hours for only two cans of beer to disappear from your bloodstream. A six-pack takes five hours. The time for gin/vodka is even longer.

If you take sleeping pills also take care. Sedatives prescribed for insomnia—particularly barbiturates—can have dangerous side effects when mixed with alcohol or antihistamines (drugs given for travel sickness and hay fever). Sleeping pills can, in any case, bring about bad judgment, poor coordination and mental confusion. You should check with your doctor first.

Many people on trains and buses will not take sleeping pills because they are scared of missing their stop. Nothing can convince them to close their eyes for long. These fears are ungrounded. In most cases the bus will make a long rest stop in a big city. All passengers have to alight while the bus is driven away and cleaned. So the driver wakes anyone who is sleeping. If you are on a train or bus that is passing through and only stopping briefly at your destination, however, ask the bus driver, the conductor or brakeman to wake you. (And offer a tip.) Another help is not to empty your bladder before sleeping. As this fills during the journey, it will bring you awake gradually like an alarm clock.

It is not a good plan—if you can avoid it—to take pills for travel sickness. Side effects can include blurred vision, lack of concentration and a general drowsiness long after you should have been awake and on the ball. If you take alcohol as well it worsens the effects.

It is not only on ships that you feel sick. The same effects can trouble bus, train and plane travelers. Motion sickness affects 90 per cent of us, some so easily they feel it in elevators, on escalators or swings, and climbing down ladders. Yet the chances are you have only yourself to blame. In these 90 per cent of cases, travel sickness is preventable without pills.

The most universal remedy is simple. And it works.

If you stay calm and collected and stop feeling sorry for yourself when on board ship or in the sky, the chances are you will not be sick. Most people who are travel sick think themselves into it. But if you are one of the genuine motion sickness victims, see the doctor. That way you will get the pills that are right for *you*. This is important because the two main drugs—antihistamines and hyoscine derivatives—affect people differently.

You should not take travel sickness pills if you are going to drive on arrival at the terminal. (If you must, then wait at least six hours after taking the pills or you may find yourself driving under the influence.) Pregnant women and children under three should not take the pills either.

There are other pills, too, which may have a harmful effect.

Tranquilizers: the "minor" tranquilizers are most commonly given for nervous disorders. They can bring drowsiness on arrival and mental slowness. Avoid alcohol with them. Amphetamines: For depression and dieting. These are not now recommended except in very special cases.

BEING WIDE AWAKE

There are certain effective ways to jolt your system awake 30 minutes or so before arrival at the city terminal. These will quickly dispel the awful bleary-eyed, buzzy-headed and bird-cage-floor-mouthed feelings on coming to in a train, bus or plane seat.

Best of all methods, especially when your time is important in the city ahead—say you are on business—is to freshen up for the trip before you embark on it.

If you face a lengthy flight which passes through time zones it pays to adjust your body clock well in advance so that your natural rhythms have a chance.

Say you are an executive flying 6,000 miles from America to another country on a vital assignment to spearhead an industrial purchasing commitment of over $5 million:

1. When your time in the foreign country is critical but the time in America is not, then live by the foreign time for two to three days before leaving the United States.
2. When, however, the time in both countries is critical, take a flight with an estimated arrival time equivalent to midday in America so that you are nearer your peak performance on arrival.

Then, 30 minutes before touchdown—or, in the case of travelers on a bus or train, before entering the city station . . .

Go to the rest room. (Take your children too.) Empty your bladder and run the underside of both wrists under the cold tap—so the chilled water stings the viens which are near the surface of the skin here.

As many taps produce only a trickle of water toward the end of a bus, train or plane trip, place the tip of the forefinger of the other hand under the tap to squirt the trickle in a fine cold jet.

Brushing your teeth, pushing your face into a basinful of warm water, then rinsing with cold water and combing your hair all help.

Any kind of sick feeling, whether drunk sick, travel sick or simple biliousness, can be eased by placing a dab of strong toothpaste on the very back of the tongue. The taste stings and helps keep you from vomiting.

If you are not at your best, it can be a silly little frustration that will tip your temper. Try to minimize these troubles.

It may be an empty toothpaste tube when you thought you had packed a full one. Place it under the hot tap for several seconds and the warm water will make it usable for one more good squeeze onto the toothbrush.

Or your shoes may be filthy because of a last-minute rush through airport slush hours ago. Your normally businesslike morale leaks away. The answer is to save the apple core, orange peel or banana skin from the last meal on the plane and rub with toilet paper or a tissue. Give a final polish on the backs of your trousers. Even damp shoes respond.

If you did have shoe polish but stained your dress as the bus lurched—clean it off with toothpaste.

Soot marks from boat, train or plane engines can be cleaned with a dry crust of bread.

Get rid of the blood that dripped on a shirt collar in that last-moment shave by immediately dabbing the shirt with cold water. Keep dabbing.

Just before arrival pull away the toilet or cigarette paper

which you stuck on the shaving cut by licking a finger and dampening the paper first. (Rip it off dry and caked with blood and the cut will bleed again.)

Practice an imitation yawn. When done properly, this will bring delicious relief and freshness.

The actual physical movements of brushing and washing and cleaning and rejuvenating your appearance will wake you up and regenerate the thrill you probably felt at the start of your trip. This is a tremendous aid to you. *Excitement* at the prospect of something new, the city, can prove one of the principal factors in helping to compensate for the impairing effects of sleep loss.

If stacked above the airport in thick fog, meaning a frustrating delay, keep loosened with these tactics: lift both heels from the floor and wriggle ankles . . . lift toes off floor and keep curling them . . . turn torso and left shoulder to the left, breathing in as you do . . . exhale and relax and then repeat exercise on your right side . . . sit upright and let arms hang by your side . . . pull in diaphragm, inhaling slowly, and flex your sitting muscles.

Now that you have kindled wakefulness again you are in a far stronger position for the trials ahead.

KEEPING UP YOUR ENERGY

Energy is important at the terminal.

Energy helps you fill in documents more quickly, lift suitcases more easily, and draw a redcap's attention more assertively. It helps you to bypass terminal pests, like the panhandler ("You look as if you could spare a dollar") in the velveteen coat and ruffled shirt whose huge dark glasses mirror your anxiety—and who blocks your way.

You can get extra energy from sugar cubes, yeast tablets, glucose and dextrose tablets and cheese/nuts/dates/raisins chewed in the last 30 minutes before disembarking from plane or train.

MAKING FRIENDS ON THE TRIP

Fellow passengers can prove a moral and sometimes physical support. They can help with lifting baggage, waking you up in time, pushing through a crowd—and in dozens of other ways. This assistance can often be won from the fit and strong by someone who is old, sick, failing or jaded.

It is much harder to make friends, however, when you are in this condition. Your general feeling of disability leads to an irritability you cannot check. But, where possible, try to conceal these feelings. It is worth the effort of at least not rubbing others the wrong way when you may badly need their backing in a few hours' time at the terminal.

MOVING WITH THE FLOCK

If you are elderly, timid, frail or in some way incapacitated you can experience great difficulty handling baggage. You might have to keep resting as you grip bags in arthritic hands, fail to keep up with the other passengers from your flight and thus get separated from the main stream heading for immigration, customs and so on.

The first rule is NOT to stampede from your seat in the plane or bus when it stops. Keep seated, helpless as it may make you feel, until most other passengers have filed out, then walk out unhindered and take for free the magazines left lying on seats— something to read in case of delays to come. You will still arrive at the baggage claim ahead of your suitcase—and you will not have so long to wait until the luggage appears.

Although this may seem a trifling matter, you are now following a key principle. Conserve your strength, no matter how limited your powers are, when you need every ounce you can produce; in any survival scene, fatigue is an ever-present source of strain and reducer of efficiency. It can leave you wide open to crises of every kind.

Wherever possible, REST, no matter how brief, is the basic factor in recovering from fatigue. Rest counts here every time you stop and take a breather—ever if it is only to perch on a suitcase.

If possible get a baggage cart and stand with it by the conveyor belt. Load your baggage onto the cart immediately. Mentally handcuff your fists to the handle so that no one else can wheel your cart away "by mistake." But don't be tense; just stay watchful and relaxed.

When there are no carts available, hail a redcap/skycap/porter to carry your bags for you.

If you can't get help right away, wait. Especially when there are more than two heavy suitcases or you lack the strength to lift even one. Sit on your suitcases and read the magazines you took. Wait. Eventually a porter will be free; don't panic.

You may be too hard up to tip a redcap or too shy to yell for one above the terminal din. You may even be independent enough to wish to carry your own luggage. . . . If so, some tips:

Heavy suitcases and trunks are best wheeled along on a cheap, strong and lightweight luggage carrier. These fold flat inside a case when not in use and secure a big case with nonslip straps to a pair of wheels. You simply pick up the handle of the carrier and roll it away.

You may only be carrying two fairly light suitcases plus hand luggage—a briefcase or vanity case, say. But how you carry them becomes important when facing the acres of a vast terminal concourse floor.

When you are elderly or fatigued, every yard gained is a small triumph. Carrying just two bags can become a struggle. Remember to:

Lift a heavy suitcase or two hefty pieces of luggage by bending your legs, *not* your back. Keep the spine straight, let the legs give at the knees, grasp the handles and straighten your legs. There is now far less risk of straining your back, heart or hernia-prone parts.

Pick out your destination across the concourse. Head for it by looking at the floor immediately ahead of you. This makes carrying less effort and you can get bearings when you stop for short rests en route.

The person for whom this struggle with suitcases is the heaviest physical effort for months should take frequent rest breaks. Always stop and lower the suitcases *before* your fingers seem to be giving out and arms about to drop off. Walk at your normal rate instead of going uncomfortably fast.

The way in which you carry the suitcases has a great say in reducing fatigue. Economy of effort is best learned by rhythmical movements practiced before you leave home.

When you are carrying one heavy suitcase in one hand and a piece of hand luggage in the other, try starting with the suitcase in your weaker hand. This, because the muscles and sinews are still fresh and will get you more paces across the concourse floor before you have to stop and rest.

At this point place the bags on the floor and wait a few moments. Now pick up that heavy case again with the weak hand

Conserve your strength when carrying suitcases. Change hands by turning the body rather than crossing the arms.

and start walking. From here on swap the suitcase to the other hand and then back again as the fingers begin to slacken.

Say you are carrying one heavy and one light bag. You will need to keep swapping these whenever the heavy one pulls hard on an aching arm. Instead of struggling to cross over arms as you dump bags on the floor preparatory to relifting, do it this way: just before placing the bags on the floor, turn around to face the opposite way and then lower them. Chafe your wrists, then turn around to face the way you are heading and pick up the cases. The heavy one is now in the new hand—and no effort was involved in crossing over.

When you are carrying an assortment of baggage, which can include portable typewriter, briefcase, wig box, cosmetic bag, folding wheelchair, guitar case, pack frame, rucksack, overnight bag, suitcases or soft-type luggage of cloth/canvas/plastic, practice the ways your hands will grip them before you leave home.

Always carry a suitcase with the lid against your leg. This keeps the contents from tumbling out if the catches go. It is also easier to carry this way; the handle is offset toward the lid rather than being in the center.

But when you are carrying four suitcases, two heavy and two light, or when one arm is in a sling and you must therefore carry two cases with one hand, learn the best way to grip.

Carry the smaller case on the outside, its lid turned in to rest against the lid of the larger case. The adjacent handles you are holding should lie as close to each other as possible to ease the strain on the hand—and also to stop the skin from getting pinched in the crack between the cases. This happens when you carry a suitcase with the handle offset toward the lid and the lid is next to your leg. If you grasp a smaller case or portable typewriter on the outside in the same hand, the leverage created by having the handles some distance apart will hurt your hand very quickly.

People who get flustered easily sometimes carry a customs declaration form or immigration document in the same hand with which they are clutching a case. Don't. Just one piece of paper can weaken your grip by half. Do not keep entry forms, health certificate, passport and other travel documents in checked baggage either. The proper place is together in an envelope secured with a safety pin in the inside pocket or in a zippered compartment of a purse.

EXPECTING THE WORST

Being resigned to the worst aspects of arriving at a terminal is a strength of the sheep. If you are not stoical under these circumstances you fail to blend with the majority, and this can lead you into trouble. For example:

Standing in the slowest line. Waiting for long periods in the baggage claim. Endless delays at the customs or immigration barriers. What may seem insulting, rude or abrupt behavior from others in this new environment where customs, manners and language are different. And a general travel soreness which makes everything seem a personal Gehenna.

It is the person in pain who suffers most. The pills and medications we take tend at such times to fail to work. However, concentration on the task in hand helps to relieve pain. Try not to think about the pain. Think instead about the next step in the terminal procedure, keep busy mentally checking that everything is in order—documents together, bags locked and together, etc. Think about the city ahead as being a challenge and that— when the goals are your safety, your life, your honor and your enjoyment and you value these highly enough—you can tolerate anything. It is amazing how such fiercely positive thinking can help to give you a white-knuckled determination.

GREASING THE WAY

Be resigned to tipping *anyone* who can help you, however much it may go against the grain. For by this YOU gain.

Always carry a pocketful of small change. The weight of the coins encourages you to lighten the load and to fish out payment to thank those who have done you a service, to prove in advance you are willing to pay for help and, to get rid of nuisances like the aggressive panhandler/huckster/derelict—often drunk, menacing and profane—who come into the big terminals off the streets.

There are other advantages. You will never miss a bus in the city where the drivers don't make change, because you have the exact fare. The coins also form a hard core of metal to squeeze and squash when nervous tension caused by terminal delays threatens to make you boil over in public.

Look on the expense of tipping as the necessary payment for an easier entry into the city. It gives you confidence to know you are prepared to tip even though you may be poor. Be ready to go without something else instead. And never tip too little; the people who do you a service in an enormous city expect a higher rate than elsewhere. Try to find out from people who have been to wherever you are visiting what the standard rules are.

The Canny (Cagey)

Think carefully before arriving in the city and make due preparation which will stand them in good stead from the moment they arrive.

Here is what they do to make safer the life they value and the things they possess.

SAFETYPROOF THE SUITCASES

Do not buy expensive, beautiful custom-made bags with superior-looking locks. These are a target of the baggage thief who can obtain a good price for the luggage alone, regardless of its contents.

You should not wrap valuables in paper, grubby waxed bags or misshapen and lumpy cardboard cartons held with string. All these attract the casual thief who could, because of his predicament (probably desperate for a drink/fix/meal), carry a weapon to make sure he steals what appears to be at his own level.

Buy hard-wearing, lightweight, mass-produced suitcases. These will blend in with the other baggage and are less likely to be stolen.

Three suitcases for an average trip will measure approximately:

18″ (× 12″ × 7″)
24″ (× 16″ × 8″)
27″ (× 18″ × 9″)

They ought if possible to be soft-topped to take that extra little bit. The sturdy modern vinyl-covered frames will stand up to wear and tear and resist scuff marks. The handles will be strong and comfortable to hold, and the tough polyester zippers will not rust or damage your clothes if accidentally caught. The bases will be protected by studs and the two larger cases will probably have straps and buckles as well as locks, for extra safety.

Know also that it is NOT only the casual thief that you must thwart. There are also the dishonest airline loaders who open the most likely suitcases and who, by the time the theft is discovered, are thousands of miles away. They look on their thieving as a "lucky dip" practice.

Two things will help:

1. DON'T PUT ALL YOUR EXTRAS INTO ONE BASKET. Distribute your wardrobe/possessions/valuables over several suitcases. And women, carry a versatile Pucci and a change of underwear in your hand luggage in case *all* baggage goes astray.
2. STRAP YOUR SUITCASES either with string if they are of the old-but-faithful style of baggage OR with a strong strap and thong-tied-down buckle. Loaders can't usually be bothered with fastenings like these when there are so many more vulnerable and yet bulging suitcases around them.

It is a great advantage, of course, if you can travel light and put everything into one lightweight travel bag, available from most department stores. This counts as hand luggage—so obviating baggage claim delays. You just walk out of the plane, go through customs and get into a cab.

The average measurements will be around:

22″ × 13″ × 9″ when closed

And it will weigh under 5 pounds before packing. These bags have plenty of space inside and can hold clothes, shoes, gifts, goodies, etc., in a roomy compartment. Large side wallets and side pockets expand to include last-minute extras. A special crease-free suit-hanging unit is also incorporated in the handy and efficient design. Toilet articles, a change of shirt and underwear, and other essentials should go in your hand luggage too. NEVER leave documents or travelers checks in a suitcase that has been checked through.

Remove old baggage tags and check that your present destination is properly written. Then write your name and destination on both the outside and inside of the bag. Use rip-proof plastic or leather tags attached to the handle mountings for the outer name, a card taped inside the lid for the inner.

If you forget to do this, ask the ticket agent for identification tags at the terminal where you start the trip.

Important—check the girl has put the correct flight label on your luggage at the start. Suitcases can often be pushed on the conveyor belt with the wrong destination label or with none at all. To be certain, label bags with your hotel, destination, airport and address.

Cover any baggage disaster with comprehensive insurance.

Lock all your luggage. But realize that locks are not foolproof. Look on them as burstproofing instead—and watch them all the time.

The same goes for combination locks on briefcases and attaché cases. Because they are stronger than normal locks and are supposed to be impossible to open if you lack the correct sequence of numbers or letters, you may be tempted to be casual in handling such baggage. Thieves can still butcher such clasps with a special wrench which is held in the palm of the hand.

So watch even these closely all the time.

Distinguish YOUR bags from a distance by painting or sticking a bright and contrasting band of color around them. Many suitcases are sold with such stripes, but you should make yours stand out even more by neatly repainting the original stripe a different and unusual color. Circles, stars, triangles and blocks of solid color will also help you to identify a suitcase from any angle when it first comes into view on a piled-high baggage conveyor. A'thief is less likely to try and snatch it because its marking is unique.

Keep on your guard, however. Suitcase snatchers know this too. Sometimes they pretend they are color-blind.

PACK SUITCASES PROPERLY

Not only does a well-packed suitcase give you a pride of ownership which makes you supervise your baggage all the more closely, it also cuts custom delays to the minimum.

Pack suits to go in a suitcase separately on hangers. Turn the jackets inside out, place them lapel to lapel, draw down the sleeves tightly, then fold them over before putting them into the case.

Now pack the trousers with one leg hanging out of the case. Place your other garments on top. Then fold the outer leg over —this prevents deep creases in the pants. Roll ties with their seams outside. And along with rolled-up socks, push these inside your spare shoes to save space.

Women's clothes, if made of the crushproof fabrics that are now everywhere available, are far less trouble to pack. But skirts should be laid the length of the suitcase, and pantyhose and underwear should be rolled and wedged into corners. Small items like costume jewelry can be packed in extra pocketbooks.

Never ship compressed gases, corrosives, explosives, munitions, fireworks, flammable liquids and solids, oxidizing materials, poisons, radioactive materials, mercury, magnetic objects or offensive and irritating substances.

WEAR APPROPRIATE CLOTHES

Anyone who wears his best clothing obeys a natural instinct to show off when visiting a city. But expensive furs, well-cut suits, flashy rings and well-stuffed wallets all advertise goods for the taking.

It is more prudent to pack or store your quality clothes and dress comfortably and modestly for the journey.

Wear clean, loose-fitting clothes to give your blood a chance to circulate freely and your sweat glands an opportunity to function efficiently.

A well-worn suit, jeans-and-sweater or easy-fitting outfit or dress makes you blend with the rest of the terminal traffic more safely.

They make you feel better in the long run. Not lumbered with anxiety about crumpling the fine material of your best attire—a common tendency as the hours of traveling take their toll and any garment begins to feel itchy, soiled and rumpled—you have a more restful journey.

A sweater is always useful—as a pillow, mini-rug, extra clothing or towel when, at the end of a journey, all the paper towels in the rest room are used up.

Wear a comfortable old pair of suede shoes or sandals. Leather soles become slippery after treading the carpeted floors of jets and slip too easily on skiddy terminal floors. (But they can be made safer by wearing stick-on rubber soles or by sticking strips of adhesive across the soles.)

CARRY MONEY SAFELY

Never stash all your money in one pocket. Even the most cleverly tailored suit will show a suspicious bulge.

Most men's suits have about fourteen pockets. The safest are near the most sensitive parts of the body—the nipples and the crotch—which are quick to detect prying fingers.

It is a good plan to carry some folding money in the two side trouser pockets. These are even harder to pick because they are the deepest pockets.

Carry bills of smallish denomination in one side pocket and larger bills in the other. Remember which is which and be ready to pay your way from terminal to hotel or apartment with the money in the pocket containing the smaller bills.

The wallet, containing more bills, should be jammed across

the inside of an inner jacket pocket secured to the coat with a strong safety pin.

It is wise not to carry in the wallet any more money than is likely to be needed on your journey. The same applies to checks and to any membership cards or other documents that can be used to establish identity. Such cards, particularly credit cards—especially if accompanied by a driver's license, or library card—can be used dishonestly to obtain substantial amounts of goods at your expense.

The only money you should keep in the side pockets of a coat is the small change needed for tips. Otherwise never keep anything of value in any side pocket. Or in a hip pocket. They are all easy to pick.

Do not have complete faith in zippers, buttons or the safety pin fastening a pocket. A topcoat worn buttoned-up over a suit will not stop the ace pickpocket, who can still find ways of getting into the suit pockets.

Any open pocket is an invitation to theft, and pocket flaps fastened with buttons—whether on the breast, side of the coat or hip—offer little real protection.

When your arm is broken or paralyzed, do place your money appropriately so the good arm does not have to reach for, nor the hand fumble with, a wallet kept in its usual pocket. Switch pockets. A left arm in a sling means the wallet should now go in the left inner pocket if you have one. If you haven't, then keep the wallet in the right-hand inner pocket but carefully place bills you may need in the right-hand trouser side pocket. Separate the bills in advance so there is no need to drag the whole wad into sight every time you need to pay for something. Make sure you know in advance which denominations they are.

If you are carrying a large amount of money, stash most of it *in reserve* on your person in places where you will never need to reach for it.

The following have proved the best . . . money belt . . . special inner pocket which you asked your tailor to incorporate . . . inner jacket pocket with an extra strong zipper fitted . . . stitched inside the lining of your coat so the thread runs through the paper . . .

placed inside socks or tights so you can always feel the money is there . . . folded inside two grubby-looking Kleenexes glued together in a kind of wallet to disguise it.

It is a good plan not to use just one of these, but several.

A woman's handbag is even more vulnerable than a man's billfold or wallet. It is best to use a bag with a catch that cannot be opened easily or quickly by a stranger unfamiliar with its design.

At all times keep a firm grasp on the handle. Hold it close to the body and never place a purse in the side pocket of a coat. This is just bait for the pickpocket.

When you have a bag on a strap slung over one shoulder, do not let it dangle freely behind you—especially when it gapes open. Keep it tucked into the side with your arm, otherwise it is far too easy for a thief to rummage through it while your attention is distracted. He can even snip through the strap with a knife or sharp scissors, seize the whole bag and run.

The same goes for anything worn over a shoulder on a strap, whether it is an expensive camera or a tape player. Guard all and any of them under cover of your elbow.

The wallet is best buried deep inside a handbag—under the contents.

The newest accessory on the market is a handbag equipped with a siren which wails as the bag is snatched or the strap cut.

REPORT LOST ARTICLES

Tell the plane, train or bus agent when you have left possessions on board or when bags you checked at the beginning of the trip do not turn up.

Always report to the police when you find a wallet, handbag, purse, briefcase or other valuables missing.

There is always a chance you will get them back, especially if you know the serial numbers of cameras, the typewriter, tape recorder, radio, binoculars etc.

Always carry a note of the address of your insurance company so you can inform them of any loss or theft.

LEAVE VALUABLES BEHIND

Store expensive furs with a reliable company. Bank excess cash. Put costly jewelery, gems, cameras or wristwatches in a bank's deposit safe.

But if you do take expensive items with you, remember to register them at the customs barrier of your departure point.

TAG YOUR HOUSE KEYS CORRECTLY

Never put your name and address on keys. It is better to lose them permanently than have them return in the hands of an unwelcome intruder.

Tag them with your business address, unless you have business keys on the same ring or chain.

PLAN A SAFE ROUTE

When there is a definite risk on part of the direct route to your city, take another route. Or change your means of transport.

If, say, a section of the route has been rife with recent hijackings, cover that part of the journey by boat, bus or train, or take a longer, more roundabout route. Do this when you are old, nervous, sick or just a plain self-preservationist.

The Leery (Suspicious)

Back up their doubts of every stranger in the city with automatic reflexes. These show they are aware; consequently city foxes, every bit as savage as the wolves, tend to leave them alone and track the more susceptible instead.

Here is where and how you can telegraph that you know full well what may happen to you.

GANGWAYS/STAIRWAYS/WALKWAYS

Place a hand on the opposite shoulder and press your arm hard against your chest whenever you are pushed, crushed or jostled in a crowd. Refuse to be distracted, keep your hand and arm there and move from the disturbance.

This protects your wallet in an inner jacket pocket, yet does not indicate which pocket it is in. It also shows the pickpocket you are a wallet-watcher.

BAGGAGE CLAIM

Most people never imagine that their baggage can be stolen here. But it can.

Keep briefcases and the like between your legs or touching an ankle while waiting for suitcases. If a stranger asks for directions pick them up and hold on to them.

Take suitcases off the conveyer belt as in THE SHEEP.

CUSTOMS

Watch for, note and remember anyone behind you in the line who shows an interest in your possessions if the customs spill them all over the counter.

Also find out if there is an observation gallery where anyone can see the customs unpacking smugglers' underwear, film stars' toiletries and the innocent's guilty secrets. This is also a place from which muggers select their victims.

Scan any such observatory closely. It can give you confidence. And show them YOU are aware.

BAGGAGE LOCKERS

Say "No thank you" when a stranger offers you an empty locker space after taking out his or her suitcases. Do not store valuables here.

CONCOURSE FLOOR

Walk straight across it. Rest tired arms by standing with legs touching the suitcases. Or sit down briefly on them.

As you mentally handcuffed your wrists to the baggage cart or carrier in the baggage claim, now mentally fetter your ankles with imaginary leg irons and chains to the handles of your suitcases. Think of these as the iron balls at the end of your chains. Thus shackled mentally, there is less chance of your possessions disappearing should someone try to distract you on the concourse floor.

Look no one in the eye. It is much easier to carry suitcases if you look at the floor a yard or two ahead. When someone blocks your path and you just see their toes, step well aside and keep going. Try not to get involved with anyone, but don't be aggressive.

Be courteous, self-effacing, determinedly diffident and doggedly humorous and/or apologetic.

When you are unsure in which direction to head because you have time to kill . . . keep going. Toward the shoeshine stand/insurance counter/telephones. Or to a redcap, skycap, porter or terminal policeman and ask him *some*thing: what's the time, where's the rest room, anything.

CONCOURSE SEATS

Place a handbag or briefcase on your lap, never on the floor by your feet or on the seat next to you. It can be taken too easily —especially when you are reading or watching the pay TV on the armrest of your seat.

To sleep on seats: check the suitcases, drink two or three hot chocolates and go to the rest room to safetyproof the cash in your pockets by pushing most of it down the front of your briefs or panty hose; place the sweater you carry as a pillow.

REST ROOMS

Avoid the eyes and ears of those who comb their hair repeatedly in the mirror, wipe their hands endlessly on the towel, shout as their lips get a shock from the static electricity off a water cooler, ask you for the time, or make any veiled offer or suggestion, no matter how innocent it may seem.

Nor should you say "OOOOH!' when you unexpectedly receive an electric shock by touching a metal knob on the toilet door or drinking from a water cooler in a humid city rest room. *They* may then think of you as an exhibitionist.

The correct way to be shockproof is to pick up your feet as you walk. Avoid trailing them on the floor. Rap the door knob sharply first with your knuckles. Just before you drink from the cooler or fountain, slap it hard with the palm of one hand to rid yourself of the highly annoying static charge.

When you see notices in public toilets which say BEWARE OF PICKPOCKETS, do not pat your pockets. If such pests are present, they will notice which pockets you felt and conclude you may be worth robbing.

Keep your jacket on when it contains a wallet or papers rather than hanging it from the hook on the toilet door. If coins or a roll of toilet paper are dropped next door and roll under your side of the partition, kick them back with a toe and look up for the sign of itchy fingers coming over the top to steal.

Avoid long silences, rustling magazine pages or spending any length of time in rest rooms.

If you are an adult male in charge of a small girl ask a woman with children of her own to take her into the ladies' room. When you are a woman with a boy of ten or more, see that someone who has a wife and children present in the terminal goes with him into the men's room.

TELEPHONES

If you have to make a telephone call don't forget to keep a sharp eye on your luggage.

TERMINAL BANK

Glance to see which person is watching when you make a transaction at the counter. Block his view of your business by placing your back between your wallet and him.

TERMINAL CHAPEL

Kneel on your briefcase. Place valuables like a handbag or camera by your knees and never on the pew by your side; it is too easy for someone to reach over from behind when you are engrossed in prayer. If *sitting* in the pew, keep your handbag on your lap or your briefcase tucked between the ankles or laid flat beneath both shoes.

TERMINAL MAILBOXES

Walk away from fights or scuffles which take place anywhere in terminals, especially near mailboxes. These distractions are often staged by pickpockets who steal the wallets of those who try to intervene or watch. They slip the cash from the billfolds and then mail the wallets down the letter openings to get rid of the evidence.

POST OFFICE/TELEGRAM/TICKET COUNTERS

Fill in postcards, cables, etc. on top of your briefcase instead of putting it down by you. Tuck a handbag tightly in to your body under one arm instead of placing it on the counter.

CAFETERIA

Watch your wallet when someone bumps into you and says, "Look out, you're spilling." While both your hands are occupied and your attention is diverted, he may steal your billfold.

Trap a briefcase between your ankles and place a handbag in your lap while eating and drinking. Do not put them down on the seat next to you.

TERMINAL EXITS

Do not jump on the first bus at the airport. It may not go into the city. Some buses only run to other terminals or to a distant parking lot.

Ask the airline agent where the city-bound buses leave from and how you can identify them.

Check on yellow cabs too.

These are the taxis which are registered with the police department. The agent will tell you how to distinguish them—or their equivalent when a different color—in a strange city. It is not always easy to tell. A gypsy taxi may operate at a more expensive level than the set rate for the yellow cabs and may also be painted yellow or part-yellow, although it will lack the approved medallion decal. Ask the agent what exactly to look for.

Be ready for the taxi touts who will try to snare you into taking a more-expensive-than-necessary trip into the city.

When you are old/frail/nervous it helps to wear a hearing aid—even though you may not be deaf. Then you can pretend you cannot hear. Or simply appear not to understand. Step aside and keep walking for the bus or yellow cab rank if someone tries to hold on to your sleeve or take a suitcase and lead you to his car.

Turn down offers from strangers at the airport or station to share the cost of a taxi or chauffeur-driven limousine. It is safer and cheaper to go by citybound bus or yellow cab.

The Nervous (Normally)

Prove Winners when their anxiety is healthily devoted to self-protection and does not spill over into complete disorientation and panic.

CONTROL ANXIETY

To recognize the danger you are confronted with is two-thirds of the battle for survival.

Even so it is a strange human quirk that although we may feel we are prepared for any ordeal ahead, we probably never completely convince ourselves that "it *can* happen to us." It is doubly important, therefore, that we should have some understanding of the psychological as well as physical obstacles which we must overcome when it *does* happen to us.

The emotional states associated with any survival situation are crucial; the most important element in the determination of success or failure in any metropolitan emergency must be yourself and your loved ones. Important areas of concern to you are: how YOU react to various situations; what varied signs, feelings, expressions and reactions in yourself and others mean; your tolerance limits; how to maintain, care for and effectively use your own abilities in order to function at your best.

Nature has endowed us with biological reaction mechanisms which aid our adaptation to stress. Adrenalin, for example, gives us extra energy for fight or flight. These same mechanisms, however, *can* betray us too. For instance, you could cast reason aside and try to fight a mugger—instead of giving way.

There are three main rules which will help us to overcome our own misguided instincts: *prepare, relax, concentrate.*

There is always some emergency which will catch us unprepared. But it is not so much a matter of carrying a tear-gas squirt to stop muggers as of thinking out just what you would do if an obstructive huckster or peddler did stop you and refused to let you pass until you had given him money.

If you have never given it a thought you panic when it happens. Your face flushes, your hands sweat and you become tongue-tied—paralyzed with fright. You have lost your nerve.

But these sensations can be turned to advantage by the person who faces danger—provided he has thought and prepared against such an eventuality, and then is relaxed enough to keep his anxiety under control.

A mountaineer who looks so relaxed before the ascent as he puts up his boots and has a last smoke is probably as frightened as you.

He knows he may plunge to his death, but he has been over every item of ropes/carabiners/pitons, and concentration will let him deal with the risks when they come. . . . Such prepared nerves

are necessary for your own self-preservation in the city.
YOUR anxiety shows you recognize there are risks ahead. It
makes you more alert, enables you to see the strengths and weaknesses in a crisis situation. Without anxiety you can either be
blindly optimistic or helplessly pessimistic. People who never
admit to anxiety are less vigilant and more prone to be taken
by surprise. In a sudden catastrophe, disaster or calmity they
are more likely to do the wrong thing.
Prepare. Relax. Concentrate. Breathe slowly and deeply, let
your muscles go limp.

SHAKE OFF FEAR PHYSICALLY

Place the fingertips on your stomach just below the solar
plexus. Breathe in deeply, press hard with the fingers and bend
over forward. Hold this position and count one-two-three. Now
let the breath out slowly and stand upright. Repeat this effective
measure until you feel calmer.

This will reduce the tension in your head and allow you to
concentrate.

CONTROL FEAR IN OTHERS

You may be old and fear for your young, or perhaps you are
the grown-up children who are apprehensive for the old folk
traveling with you.

Cultivate moral support. A tightly knit group, whether it is
family or friends, has greater morale per person. Teamwork
lessens fear and makes each person more effective.

Use leadership. Especially when you are the older with the
very young, or the young and mature with much older people.
Practice discipline on the trip. A ruly group on arrival at the
terminal will always survive better than a rabble.

Be calm and controlled so that the feeling spreads. This re-
duces nervous tremblings and inspires courage.

And practice your religion, being quite prepared to pray and
unashamed of having spiritual faith.

BE READY FOR THE WORST

It helps to know that you are prepared for the worst kind of eventualities.

By counting on frightening possibilities happening, even the old and immobile can gain some strength—not to resist, but to take better measures to sidestep the trouble altogether.

Such as—

Hijackings: With bitter experiences behind, the airlines follow the basic policy that the safety of the passengers and crew is their first consideration. Most airlines direct their crews not to resist hijackers. A gun fight could cause injury to the passengers or severe damage to the aircraft.

A passenger should not by words or actions upset or provoke a hijacker.

When a passenger is confronted by a hijacker he should sit back, remain calm and not try to be a hero. The crew's instructions should be followed to the letter.

Muggings *should* not happen at a terminal, but they *do*. Security, transit and city police cannot be everywhere at once. A mugger pulls a weapon every fifty seconds on average in a really gigantic city; some of these occasions happen at terminals. The mugging takes place and the mugger who has aimed for fast money melts into the throng by the exits.

From your first step into the terminal, always carry a $20 bill loose in an inner jacket pocket (see also THE CANNY: p. 40). It is even better if you can afford a $50 bill, but the lesser one will do if you are poor. Look on it as instant life insurance.

In most cases $20 is usually as much as any street-heister expects to score from one job. And even when the assailant is as inept as the victim—for instance, a nervous junkie who needs quick cash for his habit—it is unlikely that the victim's need to keep his money will equal the addict's atrocious physiological craving to get it.

When you face someone threatening you with a gun or knife or some other weapon, pull the banknote out of the pocket *slowly*. Look pathetic. Say it is all you have on you. But do not go immediately for the money—wait a moment or two to make him think that it is your only money and you are reluctant to let it go.

There is an important warning to remember whenever you face a weapon held in the fist of an unknown quantity.

Never underestimate a criminal because he looks young or small or scared. Keep on your guard. Murder and manslaughter rarely happen out of the blue. Almost always, words or actions by the victim prompt the killer into striking.

Handbag snatchings happen regularly at terminals, where travelers carry more valuables than usual. A fast-moving thief can still hide inside a vast terminal building after robbing you.

Although the usual victim is female, men too can fall prey to the bag snatcher who steals other possessions besides handbags. It could be a camera, tape player or similar-sized possession that is costly and hangs by a strap from the shoulder or is held in the hand.

Let it go.

Do not try to resist the snatch. The person may be armed and mentally disturbed. Shout "Stop that man!" or "Thief!" if you must, but do not give chase.

Were you to catch and trip him, he—in his demented fury should he be of this temperament—can turn and rend you. Realizing you have cost him his freedom, he may stab, shoot or butcher you.

Pickpockets are usually too slick to be caught. If you do feel fingers in your pocket . . . shout. Pickpockets are cowards and either run or try to appease you with a look of outraged innocence (shoulders up/eyes rounded/mouth open).

One reason is that a pickpocket might have robbed others who, hearing your call, will feel their own pockets. If they find them empty, they close in to help you.

However, do not grab or hold on to the fingers in your pocket. This thief may be the exception prepared to be violent.

If the wallet or billfold has already gone, look on the ground. It may have been thrown there—perhaps tucked into the folds of a dropped newspaper, dropped on to railroad tracks or even stuck in someone else's pocket nearby. (See also THE LEERY, p. 47.)

Call "Hey" indignantly rather than aggressively when someone else—probably a suitcase thief—picks up your suitcase and walks away. It is not easy to run with a suitcase and the thief will usually pretend it was a mistake and apologize.

The threat of kidnappers is even worse when you are elderly or sick and taking the role of temporary guardian of the young. You have not the energy, strength or presence of mind to thwart a father slutching for his offspring.

Talk when you are cornered. This gives you time for help to come and a little space too.

Keep calm. Minds cannot control bodies when emotions take over. This is as true about dangerous hatred as it is about fear.

Keep moving even if only in short steps. Stay in balance by shuffling the feet flat-footed from side to side and never cross your legs.

Look the other person in the eye to show you are not afraid. Because eyes and the surrounding parts of the face tend to express thought, this also reveals what he intends to do.

If he grabs for the child, grasp the youngster tightly and call for help.

Call for the police. They are likely to arrive more quickly in a terminal (where city, transit and port authority police patrol 24 hours) than on the streets, where you might have to be lucky to find a cop.

The universal cry for help in any country is a shriek and a sob. This is especially true when someone has grabbed for your son or daughter, and it is quite clear there is no reasoning with him. Whatever you say or do, he is going to assert his masculine strength and take the child away.

If you look bewildered and shout, help can come from various sources. Especially when you have made friends on the trip (see THE SHEEP, p. 28). The sight of a distressed woman and child being harassed by a male could bring an intervention from someone—if only to separate everyone until the police arrive. It might be a serviceman or another woman or someone else who answers your call. Only be sure to make it loud, clear and plaintive.

GET HELP FAST

The ways to shout for help most effectively are:
Call quickly as soon as trouble hits you.
Call as loudly as possible, because you have to compete with aircraft sounds, buses revving, trains shunting, trolleys rolling, public address systems squawking.
Call continually; keep up the shouts, cries, yells, screams for HELP or POLICE. Or even, when the terminal is deserted, FIRE—the one call which will fetch people running quicker than anything else.

If you are a woman in good health an ear-splitting scream will work. A chain of such shrieks will bring help running, and also has the effect of an "offensive" grenade on your assailant's system—it attacks him and defends you.

When you suffer from laryngitis, inhibitions about screaming in public, or simply a weak voice, call for help in a low tone. This does not carry as far as a scream, but the low-register call will last longer. It can be heard after a shriek has died away. Keep calling for aid in these low foghorn tones.

Bray, bellow and bawl in the gruffest, deepest and loudest tones you can muster. It helps to shout all the louder if you place the ends of both forefingers against your ears. The noise then cannot deafen you or dampen your yell through any inhibitions. You cannot hear yourself, but everyone else can.

This low-register call then becomes a long drawn out "HEEEE-EEEEEEEEEEEEEEEEEEEEEEEEEEEEEEEEEEEEEELP!" as opposed to a quick yelp or succession of yelps.

When, however, you are too old, sick or weak to raise more than a whisper prepare in advance by carrying an alarm for your peace of mind. (But *never* a weapon which, if it works, will land you in court. In any case such a weapon is more likely to be taken from you and used against you.)

Carry a whistle. Blow this when in need. Do not wear it on a string around your neck—there is a risk that an attacker could strangle you with the cord, whether on purpose or not. Put it in a pocket you can reach easily.

The same goes for a child. It is far safer for a child to carry a whistle and blow it in an emergency in the city, than to carry a weapon of any kind. As with the tooled-up adult, an attacker can so easily snatch the weapon and use it to his or her own ends.

A whistle is good because it can be shielded in the palm of a hand before you place it to your lips and blow.

Or carry a portable alarm in a pocket or handbag. Stores sell these hand alarms—either battery operated alarm packs which emit an unstoppable series of shrieks when a pin is pulled, or compressed air alarms shaped like a hairspray container with the horn on top and producing 150 two-second blasts heard a mile away.

The Confused

Have a saving grace which will help them survive certain city situations.

Cultivating this appearance can help you survive many city situations, but you will need to work for this loutishly gauche manner to be effective. And it, by its sheer unorthodoxy and confusing contrariness, can beat the self-confident city pack and actually scare them off.

CULTIVATE UNCERTAINTY

If ever you do slip and are pulled into rapping with a stranger who cleverly draws you and the conversation out, introduce yourself as Mr. Bates, Mr. Egg, Mr. Rapper, Mr. Apple, Mr. Lemon, Mr. Winchell, Mr. Touch.

Most of these are names given for the victim in the city by the waiting wolves. And the fact that you state your name with the apparent honesty of the fool makes them uncertain. They are not sure just who you are or what you know, but they will usually have their grift sense telling them you are no loser. Not with a name like that and an element of confusion about you.

In this way you save yourself, for now you are *aware*—and it registers to their razor-keen instincts.

CULTIVATE INSOLVENCY

The fact that you have spread your money in different pockets and are possibly carrying a hidden cash reserve too means it is physically impossible to pull out more than a limited supply of cash from any one pocket at any one time.

Therefore when you cannot produce the amount needed for a prostitute, a card game or a con man trickster—not right away, at least—there is every chance that any villain will look somewhere else for his action.

Never produce a stuffed wallet or a roll of banknotes from a pocket. Apart from the mass of small change in a jacket pocket show only a few small bills in public.

CULTIVATE MISUNDERSTANDING

Should you be drawn into a conversation that has all the makings of a confidence trick—a proposal is put forward in a roundabout and devious way, although each step is quite easy to follow—purposely misunderstand.

By a combination of saying, "Pardon? Pardon?" and puzzlement which shows you cannot take it all in, the con man, if he is one, will soon be persuaded to move on to easier prey. For in his book you are a "lop-eared sucker"—a sucker who is too stupid to realize his advantages in a confidence game. And not worth pursuing.

CULTIVATE BUMBLING

It is important that you should not overdo acting stupidly. You must never be confident that you cannot be taken by a con man. They have too many ploys and know human nature far too well for you ever to be that sure.

However, it does pay at times to pretend to bumble and stumble through situations when you are unsure if you are being set up.

When you realize these tactics are paying off and you are even starting to enjoy them—for there is a frustrated actor in most of us, especially when we are allowed to hold the stage—remember: this is no game. Leave now with apologies before you give away the fact you are being clever and get hurt.

Part Two

CITY TRANSPORT

**Trains, Subways, Buses, Taxis
and Cars**

3

CITY TRANSPORT

LOSERS

BATTERED, pushed, shoved and delayed in the commuter crush or riskily alone on an empty subway platform or cabless street— that can be YOUR situation on leaving the terminal. There will be many such times when you face discomfort and danger on city transport.

How DO the lambs survive? Against the subway conductor who purposely gives incorrect directions . . . the teenagers who knock down a blind woman on a bus . . . muggers on the move . . . trains that jump switches or hit tracks that are bombed . . . strikes, traffic jams and holidays when modes of transportation are immobilized?

We can only make city travel more bearable and safer if we see ourselves as others never see us. By not dumping our own weaknesses on to long-standing and overstrained vulnerabilities of city transit systems, we can survive better than those who ignore their personal failings.

The American (Overseas)

Is vulnerable on foreign city transport. Unfair as it may seem, Americans abroad have become associated in many eyes with an international arrogance which cuts across the grain of national manners and customs overseas.

SIGNS AND SYMPTOMS

You may be a gentle and sensitive American, but the fact that you are American can make you the victim of persons obsessed with the idea that all Americans are Ugly Americans.

That you may not sport cameras hanging like a bunch of grapes, wear a cotton suit or Bermuda shorts and carry your billfold at the hip does not really matter. The fact that you speak with an American accent will dress you in this guise to the anti-American taxicab driver, bus conductor or citizen.

CAUSES

The American tends to manifest, especially on leaving a great terminal in a foreign city, the schizophrenia associated with these very areas. (Airports DO attract the mentally disturbed who have discharged themselves from hospital but who are still in need of care—and who are pulled by the no-man's-land glamour of these places; big railroad stations also attract those suffering from depressive illnesses—the reason being many schizophrenics find it difficult to cope with life and drift to these poorer areas.)

WHY the American? Because, once out of his native environment, he or she—it is often felt abroad—does a complete about-face into a tightfisted spin. Big spending is an anathema. Every transaction is looked on with suspicion.

The way of the world is responsible. America became the richest nation at a time when the world accepted—more or less— the idea of democracy. And as if to recompense for its gargantuan wealth, at this of all times, sought to ease its conscience by massive handouts to neighbors near and far.

Only it all backfired. Instead of being looked on as kind and generous, America's motives have been questioned, its advances snubbed, its coffers further subjected to charity calls. As a result the average American overseas—under the belated belief that charity really *does* begin at home—now exhibits split personality tendencies to an alarming degree.

ILLOGICAL BEHAVIOR

In the transit arrangements of any great city we daily encounter madhouse moments—whether we are in or outside the USA.

We can go by taxi, bus, train, subway or rented car and there will still be crisis situations ahead where the American, no matter how quiet a one, can revert—when unsure, rushed, lost, pushed, delayed, obstructed, cheated or insulted—to the more pushy behavior which will get him by in times of crisis at home but not abroad.

It is an anomaly that such tactics can put you in more danger in a supposedly "gentle" foreign city than in its most vicious American equivalent.

Elbowing to the head of a line patiently waiting for a bus or train ticket, for example, will cause uproar abroad. What begins with a push and ends with a push in the American city will end in a punching match in a European city. People simply do not retaliate as much in America—in case the line-jumper is mentally disturbed and armed. But in those cities overseas where brutality is reckoned less likely and the rules for waiting your turn more rigid, watch out for a broken nose.

Even when a line-jumper succeeds in breaching the line, it will now close in on that person. Otherwise responsible citizens are now more likely than ever to block, trip or trap you.

This same reaction is met by those who become victims of their American parsimony. Because of an ever-ready suspicion that he is being taken for a ride and conned when traveling in a strange city, the worst kind of American's tips are almost nonexistent. Not so his doubts, though.

Of course there are cab drivers who will cheat. But being taken for a longer-than-necessary drive in a foreign metropolis is of secondary importance to your arriving safely at your destination.

And there is nothing like suspicion to breed belligerence in the taxi driver who is doing his best. From here it is a short step to his throwing you out somewhere en route, making an even longer detour out of spite, or even becoming violent.

Gridiron football is pure Americana. Because some of its devotees treat travel in cities overseas like a piece of broken field running against an enemy backfield of whoever gets in the way, YOU, bless you—gentle, loving and kind American though you may be—must be ready for the worst.

Remedy: The Researcher, p. 90; The Obsequious, p. 124

The Provocative (Pullers)

Can draw unwelcome attention to themselves consciously or subconsciously. But here they attract danger.

We are all unknown quantities when packed tight in a crush-hour train or logjammed traffic. The provocative have ample time to attract emergencies that would pass them by on the sidewalk.

SIGNS AND SYMPTOMS

The unconsciously provocative girl may straphang with a straight back because her skirt is so short her panties would show if she bent even slightly. The consciously provocative might not wear a bra, but use Scotch tape instead. Or wear an ornamental zipper on the front of skintight pants when the zipper is unnecessary.

CAUSES

As long as city transport carries millions of people a day, something someone does in a certain way will always draw the attention of someone else and, sometimes, provoke an emergency.

It can be the cyclist wobbling in front of a cabdriver and asserting his right to the road or the motorist who carefully displays his more expensive possessions on the rear window sill before locking his car. One provokes being sideswiped, strafed and knocked into the gutter; the other, theft from any automobile thief with a master or duplicate key (as advertised and provided by mail order), beer can opener, wire coat hanger or other car-door-lock-picking device.

But it is sexual provocation that brings most discredit, shame, loss of image and physical harm. Because whatever happens—and whatever we say happened—*we* are mainly to blame.

No one else is. Not even the media which are often accused of arousing women's sex consciousness. Those sex ads in newspapers and magazines are only effective because women themselves *want* men to be aware of their sex.

And girls know of course, when they draw attention. Yet, like anyone else who flirts with trouble in an inviting way—be it that bike rider or car owner—they always feel they are within their rights. That if anything nasty should happen, it wouldn't be their fault.

Prompted by this craving to make heads turn and to force others to react to them, they gamble.

It may be due to a deep insecurity—you may feel "old" and that you are losing your pull or you may, if you're young, simply want excitement. But one thing is certain. You *did* tempt fate—and trouble is trouble no matter what are the ultimate rights and wrongs of the matter.

ILLOGICAL BEHAVIOR

The provocative always have a choice and if they opt for the decision that makes them stand out, they face potential mayhem.

If a man gets into a train compartment occupied by just one girl he has taken a step which provokes. If that female is neurotic and screams and calls a redcap, even the most innocent person is liable to have an anxious, sick-feeling time proving that he did nothing.

Sometimes, however, the choice to provoke is prompted by a subconscious desire to pull an attention which you feel you can control. You have never known yourself to fail before.

A girl in the subway car showing a yard of leg, for example, knows that she is provoking all the males in sight and will readily risk stares from them. But if a man's leer becomes so lecherous that it scares her or pushes her relatives into using violence, the man can be bound over to keep the peace or be fined.

However immune she may feel to the most searching gaze, though, she will not be able to ignore the feelings of repugnance and anger which creep up her spine and make her cheeks flame with embarrassment when she feels a hand actually fondling her bottom. Yet the man who is doing it has the beautiful excuse of touching her in the thronged subway train because the ordinary rampart of distance is removed. With every lurch he can pretend to be thrown against her.

There is even danger here. A young girl provokes a degenerate in a subway train and angers him on these grounds: although she is pushing her sexuality, she is also making it obvious he will never be able to touch her. He unzips his fly in a I-can-be-a-teaser-too retaliation.

We can all be provocative just by being *there*.

There is no clearer evidence of this than when a woman chooses to drive alone through a city center *and* look her best.

But she already does, if only she knew it—even though she may be pregnant, plagued with lumbago or have varicose veins. To many males any woman behind the wheel of a car looks unattainably sexy—as witness the male drivers who will sometimes follow women driving alone on and on through the avenues, streets, parkways, expressways and beltways.

This is nothing, however, to the fate of those women who, driving their cars alone, have become part of a giant traffic jam extending 8 miles in one direction and 6 miles in the other. The cause of the traffic holdup is a massive victory celebration in the city because Peace has been declared or the local baseball team has won the World Series.

Huge rejoicing crowds are every bit as menacing as sullen and angry mobs.

Over 100,000 drunken people in the metropolitan hub go berserk. Indulging in every kind of excess, they will all too readily turn on those who are trapped inside cars. Buses and autos are overturned, the roofs of cars collapse under the weight of the crowd climbing over them, police cars have their windows smashed and are abandoned and women are pulled from their driving seats and brutally attacked.

Pity the unaccompanied women drivers, at the mercy of the merrymakers milling around. For the sadistic ones who have already smashed fire hydrants, bathed in the resulting spray, indulged in public nudity and pranks with loaded shotguns will think nothing of taking part in sexual assault in front of hundreds of rejoicing fans who will cheer on the assailants and make no attempt to help the victims.

You may think it impossible to survive in this type of situation if fate turns against you and singles you out. The result of what happens when 3,000,000 locals, tourists and good-time gladiators hurl themselves into their yearly madness and reason flies in the face of alcoholic euphoria.

Yet by borrowing from the stuff of Winners, you *can* survive. You DO have certain lines of defense—even if you were foolish to be caught in this situation in the first place, because you chose to be in the wrong place at the wrong time.

Remedy: The Pessimistic, p. 99; The Devious, p. 118; The Obsequious, p. 124

The Long-Suffering (Upright)

Are the lambs who have become hardened to the sudden storms of rush-hour conditions. They are the easiest prey of the pickpocket.

SIGNS AND SYMPTOMS

A season ticket dangled ostentatiously in the line at the ticket gate. Standing when seats are available on the subway. Staying in the same crowded spot although there is more space to stand several feet away. Not turning your head or straining your eyes for the next bus. Keeping shoes rooted to the same spot when traveling in the train.

CAUSES

A mild and gentle disposition makes you long-suffering. But the fact that you believe in a lazy existence, in which you do not intend to strain yourself for any reason, also contributes to your vulnerability.

You have decided that the best way to survive on crowded buses, trains and subway is to bend like grass to the rocking progress. You become the perfect stoic. This is not the same as the feeling of resignation that comes over the ill or old, who will naturally go for any chance of comfort.

By no means slumped, you stand in a vertical torpor, unconsciously adjusting to every movement of the bus or train like a sailor on the high seas—a season-ticket mariner with season-ticket legs.

ILLOGICAL BEHAVIOR

Pickpockets know that in every tightly packed subway car at 5:30 P.M. there will be certain individuals whose very resignation will make them easy victims.

Obvious to them *you* are oblivious to the pickpocket who brushes your pockets with a hand while pushing past. A good pickpocket can tell how many banknotes you have in a pocket in three seconds of "fanning."

You will allow a person rushing into a train just before the doors close to grip your arms and thrust you aside, all the time claiming he is now in the wrong train. Then he rushes violently out again. But this one does not steal your wallet; he only distracts you. The money is taken by a second thief who passes it to a third—still on the train.

Or you may allow someone to put gentle pressure on one shoulder as the train moves. Rather than move your feet under the pressure, you lean forward. This old trick makes the lips of the side trouser pocket opposite the shoulder open up slightly. And your billfold or wad of banknotes can be lifted from it that much more easily.

How do they do it? A pickpocket stands facing you and another stands behind. A third stands to the side with a folded newspaper thrust casually in front of you.

At a signal, the one behind leans on your back. As you lean to give way, the crook in front begins to "reef" your pocket under cover of the newspaper. Instead of using a whole hand, he inserts his index and middle fingers and then, by bringing his thumb into play too, pulls up the lining of the pocket until the money falls into his hand. Giving a canary-like chirp to signal success, he slips it to the accomplice with the paper.

You may even allow someone to chuck you under the chin with a tightly rolled magazine as he squashes past, appearing to fend you off. This keeps your head up for a second or two while he dips into an inner jacket pocket with his free hand.

Many people will *not* stand having their chins propped up by someone else—even for a second. But if you number among the chosen few who will, then only the long-suffering who is also a wallet-watcher will survive.

Remedy: The Pessimistic, p. 99; The Devious, p. 118; The Canny, p. 40; The Leery, p. 47

The Tense (Uptight)

Lose their cool when everyone else is keeping theirs. Or if they don't, the tension is still screwing up inside them.

Transit in the city is a situation in which, if you are going to go off the deep end, there may be no holding the waves of violence you set up in *re*action.

SIGNS AND SYMPTOMS

Scratching your nose agitatedly because the train's bar car is out of bourbon. Leaping a mile as a crack in the wooden seats of a cable car nips you. Glaring at the smart ass who talks of the pollution being so "unhealthy" this morning that the city skyline could not be seen from the ferry. Being bumped on an underground train and, when you discover your wallet missing, grabbing a suspect as he steps on to the platform even though the doors have closed on your arm and the train has started moving. You are left with a handful of ripped jacket. Then your wife calls the office to say you left your wallet at home.

CAUSES

City air is more than smog. Noise and crime pollute it too. The resulting umbrella presses down on us, squashing all the senses, screwing down the reflexes and pulping his inhibitions against violence.

During rush hours in crowded streets, the traffic fumes turn the air blue. These fumes, it is found, send thousands on a minor hallucinatory trip every day. Prolonged exposure to even tiny amounts of carbon monoxide, for instance, can lead to sudden dizziness, violent coughing, headaches, sleepiness, difficult breathing and slowed-down reflexes. There is also loss of instant judgment of color, distance and direction. The air in a car becomes poisoned, and inhaling over the period of time it takes for traffic to unsnarl can make a driver temporarily color-blind. At a distance he might mistake a red traffic light for a green. . . .

Beneath is a global hell that all can experience. It forms a personal globule that is constantly being pricked from all sides too—as feet/legs/elbows constantly attack us in subway trains, taxicabs and buses. And we start to twitch.

Too much of this kind of strain can prepare us for a nervous breakdown. And city travel in these days *is* too much. It is too easy to underestimate the wear and tear of getting to work each day.

Those happy in the work which makes them take city transport daily will ride the battle better. It is when you are miserable in your occupation that there is the most long-term risk: when you groan rather than whistle your way to work.

The motorist who drives along the parkway and down Broadway each day can all too easily regard it as a symbol of manhood to slip through the heavy traffic—an indication of the male superiority and pride that his work denies him. He may actually look on those who travel by subway, train or bus as "softies," "old men" or "quitters."

One day frustration grows as he drives to his office, which is on the 26th floor and as anonymous as the guts of a vacuum cleaner. A traffic jam blocks him. Balked in the one pursuit which brings him relief and self-respect, he loses control and. . . .

ILLOGICAL BEHAVIOR

. . . feeling engulfed in this avalanche of metal momentarily suspended above the abyss of the daily comedown—*work*—he precipitates misery by accelerating hard on into the back of the car in front and wipes himself out without reason. Oblivion.

How different this disastrous behavior is from most of our other eccentricities. These can go unnoticed by many people. But we're never unnoticed when we freak out.

An individual who is himself very near maximum tension level tends to leap at any chance to jump on someone else's tension bandwagon. . . .

As when, crazed by incessantly spewn-up slush while trying to hail a cab and further incensed by a cabdriver's complaining/ grumbling/moaning as you try to nip back the creases into the trousers of your best suit, you vent your pent-up feelings by making a motion as if to batter down the mugger-proof mesh between the front and rear seats of his freezing yellow cab and pound him to death. He, maddened too by all that's maddened you, catches a glimpse of you in his rear-view mirror. He slams on the brakes, leaps out and puts a bullet into you with the pistol he always carries.

When the driver of the tiny Fiat 500 squeezes himself out on to the street at the lights and stands gorilla-tall. You had taken violent umbrage at his overtaking you—in a car of a class inferior to your own—and given chase in your smart limousine. But you never considered that HE might be bigger than you or that he might be even more wound-up than you and now fully prepared to use a knife.

Too late again when you are knocked on to the subway track below the platform because you did not say sorry to the person who first barged into you—standard survival procedure in the big city. You pushed back. But that person was twice your size and repeated his first shove so vigorously that you fell over in front of the approaching train.

Even the most trivial frustration can burst the festering boil of your irritation—and you along with it.

Remedy: The Pessimistic, p. 38; The Obsequious, p. 124

The Sybarite (Softies)

Look on comfort as their greatest need. Like lambs who slumber on the warm highway, they are blissfully unaware of all the risks.   ,

SIGNS AND SYMPTOMS

Going on your way by taxi when the others are still waiting for their luggage at the airport because you purposely left it until two minutes before your flight was called to hand suitcases to the redcap at your departure terminal! The bags (you know) miss the flight, and the airline has to deliver them to your address in the city (and so you are not lumbered with them). Wearing a Pregnancy Without Fear, a small satin pillow trimmed with antique lace and rosettes which you shove up your dress and tie around the waist with pink ribbon so that you can jump queues and always get a seat on the bus or subway.

CAUSES

It is easy to value comfort too highly. It is not all that important. Yet city transit systems manage to convert the hardy/ tough/ascetic into luxury-seekers within a few days.

Trains and buses are hot, stuffy, dirty and often packed. Anything from 3 million to 7 million people will pile aboard at morning and evening rush hours. Often there are . . . several hundred more passengers than seats . . . broken train seats . . . missing light bulbs . . . vital lights missing from signals . . . trains still in service since the 1930s. All exist.

It is tempting to cringe away too obviously from bad vibrations in a sardine-can subway car stuffed with over double the amount of passengers it is designed for . . . and jangling with scarcely hidden personal prejudices. But we can't escape.

When a subway train breaks down through faulty doors or is delayed because a suicide has jumped in front of a train, there are long waits between trains.

This means stations become crowded, boarding times become longer, delays build up and down the line—and everyone becomes more angry.

Buses, which do not have their own tracks, are as vulnerable to congestion as anything else on the roads, and this infuriates passengers waiting at windy and wet stops.

You see commuting as a personal thing—not as something related to the millions of other poor souls who are doing the same thing. After all, it is you, personally, who are being battered and barged every day. You do not see *yourself* as just a tiny fly in the most enormous pot of ointment.

But there is every reason why you should. Otherwise seeking extra comfort can become dangerously expensive—in a number of sinister ways.

ILLOGICAL BEHAVIOR

You make it clear that no one will be welcome who sits next to you. But why should YOU have the bus seat next to you empty when others are standing?

It is because you like the luxury of the space next to you. You will hate too the thought of anyone who is dirty, or otherwise obnoxious, sitting so near.

This is why there is a brand of purse snatcher and pickpocket who deliberately cultivates just this appearance.

He sees your handbag making unspoken claim to the seat next to you, and so he makes as if to sit down on that seat. You hold your breath. Then he changes his mind and sits on the seat behind you.

You relax, yet are still conscious of this weirdo just behind. You can't turn round in case you should connect yourself in some way with him. Not even when he throws his topcoat over the vacant seat and feels through its pockets, takes the handbag and jumps off the bus at the next stop.

As for the pickpocket, he eats garlic, sits next to you on the aisle side and lets go his breath. Most people's reaction is to twist away and stare tensely out of the window.

This enables the thief to bring the hand further from you behind his back and—jogging you with his nearest elbow to keep you looking away—dip it into your coat pocket. When a bus stops there is a floating motion; he takes the purse or wallet and steps off while you are still staring out of the window.

The sybarite who always goes to the rear subway car for the best chance of finding a seat at rush hour can fall prey to habit. Suppose he still heads for the last car, without thinking, between 11 P.M. and 4 A.M.?

Now he finds he is alone except for the patrolman assigned to the rear car. However, when the officer eventually walks toward the front cars, two muggers enter and force the sybarite to hand over his billfold at knife or gun point. They flee at the next station.

However, THE SYBARITE is able to sit in a bus or train at *any* time of day and still be the Loser most likely to attract sheer terror from the worst source of trouble on city transport: young thugs and vandals who crowd on board and goad the passengers.

A characteristic of the bon-vivant-at-heart is that he glares at and stares down anyone who presumes to encroach on his territory, especially when the invaders are so obviously scum. But, as we saw with the pickpockets and purse snatchers who capitalize on this trait, the glarers and starers do not continue for long before they turn away with averted eyes. But they have already signaled their displeasure to rowdy football, baseball or basketball fans entering that bus or train.

When, say, a group of youths are showing off by bumping, shoving and making loud remarks on the sexual attributes of girlfriends and wives already on board the train or bus, YOU—the carpet knight—will never fail to ignore the threat. By scowling, grimacing, gritting your teeth or narrowing the eyes—no matter how momentarily.

Such an attitude spawns an aggression that THE SYBARITE cannot maintain. He postures briefly but the muscles he flexes are imaginary. This violence is all in the mind.

The crunch of breaking bone is music in the ears of young sadists, who lose no opportunities to set about anyone (YOU?) with taunts and jeers—just to encourage retaliation. The slightest suggestion of a shove or suspicion of a sneer, and they will swarm in to the kill (of YOU): weapons bouncing off your skull, shoes or boots going in with sickening thuds and grievous wounds on your body, head and genitals (wrecked forever) as you fold up on the floor.

The fatal mistake of the SYBARITE is to underestimate these rough boys who undermine his own little world of sensual luxury. He feels insulated from the physical existence of the tough, unruly and brutal; theirs is a world apart.

Cold facts tell differently.

These warn how vital it is to be especially wary of mere kids who, though half your size and a third your age, can quickly slash you to ribbons with any one of the arsenal of mean weapons they carry.

To avoid being picked up by the police for toting *concealed* weapons—the tools with which they hope to inflict harm on *anyone* of sybaritic tendencies—they prefer to carry those which may legitimately be called "tools" or some such other daily-seen objects.

No one would ordinarily suspect a youth carrying an umbrella. Yet the sharp-pointed metal end can easily punch you full of holes, or the heavy handle pound your head to pulp. It is the same with the junior who carries a cane: the knob could well be weighted with lead, or the cane itself be constructed from hard wood or even steel to be used for your destruction. Rowdies carrying bottles of any kind, whether in a bag or out in the open—filled or half-empty; milk, liquor or soft-drink bottles—have brittle clubs which, if they break in action, will see you scarred for life.

The list of potential weapons is endless. Sharpened steel combs, heavy boots or stiletto-toed shoes, studded belts and heavy metal ornaments worn round the neck: these are as effective as the more obvious.

So constantly check on how sybaritic you are. It is well worthwhile, if only to avoid the confrontation with the teenager (less particular about being picked up for carrying concealed weapons) who stitches razor blades inside the peak of his cap . . . or who carries a piece of lead piping wrapped inside a folded newspaper . . . or who sews a length of bicycle chain inside the bottom of his jacket, the garment to be used as a flail . . . or who will wear a few strands of barbed wire around a rusty-colored leather glove and who can inflict more damage than a wild tiger.

The kind of thugs whose attention you have drawn to yourself on a train, subway platform or bus can never be dissuaded by philosophical chat aimed at pointing out the error of their ways.

By then it is far too late. All the bully can think about is satisfying his itch to hammer you into the ground.

We are all guilty of grading comfort too highly: it is the result of our living in a parlor society where, cushioned and pillowed against the spikiness of the concrete jungle, we turn into rolls of physical fat and mental flab. But the quicker we realize the kind of occasions when we give this away—usually over unimportant issues—the safer we will be.

Remedy: The Researcher, p. 90; The Pessimistic, p. 99; The Obsequious, p. 124

The Dependable (Worthy)

Put stress factors on themselves by obligations and promises which they feel must be honored *at all costs.*

SIGNS AND SYMPTOMS

Peering anxiously up the street/rails/platform for a cab, train or bus, but never down. Asking others for frequent wristwatch checks. Line jumping to buy a subway token. Begging the right coin to make up the exact change for the bus when the driver does not make change and you must have the exact fare. Letting the imagination run riot when you miss the exit from a strange subway platform to the street.

CAUSES

There are two forms of promise which can endanger you. One is when you promise someone that you will be at a certain place on time: "Honey, I'll be there at 6 sharp." The other is when she, or he, gives *you* a promise: "You be ready too—I'll be waiting."

Either way fulfilled promises can endanger more lives in the city than broken ones. We all, from time to time, have been guilty of setting ourselves an impossible schedule, only to be delayed. And the promise which you feel has to be kept at all costs creates a dangerous situation that makes you very vulnerable.

If you are always making promises and keeping them (proud of it too, no doubt) you do yourself a disservice. Home pressures, for instance, that overrule the fundamental basics of city survival are usually caused by promises and result in wildly idiosyncratic traits. Of course, a loved one may get mad if you break your promise and turn up late, but surely it's better *to* arrive than end up in a city hospital. . . .

ILLOGICAL BEHAVIOR

It is the law of averages which sooner or later will catch out the perpetual promiser on city transport. The time to be warned is when you find yourself daily trying to burst into an overflowing subway car as the metallic voice of the public address system warns, "Watch for the closing doors."

If pickpockets don't get you, Forest Lawn will. For example, it is the person who is robbed as he dives through subway doors at the last minute who is also liable to be killed outside his parked car.

It is the person whose wallet is taken while boarding a taxi who could also be killed on the tracks below a subway platform.

The reason in each case is get-home-itis or get-to-work-itis, which pricks people into attempting the absurd.

The pickpocket well knows that anyone so afflicted is blind to everything but getting on that stuffed train. You can rip a pocket off a woman's coat and still she will not notice when she is intent on pushing through a herd of people also all trying to get on board.

The same applies to riding a cab. If a permanent promiser spots one, hails it and then finds others climbing in, she forgets all reason in her fight to assert her right and claim the cab as her own.

In both cases, they—the pickpocket pack—hold open the doors of the subway car or taxicab to stop it moving. At the same time they take advantage of your distracted mood and pick every pocket clean as they jostle around you. Only then will they let you climb aboard.

When the subway doors are nearly closed, there is even more danger. Say you thrust an arm or leg through in an attempt to keep them apart and stop the train so you can get in. . . .

But subway doors do not always open when a foreign body (yours) is trapped between them. Nor is it true that a train cannot move if one door is still partly open. They can and do when the door is faulty. It may be stuck an inch or two open, trapping your elbow or knee or shoe, and still the train moves out. If you are boarding near the front it is quite possible you will be dragged off the end of the platform because you cannot free the trapped limb in time.

Then cars. Most cars weigh over a ton. The unaccustomed strain of pushing a car that won't start as far as a slope can kill someone. He need not even be middle-aged, out of condition or recently ill. He may have seemed to be in the best of health. . . .

Digging snow can also produce a coronary in the 30-year-old

when the work is the only really hard physical labor of the year. Shoveling snow in wintry conditions accounts for many deaths between December and March in large cities.

Just as bad is many a promiser's decision to abandon the car trapped in snowdrifts and, despite the deadly blizzard, attempt to reach a telephone when on the outskirts of the city limits.

For motorists caught up in winter storms such a decision may mean death—as compared with the varying degrees of misery to be suffered by those who stay in the car. These catch cold, but survive.

Any distance at all, whether a trek across fields or "half a mile down the road," involves the risks of exhaustion or stumbling off route. Having perhaps covered no more than a few yards in the blizzard you disappear into a hidden ditch or pond. And it is often too late to turn back for the car when you try; you can no longer find it in the storm. And a snowstorm can be a killer.

The strange part of it all is that there is nothing unique about such deaths; they happen every winter where snow falls.

Not that this lets out, however, the dependable people who live in the sun all year round. While on a visit to the north in a rented car they are even less likely to know what to do when a snowstorm hits them. Persistent promisers live everywhere and can suffer as a result *anywhere*.

There is another threat to life from driving under the pressure of time. You may meet the type who cannot bear to be passed. Psychiatrists call this behavior the Pass Syndrome: a man's car is part of his ego, and he will look on it as a personal insult when YOU—racing to honor an obligation—pass him. He will chase you and when he catches you is quite liable to shoot, stab or at least beat you up in his fury.

This is why the warnings go out each hot summer: "Drivers, watch your temper." But YOUR promises and obligations, which encourage you to disregard time and again the sounder precepts of city survival, should warn YOU.

Remedy: The Pessimistic, p. 99; The Obsequious, p. 124; The Canny, p. 40; The Leery, p. 47

The Duchess (Stubborn)

Is the frail, elderly or crippled person who is liable to dizzy spells, fits and blackouts; regal disregard of his or her condition makes for a pigheadedness which can kill in city transit.

SIGNS AND SYMPTOMS

Taking a cab because to walk any distance you need a stick—but are too vain to use one. Standing near railings because you know that if you fall you cannot get up without something to pull yourself up on. Stepping off the sidewalk and in front of an oncoming taxi to stop it because you think, "They always stop for me," but risking injury if the cab driver turns nasty, since, though you won't admit it, you can only move at snail's pace.

CAUSES

Variety can maim or kill the old or ailing, whether they are poverty-stricken or live in a penthouse.

If you have to make a journey in the city, then you have to. But *do* you have to?

Is it not right that, on fifth, sixth or, anyway, seventh thoughts that your journey is not really necessary? That it is partly a flinging down of the gauntlet in the face of advancing years or cramping disability, a gesture just to show the world what you can still do when really up against it.

Very often this is so. And each time you make an unnecessary city trip to assert your independence, to show there is life in the old dog yet, and to generally flaunt your refusal to take things quietly, you tilt with fate. . . .

ILLOGICAL BEHAVIOR

Many fit and mobile people find traveling in the city a strain. But even the shortest trips are hell for those just recovering from operations, or unwell or old and frail.

You have very little control over any situation when tottery and unstable, and yet your dangerous state of mind is, "I'll show them."

Such an attitude is unrealistic. Many things can go wrong in the city which inconvenience the fit but seriously threaten the weak or ill.

As when the subway train on a stifling evening is one of four which break down between stations and which, together, trap 6,000 citizens for two hours. Overcome by heat or claustrophobia many panic or faint or even hammer on the windows for relief. When eventually freed from this nightmare in a tunnel the fit are shaken—YOU are seriously ill.

Which country or what city you are in at the time does not really matter. These are universal crises when, too intent on making your trip come what may, you fall prey in any subway system. . . .

You get caught up with a frantic line as it rushes on to a train or bus going to a destination you've never heard of. You have to give way, but what you hoped might be a short journey turns out to be a nightmare trip into the unknown concrete jungle.

Is taking a taxi the answer? Not if you have no money or lack the courage, know-how and agility to hail one.

And when you do catch a cab and inch yourself on board you may find that, due to a stiff arm, paralyzed side or sudden shooting pain in the chest, you cannot close the cab door. It is out of your reach.

In a really violent city it is too much to expect that the cab-driver will get out and do it for you. Today's yellow cabs have bulletproof partitions between driver and passengers and a locked cash box bolted to the floor. Both have helped stop the rise in the number of cabdrivers being murdered for their money. So why should your driver—when YOU could be a decoy planted by a gang—get out to close the door for you?

Whether YOU go by bus, train, subway or taxi, your TED factor is of longer duration than anyone else's in the city. TED means Time Exposed to Danger. It stacks up the odds against anyone who is elderly or ailing.

These fall into danger on city trips that for those who are younger and in better health are commonplace.

Remedy: The Pessimistic, p. 99; The Nervous, p. 52

The Cavalier (Casual)

Cut a dash by appearing not to care if their possessions are stolen, their lives threatened or their loved ones hurt. This is a grossly irresponsible attitude; others suffer for it.

SIGNS AND SYMPTOMS

Turning up the car radio to drown the sound of a sudden loud knock in the motor.

A clean windshield—but only because you burned the ice off with hot air from your new red-barreled defrosting gun. Exactly the right change at the toll booth—but only because you use the new pistol-shaped toll gun which fires nickels and dimes into the wire basket to one side. But for all your slickness you still leave the car unlocked, with the baby fast asleep under a blanket on the rear seat as you dash, so handsome, into a store.

CAUSES

There is an 007-element in all of us. We rebel against the uniformity and drabness of city life, in which it too often seems the only real action lies in side-stepping responsibilities, jumping to conclusions and pushing our luck.

We tend to take up this cavalier attitude—we know we have it, but what the hell—when things are going well. . . .

When the life insurance is fully paid, the hospital and medical insurance is up to date and there is money in the bank to replace anything that is lost or stolen.

It happens particularly when things have been handed to us on a plate. We are cheerful. Wanton carelessness can result from a run of good luck, in which life has seemed tailor-made to our requirements.

There is a widespread notion that it is a sign of insecurity and weakness to take pains to protect the family you love, the things that you own and even the future you want. A stupid notion, but. . . .

The person hell-bent on self-destruction chooses to tempt fate with a panache he believes is attractively casual; he thereby makes a rod for his own back.

But the beating may come too late. The lesson is never digested if you hang yourself because thieves took your automobile with the baby sleeping peacefully on that rear seat—and it was then involved in a hideous crash.

ILLOGICAL BEHAVIOR

It is not a very sexy, potent or virile characteristic to go over your newly rented car looking for faults. It seems overfeminine, fussy, to lock all the doors before leaving your car, or even to fail to pick up a hitch-hiker as you drive out of the city.

Or so it seems to those who are with people they wish to impress. They feel that their passengers may secretly mark them down in their estimation if they play safe.

"So what if the car is stolen?" "The insurance will pay." "Who would want this heap of crap, anyway?" "Sure this rented car's okay—they wouldn't put a bad one on the road."

These are the kind of comments which spur the irresponsible, those who never grew up, into shameless behavior that leads to certain downfall in a great city. Because they are afraid to look like a granny, they would not be seen dead checking this, locking that, securing these or alarmproofing those.

But look at the facts.

Rented cars *are* often unsafe. In various surveys, in many different countries, a third of the hired cars examined should never have been on the streets. Investigators have regularly found loose safety-belt mountings, low tire pressures, flat spares, severe front-end vibrations, wheels out of balance, oil leaks near the front brakes, throttles that stick open, rear brakes binding, gearbox oil too low, horns not working, wipers out of unison, wheel nuts and steering column clamps loose . . . all dangerous.

Our cavalier, who is unlikely even to kick the tires for hardness (let alone go down to them with a tire gauge), look at the oil level, check all the lights and flick the fan belt with a finger for slackness before taking over a rented car, will also show a lunatic disregard for safety on leaving the car. He won't even lock the door.

He has the key—that's enough. (No one will despise you for whipping that out as a safeguard; it can be done with a flourish too.)

But it is certainly *not* enough.

If a car thief wants your car badly enough he can take it. Don't worry about that. He can back a repair truck up to it, slide a towing trolley under it and pull it away. After all, who is going to query a couple of overalled mechanics?

YOUR leaving the car unlocked, however, means virtually *any*one can climb in and drive it away. This is why at least 200 cars a day are stolen in any great city, where a minimum of 2 million cars will be parked in the open every night—goods which represent a value of over a billion dollars, of which the car-thief gangs help themselves to at least $12 million worth a year.

Look how the incompetent, nervous or cowardly runt takes advantage of your swashbuckling idiocy. . . .

He opens the door and squats behind the wheel. In a flash he is under the dash connecting leads—jumping the ignition with his trusty wire and crocodile clips. He is taking a risk carrying a "jumper" in his pocket because it is a sure giveaway for the police. But without it he couldn't steal a car. He knows absolutely nothing about what goes on under the hood. The jumper, however, shortcuts this for him. The car starts with piston pulse.

Perhaps you have at the back of your mind the reassuring thought of the insurance company waiting to pay out if the worst happens.

This, however, may cost you a larger premium for the next

insurance. You might have to find the cost of any repairs if the car is crashed (many stolen cars are). If the car is a total wreck, or untraced, you receive less money from the insurance company than the cost of buying an equivalent vehicle to replace it. One of the things insurance companies can rarely do is to replace the car immediately—it may take weeks to get a settlement.

Nor is the private motorist always immune in a case of injury to someone to whom he is giving a lift. Many policies do not include such cover. You could be open to a substantial claim arising from accidental injury to any passenger you may be carrying.

Not to mention the risk you take if that hitchhiker turns violent and decides to rob, rape or kill you.

It is sometimes said that car drivers with friends or relatives traveling with them can give lifts safely.

But this is not true when it is because of wanting to impress these very people that you stop. You now place *them* in danger too: perhaps from an experienced gunman, con man or rapist.

It may be only one hitchhiker you pick up, but if he has a pistol filled with six bullets he can kill the three of you twice. . . .

Remedy: The Pessimistic, p. 99; The Devious, p. 118; The Obsequious, p. 124

4

CITY TRANSPORT

WINNERS

Entering a city from the terminal we leave a mini-metropolis—the airport or bus depot with its fountains, banks, bars and drugstores—for the real thing: *the* concrete jungle. Transport from one to the other is a transitional stage.

It is not a gradual but a brutal breathing space. There is no gentle acclimatization from the great depot to the hard reality of the city itself. Thrown in off the deep end, there are only four Winners capable of buoyant behavior now.

The Researcher (Interested)

Does his homework in advance when he is genuinely and enthusiastically passionate about the conurbation ahead of him. His is a strength founded on preknowledge. It counts for safety all the way.

KNOW WHERE TO GET INFORMATION

The things that matter most about traveling in the city should be learned before you reach it. Obtain information from the most reliable source you can.

By advertising in the personal columns of the papers back home that you are willing to pay a small fee to anyone living locally who is from the Big City—and who can help you with material for a research project. By meeting natives from that city in your local bars, clubs, dances, church organizations, parks. By telephoning local newspapers to check when the next delegation of visitors (if any) is due from the great metropolis. By visiting the consulate or foreign-speaking unions of the city you are bound for. By searching for, in each case, an individual who will help answer your questions. Or individuals—even better.

By visiting the library to read travel books, guidebooks, maps, magazine articles, etc. *before* you reach the city. (Children's libraries are often best for information laid out simply and quickly absorbable.)

By drafting the basic map of the city center on the back of an envelope as you fly, ride or sail toward it—from the guidebook you obtained in advance. Memorize it by leaving out all the streets except the main ones: your main impression then will be of circles, segments, squares, triangles or a grid with each geometrical facet a thoroughfare.

By making friends on the journey in with a native returning to the Big City. And who will drill you on all the city matters you need to remember.

By getting any unanswered queries solved at the city's tourist board free service—at the city terminal—on arrival. Or, if there is no such service here, by phoning the tourist board or bureau as soon as possible.

KNOW WHICH CITY TRANSPORT TO TAKE

If solvent, take a cab. If not, a city bus is better than the subway, which can prove too complex an introduction to a strange place after a long trip.

The taxi gives you the presence of the driver, who is an expert in his own terrain, like the sherpa on a Himalayan peak. Going alone on bus or train in the city makes you more dependent on casual help if you need it; it is the kind of assistance that can prove nonexistent or fatally unreliable.

If you are hard-up, the chances are you will be staying at a low-priced hotel or hostel somewhere near the bus or railroad station.

Stash your possessions in a locker and walk to the hotel to check in. Return later for the suitcases after first casing out the streets— or buses if your accommodation turns out to be too far away to walk.

When you board a city bus you will need to have the exact fare in small change in one hand; the amount can be ascertained from others waiting at the bus stop if you are not sure. As you drop this into the slot by the bus driver ask him to drop you off at the street nearest your destination. Offer him a tip.

Those who are too broke to do this should still sit near the front after asking the driver to say when. But it is also wise to check with other passengers seated nearby you, since busy bus drivers do forget.

Remember it is your approach that counts. Bus drivers and conductors (where they have them) are sensitive people. Contrary to what some of the public may think, they are not all petulant characters, skilled at rushing past rained-on you or giving passengers a dressing down along with their tickets. But there is no doubt that dealing with the public all day drives some bus drivers toward the verge of breakdown. And many leave their jobs because of the paranoia induced by citizens venting angry feelings on them.

It pays to look on a bus driver as someone who has—and *needs* —the concentration of a racing driver, the dexterity of a taxi driver, the smoothness of an ambulance driver and the endurance of a cross-country truck driver. *And* the attributes of accountant, diplomat and walking encyclopedia. . . .

Apologize for being a nuisance; ask quietly but firmly to be put off at your street. Know the exact address and have it ready at the tip of your tongue. (It also helps when you can describe the city landmark nearest to it.) Show you will appreciate his help by smiling rather than frowning.

Approaches such as this are the drips oiling urban cogs—only it must be you who applies them.

If you are picking up a rented car at the city terminal and have never been here before, avoid steering straight into the thrust-and-cut of downtown traffic during the daytime and early evening unless it is absolutely necessary.

It is far easier on the nerves to go first by taxi to your hotel then to pick up the car around 5:30 A.M. and accustom yourself to driving round the city streets when they are at their quietest.

Before driving into the city center, at any time, buy the latest morning or evening newspaper. Check if there are going to be massive demonstrations, processions, public holidays, annual sporting occasions, great carnivals—or if a war has just ended.

Before leaving for the city, ask a terminal policeman if there are likely to be large gatherings in the main streets and avenues.

If he says yes stay in the terminal until the metropolis calms down or take a subway train to your midcity address after leaving baggage in lockers. Or take a cab and ask to be taken by the safest route, which need not be the shortest, but which you should be prepared to pay and tip for.

KNOW HOW TO BEHAVE IN THE CITY

Urbanites are as parochial as villagers, as quick to spot the out-of-towner as they are to sense the city dweller—with whom they feel more kinship.

Bus drivers, cabbies, subway conductors and train conductors will be more helpful if you commit these gilt-edged assets to your memory bank.

Try to *look* city. This can be done by dressing formally, casually or in-between. Do try, however, to subdue, if only a little, the overdone appearance of the *tourist*: see THE AMERICAN, p. 65. It is important to try to strike a balance by not being too flamboyantly wherever-the-country-overseas-you-come-from, even though you are understandably proud of your origins and mother country.

Do not be carried away by the en masse beauty of city girls. Head turning is against the rules. Once a girl has passed, you should be happy with the memory. Of course, if you are creative enough to invent some reason for turning round—like stopping to tie a shoelace—it might be permitted, but it must be done smoothly.

Highly developed eyeball training is a desirable goal. Aim for the most refined all-round vision possible—by swiveling the eyeballs and keeping the head still. Later, you will find this can help save you from criminals too.

Find out about city terminology before arrival, so you know some of the local expressions. New Yorkers, for example, will ask for Sixth Avenue, never The Avenue of the Americas, which is the newer name used by the noninitiated. The San Franciscan will call his city "The City" or "San Francisco," never "Frisco."

Do not scatter your pleases about too profusely, but always be ready with thanks for favors done.

Always have the right fare for city buses as well as small change ready for tips (see THE SHEEP, p. 28).

Do not climb into a yellow cab after your girlfriend, wife or mother. Climb in first to save her the longer trip across the seat, a mark of the urban traveler.

Ask a cabdriver, "How's the weather been in town this week?" "Which route will you take?" "Did you see that Mets/Jets/Knicks game last night?" Don't try to be too clever, but be interested, like someone who, notwithstanding the foreign accent, sounds as if he lives in or knows the city.

Any reference to football, baseball, boxing, soccer—whichever is the big sporting event of the day or evening before, a fact you ascertained from the paper you bought at the terminal newsstand —is valuable. The cabdriver may not follow the sport, but he will follow you—especially when you use the local nickname or abbreviation used for a city team, like "Knicks" instead of "Knickerbockers."

Try, no matter how approximately, to get and keep your bearings. Keep glancing at the back of your envelope where you drew the basic map of the city. The sun will help you note the direction. It rises in the east, sets in the west and is, more or less, around the south at midday. When the sky is overcast hold a plastic credit card vertically on a thumbnail and slowly rotate it. Unless the day is gloomy, or you are standing directly in the shade of tall build-ings, the sun will cast a faint shadow.

KNOW HOW TO HAIL A CAB

It is not always easy to get a taxi in the city. In some cities, never. In others, at certain times of day and night.

If you want to stop a taxi in Moscow, for example, dress up in peasant clothes and try to look simple. Moscow cabdrivers are notoriously selective. They choose their fares according to how much they think they can get out of them. They divide people into three groups: (1) the peasant types—farmers, their wives and ordinary people not used to traveling around the city, whom they consider easy picking; (2) the sports jacket types—out-of-towners who may be alert to obvious overcharging and whom the cabbies feel can be tricked only with caution; (3) the fur hat types— usually well dressed and educated, who will check their change carefully unless they are drunk. The taxi drivers ignore the fur hat types unless it is unavoidable or they have had a poor day. They prefer to drive around the suburbs where there are plenty of peas-ant types laden with luggage, anxious for a lift. Thus it is hard to get a taxi in the city center; usually you need to book one by phone at least four hours in advance.

Find out the taxi situation in *your* city before you get there.

KNOW HOW TO RIDE A CAB

Take the number of the taxi before getting in. In case you should leave anything. Or wish to report gross overcharging to the police later.

Know the simple way of doing this (a gimmick used in mathe-matics to remember formulas). Develop your own code. Say the number is SA7 9RY. It looks like SAY DRY. Another, BS11 OAX, could be Be Safe Eleven On A Crossing. EC4Y OJA can be Easy For Why, Others Jobs Aren't. Practice soon gives a flash response to this mnemonic aid.

Ask the cabdriver about how much the trip will be if you are hard up. If he is surly, angry or noncommunicative take another taxi.

See that he switches on the meter at the start of the ride. If he does not, mention it. Even if he says his meter is out of action, you have registered that you are aware. Say, "I hope you have a head like a taxi meter."

Keep your purse or handbag on your lap so there is no chance of accidental loss.

If the cabdriver asks the way he may genuinely not know. Do not assume he is trying to trick you into taking a longer trip.

Keep cool if the cab is heading in a different direction from the one you think is the way. Give a cabdriver the benefit of the doubt —getting there is more important than being cheated over a matter of peanuts.

Sit back and relax. This saves you a bump when the taxi makes a sudden short stop. It also helps you gain the correct attitude of a calm air rather than one of nervous tension induced by watching other traffic and the meter.

Resign yourself to disaster—and when it fails to happen congratulate yourself on your abundant good luck. Tip the driver well, about 20–25 per cent.

KNOW WHAT TO EXPECT ON THE SUBWAY

Ask for a subway map at the ticket or token booth when you are new to the city. But still expect the initial attempts at finding your way around the honeycomb of subterranean passageways to be difficult and at times desperate work.

Don't be taken in. Once underground, we tend to lose all perspective of distance traveled by train and mileage trod. In many cases, in the course of a short journey on a subway train, we cover half the journey by plodding corridors/stairways/platforms—paid for in advance. The same happens once we disembark from the train; there may be an even longer trek to street level.

Remember: it may be quicker, easier and less strain to take a slow-crawling bus for a short journey in the heart of the city.

Crush-hour subway trains impose physical strain on day-to-day commuters. Examples—

1. False Angina, a pseudo heart attack bringing pain to the left chest and arm . . . caused by the tension of standing cramped in an unnatural position (being unable to lower the arms, say, which would have to push past the large breasts of the female standing by you).
   Remedy: Get out at first chance and wait for next train—or push back into another car at the next station.
2. Nagging Preoccupation that you MUST stretch your legs (which are jackknifed up because of those commuters standing in front of you).
   Remedy: Twiddle toes. Rotate ankles. Move foot muscles. Wriggle body. Breathe deeply (reoxidizes blood).
3. Aching Legs caused by suffering from the same Misery Syndrome.
   Remedy: See Nagging Preoccupation.
4. Sudden Cramp in the legs because of lack of movement. Or could be in the arms which you had folded across your chest or held up in the air on entering the solid-packed train (and now you can't move them to a new position).
   Remedy: Stretching combats cramp. And cramp twinges give warning of cramp attack to come. When warned, stretch muscles at once . . . in foot, press toes on floor so they are forced toward your knee; in calf, straighten leg, try to bend toes toward knee AND force foot back toward shin pressing heel away; in thigh, bend knee and stretch thigh forward.
   When you can, knead with fingers until cramp knots go.
5. Drowsiness, another symptom of the Misery Syndrome found in crowded subway trains/buses/private cars.
   Remedy: Yawn (see also The Sheep). Also . . . stretch your neck up carefully—and down again. Keep repeating. Breathe deeply. Search for new ads to read in the train.
6. Migraine, a headache caused by sitting too long concentrating your sight within a narrow field of vision.
   Remedy: Pull your head up higher; straighten the neck. Turn the head in different directions, but keep your head held high (good health reasons for this too).

KNOW HOW TO PLAY THE COMMUTING GAME

If you live more than a few blocks from work, there is only one way to keep sane. Look on the everyday trip as a game. Commuting to work can be looked on as a series of baffling checkerboard strokes and shots to reach the king row.

Research and make up your own game, depending on your preferred method of travel. You will find it gives you a therapeutic diversion in the most awesome and breath-squashing crushes.

Such a game may be expanded by the subway traveler from this simple idea: the main aim in subway travel takes place as the train arrives at the platform. Once there, it is the duty of all passengers inside to get off while letting the absolute minimum of travelers get on.

Embarkers, on the other hand, must ensure that as many as possible get on, while making it impossible for anyone inside the train to get out.

The crush in the doorways may be tremendous. The disembarkers forge forward on to the platform as the embarkers force back into the train. If more boarders can bulldoze their way on than those abandoning the train can charge their way off, the boarders can be said to have won.

Score like this . . . 2 points for every passenger so frustrated WITH 1 bonus point for every passenger carried on for more than one station beyond his or her destination.

Not that YOU, who aim to blend, put this into practice and thus obstruct people. It is the thought, however, on observing subway doorway tussles, that brings the grim ordeal into perspective. You are the silent referee, who, by keeping score, keep your own senses too.

KNOW THE INSULTS OF THE CITY

When it comes to offending the greatest number of people on buses, trains, subways and cabs in the quickest possible time, it is not what you do or even the way you do it that matters—it is *where*.

Insults do not travel well. A noise or a gesture that will turn the citizen of one city into a homicidal maniac might not raise an eyebrow in another metropolis. Such as—

Pointing a camera at anyone.

Beckoning to a woman.

Jerking a thumb upward.

Clasping the right bicep with the left hand and jerking contemptuously at the object of your displeasure.

Jerking the first two fingers, palm upward.

The same V-sign, palm outward.

Jabbing the V-sign horizontally, palm down.

Your explanation that you did not know that such and such an action was insulting will almost certainly be too late . . . .

There is danger here. So find out first which insults apply—there are many more—to the city where you are going.

The Pessimistic (Prepared)

Expect trouble while traveling in the city but are not put off. Instead, by learning from the experiences of others—as well as their own—they make provision against emergency.

Thus it *is* possible to ride the daily hassle of metropolitan travel not as brooding Jonahs but as sensible avoiders of trouble.

DEGENERATES

Say "Do you mind" in a loud voice when a hand strokes or pinches you.

Turn round and look steadily at the offender.

A woman is perfectly safe from an exhibitionist if other people are in sight. If, however, there is no one else about she should not risk violence through humiliating him. Pretend not to see him. And leave the train or bus at the next stop and report the man to the guard or a policeman.

ROLLERS

Do not fall asleep on a subway or bus after you have been drinking or working late. Rollers who rob drunks work in threes. Two sit on either side of the sleeper; one stands in front reading a newspaper. They then go through the dreamer's pockets.

MOTORIZED PESTS

There are several kinds in the city. Because in some cases you need to keep driving to escape such nuisances, make a habit of regularly checking your gas, oil and radiator.

A good rule is never let the gas tank run lower than a quarter down. If you do a lot of expressway driving get it refilled when it is verging on the halfway mark.

Do not rise to taunts such as violent cutting in front of you by another car, the rotten pear that is thrown to splatter your windshield (never switch on the wipers first; turn the windshield jets on instead) or the moron who burns past you and then waggles a boot as if driving with one leg out of the window (in fact, it is his arm in the boot).

Keep driving normally and do not speed. If the harassing continues pull over to the side and let the nuisance get ahead.

When you are a woman driving alone and being followed by a male driver, keep going. Do not look sideways, but imagine you are wearing blinkers. Avoid slowing down, then speeding, then slowing down. This can excite the driver whose fancy you have taken. Drive slowly and steadily and, when sure he *is* following you, pull in at the nearest police station or parked patrol car. Stopping at a garage, store or restaurant is an alternative. Do not drive home if you live alone; this is the last place you want to bring trouble.

A car sticker helps deter reckless drivers. From a distance the sticker appears to display one word—POLICE. But there is small print above and below it, and on closer inspection the sticker reads, "support our POLICE force."

PROSTITUTE

The john urgent for a woman will curb-crawl his car and proposition females in the downtown areas where prostitutes patrol the city streets. This can only lead to trouble.

Never take up the offer of two girls for the price of one. They can both turn on you and rob you after you have driven them to a more isolated part of town, or one can nibble through your pockets while you are in the heat of passion with the other. If you must take this risk, only carry the amount of money you intend to pay. Hide the rest, including your wallet, in the trunk of the car.

When a girl gets into a front seat to discuss business, never be insulting. It is all too easy to trigger a prostitute into an act of venal and vicious violence. Such women, ultrasensitive to insult, have you at their mercy inside a car—where a flashing blade or a splash of acid is the answer to the jibe or to the john who fails to hand his wallet over.

Keep a hand on the car door handle during your discussions with business girls. Be ready to make a quick exit.

It is a little safer to drive a hooker to a quiet place than to ferry her back to your apartment or hotel. Rush her home and you make yourself vulnerable to robbery, blackmail or burglary—if not now at a later date. Not to mention trouble with hotel detectives.

Never drive a prostitute to the parking place of her choice. She may have accomplices waiting there to rob you. Find your own quiet site some time previously.

Make sure all the doors are locked and the windows are rolled up when you stop.

If at any time you have to leave the car or room, take your trousers (never remove these in any case) and jacket with you. Then she can't go through the pockets of your garments where there may still be something of value in them.

VISITORS

When parked in a car with a girl, or on any other occasion at night, never roll the window right down if a stranger taps on it. He might slug you on the head, rob you or do other damage. Slide down the window an inch only. If he acts suspicious—drive away.

If you can't get away, stay put inside the vehicle. Lean on the horn to produce intermittent blasts, rather than one long one, if he tries to attack you.

Women in automobile breakdowns should wait for the police; never go with a stranger who offers a lift to the police station or nearest garage.

UNRULY TEENAGERS

Avoid entering subway cars or buses full of teenagers if you are elderly or nervous. Choose the ones where there are older people. If none, wait for the next train or bus.

Avoid the rear (when the door is at the front) of buses late at night. When teenagers move in here, you should go to the front.

Always go forward toward the driver when changing seats on the bus. If teenagers enter the empty bus or subway car occupied only by you—leave it and get the next one home.

When jittery and frail, enlist moral support from a reliable-looking person. If he is sitting ahead of you, stare hard at the back of his head. He may begin to feel your gaze, start to fidget and turn round to see your predicament. The fact you are concentrating on something also helps calm you.

MUGGERS

City transport muggings are not always vicious and dangerous —all they need is your silence and fear.

Wait by the change or ticket booth on a lonely subway platform.

Sit by the subway driver and/or a door. Any subway car near the front holding several passengers is safer. If the car empties, move into one where there are other people.

The *worst* crime time in the city—although, remember, crime is a 24-hour deal here—is from 11:00 P.M. to 4:00 A.M. Take a cab or bus to be safer.

In any case always carry the $20 or $50 bill loose in an inside jacket pocket (see THE NERVOUS, p. 52). Be prepared to pull it out slowly and plaintively and to hand it over.

PICKPOCKETS AND PURSE SNATCHERS

Avoid piling on to trains and buses in a frantic crush of people. But if you are surrounded keep your mind and if possible hands on your wallet and purse.

Keep cool when people bump, obstruct, pull, shove, barge or blow garlic, onions or beer in your face. If people drive through closing subway doors or down the stairs from the top deck of a bus, knocking you down in the process, let your hand grasp your opposite shoulder (see THE LEERY, p. 47) rather than fend them off. And save your wallet.

Sit in the outer seats of buses, not on the inside by the window. Stick your outer hand on the aisle side into the side pocket when it contains small change, keys etc.

Move your feet occasionally when straphanging on a bus or train. When a space clears, move into it. Do not respond to gentle pressures, but move away from them altogether. If this is impossible because of the crush, keep your hands near your wallet or purse and think about it.

Keep a wallet in your hand or in a handbag held firmly. Do not put it down on the seat by you. Nor in the side pocket of a coat —an instant target.

If you do find your wallet missing and make it obvious (see THE NERVOUS, p. 52), look on the subway or railroad tracks— a favorite place for pickpockets to drop a wallet or purse when the victim discovers in the nick of time that he has been robbed.

Do not jump down on the tracks. Modern trousers will not let the legs bend sufficiently for you to spring back on to the platform easily—and an approaching train may catch you.

Leave the wallet there. Report it to the token or ticket office, a porter or a policeman. But if it contains a lot of money then stand guard over it until help from the subway staff comes.

PLATFORM PUSHERS

Do not stand right at the edge of the subway platform. It is too easy to be pushed over by the sudden surge from behind as a train approaches.

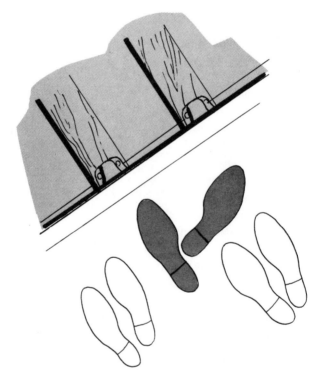

Resist the pressure of platform pushers.

If you are shoved to the edge and can't get back, brace yourself in the strongest position. Stand with the feet at right angles, so the right foot points at the tracks and the left shoe is behind and crossways.

Brace and flex the right leg to buttress yourself against any sudden strain caused by crowd movement behind.

DRUNKS

Give empty subway cars and buses a miss late at night. Go for those where there are other passengers. If they prove drunk— or rowdy drunks climb aboard—swap your transport once more.

Check previously whether this is a date when all the city celebrates. If so, take a taxi—but check those traffic jams.

CHILD MOLESTERS

Realize that children old enough to travel alone by city transport can attract the degenerate's attention no matter what they've been told or how well they've been brought up.

If a girl is returning from school she should travel with other children. But when she does find herself alone—

She should never climb into an empty subway car, but always choose one where there is a woman or women. If those women get out, she should move to another occupied subway car containing women.

In any emergency, a child should always go to a woman for help, not a man (unless a policeman).

FALLING ASLEEP

Tired or drunk commuters often doze off in the warmth of a rocking train and sleep well past their station.

Some people can fall asleep as soon as they get on their train, but always wake up a few minutes before they reach their station. Their subconscious mind has learned to recognize the particular noises the train makes when it gets on to the homestretch.

Persistent railway oversleeping, however, is a habit. Break it by reading, writing, chatting or playing cards (see THE CONFUSED, p. 59).

Avoid going to the toilet before the ride so that your full bladder makes for an irritant which blocks sleep.

Tell another passenger where you want to get off, but make sure he is not a train sleeper too.

HOMOSEXUALS

In a tightly crowded train avoid the eyes of anyone of the same sex when those eyes tend to linger. Forget about brushing that loose hair from your forehead; it's a sign, in some cities, of acquiescence when it follows momentary eye-locking. Universal body language.

Recognize the standard procedure so that you do not mistakenly fall into any such trap when *you* are a normal heterosexual.

The half-smile from a homosexual will, he hopes, get you to respond with a deliberate yawn and gay acquiescence. Should you do this, he will inch forward on his seat, returning what he imagines is a response to your reaction.

Do not be drawn into these games when you may well be out of your depth, unsure of yourself in such situations.

There is a type of homosexual who, if he suspects you are playing him along for kicks, can prove vicious.

MECHANICAL BREAKDOWN

The train that breaks down underground between stations can cause some to break into complete panic. They scream, yell, hammer on windows, throw themselves at the doors and hurt themselves in the crush, when in reality they are perfectly safe.

Prepare in advance if you have a phobia of this type.

Make up a survival kit for it, and carry it in your pocket, handbag or briefcase. It should be small, compact and contain those items which are known to give a sense of security to those with claustrophobia (dread of confined places), nyctophobia (fear of the dark) or thanatophobia (fear of death).

Two kits have proved best. One contains two glasses and a small bottle of Martini, carried in a small shoulder bag. The other is a pen-type torch, a felt-tipped pen for doodling and a screw-driver-like tool. The tool will not allow you to break out, but it gives many people trapped in trains a certain comfort.

In any event, know that broken-down trains can and in due course *will* be pushed or pulled out of a tunnel by other trains.

If the train is derailed it will be evacuated car by car and the passengers led to safety. Most stations are less than half a mile apart. When they are further apart there are always escape stairways leading to the streets in between.

It is very important to check a rented car in advance for the possibilities of mechanical breakdown in a great city center.

Carry out these checks at the terminal.

Switch on all lights and flashers and walk round the car to see if they are working. Check the tires with a gauge or a swift kick (the shoe should rebound sharply). Wiggle the steering while driving slowly. Pump the foot brake and see that it works. Stop on a ramp and test the hand brake. Bang the horn. Look at the seat belt mountings. Flick the wipers. Check oil and spare tire and warning lights on the dashboard.

You do not need mechanical knowledge to recognize sounds indicating trouble as you leave the parking lot for the city.

BACKFIRE may show improper timing of ignition or a bad valve or faulty carburetor. KNOCKS OR CLATTER may mean an engine badly needs an overhaul; or it may be a fuel knock, meaning you need premium gasoline; a bad spark plug can cause an engine to run unevenly; a heavy thumping knock may mean end play in the crankshaft, while sharp distinctive knocks could be bad bearings. RATTLE may be due to faulty springs or a loose exhaust pipe. If heard when the brakes are applied, SQUEAK means worn brake linings; brakes also squeak when wet, but they soon dry out and return to normal.

ROGUE DRIVER

Anyone who gives someone else a lift, whether that other person has broken down or is just hitching to some part in or out of the city, has the person picked up temporarily at his mercy.

If you *have* to hitch—despite the fact that the police will always say NO—know what danger signs to look for.

Truck drivers are best. If they make a suggestive remark and a girl hitchhiker shows she is not interested they drop the subject.

Never trust car drivers. There are two types particularly to avoid: (1) the male driver who has other males in the car and (2) the male driver who addresses your body but not your face. The best way to turn them down is to say you thought it was someone else—friends you expect along any minute who will pick you up.

When you DO take the lift . . .

ALWAYS—

1. Fail to shut the car door properly.
2. Open it again so you have to slam it closed . . .
3. . . . At the same time inspecting how the door opens—and whether there is a lock which has to be released first.

Listen for danger signals. If a driver asks casually if you have a boyfriend or whether you would rather take a more picturesque route, beware. Say YES to the first, NO to the second—loudly—and chat about anything not associated with sex. If you smoke, light up—ready to jab the burning end into the would-be rapist's cheek.

No matter how highly persuasive a driver may be to buy you a drink/meal/sandwhich in town, refuse the offer politely.

In emergencies, leave the car quickly. But keep calm. Say you feel ill and are going to be sick, even start to make gagging sounds, ask will he stop a moment. Once you are outside you can get away fast.

If this subterfuge fails, wait until the car stops at traffic lights. Remember how the door lock worked, open the door and climb out quickly. Make sure, however, that the lights have just turned to red. If they swap to green too soon you may suffer a bad tumble as the driver speeds away.

The woman driver—accompanied by a young child—is the potentially safest lift.

ROGUE HITCHHIKERS

Know what to do if a young girl you have picked up threatens to shout "rape" after ripping her blouse. Her object is money.

Either give her cash or drive to the nearest police station or parked patrol car, whichever is the easiest for you. Only keep calm.

There are also occasions when thugs use a good-looking girl as bait to stop trucks and cars. Once the driver stops, the others emerge from shadows or round a corner and pile into the vehicle and force him to drive on.

Remember that hardened criminals who are being sought by the police do not travel by public transport, because it is so easy to get caught. They travel as hitchhikers and think nothing of pounding you into oblivion and then taking your car.

Never pick up a hitchhiker at night, whether it is a figure waving a gasoline can by a car, someone in U.S. Marine uniform, a student standing hopefully in pouring rain, or a group of girls.

When flagged down because of an accident ahead, slow down, checking the doors are locked and the windows rolled up—as they should always be when driving in the city.

Look the situation over. Slide down a window an inch to hear what is wrong. Offer to go for help, but do not get out. Only open a door when a policeman shows his credentials. Otherwise be ready to drive away at once.

DANGEROUS AREAS

Look on ALL parts of the city at night as risky areas. Have your car keys already in your hand when you go to your car. Thus you cannot be caught suddenly unawares while fumbling in your purse or pocket.

If you are forced to park in a really bad area because you run out of gas, look around first before getting out for the spare can of gasoline you should always carry in the trunk. When you do have to walk for the gasoline check that there is no one crouching behind the driver's seat on your return. It is a precaution you should always take before stepping into your car in the city.

Always keep the top up when driving a convertible in city streets at night or driving through unfamiliar areas or likely trouble spots.

If you do break down in a bad or unfamiliar area try to limp on at all costs to a safer, better-lit and busier section of the city. Inch along on a flat tire. Or move on the starter motor alone, if the motor will not fire, to the edge of a slope that might roll you downhill to a safer position.

When you can go no further raise the hood and trunk; tie a white rag or piece of clothing to the radio antenna or door handle on the traffic side and stay inside with locked doors and turn on whatever flashing lights you have.

If you find a flat tire on your car when parked in a dark street look around carefully; muggers may have slashed the tire and be ready to jump you. They may even scatter black thumb tacks to puncture your tires as you drive then lie in wait for you when you stop. Limp out of their range.

Lose the ignition key and you can still start by making a connection with any strip of wire, from the terminal of the battery which is not grounded to the terminal on the coil marked + or "bat." You *must* disconnect this wire at both ends when the engine is stopped.

CITY DRIVING HAZARDS

Assume that every driver other than yourself is either a raving lunatic or someone who has been used to steering a boat and who is unsure which way to move the steering wheel as a result.

Wear a seat belt on every little trip—even driving down to the store or public library. Even at 26 m.p.h. or less the impact of a sudden stop may cause serious injuries. Rear seat belts will also protect you. And harnesses in the rear seats will save your children too.

In accidents where seat belts are worn, serious injuries are reduced by more than half.

Defensive driving means taking into account all crises that could hit you.

FITS, FAINTING, DIZZY SPELLS. Do not drive into the city after a long journey when you have been drinking and/or taking pills. Not only should you never drive home after drinking—take a taxi—you should leave the car behind next morning too. Driving ability does not improve until the afternoon after the morning after the night before.

Certain drugs and illnesses impair driving. If you are in *any* doubt, consult your doctor before you travel.

DANGEROUS CROSSINGS. You may regularly have to cross streams of traffic at points which make you vulnerable. Work out a new route so that you always turn with the traffic stream and never cross it, even if this makes your drive longer. The extra safety will compensate for the longer route.

Know what to do in the following emergencies:

SKIDS. Expect them when rain follows a long dry spell or when the temperature is just cold enough to freeze water (braking distance on glaze ice is twice as long with the temperature at 30 degrees as it is with a zero reading). *Rear-wheel skids* are the most common; steer into them by going in the direction in which the back end is slipping. Try not to overdo it or you will set the car skidding the other way. *Front-wheel skids* happen from taking a corner too fast. Do not try to turn further into the corner, the instinctive reaction. Ease the throttle, straighten the front wheels and jab the brakes. *Four-wheel skids* come from too harsh braking. Take your foot off the brake, then dab down again.

STEERING WHEEL COMES OFF. Slide it back on the end of the steering column. Only start to brake then—with the parking brake.

WINDSHIELD SHATTERS. Take your shoe off the accelerator, maintain direction and punch your fist through the milky glass. Try not to swerve. Pull in as soon as possible and stop. Clear away broken glass to give a better view and close all windows to reduce the risk of remaining areas of glass collecting in the car because of wind pressure.

DOG IN THE STREET. Do not brake or swerve with other vehicles behind and approaching. Hit the dog.

BLOWOUTS. Do not panic and jerk the steering wheel as you hear the loud bang and feel the pull to one side. Grasp it tightly instead to maintain course. Brake very gently—using the parking brake with only small pressure on the foot brake if it is a front tire. Pull into the side, knowing you should still be able to hold the car straight against the most violent dragging effects of a spent tire.

Never try to change a tire yourself if you have a weak heart. The strain of lifting, jacking and working wrenches can be too much for you. Always carry the aerosol, obtainable from auto stores, which inflates a flat for long enough to enable you to drive to a garage. Or telephone for a garage repair service to help you.

It always pays THE PESSIMIST to carry one of the lantern-style flashlights. Like the type of lantern used by railroad men, it is not intended to throw a beam. Instead it blinks, winks or flashes SOS when you are in distress. You can place it near the rear of the car when changing a tire or when you run out of gas or when something is wrong with the motor and the car will not move. This lantern will help save your battery too.

CHILD OPENS A DOOR AS YOU DRIVE: Look ahead, steer straight. Feel for the door. Shout a warning and brake. Do this gently or the door will whip right open. Wind pressure will help keep it shut.

LIGHTS FAIL: In the unusual event of both headlights cutting out, slow up as quickly as you can and look for any other source of illumination you have. Dimmer. Fog lamp. Spot lamp. Near-side direction flashers . . . all can help you drive or crawl along a dangerous stretch of road.

A SNEEZING SPASM: Slap your thigh hard. Brake and pull in if practicable.

WINDSHIELD WIPERS STOP: Keep going straight ahead. Crouch over the wheel, face up to windshield. Brake gently on the wet road. Pull in.

BRAKES FAIL: Pump the brake pedal and apply the parking brake quickly but steadily. Do not yank it. Start engaging lower gears to act as a brake on the engine. Bang on the horn. Switch on lights. Run the edges of the wheels against the curb, and if you are still going too fast aim to side-swipe an empty parked car when there are no escape routes.

Test the brakes often by making a light dab on the pedal before they are needed—especially in a newly rented car or your own fresh from the car wash.

ENGINE ON FIRE: Pull into the curb after checking the traffic behind; switch off. Take the extinguisher (you should have one), lift the hood and direct the jet at the source of the flames or smoke. Or smother the fire with a coat, rug or floor mat.

FLOODED STREETS: Walk through carefully if you have to check the going. If the water does not come to your knees you should be able to drive through if your exhaust pipe isn't unusually low. Use a low gear, drive at walking speed, and if the exhaust bubbles under water, slip the clutch (if the car has one) and press harder on the accelerator. Brake frequently afterward to dry and test the brake linings.

JAMMED ACCELERATOR: Shove your toe under the pedal and try to ease it up. Do not de-clutch. When time and space are limited switch off the ignition and brake to stop. When the traffic is behind you switch the ignition on and off to keep you going until you can pull into the side.

TRAPPED BEE/HORNET/WASP: Do not swat. Open a window, pull over and switch off the motor. Shoo the insect out.

LAST HALF-GALLON: Keep a relatively low speed in top gear avoiding sudden acceleration. Cut the motor to coast down slopes. Switch on near bottom of slope and ·engage high gear to start.

STRONG GUSTS: Grasp the steering wheel firmly and cut down your speed. Be wary when traveling in and out of shelter: big trucks, high walls, etc.

TORNADOES: Spot the most violent wind on earth by the funnel-shaped cloud spinning rapidly from the base of a thundercloud to the earth. Pull into the side, get out and find a ditch to lie in. But if you have time to move out of the twister's path drive at 90 degrees to the storm, averaging 50 m.p.h. to be safe.

EARTHQUAKES: Pull into the side and dive for the floor. Stay below seat level because upper structures may crash down as far as the seat level. If a live wire comes into contact with the car forget about debris and sit up straight. Sit still and do not touch interior metal. Leave the vehicle only when a policeman or power linesman comes to help you—not when well-meaning citizens motion you out.

SNOWFALL: Do not let air out of the tires or put extra weight into the trunk. Start in as high a gear as possible; avoid low gears. Handle the accelerator like a thin-shelled egg. Test the traction occasionally by touching the brake lightly. To climb hills build up a little speed first—in the highest gear possible. Wait, if necessary, until the slope is clear of slow-moving traffic. If you have to turn round in a difficult and constricted place on ice, just get out and push sideways on the front of the hood, but not too strenuously. The car will pivot round.

Remember to turn the steering wheel to the curb when you stop on snow or ice. If you are banged from behind by someone who fails to stop, you will not be knocked into an intersection at the lights. It also deflects you from an end-on collision with the car in front.

CAR THIEVES

Always roll up the windows and lock all the doors on leaving the car. This is especially vital if you have a four-door car. Frequently, if you have the car washed or carry passengers in the back, you overlook the doors that are left unlocked by others.

Avoid parking on dimly lit streets. Make full use of a street lamp, well-lit house or illuminated store. Try to find a parking space near people: shoppers, theatergoers, commuters.

Public parking lots whose attendents insist you leave the ignition key in the car should be a last choice. If forced into this, then leave *only* the ignition key in the car—take all other keys with you, trunk key, gas tank key, house key, office key, etc. Insist you get a claim check from the lot, and make it obvious that you are noting the mileage on the car as you leave it.

Make it a habit not to keep your car and house keys on the same chain. When you turn over your car to an attendant, he could have duplicates made of your house keys in your absence.

Take everything of value—credit cards/registration papers/letters—with you. Thieves always look in the glove compartments of cars for documents which, with the car, give them a complete package.

Never leave the car park ticket inside the car; a spare key on the sun visor or in a magnetic box under a fender; or the trunk key under a rubber floor mat. Thieves know all the hiding places in a car—right to looking in the bottom of the spare tire well in the trunk.

Stow valuables in the trunk only during the trip. Take them out on arrival. Trunk locks are easily opened with duplicate keys. If you *have* to keep valuables—portable radio, tape recorder, camera, binoculars, musical instruments, guns, fishing tackle, etc. —in the trunk for any length of time, use a sturdy, case-hardened link chain, a hardened padlock, and strong mounting brackets inside the trunk. Then the trunk lid can only be lifted 2 or 3 inches unless the padlock is unlocked.

Your hope of recovery when your car IS stolen lies in submitting a detailed description to the police: year, make, model and color; serial number, license; tires—size, brand and serial numbers; extra equipment—the make and serial number of your radio, tape deck, air-conditioner; identifying marks—dents, scratches, blemishes and other flaws. Keep such details noted in a diary or your wallet—along with your spare car keys.

Motorists should always insure themselves against loss. Take an inventory of your possessions not only to determine exactly how much you have and what it is worth, but also to be able to notify such a loss to the police as well as to your insurance agent. A police report substantiates that a theft did take place and that you did suffer loss.

Thiefproofing (except audible alarm systems; see below) must be *seen* to work best. This persuades the thief to find an easier car to steal or to steal from.

There are many theft-prevention devices. They work on three basic principles.

VEHICLE LOCKING DEVICES: Standard locks fitted to cars are suitable for stopping people from falling out of the car, but they will not prevent a determined thief from breaking in. For extra protection special security locks of the dead-lock type should be fitted.

Locking all the doors and windows is not enough. The trunk, the hood and car accessories are vulnerable to the really determined car thief—a fact which hits you when your car is stripped of its valuable parts.

Fit dead locks to all doors . . . to the trunk . . . and also the hood.

Fit locking nuts to all wheels . . . and also gasoline lock cap.

A word of warning: gasoline caps, like a car door lock, can ice up in winter and it is dangerous to try to free them with a naked flame, such as a match or your cigarette lighter. A drop of oil before winter sets in will prevent the trouble.

VEHICLE ALARM SYSTEMS: Nothing worries a thief more than the prospect of being caught in the act.

Audible alarm systems have just this unnerving effect and give positive security warnings at any time—day or night.

It is essential that the warning system—the horn blows when someone tries to break into the car—should protect all openings: doors, trunk and hood.

Some systems utilize existing electrical circuits; others are separately installed. Most are operated by a simple key switch. However, a separately installed horn is worth considering. Its pulsating note stresses urgency and is a greater deterrent than a standard horn.

Conceal *this* alarm system: experienced thieves know how to disconnect it. Hide the wiring and use wire that matches most of the car's own electrical circuit. And conceal the alarm switch.

Never place it in view either on the dashboard or in a place out-side the car where it could be corroded by road spray. Ask the garage for advice.

VEHICLE IMMOBILIZERS: The steering column lock which incorporates an ignition switch is a good mechanical car im-mobilizer. It must be fitted by a specialist. It is now standard equipment on most new cars.

There is a wide range of other immobilizers varying both in cost and security value.

Although steering column locks do a great job, it is usually after the damage has been done. Thieves will smash up a car to get inside before they realize that the vehicle has been immobilized. A visible deterrent is therefore needed.

Among the best are locking rods which hold the steering wheel to the clutch or brake pedal. While they can be broken or cut, it takes time to do so, and a thief will rarely risk being caught red-handed. He will look for another car with no obvious safe-guards.

Other methods include securing the steering wheel to the clutch pedal with a strong chain; locking the gear lever with an obvious and simple device; making the parking brake "dead" with a special combination lock.

Electrical fittings are available to cut the ignition circuit; devices of this kind are sold in kit form and can be installed by car owners. It is not too difficult for a motorist who has a knowledge of car electric systems to design such a device for himself.

There are also two other effective immobilizers.

Conceal a small gasoline cutoff valve somewhere inside the car—to be flicked off whenever the car is parked.

Make the car immobile by removing the rotor arm in the dis-tributor. The thief cannot drive without it and it would be difficult for him to carry a selection of rotor arms about with him.

A word of warning: beware of theft prevention devices which work on a time limit. Anything that could lock the brakes or transmission once the car is moving can be dangerous.

The Devious (Foxy)

Do not get into trouble because they train themselves to think on the wavelength of the more crafty among the wolf pack.

RECOGNIZE SUSPICIOUS BEHAVIOR

Watch out for certain patterns of behavior in others. And suspect:

Anyone who walks along the curb glancing into cars; he may be a sneak thief, looking for anything of value lying in a car. Honest people usually walk on the inside of the sidewalk.

Anyone standing around or propping up a bicycle on the sidewalk by traffic lights which are on a slope. He may be another type of sneak thief. He waits until a woman driver, with the top of her convertible or window down, stops at a red light. As the light changes to green, the thief jumps out to snatch a handbag or anything else he can reach—and runs or pedals away as the woman stalls the car on the gradient.

Anyone who holds a subway door, bus door or taxi door open for you until you are on board. He may also be a pickpocket (see THE DEPENDABLE, p. 80).

Anyone who looks down a subway platform, *away* from the approaching train, could be a pickpocket. Most people look toward the oncoming train, but a thief is looking for people with wallets and is not interested in the train.

Anyone who waits for train after train to go by might be a purse snatcher or pickpocket waiting for the right victim.

Anyone who stands *facing* you directly on a subway train in the commuter crush when everyone is pushing could be a pickpocket about to riffle through your trouser pockets—especially if there are rolled or folded newspapers in evidence in front of you (see THE LONG-SUFFERING, p. 71).

Anyone who sits behind your empty seat rather than behind *you* on a bus could be a purse snatcher hoping you will put your handbag down on the seat by your side—so he can reach over (see THE SYBARITE, p. 76).

Locking the clutch to the steering wheel effectively immobilizes the car.

Anyone who is wearing a topcoat on a warm day and has a gloved hand or steel hook protruding from a sleeve might be wearing a "third mitt," an artificial arm which leaves his own perfectly sound arm and hand to do the stealing as he sits next to you. (The sight of the polished hook makes many people turn away in embarrassment.)

CHECK ON POLICEMEN

When a policeman stops, or stops at, your car, never roll the window down more than an inch or so. He may be posing as a cop. There are hundreds upon hundreds of such cases in police records in every city. Remember that credentials may be phony.

Leave the motor running and be ready to drive away. Cover the ignition key with your hand. WHY is the motor running?

Is it because the car has been stolen and has been got going with the use of a jumper to connect the ignition wires behind the dashboard?

Any real policeman will make sure that he sees the ignition key *and* will ask you to switch off the engine and pull out the key (thieves sometimes use a half key which does not actually fit in all the way, but which seems to once their jumper has started the engine).

DISSUADE CAR HEISTERS

Make your car look not worth stealing or even too dangerous to take. Remember that it is the powerful cars that are not necessarily too conspicuous that are the main target for stealing gangs.

The life expectancy of a Chevrolet Corvette, for instance, on a New York street is just one hour. In London car gangs mark down Rovers, Triumphs, Jaguars and Fords in the same way.

The following methods have persuaded heisters to look elsewhere.

ERRATIC PARKING: Vary your parking habits all the time, never choosing one favorite site. Have lots of them.

MECHANICAL FAILURE: Simulate some form of breakdown. Stick a note on the steering wheel or windshield, ostensibly to inform a policeman or traffic warden, but really to warn off a thief. It can say: "GONE FOR GAS," "SUGAR IN GAS TANK," "STARTER MOTOR DEAD."

Leave mechanical bits and pieces scattered on the driving seat with instructions to a mechanic jotted on the back of an envelope. Or have the note signed, "GONE FOR REPLACEMENT PART." (But make sure the mechanical parts are not valuable, as this may encourage a break-in.) Add a couple of old spark plugs, an oily cloth and an old wrench and the deception looks complete. (Arrange the pieces on an oily newspaper. Place this on top of a plywood base. Drill holes in this so that thin fuse wire or string can be passed through to tie each mechanical bit in place. Conceal the wires or string under a smear of grease. The board can now be kept under a seat, ready to be put into position wherever you park in a new place.)

UNUSUAL SAFEGUARDS: A thief will often leave a car alone if he is unfamiliar with the kind of security device by which it is immobilized. This can simply be an old and rusty, but *strong*, chain looped through the steering wheel with the ends tucked out of sight under the driver's seat—presumably padlocked round a seat leg. Use it in addition to conventional safeguards.

A thief will hesitate when faced with an unfamiliar security device.

TRAPS AND SNARES: One of the best ways to deter the professional car thief is to mark all the windows with the car's registration number, using a do-it-yourself Identicar kit bought in an auto store. The registration number is etched on the glass and cannot be removed with disfiguring or by breaking the window. The effort and cost of removing all the windows, especially the windshield, from a stolen car and fitting unmarked glass is so great most thieves would ignore a marked car. The etched numbers are ¼ inch high and 2 inches long, so they do not obstruct the vision; the best place for them is on the side windows just above the door-key slot where a thief will see them. The Identicar kit includes a container of etching fluid, a brush for applying it, a set of stencils of your car's numbers, a duster, complete instructions—and a piece of glass to practice on.

Also identify your car by slipping an old excise license down the rear seat; making distinctive marks on the car's body in concealed places, say with a file on the chassis; scratching your initials inside the trunk or under the hood; dropping a business card inside the door panels; placing a strip of Scotch tape across the registration number in the registration book—to thwart the forgers who can normally erase the ink and write in a new number for the stolen car. For now the paper will be marred if the tape is peeled off.

CONCEALMENT OF GOODS: Keep possessions out of sight in the trunk. Unload this at the end of a journey. But when shopping in bad weather, and opening the trunk is too bothersome, carry boxes with a false botton apparently containing moth-eaten old flowers or scrap metal or poisonous insects or reptiles. Stash your parcels inside the empty space below the false base. Such containers will be too large and awkward for a thief to bother with, even if he fancied—for some weird reason—their worthless contents.

CHECK ON USED-CAR BARGAINS

Has the car you are about to purchase been stolen by a gang of professional car thieves? Perhaps it is an amalgam of various parts from a number of stolen cars, all fitted together as one?

Always be suspicious of a bargain that is too good and of "dealers" with no apparent address—"Call between 6:00 P.M. and 7:00 P.M."—who offer to drive the car to your home for appraisal.

The telephone number in the advertisement may be that of a pay phone.

Suspect a two- or three-year car that has been resprayed and fitted with new chrome and eye-catching accessories.

If it has been built up from various stolen vehicles the welds will have been filed down. But there may still be telltale welding blobs under the carpets or across the chassis—perhaps covered with sealing compound.

Look to see if chassis and engine number plates look unusually clean, have drill marks on them or fresh rivets/screws to hold them in place.

Study the registration book closely for alterations to registration letters or numbers and for faded or discolored patches that may suggest an endorsement has been erased.

ACCOMPANY YOURSELF

Many men cannot bear to see a woman at the wheel of a powerful car, especially when she is alone and vulnerable. They see her as a challenge, a target. Some will almost burst their engines to get past fast, or their gut to thwart, block or molest the woman.

No one driving alone through the city at night is secure. It is much safer to give the appearance that you are NOT traveling by yourself.

Of course, two people in a car can still be attacked. But the chances are less.

Use any means available of giving yourself company in the front passenger seat.

An inflatable vinyl dummy of a human figure is best always carried in the car of the solitary driver. It looks like a man from a moderate distance. These can be bought from many large department stores under names like "The Silent Partner."

Or improvise your own silent partner in the passenger seat.

Buy balloons and blow them up and stuff them down the sleeves and inside the space of a buttoned-up coat or jacket. Sit this buoyant object on the front seat and strap it in place with the seat belt. The head can be made from a round balloon, a sweater bundled tightly into a ball and tied with cord or your own home-made head consisting of a novelty store mask (Frankenstein-style) backed by a balloon or rolled-up pullover and covered by a snap-brimmed hat.

If you have a weak heart and need to blow up balloons in a hurry, use a balloon pump or the kind of air pump designed for air mattresses. The strain on your heart can prove too great if you have to puff up a number of balloons at speed.

An emergency passenger may always be constructed by lifting the spare tire on to the front seat, draping a coat round it, placing the jack between the tire and seat so it forms a neck, and tying pieces of clothing on to this in the shape of a head. Strap the figure in place with the safety belt.

From any distance in the dark any of these look sufficiently like a male figure in the seat next to you to make a potential attacker think twice. And the more bulky and menacing your silent partner looks the better.

The Obsequious (Kneelers)

Survive when all else has failed. THE OBSEQUIOUS, however, do not copy all the fawning and servile mannerisms of cringing, abject sycophants.

Instead they pick only those aspects of the type of personality that can help them face danger. It is an attitude where you *do* take it lying down—and live to finish the game as a result—the char-acteristic that separates Winners from Losers.

FACING DEATH ON SUBWAY TRACKS

Throw yourself flat.

In many cases there will be a trench between the tracks, made to accommodate anyone who is pushed off the platform by acci-dent in the subway crush.

The train will pass safely over you.

Although, as the diagram shows, most subways have two elec-

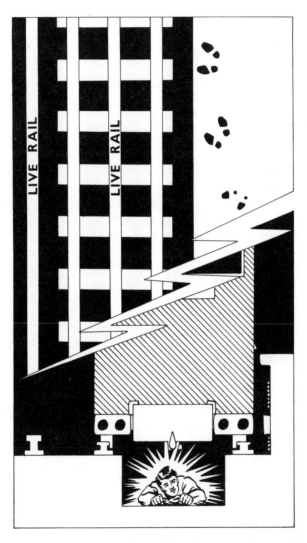

Two types of subway track. Top: A live rail runs directly over the trench between the tracks for the train. There is room to dive below it. This live rail, moreover, does not carry a live current when passing in front of a busy subway platform. It is the fourth rail, furthest from the platform, that is live. Bottom: There is a shallow channel between the two train tracks and only one live rail, the third rail, furthest from the edge of the platform.

trified rails, only the furthest from the platform is live in front of a busy platform.

SEEING A SUBWAY SUICIDE

Don't look, as is so natural, and risk extreme distress or even sudden death from shock.

GRIPPED BY A SUBWAY DOOR

Go limp. Relax completely. Sag down.

The "give" in a subway door is from 3 to 5 inches. It is enough to pull out a trapped arm, elbow, foot or knee when the limb is not swollen, rigid or taut with panic because you feel the train beginning to pick up speed.

PUSHED ASIDE BY A STRANGER

Apologize.

It is safer to say "Sorry" in the city than it is to get sore.

BEATEN TO THE BUS SEAT YOU WERE ABOUT TO SIT DOWN ON

Shrug your shoulders and say nothing.

Stamp down the approaches of any hysterical outburst when you are tense by grasping the small change in your pocket and crushing it; squashing balls (golf/squash/pool) in each hand in your coat pockets until the muscles in the wrist yell for mercy; ripping a dollar bill into quarters in a pocket (Scotch tape it together later).

Some find the opposite method more effective: relax every muscle in the body. Smile. Concentrate on the relaxing.

FACED WITH BUS OR SUBWAY ROWDIES

Do not antagonize thugs by, for example, telling a bus conductor they have not paid their fare. Mind your own business.

If they start on you by goading—about, say, the sexual attributes of your female companion—or if they pin you against the wall and spit out insults, turn the other cheek.

Freeze. Try to forget their presence. Do not glare back. Drop your gaze and concentrate on the tip of your shoes or the knot of a tie some distance away. Lose your face in the high-held printed pages of a newspaper. Examine the route map in the subway car, reading and memorizing the names of stations listed.

Never try to stare them down. Nor make any comment about "young punks."

Look and listen instead for signs that they may be football or fight fans so that you know where their allegiance lies (see THE RESEARCHER, p. 90). Are they carrying souvenirs or programs? And chanting the names of a football, baseball or soccer team?

Back the team (or whatever) *they* are supporting. Listen to catch the names of the star players, recent wins/losses, current form. Try to remember what you researched in the papers, for you need that information now.

Make it obvious that you support *their* champions, although this may be anathema to you. And not halfheartedly. Join their boorish, brutish chants when the back of your neck prickles with the warning signs of danger.

Let THEM have their say. Do not bristle or try to interrupt. Blot up their invective and constant attempts to provoke you by listening and agreeing.

It helps to simulate a glassy-eyed drunkenness. To pretend you are not with it—but that if you were you'd be with them all the way.

Take any bottle or beer can lying empty in a garbage pail, in the gutter or on a subway platform if you anticipate trouble. Put it in a pocket.

Now pull it out and drink from it. Offer it around when there is liquor in it. Sway. Stagger slightly. Slur your speech.

VIOLENT DRUNKS

Act drunk too.

Wobble, stagger and trip. Your eyes, if they do meet theirs no matter how briefly, should assume a faraway and fargone look.

Take a full bottle to fit into a pocket when you anticipate wholesale drunken behavior in the city—say on New Year's Eve.

Offer the bottle in any confrontation with obstreperous drinkers as a sidetracking device by which you can get away. But do not forge a bond—for there is no love like that of one drunk for another.

Make a reasonable excuse (drunks are ultraobservant) and leave or persuade them (drunks are easily sidetracked) to pester someone else.

TRAPPED IN A SUBWAY TRAIN UNDERGROUND

Do nothing.

Know you will be rescued (see THE PESSIMIST, p. 99).

When smoke from a tunnel fire finds your subway car place a handkerchief over your mouth. This will not prevent noxious fumes reaching you, but it will stop coughing and helps prevent panic. Know that in the last event—if the smoke becomes too thick—the cleanest air is near the floor.

Steel yourself against dreaded claustrophobia. If you have no survival kit for this eventuality (see THE PESSIMIST, p. 99), take a strong grip on yourself, think of something else, don't succumb.

Count those blessings: You are alive, uninjured, can easily last for many hours if necessary. Keep cheerful by seeing the funny side of it, and listen for humorous understatements from others. If you can make them yourself for the benefit of others—especially loved ones in your care who are feeling the strain—so much the better.

Restrain anyone gripped with fear. You neither want to hurt them nor have them harm themselves. Calm, comfort and reassure them, and only slap across the face when hysterics take over.

It is too easy to faint or go dizzy in such crises when, really, there is no need at all for histrionics. Everyone is perfectly safe, despite the sulfurous, fetid, filthy scene where dirt, sweat, stench and crowdedness make for such a nightmare setting.

Quell any rumors that reach you, for they spread like wildfire and add to the general panic.

It is those people whose mouths are like torn pockets who will spill out misleading and harmful "facts" about the situation. Born of hysteria and wish-fulfilment, such wrong information leads to mass hysteria and death—as when passengers from a stranded train stampede on to electrically live tracks because the rumor goes that the blaze is near and the rails below are safe.

Test a rumor against established facts. It will quickly pale into the ridiculous. Insist on knowing the source of the information. Curb other passengers' desire to pass on possibly false information. Assume the subway officials involved are responsible people and are doing all they can.

SUBWAY CROWDS CRUSHING YOU (see also PLATFORM PUSHERS)

Take a deep breath.

Aim not to fall down and be trampled on when the crowd suddenly sways on a platform or inside a train. Hold your elbows by your sides and sticking out, fists clenched in front of the stomach and held away from the body. Brace yourself in this position; the most buoyant available.

Never have your hands in your pockets or above your head; don't let yourself be pushed against a wall. Keep in the middle and avoid getting your feet trampled on if straphanging—anticipate the danger. Lower arms in time.

VIOLENT CAR PASSENGERS

Do as they say and drive on.

But stall the auto at a green light and feign a breakdown. Appear to try to restart the engine, only to fail. The buildup of frustrated drivers behind you has placed you in a stronger position. Say you will have to get out and see to the trouble—and then run. Or hand over the $20 bill you always carry (see THE NERVOUS, p. 52).

DRUNKEN DRIVER

Be sick.

Either claim you will vomit all over the interior of the car or actually do it by sticking the first two fingers down the throat and gagging.

As soon as he stops the car, get out and walk. Or phone a taxi.

Never reach for the ignition key when someone else is driving. It is too risky. (Best safeguard: have your seat belt fastened.) When a friend or relative is the drunken driver, however, slide out the ignition key when he stops.

PURSUING MOTORIST

Shoot yourself.

Cocking the thumb against the barrel of the first two fingers and raising it to your temples is the best apology possible when you have just rashly passed someone (or possibly your driving was quite in order) and they protest angrily on the horn and follow you.

Do not make any other gestures. An ordinary wave can be construed as insulting. Jerking a thumb upward might enrage even further. Making the fingers-uppermost V-sign will always do just that.

Drive on if the other driver is not appeased and stop at the first police station, policeman or patrol car.

But before you drive on, pull over and slow down and let him have a chance to make one more violent fist-wave. Be ready, however, for the driver to brake across your bows and try to force you into the side. Brake hard yourself, nose out and then drive in search of the police.

Check, as you drive, that the windows are rolled high and the doors are locked.

Do not be afraid to go to the police. Even if you feel you *were* in the wrong and that the other driver does have a legitimate complaint. It is by now quite clear that that other driver is verging on the border of, if he has not yet actually arrived at, homicidal mania. Do not take chances on trying to argue or plead this case without a policeman there as well.

The following maneuver works when a madman is tailing you. Slow down and stop at a green light. As the lights change, drive through the intersection at amber and hope the other drive is now blocked by the dense crossing traffic.

Ditch your car at once in a side street. Leave the scene until later, when it is safe to return and drive on.

If he does stop you, stay in the locked car. Although the rolled-up windows will not stop a fist, rock or bullet you can gain time by lowering the window slightly and apologizing. Any attempt to smash in the window is a signal for you to sprint across the seats and leave the car by the other door. Run.

Other measures can work. Banging on the horn as an SOS signal (do it in short blasts rather than in one long one); slamming the door on the attacker's hand if he has managed to wrest it open; flashing the headlights; rolling down the window so the enraged head sticks through in an attempt to get at you—and then rolling it up to lock the neck in place. But don't roll it *too* tight, just enough to trap the frenzied assailant.

BROKEN-DOWN AUTO AT RUSH HOUR

Limp a crippled car to the curb.

When the car will not budge, NEVER push it. Skip all thoughts about the massive traffic jam you are causing and which is psychologically breathing down your neck. Save your strength for lightweight but vital jobs. . . .

Set some signal on or near your car to show it is in trouble (see THE PESSIMIST, p. 99). Whether daylight or nighttime use a red light, slow-burning flare or red triangle. Your ordinary auto lights are insufficient at night; a driver approaching from the rear may not realize you are standing still, and so crash into you.

Switch on your directional signals so they wink for a curb-direction turn. But also leave on the parking lights and place your signal lamp, flare or triangle as far from the rear of the car as possible.

A raised hood and trunk is a universal sign of distress among motorists. Raise both. Tie a rag, cloth, duster, hanky or piece of clothing from the tip of the radio antenna.

TRAPPED IN A SNOWBOUND CAR

Cringe and shiver inside the car.

Avoid overexertion and exposure when the auto is stuck in snowdrifts on the beltway or expressway and some distance from telephones or buildings.

Stay put. Do not panic. Think things out carefully first and know you will survive.

Keep fresh air in the car. Freezing wet snow and a driving wind can seal it up completely.

Watch out for the "gentle killers"—carbon monoxide and oxygen starvation. Run your motor and heater sparingly, and only with your downwind window open for ventilation.

Exercise by clapping your hands and moving your arms and legs vigorously from time to time. Do not stay in one position too long. Know that shivering is a body mechanism that is fighting the cold for you. Help it out by stuffing newspapers, magazines, an old spare topcoat or ripped-up floor carpeting inside your trousers and jacket and topcoat.

It helps to drape a topcoat over you like a cloak—but button it up. Extra warmth is gained by not having both arms down the sleeves.

If you go outside to check that the tailpipe is unobstructed (you MUST do this when the engine is running properly), shake off all wet snow before reentering the car. It is vital that you should keep as dry as possible inside the car. Best of all: carry some covering—rubber floor mats, say—held over your shoulders as a form of umbrella.

Turn on your inside light (if you have one) at night so that your car can be seen by work crews.

Keep watch. Don't let everybody in the car sleep at the same time; take turns in keeping awake.

If you are so jammed in a drift that neither doors nor windows will open, try that trick of pushing out the windshield (or rear window) with your feet.

When you need something in the trunk, expect the lock to be frozen. Have your cigarette lighter ready in your hand to thaw it (or the cigar lighter from the car's dashboard).

It is worth remembering that your radiator may freeze. The temperature indicator will register in the danger zone: HOT. Your car should be towed or moved inside a warm garage. If this is impossible, pour as much water as you can get into the radiator and then cover the radiator grill. Start the engine and let it idle. This should thaw out the radiator.

Decide to shovel only if you are fit and are sure that you can work the car out in time. . . .

Work slowly and not too hard. Take a break every few minutes; leave off if you are getting tired.

When shoveling use the whole of your body, starting from the legs and using the back. Get your weight behind the spade. Do not just lever it with your arms.

Do not smoke while you are working, or drink just before. Smoking and cold blood do not mix, and a drink may make you think you are stronger than you are.

Avoid lifting too much snow at once. Remember that wet snow is heavier than the powdery type, especially when you are using a large shovel.

It is better to shovel bit by bit than to dig yourself into an early grave.

FACING A CAR CRASH

Swerve.

And brake. But do everything in your power to make the blow a glancing one and to lessen the speed of impact.

Steer the car, if possible, so the collision is turned into a sideswipe. Aim for the impact to happen at an angle.

This is especially important when facing a head-on collision with an oncoming car. Any impact on the slant is better than going full tilt into each other. For example, if you cross the lights at green and another car jumps the lights from your left, steer sharp right to create a less violent impact.

No amount of good driving will make up for your not being firmly buckled into a properly secured belt.

But even a good seat belt leaves your body exposed to flying glass or to some part of the car's bodywork distorted by impact. Try to save yourself by raising your arms, covering your head and face, and risk broken limbs rather than brain damage or disfigurement . . . but only when, as the driver, you have tried to steer out of trouble and failed.

If you are wearing a seat belt and the front seat passenger is not, throw out an arm to try and hold him or her back.

You may not have fitted children into the special harness sold for them; then you should at least insist that they ride in the back—never in the front. If you can reach back in time, hurl them to the floor.

(When driving without a seat belt all you can do is rest your head against the wheel. Grasp it hard with both fists and hope.)

The front seat passenger who is unharnessed stands little chance. Wrap both arms around your head, turn your thigh sideways along the front of the car and hurl yourself forward to go *with* the car. This takes some advantage of the shock-absorbing qualities of the hood as it crumples (a lengthy expanse of sheet metal is an effective shock-absorber if you can make use of it).

Your chances, however, are slight when you have ignored the seat belt. They are a little better when unbelted in the rear seat —if you can dive for the floor in time.

VIOLENT CROWD ATTACKING THE CAR

Bleed.

By making yourself look as if others have got to you first when crowds are rocking, smashing and trying to break into the car to get at you . . . you stand a chance.

They may not think you worth bothering with and move their attention to another car nearby. Remember, you are very vulnerable. It takes little to smash a car window and grab for you and your loved ones.

Lots of blood is the answer. Swamp yourself in it as if you had been hit in the head, stabbed in the chest and are bleeding and frothing at the lips. So slimed with blood, others—whose blood is up—are more likely to look elsewhere.

Carry the "blood" in a bottle in your glove compartment for any such emergencies. It can be made from the contents of a kitchen cupboard or shopping basket. Here is one effective recipe:

Boil together ½ pint water, 2 teaspoons instant coffee, 2 teaspoons yellow food coloring, 4 teaspoons red food coloring.

Mix separately 4½ teaspoons flour, 4 teaspoons water.

Add this when well mixed to the boiling liquid, stirring constantly, and boil for three minutes. Cool and add ½ teaspoon concentrated foam carpet shampoo. This thickens the "blood" a little, but acts as a preservative too. (Such a bottle of blood, screwed up tightly, can last for 18 months.)

When cold this blood will be thick, but it can be thinned with water.

The blood can be used most effectively when you have anticipated potential trouble with a vast crowd.

Do not be squeamish about splashing blood over your best suit, dress, coat or interior of the car. Do it lavishly to make it obvious there is heavy bleeding.

Realize that acting up a condition is essential when you decide to play injured. In this situation, however, the sheer weight of numbers in the crowd will make your terror so obvious that your message of horror and of physical hurt gets through.

Do not underplay this situation; give it everything. Put all your heart into it as though your aorta were spurting your life's blood away.

Do not stop acting just because you think no one is watching. Keep up the pretense until you are sure you are safe.

Carry a cloth with you for rubbing away the blood afterward. A small bottle of soapy water is valuable too.

Be aware of the danger of being taken to hospital despite your protests. A bloody appearance will certainly draw police protection, but you must not go into hospital. Were your deceit to be discovered, you could be sued for wasting the time of doctors and nursing staff.

Even this, however, is preferable to being assaulted and possibly killed.

If you are caught by a violent crowd without these preparations, there is little you can do but bite the inside of your mouth hard and quickly smear your own real blood all over your face.

Part Three

CITY LABYRINTHS

Avenues, Streets and Sidewalks

5

CITY LABYRINTHS

LOSERS

WHAT CHANCE have we on the sidewalks, where even Santa Claus may be an armed policeman incognito.

Slaughter on the avenues where wind blows old newspapers in our faces: four murders a day. Robberies with violence on all streets: 243 daily. Assorted escapades with shotguns and other ironmongery in the concrete canyons: 100 daily. Rapes in main and side streets—six a night. Handbags snatched and pockets picked; so many the daily figures look like population statistics.

The hazards on the streets are real. The travel folders paint a glamorous picture of great cities. But in the police headquarters, graphs which record crime in the city streets are climbing as steeply as skyscrapers. The increasing violence involves everyone and includes every type of emergency under the moon.

The Jittery (Once Hit)

Quail as the police car sirens wail their story of more murders, more robberies and more rapes.

They are the pedestrians who are terrified of crossing the street, fearful that they will not reach the other side. The sound of any fast-moving vehicle is torture.

SIGNS AND SYMPTOMS

Placing a shoe on the street crossing, hearing an oncoming car and jumping back on to the sidewalk as if the crossing contained live electric wires. Breaking out in perspiration when you see the driver who saw your hovering shoe has now stopped and is hovering too. Either taking a deep breath and galloping across OR turning away.

CAUSES

You may have been hit by a car before, or perhaps it was your mother, father, sister or brother. This kind of incident will quickly turn anyone of a nervous disposition into the kind of pedestrian that car drivers loathe in metropolitan traffic.

Who can trust motorists once you—or relatives or friends— have nearly been killed by them? How can we face them anymore?

Moreover, it is easy to believe that some drivers actually hate pedestrians. And as they splash, sideswipe, intimidate and strafe trembling US, the more jelly-like we become.

And how are we to know the "goodies"—the drivers who are as nervous and careful of pedestrians as we are terrified of them? After all, they may only be pretending to wait to let us cross— then BRRRM.

This hesitation is increased when *we* are regarded by others as the odd, the simple and the doddering—for no one is going to help us. Then crossing the great avenue or busy street is a battle to make our aching legs move faster, to keep shoes planted on icy asphalt and to ensure our walking stick or umbrella does not become wedged in the subway ventilation grid as we make the final sprint to the curb.

Even the young and presentable are not immune. There is no dread like that of the girl who, watching the traffic lights, cannot tell red from green anymore than she can see dirt stains on the sidewalk or a rainbow overhead. She is color-blind or perhaps suffers from "tunnel vision."

She could, instead, be nearsighted and dread her walk home during the winter months as darkness falls earlier. Myopics tend to be at their most nearsighted at night, and she finds it much more difficult to make street-crossing decisions. And then again, a young woman whose visual fields are so restricted that she bumps into pieces of furniture in her apartment can find the journey home from 5 P.M. to 6:30 P.M. a nightmare. Her brain is automatically depending on her good eye, which compensates for the deficiency in her weak eye. But the good eye isn't so hot either, and her overworked Cyclopean vision brings on headaches and fatigue which increase unbearably at street crossings on the homeward stretch.

The hesitation in most of us, however, springs simply from the imagination. Common sense and awareness of the rules of the road tell us that once we have stepped on to a crossing where the lights are red, the traffic must stop for us.

Only imagination is the stronger. It whispers, "What if the *driver* is suffering from color-blindness and thinks the red light is a funny shade of emerald?"

"What if it is the *driver* who is suffering from tunnel vision and who, at that moment, is staring across the street at a pretty girl, in which case the red light (and US) will not be in his field of vision?"

"What if this motorist does see the red light and US but decides to end it all in a split second's frustration and charges to his— and our—destruction on a momentary hell-bent whim?" (See THE TENSE.)

Of course, it is a fact that drivers will go to the greatest lengths to avoid pedestrians. It is our imaginations that play us false. Yet walk in the Big City we must. It is only a minority who can afford taxis *all* the time.

ILLOGICAL BEHAVIOR

More often than not we hover on the sidewalk in the hope that someone else will want to cross. We are so relieved when they do that we go with them.

But the sudden feeling of relief can be our downfall too, for we can then fail to check *where* we are crossing—and so we are struck down, whether by a speeding yellow cab in Manhattan or a royal-blue garbage truck driven by a reckless *gomi-tora* in Tokyo.

Your private theory, for instance, that groups of schoolchildren are the best to cross with in a city jungle clearing makes you even more vulnerable.

It is true that teenagers are tough and terrifying themselves; they put a driver in his place. They are real pedestrians, mafia of the road. For one thing, they have thicker skins than the elderly or sick. And, to some extent, a thick skin is a great advantage. It lets you rush in where well-brought-up or more sensitive people hesitate. But because the thicker skin also encourages swashbuckling and casual behavior, there is constant risk.

Go with a group of schoolchildren and eight times out of ten their sheer bravado will get YOU across too. There is also a fairish chance, however, that they may be the cause of your coming to grief.

You are certainly less likely to be able to leap out of the way when things do go wrong. As when young escorts outsprint you and leave you stranded in the no-man's-land a few yards to either side of an official crossing—a favorite place for juveniles to cut corners rather than making for the crossing itself.

Areas on both sides of any avenue or street crossing will always prove hazardous to pedestrians. Road safety experts claim that if in one year pedestrians had used a proper crossing only, roughly a thousand fatal and serious casualties would have been avoided.

Over 25 per cent of pedestrian accidents happen near crossings when one vehicle slows down and stops to let a pedestrian cross and another passes on the blind side and mows down the unsuspecting walker.

Yet all too often we throw reason to the wind by our snap judgments—and cross in this notoriously risky area, where accidents will always happen whatever the safety experts do to try and protect us (from our own stupidity as much as from oncoming vehicles).

Not even pouring a tin of blood-red paint over the middle of the crossing and painting thick black skid marks near the curb—as one great city did—has succeeded in alerting drivers and pedestrians alike for long. Human nature being what it is, once we get used to something we tend to forget. . . .

As when, instead of schoolchildren, we spring on the idea of always crossing the road with any pretty leggy girl. The theory is that the driver is quite glad to stop and widen his eyes. He may even seem reluctant to drive on afterward.

Not always so, however.

That motorist may be an emotionally deprived male with psychopathic inclinations, ready to drive *at* her and force her to jump because she represents a hate symbol in his warped mind. Similarly, the foot on the gas pedal may belong to a militant feminist, all too happy to squash down in a hostile move against the degrading piece of femininity just ahead.

Your unreasoning fear of crossing the street has therefore clouded your earlier judgment.

It is not that the driver may not like *you*. It is that he may not like *them*: the person or persons you are crossing with. But it is you—too old, pregnant or generally unfit-to-leap-aside—who are knocked down and become another road accident statistic.

Remedy: The Plodding, p. 170; The Comforted, p. 179; The Nervous, p. 52

The Nosy

Nurture a curiosity which manifests itself in lunatic ways. When 5,000 people gather on the sidewalk to watch a fireman rescue a bedraggled cat on a window ledge 100 feet up, we should consider the implications.

Inquisitiveness is an understandable and human trait, but it can prove a costly indulgence. By the time we have seen it all and remembered where we were going before it all started, we may be at the mercy of events we knew *could* happen but which we, in our wildest dreams, never thought would happen to *us*.

SIGNS AND SYMPTOMS

Trotting along after a fleeing purse snatcher on New York's East Side to see if he is eventually caught. Exploring a disturbance in any distant avenue.

CAUSES

We do not have to be out-of-towners to be nosy in the city. The great majority of city dwellers lie—and almost all "stretch the facts"—about their assumed cool and indifference when, really, they are bursting to see what is happening when something out of the ordinary is pulling a crowd.

Curiosity is the most natural characteristic we possess. How else could the weird world of Ripley or the freaks and monsters of carnival sideshows attract the millions on millions that they have?

We may be straight from the ranch, desperate not to miss a city trick, eager to garner every shred of way-out experience in the Big City and take home a harvest of metropolitan experience. Such nosiness, however, is no safer than that of the most seen-it-all-before city slicker when it comes to the unexpected incident that breaks the monotony of the day.

Either way we are vulnerable: *both* the nosy-parker-curious who are riveted because others are being nosy, too, and there is a crowd *and* the informed-inquisitive who know—or presume to —exactly what is happening and therefore feel safe.

The shock when we find ourselves in danger is devastating. What else can we expect, however, when—by prolonging our TED factor (see THE DUCHESS, p. 84) on city streets—we are sticking our necks out as well as our noses in?

ILLOGICAL BEHAVIOR

There is no such thing as *idle* curiosity in the city. Our nosiness knows no bounds as we busily look here and there for thrills and spills by which to satisfy jaded thirsts.

That fight on the sidewalk; scuffle in the shop doorway; man-on-the-run-while-another-gives-chase-yelling, "Stop that man"; would-be suicide perched high on a window ledge. All could be brilliantly staged by pickpockets to attract a curious crowd.

As long as that gathering is kept interested by superb acting—and long before the police arrive—wallets and purses go like leaves in the autumn.

We never know until too late. For while we are craning our necks, straining on tiptoes and pushing ever closer because others are shoving behind us, we are intent on the human drama enacted before our eyes and oblivious to everything else.

And we never realize that it is members of the pickpocket's troupe who are nudging us forward on the pretext of wanting a better view.

All *they* need to exercise are dexterous fingers (kept supple by rolling walnut shells around), a delicate sense of touch (sharpened by practicing their skills on a suit to whose every pocket bells are stitched) and tiny knife blades (attached to the same kind of rings that shipping clerks wear for cutting string—or they sometimes use razor blades) with which they slit open the base of their victim's pockets.

They use their voices, too. One or two of the thieves suddenly shout, "Watch out for pickpockets!" and their colleagues watch closely. The natural reaction of a man hearing such a warning is to reassure himself by putting his hand to the pocket containing his wallet or other valuables. Thus the thief knows exactly which pockets to investigate.

The crass unawareness of the nosy is revealed by their stupidity in wanting in some way to be part of the action that is gripping them.

City streets teem with concealed violence. Hundreds have served prison sentences. Thousands more, inclined to criminal tendencies but not yet found out, are ready to maim or kill the nosy innocent who threatens their freedom.

In the great avenues, along the immaculate sidewalks of elegant shopping areas where men in well-pressed suits and women with freshly set hair and new fur coats are eggshell smooth, down the more squalid side streets or on the tree-lined streets outside the suburban apartment complexes, the nosy will only too easily find the sinister, insatiable, vice-gripped hand of city violence.

And there is no easier way to find it than by going to investigate a disturbance at the end of a street—even when you are supposedly only going to stand on the edge and watch.

There is no such thing as the "edge" of a riot or shooting incident where armed bandits are making their getaway from armed police.

The danger of a ricochet, for instance, is far more likely than the inquisitive person realizes. The bullet from an ordinary pistol will speed on for over 1,000 yards and can end up lodged *anywhere*. Imagine, moreover, the tactics of police when trying to oust a barricaded crook. As police marksmen are trained to move in the direction of their "strong" gun hand (because the flash of their gun gives away their position), so their colleagues must know that strong hand and direction in which he will move next for their own safety. But THE NOSY know nothing of this. Odds are they will find themselves too near the heart of spontaneous action."

Only it is too late to realize your mistake if you are caught in the crossfire and have to duck into doorways and under cars . . . because against the forces of massive gangster operations—with all their attendant aspects of narcotics distribution, gambling, loan sharking, extortion rings and huge hijacking operations— you are powerless.

So far this century 800,000 Americans have been killed by the guns of civilians—more than all the military fatalities since the Revolutionary War. The present rate of shooting deaths is 57 people a day; virtually 80 per cent of these take place in the largest cities.

Any riot is, by definition, an absence of order. It is ironic that, because of this, authorities who would normally help you may lead you to your downfall.

Police raining tear gas, fire hoses and nightstick blows into a crowd cannot tell the bad from the good—their plastic shields fog up, and events are too hectic anyway.

If your fate is this untidy, consider how messy was that urgency to pry into what did not concern you in the first place.

Remedy: The Cold-Blooded, p. 187; The Leery, p. 47; The Confused, p. 59

The Avenger (Peeved)

Is always vulnerable when his vindictive attitudes are nursed in the city. Events boomerang back against any wound that has been kept open.

SIGNS AND SYMPTOMS

Thinking of taxi drivers as having no mind to keep their pestilent bodies from rotting, so that they represent, to YOU, a mass of putrefaction; a loathsome fistula on the body public, foul bubbles floating on the cesspool of city streets. Seeing policemen as having no more decency in their ministrations and advice than yelling hyenas, cursing pirates or foulmouthed harlots. Imagining all dogs as despoilers of the London lamppost/Parisian milestone/New York fire hydrant, only too ready to foul the sidewalk.

CAUSES

Everyone, to some extent, bears a grudge when walking along city sidewalks. One of the main reasons, especially in America, is the grid system.

Here where streets and avenues run north–south and east–west in a grid as regular as the rows of a crossword puzzle, the planners designed the most depressing layout ever dreamed up.

The railroad doesn't help. It always runs through the center, separating the rich on one side from the poor on the other. And always there is the wind blowing sewer steam along the ravine floors which are commercial cockpits by day and dangerously barren labyrinths at night. No wonder grudges as well as crime are bred here. No one is immune.

And cities everywhere are beginning to sprout hideous apartment buildings, huge, ugly and bare dwellings with no communal spirit whatsoever—the slums of the future. Such high rises perpetuate the same mistakes—the most inhuman solution possible in the context of increasing urban populations.

ILLOGICAL BEHAVIOR

City streets and avenues are the worst places to obstruct the police when you bear *them* a grudge. This can range from a yearlong chip on the ego to the split-second splash from a speeding police cruiser as it carves a way through the lake of post-blizzard slush and drenches you in ooze.

Either way you feel ready—when you get the opportunity—to wreak a terrible vengeance.

Even if it is only to step off a sidewalk purposely to make a police car swerve, to block accidentally-on-purpose a patrolman's chase of a felon, to refuse to cooperate in moving along the sidewalk when asked by a law enforcement officer . . . then YOU could be victimized.

You may be 19, dressed in a suit and wearing longish hair and steel-rimmed spectacles, but if two policemen came up and asked to see your papers and then asked you to accompany them to the police station as they wished to search you, would you go? Answer NO and they would arrest you and you would have to go anyway.

Under common law there is no right of search before arrest. The exceptions to this are statutory, as in the case of firearms or drugs. If a policeman has reasonable grounds to suspect you, he can ask to search you.

What are reasonable grounds? Just that he is suspicious of you. In the case of drugs your long hair probably created prejudice against you, plus the suspicion that you might have been "palely loitering"—i.e., hanging around on the street corner early or late in the day looking tired and drawn and apparently leaning against a wall for support.

Instances such as this add fuel to the most popular public

opinions that the police are never there when they are wanted; confine themselves to harassing the innocent; are dim in intelligence and pedantic in manner; catch few criminals; after initial brutality, habitually conspire to frame the conviction of many of the people they arrest; are in any case the natural enemy not merely of the criminal but of the freethinking citizen.

Blacks for a long time have looked on city police as an unfriendly occupation force. Today, however, many other sections of society are also turning to this view—especially young people (whether students or not) with long or short hair (depending on the country/state/city) or anybody who does not blend with the *straight*'s norm.

The result is that the once-popular picture of the friendly cop —although he still does exist—is quite dead. Thanks to Washingtonese belligerence between the left and right—reflected at block level between the wealthy and the down-and-out—the crime figures and police-relations-with-the-public polls mirror the political vibrations of the times.

And one fact will always rankle as long as there are insufficient police patrolling the streets: a cruise car may catch the robber, but it has not prevented the robbery in which it took less than 30 seconds to snatch the wallet and wristwatch and slash the victim's arm.

Hold this against any policeman, however, and you will regret it for the simple reason that patrolmen no longer come in ones, but twos and threes and more.

Urban troubles of all sorts are largely responsible for the police not being able to give the public full protection. They have also to look out for themselves . . . patrol-car-follows-patrol-car-follows-patrol-car just in case the first one needs help. Difficult as this makes their duties toward the public, it certainly does make it easier to show strength against anyone who presumes to challenge a policeman's authority on account of a grudge.

Remedy: The Plodding, p. 170; The Cold-Blooded, p. 187; The Obsequious, p. 124

Men over 40 ("Johns")

Who approach women on the street with a view to buying sex from the scores of hustlers strutting their competitive wares are more vulnerable than the young.

SIGNS AND SYMPTOMS

When you realize it is 15 years since you last saw an unattractive woman in the street. When you neglect running for a bus because there will be another one along in a quarter of an hour. When you resent good looks in young policemen. When you consider the young men walking by not nearly worthy of the beautiful young women on their arms.

CAUSES

The *mature* male has seen it all before—wife, wives, mistresses, random jumps. . . . From his very first affair to his latest lovemaking 20–25 years later, he has experienced a whole variety of love and sex. What he needs to turn him on now is even more variety.

This generation's attitude to mating, however, is different from that in which he spent his adolescent years. Then it was the naughty-naughty aspect of sex that was emphasized. Now it is its very accessibility which has the stress.

So when a liberated and feminine girl today says yes-please *and* expects him to rate at least 7 out of 10 in bed, he may easily opt out, intimidated by the thought of more complicated relationships about to start.

This is why the prostitute suffices. Here is forbidden flesh that can re-create whatever turn-on he needs. With no comebacks. As to *the* prostitute—it doesn't have to be. He can have a different one every night of the year in a Big City if he is so inclined.

And there's no shortage of ways to find such a partner: the old celebrity hotel lobbies and bars, the all-night drugstores, the massage parlors—all in the proximity of the great bus or railroad station around which prostitutes circulate.

ILLOGICAL BEHAVIOR

Paying a woman money to go with her is not always illogical. There may be a dozen reasons why a man must, and the prostitute is a safety valve for all concerned.

It is the way in which the average john goes about buying his comfort, however, that is dangerous. He sets himself up as a target.

Many of his fantasies depend on the hunt rather than the capture—a process he draws out, speculative moment on speculative moment, into the icy hours way past midnight, his hormones in a frenzy and his behavior slips showing.

That he may well catch pneumonia as he hunches in arctic doorways, the night air stabbing his shoulder blades, is only one risk he takes. There are hundreds more he faces at every stride of his fatigued and weary feet as they pace back and forth along the wind-blasted streets.

Ears cocked for the quiet "Hey, come here," his eyes are ever-ready to spot the hooker already deep in conversation with a potential client. Since much of his excitement stems from deciding *who* is on the game, this is a high spot in his sport, and he closes in to see if the negotiations will fall through.

His own trading instincts consequently suffer as a result when it is his turn to barter with the woman, for now it is others who are waiting for him to clinch the deal. This psychological breathing down the neck hurries him to the decision he had probably made before he spoke to her: to turn her down (he says he has insufficient funds).

For the john who walks at night searches for a dream. Rather than some elusive beauty who whisks him away to her penthouse, however, he is looking for the attainable ideal—a booted and be-wigged looker who will come with him for next to nothing or a raving beauty for whom he is willing to pay the lot (the money he has hidden in one pocket with which to pay a prostitute plus the rest tucked away in his socks, underwear or even money belt).

The only thing is it does take time and luck to find such a target every night.

Since the ladies of the evening (from around 12 P.M. on, that is)consist of the hideous-hardened-and-ancient and the unruly-and-noisy-drunk-young, he is usually compelled to keep walking. Hence the danger. . . .

In his moments of indecision, which one minute let him show a girl his big, clanking hotel key and the next help him to price himself out of her market, he leaves himself wide open. For, sooner or later, he *will* say "OK" and she will begin to follow at a safe distance behind (a precaution against any inquisitive policeman).

His mind in a turmoil, it does not take the john long to decide that it would be better to run after all—so he increases speed, rounding the nearest street corner fast and losing himself in the crowd beyond. But what now? Sure, he has lost the girl, but there is still his problem. Those urges salivating anew, he presses back on up and down the city labyrinths, oblivious to all but his desperate need. And crosses her path again—by accident.

Prostitutes are ultrasensitive to certain types of insult. The new working girls are a violent breed, not so submissive as the old-fashioned ones. So when a john refuses to acknowledge them or insults them in some other way, he faces the ever-present risk of being injured by his quarry—even when he has behaved perfectly acceptably.

A good many whores are shallow and violent, intent on robbing and swindling their best customers. The john should think hard before going in search of them.

Remedy: Chapter 6. See also The Canny, p. 40; The Leery, p. 47; The Confused, p. 59

The Rapt (Preoccupied)

Are too concerned with their own problems and thoughts to pay proper attention to what is going on around them. They may accumulate unpleasant new troubles as a result.

SIGNS AND SYMPTOMS

Having a son or grandson who is in the hospital with a broken thigh, a brother who is seriously ill in another hospital, a wife who is caring for your 80-year-old mother-in-law and a sister who has collapsed under the strain of looking after her. And YOUR face has skin drawn on the brow, is pinched at the nose, and is puckered at the eyebrows.

CAUSES

Large problems in your personal life may not be the only reasons for making you less aware. It can be your general attitude to life.

The most common cause of preoccupation in new arrivals to the city is being one-degree-under long after we have left the airport. "Jet lag" always takes us by surprise (see THE SHATTERED, p. 3).

After an east–west flight a person may feel rested enough to sightsee—because he feels excited at being in the city—yet his cardiac rhythms, hormones and body temperature may be out of phase, secretly hindering him at every step.

If you fly into town at 7:30 P.M. after crossing time zones, so that it is only 3:30 A.M. back home, your body clock is at its lowest ebb. You stand a good chance of suffering the blues in the night just as the people here are perking up for the evening.

There are other rhythms that can dampen your spark and make you behave like a remote-controlled zombie.

A downbeat period, for instance, always comes before mealtimes, when the body's blood sugar is low. Weekends or holidays can put people off their beat. When their daily routine is broken they may feel lost and broody. Overconscientious types might even feel guilty because they are not working.

The worst time of all is Christmas, when everything is geared to the idea of feeling happy. When we just don't feel it, we feel cheated and miserable. Traditionally, Christmas is a time for family gatherings. If anyone has a hang-up about going back to childhood, visits to parents, sisters or brothers may bring on involuntary black moods.

There are many occasions when we may feel a creeping depression caused by the imbalance of hormones.

The bright teenager who suddenly turns dismal because of adolescent upsets . . . the housewife whose mood crashes in the third week of her menstrual cycle . . . the restless "postmenopausal" man. . . .

All can cause irreparable damage in the city if we do not realize the effect such changes have.

ILLOGICAL BEHAVIOR

Anyone who goes along preoccupied on city sidewalks may have to endure crises, catastrophes and disasters that are nothing short of hilarious—to others.

A woman walks straight into the side of a car. Although the driver took evasive action, swerving and sounding his horn, she still crashed into him. She was preoccupied with her obsessional terror of dogs and was moving quickly to avoid a large German shepherd.

The tourist from overseas in a city full of hills could not see the approaching taxi because the slope dipped so sharply down that it was out of sight on the far side of the road. He was suffering from little knots of tensed-up muscle that pull and tug at hurtful areas on rainy or cold days.

Each year street accidents happen in areas directly below high buildings (Empire State/Eiffel Tower/GPO Tower). As tourists rubberneck at the marvels above them, they fail to check that the way is clear on the streets they are about to cross.

And these are the areas where pickpockets and purse snatchers strike at the summer crowds who come to stare.

In the most audacious manner. They get away with it because no one in the process of enjoying the city sights ever dreams that someone passing by on a bicycle, scooter or motor bike will have designs on their . . . small change . . . wristwatch . . . sunglasses

. . . St. Christopher medal . . . passport . . . shopping bag or handbag. . . .

Lash out, for instance, at the motorcyclist who tries to rip your watch off and he could grab your wrist, slow down to a walking pace and then try to take your signet ring off its finger. Only when you hit him with the other hand does he laugh and ride off.

It isn't enough to guard all your pockets. Tough thieves can get the stone from your best ring. They do this by following you and trampling on your heels. As the pain registers, the ring-stealer grasps the hand in passing as if to make a quick apology. The powerful pincer-gadget he has previously palmed now covers your jewel, and, with a quick squeeze, the "tool" removes the gem without your feeling a thing other than a pain in the Achilles tendon.

As for the lady wearing the large hat. So long as she is concentrating on keeping it on her head in the wind, all a thief has to do is press the hat down even further. She cannot see, and he then snatches her purse, package or valuable poodle (even on its leash) and—crouching—makes his way under a parked mail truck. By the time she has lifted her headgear he is on the other side of the street and well away.

It is worth remembering that if you have not had your pocket picked by the time you are 40, it is either through the most amazing good fortune or because you just don't look rich enough.

Remedy: The Plodding, p. 170; The Cold-Blooded, p. 187; The Canny, p. 40; The Leery, p. 47

The Narcissistic (Preeners)

Will always find a clear pool in the plate glass of shop windows which will mirror their reflections. They never consider the disadvantages of self-love.

SIGNS AND SYMPTOMS

Peering into the large camera lens of a street photographer to catch your image as he prepares to snap the shutter. Posing while the shoeshine man rubs your footwear, and consciously waiting for him to tap your ankle as a sign you should change feet while you look away. Gazing at everything except the girls swarming past the Plaza fountain.

CAUSES

Narcissism is not confined to men in velvet suits and ruffled shirts. And it's as common in men as in women. Moreover, the narcissist is always the last to see what he is.

It manifests itself in people very conscious of what they are wearing. For our behavior is directly influenced by the clothes we wear.

Of course, we are all guilty, at times, of stuck-on-ourselves behavior when a sartorial show is in order—for date, dance or job interview.

However, wearing a suit or uniform in which you know you look attractive can be like having a hypnotist order you to be Casanova—by which you seduce yourself too.

It can be the blue-jowled New York cop, his black tie in a perfect Windsor, his blue shirt with creases ironed in and his holster of polished leather in which glints his gun—indeed the city's finest.

It can be the steel-hatted construction worker or hide-gloved truck driver, whose language can strip enamel.

The hopes and doubts of the narcissist, whoever he may be, are as transparent as the windows at which he so greedily pauses. *Narcissists give themselves away.*

ILLOGICAL BEHAVIOR

Those who care too much about their appearance in the city are at the mercy of the elements, from a mild drizzle to a dense fog.

Here is how.

WEEKEND SUN: We shrug on a too casual state of mind. It encourages us to leave a jacket in the car and to stuff our wallet in the hip pocket of the jeans (side pockets prove too uncomfortable). Although we are normally on guard against pick-pockets, they anticipate our behavior and are ready for it. They simply use the "straight hoist" method as we wait to cross the street. They grip the protruding top of a wallet between the thumb and forefinger. We walk away from the wallet as they hold on.

SUN AFTER RAIN: After a rain do you bask yourself where you can be properly seen and appreciated? Every thief knows that sudden sunshine will make most pedestrians use the sunny side of the street. They plan accordingly. A crowded sidewalk makes for a half-step crowd (ideal thieving conditions for pick-pockets).

RAIN AFTER SUN: Do you rush for shelter when it starts to rain, anxious to preserve your hair and clothes? Pickpockets, purse snatchers and other sneak thieves exploit the sudden exodus from crowded sidewalks and parks when rain suddenly falls. Doorways, arcades, under awnings and subway stairways are all ideal places where people crowd into tight bunches, making themselves vulnerable to prying fingers.

SUN AFTER SNOW: The narcissist who deplores crossing pools of slush when it lies inches deep next to the curb can be taken "on the stride" by clever pickpockets in one of two ways.

1. If the pickpocket has decided you keep the wallet in your "insider" (inside breast pocket), he will step along beside you until you reach the lake of slush. His stall now treads on your heels hard enough for you to turn round angrily— and as you do, he robs you.

2. When the money is in the side pockets of your trousers, however, the stall will walk in front of you. On the excuse of dodging the slush, he will suddenly pause and block your way. This time the hook robs you from behind.

The narcissistic are the victims of their whims and fancies, and as we are all sometimes narcissists, we should all take extra care on city streets.

Remedy: The Plodding, p. 170; The Comforted, p. 179; The Canny, p. 40; The Leery, p. 47

The Nice Girl (You?)

Does not "get into trouble," as the saying goes. This condition-
ing should be there long before YOU, a rape victim, are met by
police attitudes which make YOU feel like the criminal—if you
report it, that is.

SIGNS AND SYMPTOMS

Having a lighter, softer skin than men. Being more sensitive
to odors than men. Enduring more emotional stress, being less
likely to become a crank and proving less susceptible to color-
blindness and deafness than men. Needing less air than a man
and floating face up in water naturally whereas men float face
down naturally. Yet only being muscularly stronger than men in
one part of your body—the tongue.

Yes, THE NICE GIRL is virtually *any woman* from eight to
80 who can, without any trouble at all, become a rape victim.

CAUSES

Rape is the fastest-growing crime in America; more than 100
women are raped every day—that is, one every 15 minutes.

Rape cases no longer concern only women who invite trouble
by walking across desolate parking lots, construction sites or
empty side streets.

The rapist is becoming more daring, approaching a woman
near her home or place of work. The bold attacker, for example,
trails a woman to her front door—not from a distance but by her
side. No matter how much she complains, he knows his best
ploy is to pose as her husband. As she becomes more hysterical
he simply and quietly asserts, "She's my wife." And it is *her*
protests that will convince most policemen that this is just another couple's falling out—something they should sort out between themselves.

It is very difficult to establish that rape has occurred. Unless the victim is very obviously distressed and hysterical—which few women like to appear—a policeman is likely to lose interest.

If the rapist is someone who has known his victim for some time it will often be assumed that he is her lover, that he had in some way scorned her, and that she is dragging him through court for revenge. Her reliability as a witness will be queried and undermined; her private life will be publicly examined. Is it, she may feel, worth it?

The rapist with a good lawyer can successfully cloud the issue when the evidence is not clear-cut. Most rapists will deny the crime. Common defenses are lack of identification or corroborating testimony; consent; insanity.

Many will plead to a lesser offense such as assault or illegal entry. But one thing is certain: when there is no corroborating testimony at all—if the woman has no witnesses to back her up— the judge will throw out the case. As Section 130 of one penal law states, "A person shall not be convicted . . . solely on the uncorroborated testimony of the alleged victim."

A raped woman is in the poorest possible condition to be coherent. In these circumstances, especially if she is no beauty, her complaint may be looked upon by the police as fantasy.

ILLOGICAL BEHAVIOR

Women who face a rapist often surrender without struggling or screaming. And for reasons we have seen they seldom report the attack to the police either.

All too often women feel that rape cannot happen to them. Consequently they are easily taken by surprise. They tend to do the wrong thing.

Like screaming when an exhibitionist exposes himself by the shrubbery around the public library. Normally such a degenerate is quite harmless—except when a female screams. Then, particularly if cornered, he may get rough because he is frightened.

Many females, however, will not raise a murmur when the rape-threat comes from a more conventional source.

Any male who looks to have the right to be there can catch

the woman at a disadvantage—and follow her into her home, an elevator or shop doorway and attack her then and there.

Often the women have been bigger and stronger than their attackers, yet few have lifted a fist to try and save themselves. Many have been in a position during the assault to reach a weapon and batter the molester. Few have done so.

That she so chooses is partly because she has no confidence in her ability to defend herself, partly a terror she will miss if she does aim a blow, partly the guilt-fear that she could not or should not protest because it is somehow her fault anyway, partly a vague memory about keeping cool, not panicking and talking the male out of his intentions.

Yet, in ultimate emergencies, it is folly to do nothing, to have NO plan whatsoever to which you can cling, no matter how feeble or ineffective it may seem.

Keeping cool and trying to persuade a would-be rapist to change his mind simply will not work when that person is a madman who may kill you as well.

Many rapists have psychiatric histories. They are schizophrenic or psychopathic, and no amount of letting them talk or chatting to them is going to help.

It is far better to rely on a positive plan of action, worked out well in advance.

Remedy: The Cold-Blooded, p. 187; The Unattractive, p. 196; The Fugitive, p. 202; The Confused, p. 59; The Obsequious, p. 124

The Belligerent (Armed) or Phony Tough

Take risks. The laws on possessing weapons tend to make criminals out of the survivors who use them to protect themselves in the city.

SIGNS AND SYMPTOMS

Packing a water pistol filled with ammonia. Stitching razor blades into the hem of a handkerchief to flick against a rapist.

Knowing that o-goshi, o-sotogari and tao-otoshi are judo throws. Purchasing a 4,000 volt electric stunner guaranteed to immobilize any attacker, even an angry bull. Toting a walking stick which conceals a 17-inch blade. Pocketing a hand-held container of gas which will cause retching, uncontrollable weeping, violent skin irritation, a rash of nasty ulcers—and, to asthmatics, possible death.

CAUSES

It is quite simple. We have a strong aversion to being stabbed, zapped, shazammed, rolled, mugged, gassed, strangled or simply shot down.

YOU are increasingly in danger of falling victim to a violent criminal in any great city of the world.

We have come to expect crime in New York, where the probability you will be murdered is 25 times higher than it is in the British Isles. Manhattan's crime rate is high—though lower than many other American cities—and is much the same in the other great boroughs of Fun City. With its burglary, robbery with violence YOUR chance of being mugged, assaulted or knifed during any walk along the streets . . . the human friction here is atrocious.

But some types of vicious crime in supposedly relaxed and gentle Britain are increasing too. The number of indictable offenses of violence against the person is up each year. Murder, manslaughter, robbery with violence, malicious wounding and assault are reaching new highs. Orthodox firearms are not used to the same extent as in America because they are too difficult and expensive to buy—so the crooks use powerful air guns instead.

Wherever the city, the dangers, in one form or another, are always present.

From the neighborhoods where lawyers, businessmen and accountants live on streets lined with trees (complete with cooperative apartment buildings, small delicatessens, bakeries and candy stores) to the grim, decaying and crammed-full tenements with

pitch-dark stairways and a man with a broken bottle always tip-
toeing at the back of your eyeball—there is a host of daily risk in
the city.

The enormous number of drug addicts is the worst threat of all.
It takes at least $30 a day to survive on hard drugs. In their des-
peration, addicts will resort to robbery and murder to win that
money. And they use their weapons quite indiscriminately, fatally
shooting the victim who has told them he has no money to give
them as well as stabbing to death the woman who does hand
over her purse, wristwatch and shoes.

Addicts know as well as they know the backs of their own hands
that they have to rob and that when they rob they may have to
kill. We, too, know that now. But taking overbelligerent measures
to protect ourselves is NOT the answer.

ILLOGICAL BEHAVIOR

The urban warrior who takes up cudgels in the city invariably
discovers in his time of need that the arms he has chosen are either
too feeble or too vicious.

Although karate and judo are effective in certain situations,
they will never deter a determined and ferocious street brawler
or vandal. Both forms of self-defense need combat experience—
not the kind you practice when you chuck a classmate to the mat
with the special grips of kyushindo (a gentle form of judo), but
the real thing.

It is a different matter when your opponent is not a partner.
You simply cannot equate the gymnasium partner with the crazy
roughneck, driven to violence by mania or desperation.

How can you remember in time where to place that head-butt
or roll-and-trip maneuver knowing that if you fail there will be
no second chance? And that whatever likelihood you had of
suffering *only* a robbery has now gone—and you are going to be
beaten into a bloody pulp into the bargain.

No amateur karate enthusiast stands a chance against the
brutal kicking and slugging vandal, vicious, unprincipled, sadistic
and ruthless. A zigzag gash in the guts will require 24 stitches

—and the knifer will disappear down the subway steps and escape scot-free.

Nor are guns the answer. The ordinary person, it has been found, will use any available pistol all too indiscriminately. If what police say about the average citizen who is stirred to lose his temper is to be believed—that an honest, decent man will *quite readily* stick a knife into his wife in the heat of an argument—think of the effect of a gun lying around instead.

We use guns in passion, we use them emotionally, our children may pick them up in the apartment, our marriage partner may fire them at us—or at best, we naively try to fire at someone who is committing a crime and hit an innocent person instead. . . . Handguns create many more problems than they solve.

Furthermore, the fact we have armed ourselves with hardware may trigger other people to use *their* ironmongery too—action they would not otherwise have taken. American civilians own 90 million guns; a new one is sold every 24 seconds.

The warlike personality can be blinded to reason in an orgy of I'll-show-them motivations. Hence ANY weapon which can cause lasting damage should be out.

Yet these are just the harmful weapons which a belligerent character will choose to satisfy his basically aggressive instincts. He isn't going for self-protection at all. . . .

The Administrative Code of New York City forbids the manufacture, sale, possession or use of any "lachrymating, asphyxiating, incapacitating or deleterious gas . . . liquid . . . or chemical, or any weapon, candle, device or any instrument of any kind designed to discharge or use these substances." (Exception: when a permit is issued by the police commissioner.)

And with good reason. If you are attacked and pull out a deadly spray you got from a drugstore, there is nothing to stop your assailant also reaching for his canister of the same lethal vapor. He will probably be wearing a mask for face protection too. And be quicker than you.

Even if he has no spray of his own, the chances are he will still be able to grab yours and fire it back against you. Or the wind will. Tear gas and other sprays have a range of about 10 feet, and any strong air current can cause a "blow back," thus giving you a faceful too.

The long-range effects of noxious chemicals and gases are not yet known. In cases where they have been used, eye damage (including blindness), burns, respiratory troubles and skin problems have been the result. The police and the public take a dim view of *any* unnecessary violence. They don't like muggers and roughnecks, but they regard the overbelligerent person as a menace, too. . . .

Watch out even if you only use the old-fashioned kind of weapon, too. . . .

Sandbags, knuckledusters, razors, blackjacks, and all kinds of knives are illegal. So are toy guns which "substantially duplicate" real pistols or revolvers—unless they are a different color from black, blue, silver or aluminum and the barrel is closed for a distance of half an inch from the business end.

For their own good the belligerent feelings that rise at times in even the meekest of people are best soothed and calmed down. How this is done depends on how secure we can get to feel by using other methods of safeguarding ourselves. It is possible.

Remedy: The Unattractive, p. 196; The Fugitive, p. 202; The Nervous, p. 52; The Confused, 59; The Obsequious, p. 124

The Conformist (Stiff)

Is a methodical, straight person who believes that everyone can organize the future as well as the present, even in a city teeming with imponderables.

This is simply not true. Those who conform, though, are the most difficult people to persuade otherwise.

SIGNS AND SYMPTOMS

Your appearance and your conscious mind say, "I care how I look and conduct myself, I am a decent citizen. My clothes fit and are not baggy (though they may not have cost a great deal), my shoes are polished, hair is cut and fingernails are trimmed. I am simply a person trying to make the best of him/herself and not looking for trouble—you can tell I am not devious by watching my eyes (it is only crooks and policemen who are constantly looking around)."

CAUSES

Most formal, orthodox people like where they live. The chances are they would never live out of the city. They are determined to make the best of the metropolis they have grown to love.

When we are of this accord, civic pride knows no bounds. Not only does it make the ordinary person feel he "belongs" (to a tangible greatness, the mass of the concrete jungle), it inspires him too. We have not the slightest doubt that this is where it all is at; that city and civilization go hand in hand.

There is no sense of belonging quite like that of being part of a city when that metropolis suffers or celebrates. Victory or despair. Subjugation or elation. We can't help but be touched by the feelings of millions when we are part of them—Big City Citizens ourselves. No matter who we are, or in what branch of the concrete forest we live.

Yet in this glow of collective security our instincts and muscles grow soggy. No amount of weight lifting, jogging or squash awakens this mind.

Primitive cunning has long since atrophied in this kind of urban mind.

The rigid pattern imposed by the city on the millions willing to be regimented has created a vast army of automata—cardboard troops who prove incapable of positive action when face to face with the sudden crisis that does *not* happen quite as they had anticipated.

ILLOGICAL BEHAVIOR

Walking city streets when you really know them is, for many people, 99 per cent boredom and only 1 per cent panic. Most of the time nothing happens. But when something does go wrong, we are called upon to use all our resources and character to get out alive.

It is unlikely, if you are a fit, agile, sober person, that anything will happen to you on most days. At least, not in the city center. You think!

Although the pattern of midtown crime is professional and aimed at high profits, in any great town much less than half the people on the streets are fit, or agile. Consequently, everyone to some extent lets his mental drawbridge down by assuming that the 1 per cent will happen to others—never to him.

So we become creatures of habit and rarely change our routine on our daily metropolitan perambulations.

Routine seems safe. We take this sidewalk for that trip to the shops or office and that street crossing for those journeys back home. The comforting security of the old routine as our shoes tap along the same old route tends to smother the vital sixth instinct which saved our primitive ancestors.

Muggers know just how the conventional individual ticks, just how illogical is the ordinary citizen's unawareness.

The "straight" person, for example, feels self-conscious about suspiciously surveying the shopping and business-going crowds on city streets; his sense of fair play tends to inhibit this conformist —enough to stop his checking the occupants of parked cars or, by glancing in shop windows, seeing anything untoward happening to his rear or by his side.

The criminal homes on to the conformist simply by appearance (see *Signs and Symptoms*). He has everything going for him because of the stiff and unbending attitude of the victim-to-be in that (1) conformists never feel comfortable without an adequate amount of money in their wallets (it is no use looking smart if you have to act cheap) and (2) they do not think of the violent consequences of a mugging so much as of the inconvenience and expense of broken spectacles and so forth. They switch off their muggers-about-antennae; their minds connect with trivia rather than face the facts.

The facts are muggers have regular tactics to deal with the

conformist. They involve the "yoke": the villain behind grabs the victim around the neck with the crook of his arm, while his accomplices place themselves in front. The mugger injects menace into his voice to terrify the victim. And the robbery is done at leisure because the yoke-man is facing the oncoming traffic and can see trouble in the form of police cars for some distance ahead.

It is so easy to mug anyone. Yet the thoroughly conventional individual never takes full precautions on the street.

Every day in the city newspaper reports tell of victims who are not only mugged, but also maimed or even killed. After all, the man wearing a neat suit represents the establishment, the law. It's not just his loaded wallet.

Remedy: The Plodding, p. 170; The Cold-Blooded, p. 187; The Unattractive, p. 196; The Fugitive, p. 202; The Confused, p. 59; The Obsequious, p. 124

The Good Samaritan

Behaves in a stupid and irrational manner. There is no place at all in the city for unthinking altruism.

SIGNS AND SYMPTOMS

Postponing your shopping when a popular person dies or a national disaster happens—because you tend to share the general grief. Hating the pimp who emerges from a taxi with the young prostitute. Taking some kind of pity on criminals who threaten you.

CAUSES

Anyone who has been through a rough time himself will usually help others spontaneously. (Working-class people beat all others for real and positive helpfulness and a friendly word.) But such attitudes, commendable though they are, are no *safer* than those of the more selfish person, who simply acts on the spur of the moment out of some self-gratifying motive, or one who feels some religious prompting. Virtue is not always its own reward in the city. So let your decency come from a calculating mind, which first weighs what's in it for everyone concerned.

ILLOGICAL BEHAVIOR

The kindly, the helpful and the put-themselves-outers show an unselfishness quite at odds with the requirements of city survival.

Offer a good samaritan who has to cross a bad area at night a hand-alarm shrieker for attracting help or an aerosol of hairspray with which he may temporarily blind an attacker, and he will refuse. This is illogical.

Feelings of brotherly love are a dead loss in any metropolis unless you are careful, canny, suspicious, leery and cold-hearted, too. Only then can you afford to indulge in the behavior that marks out THE GOOD SAMARITAN.

As when—

HAPPILY watching our children waiting in the line to speak to Santa Claus, we spot a man trying to jump the line—and are stabbed when we try remonstrating with him on behalf of our youngsters.

ASKED for a light, we immediately dive a hand into a pocket for the lighter—and find our coat or jacket is peeled down over our arms by a mugger who now has us in a straitjacket.

HELPING to push a car to get it going, we suffer from a coronary. It was not our automobile either; we just happened to be passing and jumped in to help without even being asked.

WE foil a purse snatching by two small boys on a city sidewalk. But instead of fleeing the scene the two young robbers turn on us.

A WOMAN is getting smashed, kicked and thrown on to the sidewalk. We grab hold of the man to drag him away—only the woman, his wife, then crawls up off the ground and jumps on our back to stop us.

OUR pockets are picked and everything of value is taken while we stoop to tend the elderly man who is lying on the sidewalk—a pickpocket's stooge.

When we are true bluer-than-blue do-gooders we cannot change our characters, but we can reform to some extent, by adding a touch of realism to our view of the world. The reason, after all, why we should be our brother's keeper is that by doing so we hope our brother will keep us as well—but we must not bank on it.

Remedy: The Cold-Blooded, p. 187; The Canny, p. 40; The Leery, p. 47

6

CITY LABYRINTHS

WINNERS

ONCE YOU STEP from city transport you are on your own. It is as if the vehicle had floated you down the metallic rapids of city traffic and deposited you on the labyrinthine paths along the fast-flowing rivers. Whether you are only a few strides from your hotel entrance or several blocks away from your apartment, there are many risks.

The canyon walls of high buildings block you from the rest of the concrete forest. Lost in this maze, you had best look to your own feelings first. The more deeply they affect you, the more difficult it is to avoid a telltale display of them—which can prove fatal on big city streets.

The Plodding (Pedestrian)

Treads with surefootedness in all he does, mentally and physically. It stands him in good stead, however new to city streets he may be. He keeps both feet solidly on the ground—this is how.

ATTEND TO FOOTWEAR

Badly fitting shoes distract us. Always remember the following points when buying new shoes before visiting the metropolis:

Women far outnumber men as sufferers from foot trouble. Rather than admit that they have big feet, many squash into footwear that is too small. The result is they get painful corns and callouses.

When buying a new pair of shoes, always get your feet measured standing up. This way, the toes spread naturally and a proper fitting can be given.

Remember that one foot is often larger than the other. The shoe on the larger foot should feel comfortable. If it feels tight and needs breaking in, don't buy it.

It is best to shop around at midday, as the feet swell up as much as 5 per cent of their normal size when walking.

Wearing high heels or flat shoes all the time is asking for trouble. Walking in high heels causes the ankles to bend, putting a heavy strain on the muscles. Flat shoes do not give enough support.

If you are plagued by corns, callouses or bunions look for shoes which have smooth inside seams. They should have a reputable trade mark and the stitching should not be too close to the edges.

Buy the best-quality shoes you can afford. They will last longer and prove vastly more comfortable—as well as look "city."

In winter wear galoshes when the natives do. Clumping about may spoil your sartorial image, but it gains you peace of mind to know your shoe leather is safe.

Ordinary plastic bags worn over the shoes and tucked into the tops will help keep shoes fairly dry (and protect them from salt) when you arrive to find streets inches deep in melting snow.

Keep your footwear from slipping on wet and icy sidewalks with any of the following devices bought from big stores: safety shoe spikes (hardened steel studs) attached to rubber covers which slip over the shoes; snow chains (on the same principle as those used on automobile tires) slipped over the shoes, which they grip with springs; ice creepers, a small metal claw which fits neatly into the instep or arch of each shoe, secured by a nylon strap around the foot (and small enough to slip into a pocket when not in use).

Nervous people facing a walk along icy streets and afraid of a fall can take an effective temporary measure: pull an old pair of socks over your shoes to increase the grip.

PLACE FEET FIRMLY

Watch out all the time for slippery surfaces.

When WET: any sloping or badly paved sidewalk or street surface; mashed leaves or ice and slush stamped down into a treacherous slick; manhole covers; metal plaques set into the sidewalk; panes of opaque glass with slippery metal frames inserted in the sidewalk alongside buildings; shiny tiles.

When DRY: any surface is dangerous when leather soles are highly polished—either because they are new or because you have been treading on carpet or dry grass just before.

Deliberately scuff leather soles on the edge of the sidewalk (see also THE CANNY, p. 40).

To walk on slippery surfaces, lean slightly forward so that your weight is over your toes. The worst that can happen, then, is that you fall forward on to your knees—falling sideways or backward is the cause of many broken wrists, arms and legs and also concussions.

But if you damage a knee on going down, stay down and wait for a stretcher. Any further strain on it before examination could cause irreparable damage.

Keep an eye open for three special dangers which can bring you down when crossing a busy street—in front of all those cars. They are a loose shoelace trodden on with the other foot . . . a high heel caught in the wide cuff of a pant suit . . . both feet snared in metal straps from packing cases which have fallen from passing trucks. Snag your feet on any of these and you can end up in hospital whether a car hits you or not.

When negotiating slush, walk on heel tip to keep most of the shoes reasonably dry. And check your temper.

When stepping off the sidewalk, place feet flat on the deeper snow that is found at street corners.

Test first with your weight and then press down with your shoe before stepping forward. Try to use footsteps made by previous pedestrians. The bases of these holes will be more compacted and less likely to collapse.

When waiting to cross a busy street from a crowded sidewalk, place your shoes at right angles to each other (see THE PESSIMISTIC, p. 99)—to prevent your being pushed into the street.

Climb steep slippery slopes by keeping the heels close together and splaying the feet out. If the heel of the front shoe begins to slide back, it should then stop at the shoe behind, which will be crossways to the slope.

Keep going steadily on long slopes. Place the sole of each shoe flat on the ground. Breathe deeply and look down rather than up toward your destination.

It helps to "lock" each leg behind the knee as you step up. By snapping the legs straight like a carpenter's rule as you ascend you obtain a stronger mechanical advantage.

SELECT THE BEST ROUTE

Walk facing the oncoming traffic at busy hours—so that no motorized thief can steer a bike behind you and snatch your wallet, watch or handbag.

When it is one-way traffic walk on the less busy sidewalk.

However, when the streets are quiet, walk WITH the flow of traffic. At quiet times it's easier to be mugged when facing the oncoming cars; the thief can grab you from behind, one arm around your neck and at the same time look along the street for any approaching police car.

Always use the tunnelway below scaffolding on high buildings so that falling objects will miss you. Do not cut along the street on the outside. The tunnel wall now keeps you from stepping back into safety and you are at the mercy of the traffic.

Or cross the street. Surveys show that 40 per cent of building scaffolds are in a dangerous condition; overloading and lack of metal ties to secure them to the buildings are the main causes.

Watch for falling blocks of snow and ice. The signs are an afternoon's sun after snowfall and constantly dropping snowballs. A strong wind which shakes high-rise buildings as much as a quarter of an inch at their summits also dislodges plates of ice.

Keep into the wall of a building when lost and trying to determine the right direction.

Always place suitcases parallel to the traffic on the sidewalk when you stop so as not to obstruct the sidewalk flow. Let the people past you, and blend with the scenery.

Keep in mind your position in the city by the sun (see THE RESEARCHER, p. 90), the stars and the highest building in town.

Use city guidebook maps to locate your position.

Be careful whom you ask for directions. Even policemen aren't infallible. Ask two or three people as you go.

Phrase the request carefully. Don't be vague. Know exactly where you want to go.

Remember that there are bad pockets throughout any large city as well as those notorious ghetto and slum zones covering large districts.

Shortcuts across darkened lots, behind billboards, through industrial yards, at the end of bus lines and down side streets in the very heart of the city are likely trouble spots. Never go through such an area unless it is absolutely necessary—and then only do so with your senses alert.

Avoid alleys, dark streets, slums and other underworld areas of cities. Even policemen walk these areas in pairs.

Stick to places with people, lots of light and the best chances of fast police protection.

Give all dark doorways, hallways, bushes, walls, low roofs, darkened recesses and other possible traps a wide berth.

Remember, always, that dim, deserted streets are the hunting grounds for juvenile delinquents and adult mobsters. Gang-controlled alleys and districts exist in every city—and it means instant trouble for anyone who trespasses.

Particularly dangerous are lonely unlit zones between busy night spots—sucker traps for the unwary.

If you need to get past such an area regularly work out a safer route. Even though this may be half a mile longer, the fact you now walk several streets removed from the hazard area is a comfort (see also THE PESSIMISTIC, p. 99); you find yourself ready to accept the longer trip after only one or two journeys.

If you arrive in the city late, or work late, know the bus schedules in advance (see THE RESEARCHER, p. 90). This helps you cut the time spent waiting on a street corner.

Stay close to lighted shop windows while you wait for bus or taxi—or to the doorways of shops still open.

Trust a hunch when it says danger lurks ahead. Go home by a longer, safer route. Such intuitions are often correct.

CROSS STREETS SAFELY

The safest crossings are footbridges and subways or passageways below the street.

On the street itself the safest place is the painted pedestrian crossing marked on the street where the traffic has to stop to let you cross. These may also be safeguarded by push-button traffic lights or by boxes of flags which children and old people can pick up, wave at the oncoming traffic (which stops), and then leave on the other side.

Places at which you will be told to cross—manned by a policeman, a traffic warden or a school crossing patrol—are also safe.

Traffic lights at any intersection will always help you to cross safely—even though they only stop some of the traffic. Traffic islands cut the road into two so that you can cross a busy street one half at a time.

Find the safest way to cross before you arrive. These differ in different cities.

There are various types of push-button crossing. Some have "WAIT" and "CROSS" signals; these are activated after you stop at the curb and push the button. Others may have a different visual sign, such as a Pelican crossing, with its green and red men. At these crossings if the green man starts to flash, you should not cross. But if you are on the crossing and the green man begins flashing, keep going. You will have enough time to reach the other side. Another safety device is a flashing light which counts down the seconds that a pedestrian still has left to cross the street before traffic gets the green light to start again. In some cities, life-size plastic dummy policemen stand guard over hazardous crossings.

Always walk to one of these safe crossing places even if it means going further and taking longer.

The basic road-crossing drill is

1. Find a safe place to cross and then stop.
2. Stand on the sidewalk near the curb.
3. Look all around for traffic and listen.
4. If traffic is approaching, let it pass.
5. When there is no traffic near, cross the street.
6. Keep looking and listening for traffic while you cross.

It is important to listen, because sometimes it is possible to hear a car coming before you see it—especially in fog, at dusk or as you stand at the top of a steep hill and the car is approaching from below. Take extra care when wearing earmuffs in cold weather. They cut down sound.

Cross any street at traffic lights with care. Some traffic may turn into the road you are waiting to cross. If cars are approaching, look all round again. When there is no traffic, walk straight across.

When a light is green or "CROSS" or the green man signals *cross*, still check that the traffic has stopped.

Do not walk across a street when the lights are red and everyone else is waiting for green—even when there is no oncoming traffic in sight.

Those people are waiting because the penalties for jaywalking in that particular city are strict. You will stand out a mile as you cross—and may draw the police.

Be wary of crossing in front of a vehicle which stops for you as the lights turn to red and you are just beginning to cross in haste. The danger is that another vehicle may be already passing on the blind side and may run you down.

Always keep on a pedestrian crossing itself, rather than skirt its edges. Again, the risk is from a passing car or truck which you cannot see—screened by a vehicle slowing down to allow pedestrians to cross.

Be warned when railings fence off potentially risky crossings at busy intersections. To climb over them and cross in the face of traffic approaching from a distance is not only dangerous in itself; it also leads to a familiarity which breeds carelessness. One day you scale the rails, cross without thinking and are struck down by a car speeding from an *unexpected* angle (the reason the railings were placed there in the first place was to guard pedestrians from this danger).

Allow a greater margin of distance for drivers to stop (approaching lights, say) when the road is wet, icy, or greasy with light drizzle after days of heat.

Ensure that packages, coat collars and umbrellas are not allowed to block your view of the street before stepping into it.

If an old lady or small child asks you to take her across a section of street midway between the lights, walk her to the nearest street corner with lights before crossing.

It is safer to pull a baby carriage behind you when crossing than to push it ahead.

Keep tight hold of children. They are prone to dart from the sidewalk on to the street. Use reins on very young children.

Instruct older children in the most important street-crossing rules. But set an example too.

Always make sure you have enough time to cross when the approaching traffic is a long way off. It may be moving very fast and it is difficult to estimate the speed of distant vehicles. When in doubt, wait and let the traffic past.

Walk straight across the street using the shortest distance from sidewalk to sidewalk.

Never trust motorists to be sensible. Or to turn right because their flashers are winking that way.

Crossing from near to or in between parked cars by the curb is dangerous. Drivers cannot see you until they are almost on you. And you cannot see the traffic clearly.

If there is a long line of parked cars walk through a gap and pause at the edge of the cars where you can see the oncoming traffic . . . and it can see you.

If possible always cross well away from parked cars and bends and road junctions.

A road junction is dangerous. Two or more roads meet, and you may be hidden by a building or a corner, making it difficult to spot all the traffic coming from different directions.

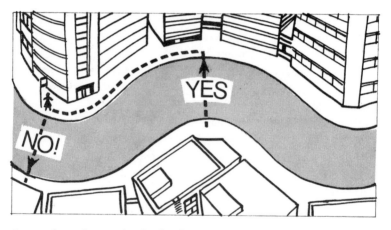

Crossroads on the outside of a bend.

Crossing at bends is risky for the same reason: you can't see the traffic for a long way and the drivers can't see you. When roads have lots of bends with no straight places in between, you should choose the place to cross where you can see a long way in both directions. This will mean the outside of a bend (see diagram) which gives the longest-reaching view.

When trapped part way across a busy street remember that the safest place is in the middle. Stand still and make yourself conspicuous until a clear line of escape appears.

WALK SAFELY AT NIGHT

The chances of being knocked down and killed are twice as great at night as in daylight. Most accidents happen at dusk and in the early hours of darkness.

The fact that you can see car headlights does not mean the driver can always see *you*. It is impossible to estimate the speed of an oncoming car by looking at its lights.

Wear something bright or white. Children's school uniforms and the somber clothing of older people and businessmen are often too dark to be seen properly.

Either make or buy a collapsible walking stick which can be carried in the pocket. Paint it white. It can be a definite help to the nervous at any time of day or night—and is not illegal.

An orange or iridescent armband slipped out of the pocket and on to an arm is a good aid in dimly lit streets.

If you become a pedestrian by accident—because your car has run out of gas or broken down—walk facing the oncoming traffic.

Take off your coat when wearing a white or light-colored shirt. Or tuck a newspaper into your waist (both front and back). A white handkerchief worn around the neck like a bib or tucked into your belt can help.

The Comforted (Granny)

Use any remedy which may seem piddling to others, but which gives the nervous something to cling to in the hurly-burly they find themselves flung into.

BE FRESH

It takes at least 36 hours on arrival in the city to recover from a long journey—especially a flight.

Do not dally on the streets on first arriving. Curb the excitement which demands to pack in all the sights at once—and go to bed.

KEEP FIT

City dwellers should check their physical condition often.

How do you feel after running for a train, walking ten blocks or climbing a steep hill?

You may be puffing, but you should not be exhausted. It should take only three minutes at the most to get your breath back. If it takes four minutes you are one-degree-under. Five means you are certainly unfit.

Grasp an empty soup tin and squeeze. If you cannot make a dent in it, your muscles are under par.

Look in a mirror. Features should be relaxed and rested, not tense and tired.

Color should be whatever is normal for you.

Whites of the eyes should be white, not yellow or bloodshot. Pull down the lower eyelids. The linings should be a warm pink. If they are pallid, you could be anemic. If they are bloodshot, you could be out of condition.

But bloodshot eyes or linings may only mean that you have been drinking. They may have been irritated by smoke, dust or bright light. Or you may have a minor infection.

Puffiness around the eyes, especially if it persists, may be a sign of illness.

You cannot be fit if you are overweight. If after knocking off 10 pounds for clothes you are not within 10 per cent of the standard weight for your age, sex and height (found on most public weighing machines) you are not 100 percent.

Other signs of unfitness are continuing tiredness, insomnia and inability to concentrate. Never-ending "blues" are also a sign you are not in the pink.

Find out WHY you are unfit before taking any action.

If you have been working without a break from early morning to late at night, have skipped holidays and spent the weekends decorating, you need a rest.

A week's holiday away from home is the best answer. Next best thing is to slow down. Take a nap in the afternoon or when you get home from work.

Go to bed earlier. As far as possible, keep weekends clear for relaxation, hobbies and family outings.

If you have a desk job, drive everywhere by car and spend your evenings watching television, the odds are you need more exercise.

Start with a brisk walk of a quarter of an hour a day. Work this up to half an hour.

The best way to slim is to cut down on starchy foods such as bread, sugar, cakes and potatoes. Keep an eye on fats. Eat as much lean meat, fruit, salads and green vegetables as you can.

If you smoke you can make yourself fitter by cutting down—or, preferably, by stopping altogether.

Cut down on drinking, too.

If you are over 30, check with your doctor before joining a health club. The same applies to sauna baths.

Fifteen minutes in a sauna will send your pulse up to 180. People have died as a result.

KEEP WARM IN WINTER

It's important to wear baggy clothes in cold temperatures to let the body air circulate. Also keep your extremities covered.

Wear long johns which keep you cool in summer, warm in winter, and which protect the small of the back, thighs, knees and calves.

These long underpants of snug-fitting whole-ribbed pure cotton will reinforce thin Levis which let body heat escape at the knees.

A substitute for long johns are ordinary pajama pants worn as underwear.

The head and wrists are the two other danger points where body heat leaks in cold weather. A balaclava is the warmest headgear. And leather mittens are warmer than gloves.

Those who wear woollen underclothes stand the best chance of keeping warm. They are more efficient than string vests and underpants.

Boots aren't warm enough without a couple of layers of socks. A headband does keep the ears warm.

But don't wear too many clothes. Many people catch cold in the city through overwrapping themselves. City dwellers are always getting out of warm cars, buses, taxicabs, subways or trains into the cold, then back into centrally heated offices or houses. THE COMFORTED in Victorian days had the right idea about keeping similar clothes on all winter so the body temperatures stayed the same. And do remember that once you get used to the cold, you don't really notice it.

Keep your mouth shut in winter. Breathing with it open in cold weather leads to loss of moisture, drying of the mouth and mucous membranes and speeds up dehydration.

Tuck sweaters, pullovers, cardigans and blouses into the trousers for warmth. Remember that two or three thin sweaters are warmer than one big thick chunky jersey.

Cut a small hole through the side of your coat sleeve just above the cuff. Stick your thumb through. Pull down. Now the sleeve will be anchored (by the thumb) over most of both hands and will keep them warm.

Take off a raincoat or topcoat when waiting for a bus. Drape it over your shoulders like a cape and button it up again. This traps a layer of heat which your body heats even more.

Watch out when you are hungry. This can produce increased sensitivity to cold, slow your heart rate, make you weak, lessen coordination and cause dizziness and blackouts.

Eat something hot before venturing into the cold. And chew dates, raisins, chocolate, candy, glucose tablets, cheese or sugar cubes while walking.

Arctic explorers eat hot cereal for breakfast, chocolate and sugar for lunch and crackers spread thick with butter. They drink hot cocoa and tea. A high-calorie diet like this gives you lots of energy—more than you probably need under ordinary city circumstances—and keeps out the cold.

Use two eggs for short trips. Boil them for 30 minutes and they will retain their heat when gripped in each hand. Or carry them in a pocket until needed; keep them warm by wrapping them in the foil from an old TV dinner.

Eat them when cool if you are still starving in intense cold.

Large stores sell pocket hand warmers. These radiate heat without a flame, have a chrome finish and are supplied in a velvet bag for the elderly.

A pocket hand warmer will comfort cold hands. The warmed hands can then be pressed to warm the face when toothache or earache pains are aggravated by the cold, or cheeks are suffering mild frostbite. Chilblain sufferers gain relief too.

Finally, do not wear *too* many clothes. The body warms up with the exertion of walking, even on a fairly cold day. You will suffer if bottled inside too many layers of garments.

COPE WITH RAIN

Mathematical rules have been devised to guarantee a moist rather than a wet walk through rain.

AGAINST rain: Walk as fast as possible and lower your head.

WITH the rain: Walk forward leaning backward. Keep a deliberate pace.

It is always possible to spruce up damp clothes in a hotel or apartment—even when you have no electric iron:

Dry out shoes by stuffing them with paper. Leave them in a warm room well away from direct heat. Never place shoes in front of a heater or fire. This ruins them.

Clean shoes next morning (even when still damp) with a piece of apple or banana skin (see THE SHEEP, p. 28).

Hang wet trousers from a hook and press the creases firmly into them again between thumb and forefinger, while they are still wet. Running a trace of soap down the inside of the creases will make them sharper.

Hang a sodden jacket on a hanger over a hot bath or running shower. Close the bathroom door. The steam will remove the wrinkles.

Suede affected by rain should be hung up (pack shoes with

paper) to dry. Rub with a cloth soaked in vinegar and then brush over the steam from a kettle or basin of scalding water.

Velvet may also be restored with the steam from a kettle.

Leather must be left to dry. Then restore by cleaning with saddle soap.

CODDLE YOUR FEET

Cure corns by taking a tablespoonful of whiskey three times a day or, if you don't drink, a dessertspoon of glycerine flavored with peppermint oil each night and morning. One improves the circulation; the other lubricates the skin through the pores.

Visit a chiropodist if you are elderly and your toenails are long and hard—you may not see well enough to trim them. Until then use a bandage smeared in petroleum jelly to ease walking.

Rejuvenate tired feet with a simple exercise: Stand up straight with the feet pointed ahead and gently raise and lower yourself on your toes for 10–15 minutes a day. If your feet are hurting badly, do this while standing in warm water.

To strengthen the toes, arches and ankle muscles, sit on a chair, place a child's glass marble on the floor and pick it up with the bent toes of one foot. Carry the marble behind the other foot and set it down carefully. Do this exercise with alternate feet for 10–15 minutes a day.

CARE FOR THE LEGS

Do not run for buses. Sudden violent movement could mean a torn calf muscle, especially on a cold morning.

Calves which become stiff and painful after walking 200 yards may be suffering from intermittent claudication, cramplike pains caused by insufficient arterial blood supply to the muscles. Sometimes drugs that dilate the blood vessels are helpful. Walk slowly.

Avoid walking on streets if a doctor diagnoses a torn muscle or ligament in the calf (2 inches below the knee). Rest, relaxation and strapping are the best cure for tennis leg.

NURSE THE HEART

A pain in the chest when walking *may* mean a degree of angina. This comes on mainly because of an increased heart rate.

You may still play golf with no ill effects (just swinging a club is not enough to make the heart go faster and thus cause pain), as walking will be the main cause of these pains.

There are tablets which may help. They should be taken only on medical advice.

Heart pains may be noticed on arrival in city streets. Heartbeats rise dramatically just *before* what you feel is a new and dangerous (even exciting) experience.

The dizziness which results from heart trouble will increase the more you keep walking. It will go, however, when you rest. This is an indication that you are being more energetic than you should.

Go more slowly and do just the amount you find you can manage.

If you sit down to rest, do not worry if you hear your heart beating. It is not a sign of a bad heart.

Anyone escorting an older person who blacks out on the street should have learned to recognize the difference between a coronary and a stroke.

When the eyes are *wide open* with a startled, frightened expression on fainting, the chances are it is a heart attack.

Dazed eyes, face drawn, deathly whiteness and a brow moist with sweat could be just a bad bilious attack.

If one side of the mouth is drooping and perhaps dribbing saliva, it is most likely a stroke.

DIABETICS: GUARD AGAINST DIABETIC COMPLICATIONS

To prevent the complications known as insulin shock (which takes minutes) and diabetic acidosis (which takes 24 hours), the control of diabetes is vital.

The following chart is a short guide only. The best safeguard against complications is to do as your doctor says.

	INSULIN SHOCK	DIABETIC ACIDOSIS
CAUSES	Caused by taking too much insulin or oral tablets for diabetes . . . not eating food or delaying meals . . . taking an unusual amount of exercise	Caused by taking too little insulin . . . injections, fever . . . eating too much food . . . emotional stress . . . nausea or vomiting
WHAT IT FEELS LIKE	Hunger, excessive sweating, faintness, headache, pounding of the heart, trembling, weakened vision	Weakness, stomach pains, aches all over, thirst, dry mouth, loss of appetite, nausea and vomiting
WHAT TO DO	Take sugar or any food containing sugar such as fruit juice, candy or crackers . . . notify your doctor . . . do NOT take any insulin or oral tablets for diabetes	Call the doctor at once . . . go to bed and keep warm . . . drink hot fluids with no sugar . . . keep to the normal routine as much as possible in continuing your diet and medication . . . keep testing your urine at regular intervals

IF YOU FEEL YOU ARE GOING TO FAINT

Or if you have been struck a blow that has made you groggy, try to loosen your collar and lie down. If you can get your head lower than the rest of your body, good. When you are lying down, your blood has a better chance to flow to your brain and carry oxygen. It is mainly the shortage of oxygen that causes unconsciousness.

COMFORT ACHES AND PAINS

With ice. This anesthetizes pain more than hot fomentations or warming embrocations.

Ice numbs skin and muscle and pain goes. Then movement becomes possible and the frozen, constricted blood vessels dilate. More blood flows, the circulation increases and the area gets hot. (As in a cold bath when your skin tingles, then becomes red and glowing.)

Ice helps to prevent infection. No part of the body that is refrigerated is likely to become infected even if it is contaminated with dirt—say, a nasty splinter run into a finger from a wooden sidewalk barrier. Germs do not spread in ice-cold temperatures.

STOMACH ACHE is eased by carrying a hot water bottle or plastic bag full of ice on the stomach inside the trousers or below the skirt. (Always call your physician if you suspect anything really serious, such as appendicitis.)

SPRAINED ANKLE can be relieved by holding a small plastic bag of ice cubes against the painful part. Also good for STRAINED NECK and SPRAINED BACK.

BURNS should be treated by rubbing an ice cube over the injured area until the sting goes. This relieves the pain, cuts down swelling and usually eliminates blisters.

CUTS AND CONTUSIONS will not bleed when ice is held on them; the cold restricts the blood vessels beneath the skin.

BLACK EYE is better handled by an ice chunk than the traditional beefsteak for relieving discoloration, swelling and pain.

SPLINTERS are best removed when ice is placed over the skin to numb it. Then probe with a needle whose point has been held in a match or lighter flame.

ITCHES can be stopped by holding ice on them.

The Cold-Blooded (Dispassionate)

Are not necessarily cold-hearted and, indeed, may well have all the attributes of courtesy, tact, sympathy, dignity, humility, gentleness and selflessness when faced with others in need of help.

BUT they do watch out.

STOP BEFORE ACTING

Any emergency on the streets can be faced better if you plan your course of actions:

S   Stop
T   Think
O   Observe
P   Plan

S—Stop. The body is designed to do three things: digest food, work, and think. It does not do any of these well when trying to do all or two simultaneously. Stopping allows us to think clearly and prevent an overhasty decision.

T—Think. The immediate and future danger to yourself and your loved ones should be your chief thoughts. Analyze the situation: prevailing conditions, your state of energy and the resources available to help you.

O—Observe. Look around you, observing the problem for possible solutions. Look for allies, resources and escape routes and determine whether the emergency is genuine.

P—Plan. After thinking and observing the crisis, plan the course of action which is best suited to you, and plan to take advantage of any nearby help.

SITUATIONS WHERE YOU HAVE A CHOICE

ASKED FOR DIRECTIONS: Say you do not know the city. Walk away. Or if you do oblige, watch your wallet. It is pickpocketing technique to sandwich you between two or three thieves who push you gently and firmly into the best position for them to take your wallet. They ask you to point out the way and your raised arm makes it easy for them, as they turn you this way and that as well.

ASKED FOR A LIGHT: It is safer to say, "Sorry, don't smoke," and walk away, all senses aware.

ASKED TO LOOK OUT FOR PICKPOCKETS: When such a warning is shouted on a crowded sidewalk, don't slap your wallet to make sure it is there. Obvious reasons.

ASKED FOR THE TIME: Give an estimation or glance at your wristwatch. Don't break your stride.

ASKED FOR SMALL CHANGE: Dole it out from your side pocket (see THE SHEEP, p. 28) and walk quickly on. If the only small change you have is in your handbag, grasp it firmly and sidestep.

When asked to change a quarter, say, on a dark or quiet street, say you have no change and keep walking.

Expect panhandlers in all shapes and sizes: blind beggar, cripple on crutches, peddler with clockwork toys, "Bloody Mary"—the woman with ulcerated legs who rifles through trash cans, "Fats" —a burly woman in brown coat, torn black slacks, blue tennis sneakers and rolled-down sweat socks, accordion player serenading commuters and Pete the Panhandler who is immaculately dressed.

ASKED TO HELP PUSH A CAR: Refuse on health grounds; there is always a risk of a coronary from the sudden strain.

If you must help, know the best way. Use the power of your legs, not the arms or the back. Turn your back on the vehicle so that it is your legs plus your weight that do all the work. Dig heels in, sink the body down, bend at the knees and then straighten the legs.

ASKED TO HELP AN OLD WOMAN ACROSS THE STREET: Watch your wallet and purse. She may be a pickpocket or his assistant who helps to take you "on the stride" (see THE NARCISSISTIC, p. 155).

Pregnant or pregnant-looking women and small children are also used as "stalls" on sidewalks, subway stairs and street crossings. They jostle and distract you.

ASKED TO STOP A THIEF: Avoid both the running man and the pursuing. It may be an armed criminal wanted by armed police. It could be a pickpocket setup (they take your wallet as they "help" you grapple with the fleeing person).

ASKED TO HELP BREAK UP A FIGHT: Never. The chances are that if you do, both assailants will turn and sock you.

Call the police. It's their job. Avoid getting sucked into street brawls at all costs. Many an innocent bystander has been crippled for life by getting involved in a fight that had nothing to do with him.

If some innocent person is attacked, then you may interfere if that person is a woman, elderly person or a child and you are fit, strong and combative.

But call the police first or get someone else to do it before you go to help (see THE NERVOUS, p. 52).

ASKED TO TAKE A CHANCE ON STREET GAMES: Walk on. If you stand and watch you will be pressed forward by people from behind—the accomplices of the performer with his cards, walnut shells or other trickery. Then they pick your pocket or strongarm you to play.

ASKED TO WATCH A DISTURBANCE BY COMPANIONS: Never. Avoid street trouble like the plague. Do not become an innocent victim of a teenage gang fight, a race riot, a strike fight or other group violence. It is the curiosity-seekers who run up to gape at such brawls who become victims. By blundering in looking for excitement, they receive much more than they bargained for.

ASKED TO ACCOMPANY CITY POLICE: The simplest way of dealing with this situation is to go along with them. If you refuse they arrest you and you'll have to go anyway.

If police wish to search you, let them there and then. It saves a lot of bother. People being searched in the street should ask a passerby to act as witness—just to be on the safe side.

ASKED TO GUIDE THE BLIND (or perhaps *you* offer to see them across the street): Be ready for them to be touchy. Let them take your arm—never hold on to them.

ASKED TO GO WITH A MAN: It depends on who you are as to *how* you refuse a stranger. But refuse.

Never send children under the age of ten on errands alone. Let them go with friends who are sensible. Impose a strict rule that they have nothing whatsoever to do with strangers—no accepting ice cream, candy, a lift in a car, the offer to stroke a pet or to go with the stranger to see his new kittens.

It is a warning that should be given as often as a goodnight kiss.

Women who are accosted on the street should turn down the

offer in the way that most suits their personality. In most cases, use the tactics which, bred in you, have saved you in such situations before.

But if he continues to pester you, it usually works to embarrass him. If people are about turn round and say "Bug off" loudly. Do not walk on like a good girl, ignoring him. He may well follow to your door.

ASKED TO GO WITH A GIRL: Avoid prolonging a proposition.

Be civil. Prostitutes live in a state of humiliation and have a ready antenna for insult. The cruelest insult is to be snubbed or ignored or tricked, and the working girl may retaliate violently if you bait her.

Don't start an approach in the first place unless you mean to go ahead with the deal, price being agreed.

When accosted be polite but never *indignant*.

Prostitutes are more likely not to bother you if, in the first place, you avoid eye contact with them.

Never get into a car driven by a working girl who pulls up to the curb and accosts you. Do not show your hotel bedroom key to a prostitute while bargaining with her as proof you *are* staying nearby.

Do not hang about streets hoping you will be accosted. A female who does say "Hi" may not appeal to you. Or you may lose courage and be insulting, thus risking an assault.

If you agree to go with her and she says she will follow you several yards behind and then you change your mind en route and hightail it round a corner so that you lose her—go some place else. The immediate streets are risky for you if you happen to bump into her again.

Avoid prostitutes if you can.

SITUATIONS WHERE YOU HAVE NO CHOICE

These are situations where something inside you dictates you should help someone else in need. You simply cannot help it. You are obeying your instincts.

So know what to do.

WHEN SOMEBODY FALLS: Do not help him up from the front in such a way that he can grasp your coat lapels or a shoulder—it is too easy for his hands to dip into your pockets as you struggle.

Go behind to lift. Place both your hands below his armpits and straighten your legs to push *you* upright rather than pull him up. But button up your coat or jacket first. And watch your wallet. One hand ready.

IF A FRIEND FAINTS OR IS KNOCKED OUT: Lie him flat on the ground with his head lower than the rest of his body; loosen his collar. Sprinkle cold water on his face, and see he gets plenty of cold air. If smelling salts are handy, use these to help bring him around.

Anyone who collapses with a pain in the chest, goes blue and possibly vomits, may be suffering a heart attack.

Dial for an ambulance. Keep him quiet. If he loses consciousness, lie him on his side. If his heart stops beating, doctor or ambulance will be too late. You must try emergency treatment yourself. . . .

Pass a finger down beyond the patient's tongue to clear the air passage of foods, false teeth and fluids.

Give the kiss of life by closing nostrils with fingers and blowing into the mouth at four-second intervals to make the chest expand. Repeat four times. Test for the pulse in the throat. If you feel nothing, place both hands on the lowest part of the breastbone and push sharply down. *Repeat once a second.* If the heartbeat and breathing start up, roll the patient on his side with the head well back and wait for the ambulance or doctor.

If the thought of the kiss of life revolts you, place a handkerchief over the person's lips and blow through that. It will still work.

WHEN THERE ARE FRACTURES AND SHOCK: People die from shock; fainting can be a sign of it. It always occurs in cases of serious accidents, however tough and calm the patient seems to be. Don't treat it casually.

Give the patient fresh air (don't crowd around) and warmth,

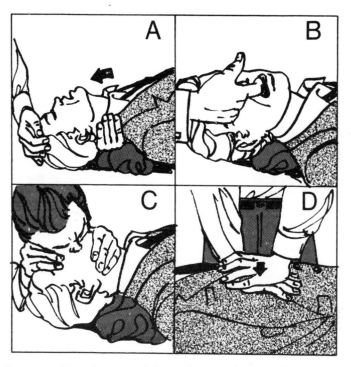

A. Stoppage of breathing=quick brain damage. Skin turns blue-gray. Turn on back, raise chin and tilt head back.

B. Pass finger beyond tongue to clear air passage of food, fluid and false teeth.

C. Carry out the kiss of life (see page 192). With children, however, seal your lips around mouth and nose, gently but firmly blow into lungs until chest rises, remove mouth, watch chest fall. With older children, pinch nose and blow through mouth only. Repeat about four times. Allow for natural exhalation in between. If still no breathing, continue every four or five seconds until help comes. Test for pulse in throat.

D. For an adult, if kiss of life fails, push sharply down on breastbone every second. If heartbeat and breathing start up, roll on side, head well back, to await ambulance. Babies: tap sharply with two fingers. Older children: don't thump breastbone; press gently with fingers.

REMEMBER: Breathing can stop for up to ten minutes while heart is still beating, but lack of air causes brain damage. So give kiss of life first.

though this doesn't mean wrapping him up in every blanket or spare piece of clothing to be found. Talk to him gently and reassure him that everything is going to be all right.

Do not give him anything to drink—if he has had an accident, he may have internal injuries which need an operation—and drink can cause vomiting and complications. In other words, if there is any brandy about, drink it yourself.

WHEN SETTING A BREAK: Inspect the limb with suspected broken bones. Look for any swelling or tenderness, especially if there is anything out of shape. Do not try to make the patient stand up for a quick test to see if his leg *is* broken!

Run both hands over it gently and you may be able to feel a break. If you have any doubts, tie the injured leg to the other. If it's an arm, tie it to the patient's side.

Treat him for shock and talk gently. Do not worry about splints —they are not really considered worthwhile these days. Just concentrate on keeping the affected limb still and *comfortable* until an ambulance or a doctor arrives.

WHEN YOU ARE FIRST AT THE SCENE OF A CAR CRASH: Keep your cool. Leave people trapped in vehicle unless there is a fire.

Injured people have been made worse and often killed by being dragged out of cars willy-nilly. A man with a broken back can be saved if you leave him alone.

Don't panic. Stop other traffic to avoid cars shunting into each other. Prevent people from smoking for fear of gasoline fires. Send others for emergency services.

Never try to right an upturned automobile with people inside unless you have a LOT of help. If the car bounches about, injured people inside could be killed. And those lifting with insufficient manpower can strain their hearts or suffer ruptures.

This advice applies to many accidents and illnesses on the streets which need immediate help. Judge whether you would do better to stay with the patient or run for help.

WHEN FACED WITH SERIOUS BLEEDING: Loss of blood in large quantities can be a killer—but keep it in perspective. Blood loss of less than a pint is not serious yet *looks* deadly.

Bleeding is worst in a standing position, less when sitting and least when lying down.

Forget about tourniquets and pressure points. Instead, simply press down with your fingers on the wound and its surroundings. If you have a sterile dressing use it. If not, employ anything— glove, handkerchief, sock.

Keep up the pressure for ten or 15 minutes (by which time help should have arrived). If the bleeding has not stopped, repeat.

Do not peel off sodden pads, but add others—a hat, say, on top of the sock being used as a dressing.

If there is something inside the wound that cannot be pulled out, keep pressing around or alongside the foreign object.

It helps to raise a limb which is bleeding badly; the uphill flow slows down the bleeding. But do not elevate a leg or arm when you suspect a bone is broken in it.

IF YOU SUFFER FROM HEMATOPHOBIA (fear of the sight of blood), there is a simple cure.

Breathe out all the air in your lungs. Just when you cannot go on without taking a breath, look at a bloodstain. You will probably find the blood does not bother you. Repeat the exercise and at the critical moment touch a drop of blood.

You will soon find that you can look at blood and even touch it without the breathing exercise. This works because big worries push little worries out of your mind. Who would think of scratching his head while falling off a skyscraper?

WHEN SOMEBODY EXPERIENCES A DRUG OVERDOSE: Get victim to the nearest hospital. Help the doctor (by taking along any pills/syringes/containers found by the casualty). Note: In most cities doctors will not inform the police.

Ensure victim vomits when overdose has been swallowed (press spoon/fork/knife handle against back of tongue), BUT have patient sitting up minus false teeth or partial dental plates.

Unconscious patient should be laid on side (no pillows); don't wake up.

The Unattractive (Defensive)

Discourage transgressors by making themselves undesirable, each in his/her own individual way (like lions/skunks/snakes). Unattractive to whom, though?

We are never too plain to be raped or too poor to be robbed on the streets. What can deter the rapist could still pull the thief. The sex maniac who was going to rape and then changes his mind could still rob, while the robber who finds that a victim has no money might rape. Nor is anybody too old to be sexually assaulted and possibly killed in a perverted way, men included.

How you defend yourself depends on YOU. There are different ways of making yourself unwanted, depending on time, place and personality. And how you react against attackers at a given time may be quite different from the way you would behave were you to meet them in another situation. Or were to meet another type of thug altogether.

It is impossible to say one mode of self-defense will work for EVERYBODY. There are too many variants depending on circumstance.

Instead, you must ACT RIGHT by ACTING WRONG.

ACTING RIGHT

Know what to do by knowing YOU.

An attractive person can still prove unattractive by behaving in the RIGHT way: i.e. putting on behaviour to put off potential aggressors. *Behavior that is suited to them.*

You can use suggestion, deception or aggression, depending on what kind of person you are. Of these, the first two are the safest tactics for most people. Fighting back is dangerous for the average person untrained in self-defense.

It is better that you should act. And everyone can when they have to: many do it from morning to night as it is.

Let danger spur you on. Acting is make-believe, but to make

people believe you must believe yourself. To make it exist you must partly dream it. It must be partly true too.

The danger of death or maiming, therefore, is a help in itself. In an emergency, acting gives terrified emotions an outlet and creates an impression of realism to those who would harm you.

PRACTICE the put-on behavior by which you put off others. You must show the *appearance* of your emotions and not just pretend to feel them.

ACTING WRONG

Do the things most suited to YOU to make you unsuitable for potential attackers on the streets.

Too Yielding

Go limp if grabbed. Many rapists are not virile: they *need* the stimulus of violence—the struggle—to perform.

Becoming a dead weight will discourage them. Force your mind to go blank. Sag down. Play dead.

Too Soiled

Keep talking when rape is imminent. Imply you have venereal disease.

Too Strange

Use surprise. It can discourage muggers and dumbfound rapists. Simulated insanity will turn off most people.

Turn a handspring. Play deaf and dumb. Pull off wig and trample on it. Blabber like an imbecile. Disarray hair. Twitch. Jabber. Throw wristwatch onto ground. Or false teeth (and jump on them). Peel off false eyelashes and eat them. Throw a fit.

Too Damaged

Use a cackle bladder to bite on and spit blood whether faced with a gang or a single assailant. This is often enough to dissuade would-be aggressors who (1) may not want the blame for the damage that appears already to have happened or (2) get their kicks from beating up someone from scratch, not one already suffering considerable damage.

Avoid any slackening off. Be inconsolable.

Too Soft

Break down and cry if a gang of toughs attack. Don't stand your ground and fight. It's not enough to cower and crawl. Wail your eyes out. Howl. Real tears come when the situation demands them. Chances are that thugs will think you aren't worth wasting kicks on and leave you alone.

But when knocked down and kicked, roll into a ball and keep rolling. Cover parts being kicked with arms, but count the head as a priority (clasp base of skull with both hands—with wrists across ears and sides of skull, pressing elbows together). Bring knees up and cross the ankles to save the genital region.

Feign pain. Gasp/yell/shout more than you need. Attackers generally leave off quicker when they think you are in agony.

Too Convinced

Feel you ARE in the right. Rape victims often don't. They secretly feel that, somehow, the rape or impending assault is their fault. And they thus give way unnecessarily by communicating their psychological weakening to the rapist.

Too Accompanied

Be—if you can—with someone else on streets, in public toilets and so on. Groups of young muggers (girls too) tend to commit muggings thoughtlessly on the spur of the moment—finding a victim alone (doddering old man/crippled woman/small child) and attacking for a few cents or empty wallet.

Tag along wtih someone big enough to look as if he can take care of himself when you don't have acquaintances or friends along as partners.

Too Time-Conscious

Travel in twos at times of day or season most favored by criminals. If alone, be *aware*. Examples: *Lunch hours* = greatest threat for mugging of housewives/schoolchildren/pensioners. *Evenings* = most assaults on lone women, senior citizens and businessmen returning home from work. *First day of each month* = risk for the elderly when taking pension checks to the banks to cash them. *Christmas* = threats from sidewalk Santas who could be crooks.

Too Pacifist

Be philosophical about having a wallet or handbag stolen. Never run after the thief; he could stop and stab you. You would then be the architect of your own downfall by not having priorities right.

Keep calm and don't resist when robbed. Murder out of the blue, in which the victim is struck down without saying or doing anything, is rare.

Too Cheap

Don't draw attention to yourself. Wearing a cheap but flashy wristwatch, which you intend offering if a mugger strikes, is wrong. The sight of the watch alone can draw the mugger—who might not have noticed you otherwise.

The person who carries a briefcase full of trash when he has no need for a briefcase is also in danger. He is mugged, hands over the briefcase as planned, but the criminal forces the lock on the spot. And angry at the deception, he could stab or shoot when he finds the contents worthless. The same goes for the decoy wad of money. If you hand this over to a mugger and he examines it, he might turn vindictive.

Consider every factor. Businessmen in dark suits are vulnerable crossing busy streets, but wearing a brighter suit more easily seen in car headlights could result in your standing out that little bit to the ever alert hold-up man.

If you must dress rather ostentatiously, then be alert yourself. Travel by taxi when carrying more money or valuables than usual.

Always carry $20 or $30 to hand over if you are mugged. Children should carry one or two dollar bills separately on the streets for the same reason—to hand over if assailed.

Too Familiar

Tell a potential assailant that you know him. Or of him. "I know you" can break a criminal's intention if said with enough conviction. (Rapists often use mistaken identity as their defense.)

Do this early. The rapist may kill the victim who is convincingly familiar enough, but who claimed identification too late.

Too Stoic

See also TOO SOFT.

Many thugs will ease up on a victim who is reduced to pleading/sniveling/groveling.

The mugger with a sadistic bent, however, will do the opposite. The more you cry for mercy, the more he will hate you for it. *Especially when you look as if you can easily afford more than he has managed to steal from you so far.*

Bite lip/chew gum/clench teeth instead. Be stoic. Don't plead when you have a nice watch, good suit, full wallet, polished shoes, happy home.

If it's in you to be a martyr, now is the time to play it. And possibly escape the worst. Endure the pain. Say to yourself *even this will pass.* Pray silently. The chances are your assailant will strip you of everything then go off to look for someone else soft enough to beg for mercy.

Too Gutsy

The victim who sees red and loses his temper is the most dangerously placed. Yet there have been thousands of occasions when a person has been unable to stop her gore rising. She flung herself into the fray and routed her assailant. So strong was her fury at being victimized that she succeeded against all odds. When nothing will hold YOU back . . .

BITE the ends of fingers/toes/noses (false teeth are most effective as they have no nerve ends telling you when to stop); CHEW ears, cheeks and other sensitive spots; ROAR with all your might into attacker's ear to shock; TUCK HEAD IN, hunch shoulders and charge like a mad bull; or if held from behind, TUCK HEAD DOWN then smash it backward; RAM SHOULDER into attacker's stomach to hit lower ribs and jolt internal organs; DRIVE ELBOW into aggressor's face to shake teeth loose, smash it into ribs with elbow point, rive it up side of jaw; JAB TWO THUMBS into antagonist's neck to cut off breath and hurt esophagus; STAB THUMB in carotid artery of neck to dam blood flow to attacker's brain; RAKE FINGERNAILS across face; PRESS POINT OF FINGERNAIL into attacker's temple and twist finger like a drill; NIP tender skin of upper lip between two fingernails; AIM FINGERNAIL into corner of eye and twist finger; HOOK BOTH THUMBS into attacker's mouth beneath cheeks and yank outward; STICK FIRST FINGER straight into other's mouth, fish hook it over bottom teeth and force fingernail into soft flesh below; TWIST BOTH EARS off (try to); or CLAP BOTH HANDS over ears so they sound like gunshots to enemy's eardrums; REACH UP as if to grasp nose, but open hand and hit nostrils with "V" of thumb and forefinger; or HIT WITH HEEL OF HAND on this tender spot; GRAB HOLD OF FINGERS and twist them into paralyzing grip—increase pressure to force submission.

If you are going to meet brutality with ferocity, when life is endangered *enough for you to react as you are doing now,* do your best to do your worst.

The Fugitive (Momentary)

At least, as a last resort, manage somehow to block the blow or knife when everything else has failed.

And by such fleeting delaying tactics, they draw the attention of onlookers who may be persuaded to help or call for aid at the flash of the blade or thud of the kicks assailing them.

Much depends on a quick brain and a good physique for combative (and scientific) self-defense, but most have arms and legs which, used to their best advantage, can offer good passive resistance. They help ward off a potentially murderous attack and give a chance to escape.

FIRST LINES OF DEFENSE

Avoid getting into situations on the street where you can be attacked. Stay alert by using your head/eyes/ears. Expect anything to happen at any time.

If you MUST go through shady areas be suspicious of the character who approaches you or who appears to be waiting for you to pass him. If you are actually threatened by someone with a weapon, retreat to safety if at all possible. Or, as a last ditch resort, keep out of reach.

This can mean running for your life—if you can do so without leaving yourself wide-open to attack.

RUNNING (1)

"Run" when followed; that is, lose them.

Check that you *are* being followed. Look round without making it obvious. . . .

Turn your head with wristwatch up to your ear as if listening to it . . . go down on one knee to tie a shoe lace and the head will swing around normally . . . stop and raise a shoe behind as if to flick a chunk of grit from under the heel; this lets you look behind quite naturally.

Or STOP and drop coins/buy newspapers/shine shoes. If the person passes you, follow him slowly. If not, return in the opposite direction, walking past him and pausing to look in a shop window that reflects the street.

If he turns and follows (toward your "mirror") . . . walk briskly round the first corner. *Stop.* And do shoelaces/heel grit/wristwatch check (whichever you haven't done so far). He will never expect you there—you were supposed to keep going.

Use whatever the situation offers to throw off a shadow. Different exits or stores and car lots. Up one escalator, down another. Jumping on a bus for a couple of stops and leaping off as it begins to move.

Be aware of three people following. Two trail behind in the A-B positions while the third walks across the street abreast of you. Every few blocks they switch positions to avoid identification.

When you need to pass through a dark passage which you know leads to safety, but are afraid: don't argue with yourself about it. Drop your lower jaw. Try to relax and carry on.

Walk backward. This enables your eyes to get used to the dark better than facing into pitch black space. It also fools a potential attacker who is waiting. And puts YOU in the best position to fend off an attack—by kicking behind you with both heels alternately.

A woman who hears footsteps at night should walk faster. If the following steps quicken too, she should run to the nearest street where there are people.

RUNNING (2)

Desperation can give almost phenomenal strength. Enough to help you sprint at 20 mph to the nearest street light, friendly doorbell or busy street. Adrenalin is the booster.

Even the elderly, paunchy or pregnant can run short distances *when they have to.*

1. STAND TO ATTENTION.
2. SCREAM.
3. KICK OFF HIGH-HEELED SHOES.
4. PULL UP SKIRTS.
5. SPRINT.

RUNNING ROUND A CORNER: Hop around one-legged on the inside shoe instead of having both feet on the sidewalk.

RUNNING UPHILL: Turn sideways so the shoes are placed across any steep slope.

RUNNING DOWNHILL: Lean forward so your weight is kept right over both shoes—especially in winter.

RUNNING UP STEPS: Tall people take them two at a time; shorter people, two at a time, then two individually, then two at a time etc. (fastest sequence).

DISTRACTIONS

Talk when cornered. You must prevent the assailant from striking, and give time for help to come. But when the blows are about to fall, the blade poised to stab . . . know the law.

If you are approached on the street, you are under some obligation to try to avoid violence. And to "retreat at least part way if possible before striking a blow in self-defense." If you ARE attacked, however, you are allowed to use any reasonable force to repel the attacker. Only if you really think you are in danger, are you justified in using force, even if the assailant doesn't strike after all. You become the aggressor, though, when you use a force out of all proportion to the threat of attack.

If you have to go where you are liable to be attacked, prepare for the worst with various aids to distract any such oppressor, which will give you a brief psychological advantage . . . and let you escape.

GETTING HELP: See also THE NERVOUS, p. 52.

It is tougher to get help on the street than in the TERMINAL. Police are always nearby in bus depots/airports/railway stations. So are newcomers to the city who are not yet brainwashed into citadel survival and who may help. On the sidewalk people will pass by. Those who stop are likely simply to watch. However, really urgent pleas for help can (1) dissuade your attacker who is only too conscious of the attention you are causing; (2) persuade someone, THE GOOD SAMARITAN (p. 167), to get help fast.

SCREAM OFFENSIVELY (karate attack yell style). Build up

an explosion. Look at sky. Clench fists. Open arms. Show teeth. Scream/roar/bellow to intimidate as well as call for HELP.

BLOW POLICE WHISTLE (carried in pocket). A series of sharp blasts is most noticeable. Or—

LET OFF PORTABLE SCREAMER (best kinds have 118-decibel sound at least—118 decibels = threshold of pain). Stab button to spurt out screams. Remember passersby may keep walking because they think the scream is squealing brakes or a child letting air out of a balloon, but your attacker *is aware that he is no longer blending with the city because he is with you* (creator of noise). Or—

THROW BRICK (through window). Break glass with shoe. Ring fire alarm. Get to police call box. Ring door bell (other than your own home). Jaywalk in front of a police car. Throw bank notes on sidewalk. Do anything to get attention.

USE WEAPONS IN SELF-DEFENSE. Distract your attacker and give yourself more time. Or the chance to escape. You may even make him decide to run for it first.

But which aids are best?

INADMISSIBLE

Weighted blackjack with flexible whalebone or sprung steel grip (illegal)

Noxious liquids and gases (Mace, ammonia, alcohol, acid etc.) or any bootleg killer spray—some incorporating indelible ultraviolet dye in the liquid—in aerosols, water pistols, fake fountain pens and lipsticks, syringes and tennis balls pricked with a hole or two (see THE BELLIGERENT, p. 160)

The criminal could sue if maimed and get substantial damages for assault and battery. There is also a blow-back hazard in wind

PERMISSIBLE

Small bludgeon, but it must be rigid (usually ineffective for the average citizen)

Folding penknife if blade is less than 4 inches long (but would YOU know how to use it? Worthless really, with little effect and exposing you to a criminal police charge if the defense works)

Vegetable knife, screwdriver, ice pick, sharp scissors (law states that where evidence doesn't establish beyond a reasonable doubt that defendant carried ice pick, etc. with intent to use it on another person no charge can be made—but watch the circum-

INADMISSIBLE

where a lethal spray can backfire on YOU. An attacker may also wrest your spray/ gas gun/aerosol from you and turn it on you

Many gas guns disguised as lipsticks/cigars/cameras are ineffective, with a range of only a few feet

A simple ammonia or alcohol spray, furthermore, must come into direct contact with the membranes of eyes or nose and calls for too much accuracy

Pistols (too much risk of missing, hitting other people, provoking a criminal into firing a gun and being sued by the criminal whom you maim)

Un-guns that don't shoot to kill, but fire to stop (nonlethal weapons that look authentic and which perhaps propel a small bag of metal shot; they can make a criminal mad when hit—and can provoke a thug into pulling a real gun)

Switchblades whose blades fold into the handle to be released by a spring (illegal)

PERMISSIBLE

stances; it CAN be construed as a weapon in any crowd from a football crowd to New Year's celebration)

Big-mouthed pot of laundry detergent, sand, soot, salt, pepper or cinders to throw (gives victim some psychological advantage and blinds the attacker momentarily) *Aerosol spray of disinfectant* (with ammonia) does same. So does— *Can of hairspray* with label off or brand name covered with tape, *pepper spray dispenser* (looking like pocket breath freshener), *powdered aerosol spray deodorant* or *plastic yellow lemon* filled with concentrate which, when squirted, shoots 15 feet (lemon is refillable)

None of these sprays can really be construed as illegal weapons, but all can temporarily blind an attacker to give you a chance to run

Ordinary comb with teeth run beneath nostrils of an assailant (good because it is an almost universal possession, with you all the time)

Hat pin 6–7 inches long made from tempered steel with handy grippable knob at one end (also good because it is easily hidden and no policeman will arrest a woman for using it)

Fistful of coins (not so much a weapon as a decoy—Scatter the coins by throwing them in the face of an attacker)

INSTANT DISTRACTIONS (anytime) = thin end of belt swung so buckle end whirls around (or is used as flail); fistful of dirt/face powder/flour flung into attacker's eyes, making it impossible for him to hit you with his weapon and giving you a chance to flee; coat/sweater/handkerchief thrown in his face (if you can set fire to the fabric first, even better); a tightly rolled newspaper can be a prodding rod, one end driven under assailant's chin (preferably toward the Adam's apple, which interferes with his breathing mechanism); an ordinary bunch of keys (holding case or ring in palm of hand, keys projecting from the fist) driven hard into some tender part of opponent's anatomy; wristwatch slipped forward around fist so glass protrudes beyond the knuckles —a useful punching aid for hit-and-running; ballpoint pen or pencil gripped between the center knuckles and sticking out from the fist enabling you to stick it up nose/in ear of assailant (if pen or pencil broke, the short jagged bit could do even more damage); lighted cigarette or cigar thrown into transgressor's face or stub-lit cigarette into attacker's skin; book or box of matches set alight and flipped into thug's features; shoe used as club to batter with before throwing away and running—any heel from a sharp stiletto to a thick wedge can be effective.

PARRYING

Stave off an attack. Use elementary defensive self-defense. Just placing your body and limbs into the right position will help. And give you extra seconds.

BLOCK KNIFE/CLUB/BOTTLE with raincoat carried over an arm wrapped around that arm to "catch" the first thrust or blow and give you a chance to disarm the villain (keep the padded arm horizontal; move it up and down parallel with the ground) with lid of garbage pail held up in front of you like a shield—take blows on the lid, then strike him on neck/face/head with edge of lid if you have the chance; with garbage pail shoved between you and the attacker—so he has to keep his distance; with umbrella or any long-handled implement which you ram bayonet-style into his guts/groin/face (stab forward, both hands grasping the object) with attaché case or briefcase used as a shield in both hands—a cover from blows, kicks, or a blade.

BLOCK HEAD-DOWN CHARGE by raising a knee with all the zest you can gather (when you can't get out of the way)— and lunge it up into his face. But lean right over his back too so that you are not knocked flat on your back (his aim in charging).

BLOCK BLOWS FROM CLUB by stepping toward attacker, crossing both wrists and extending your arms in front of you to catch his weapon between your wrists (which will absorb the blows). It will hurt him more than you.

THWART ATTACK FROM BEHIND by moving as fast as possible when someone jumps on your back, his arms pinned round your body. Step aside with one foot, reach down between your ankles and grab one of your antagonist's ankles in both hands. Grip hard and shove the ankle forward and upward, also squatting down a little on to his thigh. The grip around your waist will be broken and he will crash backward . . . because of the leverage you have exerted and the pressure against his knee.

STOP STRANGLER BEHIND YOU by stepping back in the direction of his pull—whether from a noose or bare hands—lift up your right foot and stamp the heel HARD on to his right toes to break his hold.

SNAP STRANGLE FRONT HOLD by clenching both hands together, fingers interlocked. Drive them up between his arms. When your hands pass your face flip them apart to jolt your forearms against the insides of his elbows. This will drive his arms apart and break the grasp of his fingers on your throat.

BLOCK ATTEMPT TO STRANGLE by either of two simple methods when attacker is coming from the front: (1) Raise both arms up and forward, just above shoulder level, hands 6 inches apart; this keeps strangler at arm's length and puts your straight arms between him and your windpipe. (2) Cross both arms in front of your face with arms raised to shoulder level and palms facing out down in front of collarbone.

FEND OFF ONCOMING CAR by leaping up on to the hood (when obvious it is going to hit you). Try to make it obvious to the driver which way you are going; you don't want to leap left if he's going in the same direction (so that you collide trying to avoid each other). OVERACT; if you're going to jump left swing your arms that way to make it obvious from the beginning.

BLOCK KICKS by doing whichever suits you: (1) Crossing both arms in front of your stomach to catch savage kick on the wrists—kick will be absorbed by your arms, you can catch his foot and return a kick between his legs. (2) Holding out one arm, fist clenched and knuckles down so that you block kick on shins with the fist—at the same time moving out of the way. (3) Blocking his kick with one of your own by simply turning sideways, lifting your nearest shoe and chopping it on his ascending shin bone.

BLOCK ATTACKS WITH YOUR SHOES by kicking (the most common defense for the average citizen). Use combination of kicks to parry any attack on you. AND KEEP KICKING. Lift foot closest to adversary and kick under kneecap with outer edge of shoe; force welt against shin and scrape it all the way down; finally stamp on his instep or toes with all your weight on top—and twist it around. Turn your back on him, kick back with a foot and drive it into his shin or below his kneecap so your body is out of reach.

Part Four

CITY DWELLINGS

Hotels, Apartments and Houses

7

CITY DWELLINGS

LOSERS

INDOORS AT LAST, we are still vulnerable after crossing the threshold and securing the door. Even when protection includes electronic burglar alarms, double-bolted locks and bars across the windows, it is not enough.

Burglary heads the FBI Scale of Major Crimes; it occurs more than any other crime. Every 27 seconds sees another break-in in the city. And there are other closely tied risks—quite apart from the $600 million worth of property that vanishes each year in America—the scores of thousands of men, women and children who come to bodily harm, the $100 million wheedled by tricksters and confidence men from unsuspecting souls.

Yet if we cannot find safety at home, where can we? The answer is IN the home. But we must not expect the physical presence of walls, doors and windows to stop the intruder. It is the weaknesses in ourselves that we should first root out and secure before we put our houses in order.

The Accommodating (Gullible)

Take in anything anyone else tells them at their front door, over the telephone or by the mail. As a result they are quickly taken in themselves, and to their cost.

SIGNS AND SYMPTOMS

When the stranger at the door says, "Good morning, it's Mr. ah ... Mr. ....?" you invariably volunteer your last name. Sending $5 in answer to the ad in the paper—"a guaranteed, radical and successful method of curing greasy hair"—and receiving a piece of paper saying, "Simply shave your head completely and you will no longer have greasy hair." Letting a salesman clinch a deal by telling you that when Winston Churchill was involved in tough wartime decisions he would take a blank sheet of paper, draw a line down the middle, write YES at the top of one column and NO at the top of the other ... then he helps you make out the Yes column, listing all the benefits of his policy or goods, but shuts up when you go to the No column and you cannot think of any disadvantages.

CAUSES

Despite our locks and burglar alarms, most of us prove vulnerable to the doorstep caller with the right approach.

Vanity, sympathy, fear, the desire to save money—all make us more likely to be victims in our own homes under city pressures.

A pleasant manner, for example, will often enlist the sympathy of the housewife. Especially if it is raining and the caller looks wet, cold and miserable and is posing as a student (actually just the conditions this type of caller prefers).

Most people will wilt, too, when faced with the doorstep caller, who, rather than rely on high-pressure fast sales talk, uses psychological selling tactics. Such a caller is discreet, disarming—and dangerous.

Be warned when you find yourself saying YES to everything he says. "You do want to save this money, don't you?" . . . "Is this the kitchen?" . . . "You did say there were four in your family, didn't you?" . . . It becomes increasingly difficult to say NO when he suddenly produces, say, an agreement to be "okayed" (never "signed"; that's too obvious).

The need to get back to the children and a lack of self-confidence which cannot say "No, go away" are only two of the reasons we say "Yes" to any apparently reasonable request so long as it gets rid of the caller.

There are reasons, too, which prompt you to ask him inside. The loneliness which craves a chat with anyone. Greed, which blinds us to the "salesman" who is apparently offering a bargain. A subservience to officialdom (many salesmen pose as officials). A pride in your home, which you want others to admire.

ILLOGICAL BEHAVIOR

We seldom ask callers for identification. The natural reaction when a stranger knocks at the door is not "State your business and prove who you are," but "Come right in."

We are too easily taken in when they "prove" their identity—simply because they *look* the part. A friendly smile, a quick step, a plausible story and an authentic-looking uniform work wonders.

Yet any criminal worth his salt can get hold of a uniform and peaked cap that looks genuine. Sometimes they are genuine.

Anyone with nerve and a ready story can pose as the hotel manager, hotel detective or chambermaid and enter your hotel room by simply knocking on the door and announcing himself in his phony role.

Your apartment? The superintendent or janitor has every excuse to come inside. And so does the impostor who pretends to be one of them when you have just moved in.

As for private homes, there are in every city literally thousands of genuine officials from national and local government agencies who have reason to enter your home—whether you like it or not.

Gas or electricity men must be allowed in your house to read the meter—or they cut off your supply. Census takers, police detectives, fire inspectors, bill collectors, meter readers, Social Security inspectors, housing officers, tax collectors, public health officials, school medical officers. . . .

This means that the burglar's assistant (who "fingers" you for a burglary at a later date) is able to masquerade as virtually anyone and case home after home. He will check the quality of the furni-

ture, decor and general signs of prosperity—and then advise his
partners in crime whether YOU are worth a visit.

So you let him in. And you suspect nothing if he protests when
you try to check, despite the fact that a plainclothesman making
inquiries or a journalist on an assignment (two much-used dis-
guises) will not object to showing you his credentials or waiting
while you check his authenticity over the telephone.

You also close your eyes to the possibility of robbery on the
doorstep while your caller is there. But many a face-to-face salesman has picked the victim's pocket while smiling into his/her
eyes. Few housewives can resist his charms.

There are countless variations on this theme. From the children
who ring the bell, asking to wash your automobile and who—as
they go through the house—fill their buckets with many other
things besides water . . . to the "salesman" who is selling new
locks and burglar alarms. The locks and alarms are not as expensive as those at your local locksmith's. For one thing, they
are inferior and easily picked; for another, he has a copy of the
keys anyway.

The majority of people who need help in the home merely
phone an employment agency. If they check references, they
never evaluate the references carefully enough. One quickly
checked fact—often overlooked—is the employee's address: Is he
or she actually living there?

Dishonest help will, after all, only stay on the job long enough
to know where the important jewelry and furs are stored. Then
they abscond with them or tip off friends on the outside about
them. When the coast is clear, they come in undisturbed and
make their haul.

There are the people—they never lack victims—who knock on
the door saying they are "specialists." They offer to provide an
on-the-spot service—for example, household appliance inspection.
They wear coveralls bearing the name of some famous company,
will look clean and presentable and have a number of small tools
protruding from their pockets. Do we require a free electrical
inspection which covers all cords, plugs, vacuum cleaner, toaster,
stereo, lamps, hair driers, power tools, etc.? But what a good

excuse for a potential burglar, rapist or simple fraud merchant. They can always find something expensively wrong. Just think of the damage they can do (so they can put it to rights) to a television with its thousands of parts.

And the frauds can cover many fields: TV repairmen, lawn mower sharpeners (they come to collect the machine; the wife, thinking her husband has arranged it, pays the fee as they load it on the truck—the last she sees of it), automobile mechanics, heating and air-conditioning engineers and exterminators. . . .

How do criminals get fake identity cards? One much used way is this: the thief or would-be rapist goes to the Social Security office and tells them he wants a card because he never had one. They may look skeptical, but what can they do? He then takes this card along to the license bureau and obtains a driver's license in that name. The man at the counter doesn't care so long as he is shown something that looks legitimate. Often, the burglar will say insurance is his line when collecting his fake ID. All he has to do is to call a few insurance salesmen, ask them to come and see him—and listen hard. After he has seen one or two of them he can imitate their line. Business cards, letters (with phony letterheads) and so forth can now be faked based on the details of the Social Security card and driver's license.

Furthermore, when he does call on you, he may well have a telephone number to back up his claim if you wish to double-check by calling his office. Only it is his friend on the other end at a private number. . . .

Hard as it may seem for the ordinary citizen to win when facing such situations, there are ways in which to make our natures, however accommodating, wary when necessary.

Remedy: The Beaver, p. 278; The Confused, p. 59

The Penny-Wise (Tight)

Are the dollar-foolish in the ways they pinch pennies in the daily routine of housekeeping. It can be as open an invitation to a burglar as wide-open windows and doors.

SIGNS AND SYMPTOMS

Never running hot and cold water into a bath at the same time. Leaving the oven door open when you have been cooking to let the heat out into the apartment. Setting the control dial on the freezer lower in winter than you do in summer.

CAUSES

These signs of thrift at home *do* cut electricity bills and are all reasonable in themselves, but much thrift can be misplaced, even during an energy crisis. If we find ourselves *over*thrifty we ought to look for causes.

Even if you are now fairly well-heeled, the habits of a poverty-stricken youth stick hard. Sometimes they are unnecessary and make you seem eccentric.

No one is exempt. You may live in a poor part of the city, in a smart apartment or in a large house; tightfisted behavior can let you down.

For here is the one area of the city where we think that others see us least—at home. So we make economies that leave ourselves —and our families—totally vulnerable to the intruder.

ILLOGICAL BEHAVIOR

Not changing locks on new apartment or house doors is criminal. Burglars obtain keys from lawyers and agents to look at homes up for sale, copy them and return at a later date to see if the locks have been changed. If they haven't . . .

Here are some ways in which small-minded money-savers let themselves down once the burglar reads the signs from the street. . . .

LEAVING the grass to grow while you are on vacation because you are not prepared to pay the neighbors' children to cut it.

HAVING a mailbox that hangs outside the home rather than fork out the cost of replacing it with a slot-type inside the door, so that your mail falls into the house.

THE PENNY-WISE will usually remember to cancel the newspapers, however—a big giveaway to prowling burglars.

SWITCHING off the radio when you leave the house for a shopping trip or evening out. Yet a radio loud enough so that you can just hear it when standing near the front or rear door will always form a doubt in a thief's mind.

INSUFFICIENT tipping to the superintendent, doorman, janitor, postman, garbageman, bell captain . . . all of whom will look after you better if you have tipped them well.

PULLING down blinds, drawing draperies tight, and closing shades and venetian blinds so that sunlight does not fade the furnishings or wallpaper—which immediately tells the passerby there is probably no one in.

TURNING down the heating when leaving home for several days in winter. A thin skin of snow collects on the windowsills.

LEAVING snow unswept when you are away. It costs little to pay someone to sweep it. The fact you don't means a burglar will know the house is a sitting target.

ALLOWING footprints to point one way only in the snow on your drive—out to the street. Or having just one set of car tire marks going the same way—both signs that your house could be empty.

BURNING only one small light in one room or the hall on leaving the house. Overexposed as a safety tactic, you are inviting not only the professional burglar but also the incompetent one. They will telephone the house if they see one light only (especially in a day room)—and then break in when no one answers.

ECONOMIZING with lights on front and rear porch, patio and garage. And in not using floodlights to illuminate the rear and sides of large houses. But lighting is not expensive compared with the good it does to scare off burglars; they hate *bright* lights.

Intruders outside our homes depend a great deal on the outward signs that we are away from home. So often it is petty economies that give our absence away—whatever the state of our bank accounts.

Remedy: The Guardian, p. 246; The Noisy, p. 258; The Addict, p. 266; The Beaver, p. 213

The Advertiser (Daily)

Is careless, often through vanity, and tells the world everything a burglar wants to know. For anyone who cares to listen—and there will always be willing ears in the city—such information is priceless.

SIGNS AND SYMPTOMS

Talking about valuables in a public place. Checking the new telephone directory to see they spelled your name correctly. Using long words to describe your hobbies in order to sound impressive.

CAUSES

Keeping up with the Joneses draws attention to our life-style.

Deep insecurities taint our behavior. Such is the character who is always trading in his car for a more recent and expensive model or who always picks up the tab in a restaurant—even when he can't afford it.

This is linked with an "it can't happen here" attitude, and we do nothing to protect ourselves. Especially when we come from comfortable middle-class homes in the suburbs. We realize the crime rate is going up and up. However, the fact that so far (knock wood) it has not hit the neighborhood produces the attitude "and I won't really believe it's ever going to."

In this way we draw attention to our vulnerability. And our desire to impress has a backlash; we care too much what others who live nearby think of us.

ILLOGICAL BEHAVIOR

We make a plea to the burglar every time we advertise in the personal ads in a newspaper and carelessly give our address or telephone number instead of a box number.

Burglars scan the want ads of newspapers daily. If they read that someone is advertising an expensive item such as a diamond engagement ring or a car, you can be sure they will be interested. Especially when the ad says, "Call after 9 P.M." and adds the phone number.

Once the burglar has your phone number, he can find your address. As he knows you have at least *one* possession worth stealing, he may decide to search your house before 9 P.M.—as there is a good chance that you will be out.

Not that jewelery is his only target. Advertise stamp collections, musical instruments, guns, furs, hi-fi equipment or scuba diving gear and it all gives a pointer to other valuables being in the household. Furthermore, he will be particularly eager when he knows he can sell the advertised items at a fat profit.

He may even take advantage of a funeral or a wedding, if he knows about it, to break into your house.

In these instances we advertised our situation to possibly thousands of people via the media . . . and never tightened the security on our homes and families in the meantime.

But it is not only advertising in newsprint that spells our doom. An ad on the bulletin board in a supermarket or drugstore can also pull criminal elements. And quickly.

Our next sphere of advertising lies in our behavior *at* home. Most people, for instance, always want to park their cars in the same place when they are home and leave the same gap when they are not. Women who do the shopping tend to do it at the same time on the same day. People with houses in the country often leave town each weekend.

The burglar of residential districts will get a good idea of local families and their habits, based on careful observation. For example, he will drive around a suburb each Sunday morning noting the cars being filled with picnic baskets and fishing rods ready for a day's outing.

Some burglars prefer to call completely unannounced. They look at the nameplate on the door or the mailbox in the lobby which advertises our name, check the telephone directory for the number, dial it and return to the apartment if no one answers the phone.

To have an unlisted number is safer from all points of view. But don't be too complacent or smug about it. The experienced burglar has ways of getting round even this.

Remedy: The Beaver, 278; The Devious, p. 118

The Smug (Righteous)

Go off half-cocked, even though they appear to spare no cost in making their homes secure. Unfortunately their fancy locks become a Maginot Line, and their homes are breached in other ways by the intruder.

SIGNS AND SYMPTOMS

Sleeping soundly because you "know" the slightest sound will wake the family and NOT knowing what a burglar knows about our sleeping habits . . . that people are usually in their deepest sleep between 2 and 3 A.M. We all sleep lighter an hour before going to sleep properly and an hour before getting up (which is why burglars eat mints to get rid of the smell of alcohol; sometimes the smell alone will waken people in light sleep periods). Yet you can drill into a safe hidden in a child's bedroom with a diamond-studded bit and the child will still sleep.

CAUSES

A superb lock can blind us to how easily a burglar can still gain entry by other ways. It can make us feel *too* safe.

A dangerous reason for buying an expensive lock in the first place is a feeling of oneupmanship.

But burglars know us as mugs. For often our choice of new lock or locks is expensive, superfluous and inappropriate. And because of our preoccupation with beating out our friends as well as the burglar, we tend to think no further than the efficiency of the locks themselves.

Such complacency is very human. Yet in our haste to **put up** the shutters, we lose our sense of perspective. And still leave ways by which a thief can get in.

ILLOGICAL BEHAVIOR

Let's look at locks.

On our first night in town we ourselves can render a lock worthless. We double-lock the hotel bedroom door, put the chain on and go to sleep feeling secure. Yet we had never checked that the Servidor—a door inset in the main door so that the valet service can hang newly cleaned and pressed garments into the door without disturbing us—was also locked. And so a prowling thief gains access.

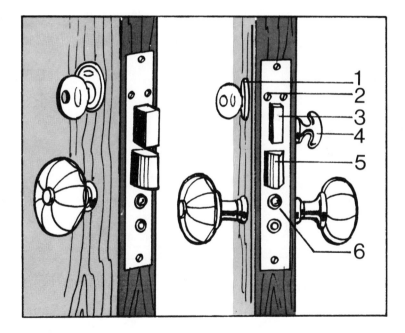

1. Face of lock (burglar will know if it is familiar to him)
2. Setscrew (approximate position for safety reasons)
3. Dead bolt
4. Thumb turn
5. Convenience latch
6. Latch locking button (position varies from lock to lock)

It is on this principle that so many locks are bypassed by the burglar. He does not even need to pick them; he can use methods far simpler than that.

Properly chosen, expensive locks are a good investment. BUT BEWARE!

Mortise locks (as shown) provide security because the locking mechanism is inside a tough metal enclosure in the door. A thief could pound off the door knob and the door would still remain fixed.

Mortise locks have two devices that slide into the doorjamb: a convenience latch and a dead bolt. The latch can be set so that it opens whenever we turn the outside or inside knob. But it can also be set so that it locks from the outside when we close the door—yet it will still open from the inside by turning the inside knob. The bolt, however, is worked by a key from outside the door and with a thumb turn on the inside of the door. The bolts on mortise locks are rugged chunks of metal and add terrific power.

Unless, that is, there is a big gap between the door edge and the jamb. This gives plenty of leverage if a crowbar or other type of burglar's jimmy (lever) is inserted. However, as such excessive clearance in the dimensions of the door would be obvious, we can discount this weakness for the moment. Our door and door frame are a snug fit. Jimmy-proof.

Now let us look at how our illogical behavior can weaken a first-rate lock of this kind.

The convenience latch is beveled and is not *meant* to keep the door securely locked. That job is for the bolt. But so many of us set the latch to lock when we close the door; we take the key from the lock outside the door and imagine the door is now burglarproof as we go for a five-minute journey to the store. When the latch of the usual mortise lock is not guarded by the bolt it can easily be pushed back with a piece of plastic (a loid).

The latch, unguarded by the bolt, can also be slid aside in the following way: a doorstep salesman or delivery man calls and we step inside to get some money or a pen. While we are away, he presses the latch locking button in the edge of the door and now—unless we use the deadbolt—the latch will open with a twist of the knob from the *outside* too. He comes back later, knocks on the door and if there is no answer simply turns the knob and steps inside.

A springy door frame can be levered apart with a car jack. Two blocks of wood are placed at each end of the jack, door slides are pressured apart. Once the gap is open further than the end of the mortise lock bolt, the door can be opened.

It is so easy to forget that mortise locks are only really secure when locked with the bolt and NOT with the latch alone. The typical mortise is bolt-locked from the outside only when you turn the key, never when the door is simply just closed. (And the bolt is shot from the inside only when you twist the thumb turn.)

Even then, with the bolt shot home, we can *still* let our good lock down:

By the doorstep caller again. As we root in our purse, he unscrews the set screw holding the cylinder of the lock in which we insert our key in position. As the set screw is in the lock face on the edge of the door (in some locks it is protected with a metal plate) it is in a vulnerable position—ready to be loosened quickly. When it is loose the lock cylinder (see diagram) can be removed from outside the door. The criminal returns at his leisure and can release the bolt and latch with his finger or a tool.

By failing to inspect the door frame properly. If it is rotting slightly, the burglar can insert a strong screwdriver and level the space between the door and the frame in the zone of the lock until the door can be forced open. (On a standard mortise lock, the deadbolt is an inch long—adequate only when both door and frame are firm and solid.)

By inspecting a door frame for rot, finding it solid, but not going further and testing its bendability. If we push one side of the door frame with our feet and the other with our back we can see if it "gives." A door frame that is springy can be levered still further apart with a car jack (as shown). By levering apart the two blocks of wood he places at each end of the jack, the thief can slowly pressure the door sides apart without breaking anything. Once the gap is further than the end of the mortise lock bolt, he simply opens the door and walks inside.

Knowing this, we may take the extra precaution of buying a vertical-bolt auxiliary lock (as shown). This is a simple way to buttress the security afforded by a mortise lock; the vertical bolt lock is fastened to the mating plate, rather like a door hinge is secured with its pin, and it is almost impossible to jimmy, as long screws fasten both lock and mating plate in place. It would be also extremely difficult to pound the lock into submission.

But our human frailties can let even this lock down, too, in a number of ways:

By forgetting to look at our door panels. These are a weak point in the door, easily booted in or destroyed with a chisel or screwdriver. The burglar then crawls through the hole.

By thinking the hinge pins will hold. But did we *really* look? Hinge pins on an outside door, for example (they exist on oldish houses and apartment doors in some countries), can easily be levered out with a long screwdriver. And when the door hinges inside our modern apartment are fastened with short screws or with long screws in soggy wood, or the door frame is past it, a few fast wrenches with a screwdriver or wrench will bring the door from its hinges.

Not even the Fox police lock can work when WE don't give it a chance. This is the lock which has a steel strut—a brace bar—propped up against the door so that any force being used on the door is transmitted to the apartment floor; it is impossible to break the door open through brute force.

But weak door panels which can be kicked in are one loophole

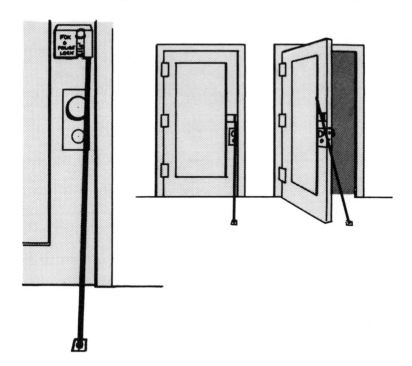

The Fox police lock

for the thief. Another is when the door is of flimsy sheet metal; it can be buckled by using the bar as a pivot point.

Too noisy? Not when power tools (lawn mower/hedge clipper/saw), a vacuum cleaner, automatic washer or hi fi stereo are being used nearby. Any of these will cover the sounds of a burglar kicking, splintering, wrenching, riving and butchering woodwork or metal.

Even if the front door is adequately protected, it is likely that the *back* door will lack good locks or its frame may be too frail. Possibly there is a pane of glass which can be smashed by a robber. He simply slides his hand through and opens the door. The garage door is another weak link. So is the connecting door between garage and home. And are the skylights and basement windows *really* secure? Both are often overlooked by complacent householders as possible entry points.

As are windows. Any ordinary window catch is easy to open once the glass is broken. Yet window locks are not expensive. We can buy them so that one key will fit all the windows in the house. The thinking behind such locks is that a burglar who breaks the glass to slip the catch will go next door—rather than face the task of taking out all the glass to make enough room for him to squeeze through.

There may be a costly unpickable lock holding our front door. This particular lock can only be opened with a special key at certain times each day by the owner of whatever is inside—but what about those door frames, door panels and the hinges? And the windows/skylight/rear door?

Remedy: The Guardian, p. 246; The Addict, p .266

The Loners (Recluses)

See all their safety precautions come to nought because they split themselves off from their neighbors. But, as any burglar knows, your neighbor is your best lock.

SIGNS AND SYMPTOMS

Not buying less than a .38 pistol because you know, unless you're an expert marksman, that with any gun smaller you run the risk of wounding your intended victim superficially and enraging him. Peering through the spyhole in your door for *how* the caller wears his topcoat. If the button between the top one and third one is undone he could be wearing a shoulder holster for a pistol; if the button is left undone just beneath the belt he could be wearing a pistol clipped to a belt.

CAUSES

Your need for privacy need not mean your being hounded by the law, gunmen or erstwhile enemies—as the above signs would indicate.

There may well be other causes to be found within yourself.

Living in a neighborhood which you consider is "beneath" you seems a good reason for cutting yourself off from neighbors. The fact you appear aloof from them makes you feel better.

Having once been burglarized through carelessness. "I was hugely indignant, depressed, angry about it all and felt much more vindictive toward the burglar than I ever would have imagined; revenge, I suppose," said one burglary victim. Retribution is a widespread goal once a person's place has been ransacked.

Not only do we hurry to the nearest locksmith to buy such hardware as locks, chains, bolts and burglar alarms (often the wrong kind), but we harden our attitude to those around us in a defensive reaction.

It is often only a passing phase. After a month we are back at the old routine.

There can be LONERS by accident too.

The new arrival at the hotel or the newly moved into an apartment or house. We simply have not had time to get to know the neighbors.

It is during a time of isolation, whether self-imposed or not, that we face the biggest risk and give the intruder his best opportunity.

ILLOGICAL BEHAVIOR

How brave is the man next door? A lot more courageous than you may think. Although he may be the type who looks as though nothing could ever happen to him, you might be surprised.

A BURGLAR may call on your neighbor when you are out and say he wishes to contact you. He asks the neighbor for the times you are likely to be in through the week (and possibly for your phone number too, so he can call and make an appointment).

A BURGLAR in desperation may try to drill the cylinder (where we place the key) out of a good lock or even blow it up. This attracts the attention of neighbors. They won't care to be involved unless you get on well with them. And the one thing a burglar cannot stand is a nosy neighbor.

A DOOR in your apartment is kicked in. The muffled thuds reach the ears of neighbors. Yet why should they bother to investigate if you have spurned them in the past?

THE ALARM goes off in your apartment. And the person next door may feel actively glad you are having trouble if he has no reason to like you.

A PIECE OF PAPER looking like an advertising flier has been sticking out from beneath your door for days. This is a burglar's trick to determine if anyone has been through the door since he last made his reconnaissance here. The neighbor who is looking out for you in your absence will throw the paper away.

THICK SHRUBBERY used to cut yourself off from neighboring houses is a godsend to the burglar. He likes a back door heavily shrouded with greenery, a basement entry well concealed by plantings and heavy foliage under all rear windows—these give him a place to hide.

AN EFFICIENT YOUNG EXECUTIVE calls next door the day you have left for a two-week vacation. He says he has come to see about moving the furniture. Met with puzzled frowns, he consults a letter and says, "You are Mr. Jones, aren't you?" (your name). He is extremely apologetic for making such a stupid mistake in calling at the wrong house and promptly goes—to repeat the same act at the neighbor's house on the other side. He has now broadcast to both your neighbors that you (Jones) are moving out furniture on the following Monday. On that day a group of men in coveralls drive a truck up to your front door and coolly gut the interior of your house . . . while the neighbors you neglected let them go with every stick of furniture.

KEEPING VALUABLES (say valuable jewelry) inside your home in what you think is the perfect hiding place, you lose out when a burglar calls. He ransacks the apartment—and your neighbors don't bat an ear at his bull-in-a-china-shop tactics, even though he can be heard through their walls.

Burglars DO wreak havoc when searching for the prize they know is there; often there is nothing furtive about their entry— they do it boldly and directly. They switch on all the lights and search from wall to wall. They open every drawer, cupboard, cubbyhole, box, bag, suitcase, even the piggy bank. They strip the bed. They pull the blinds down to see nothing has been rolled up in them. And much more.

LONERS often depend on fierce dogs to keep people away. Often these are large dogs. Mastiffs, Newfoundlands, Great Danes, malamutes, boxers, Dobermans, rottweillers, German shepherds, Russian wolfhounds and even huskies. Not all these are effective city watchdogs. Some of them don't bark—but wait for the intruder to enter and then pounce! By then he's IN. When you are away from your home for an extended period, your dog isn't likely to be around either. And an empty kennel—the kind that would house a large dog—is just another go-ahead sign to the burglar.

There are, too, many ways in which a burglar can silence any dog. He can toss it drugged horsemeat, hamburger or steak. He may rub a beef bone on his hands and legs to give off a scent that wins friendship. Others use a fire extinguisher as a pacifier. Or a punctured tennis ball full of ammonia.

Small dogs, such as a Chihuahua, which are very alert and yelp and move quickly are the best burglar alarms, but THE LONER could well opt for some larger breed instead. For these will intimidate the neighbors too. . . .

Keeping to ourselves, a factor which often helps in other areas of the big city, does not help in a honeycomb of apartments or mesh of houses.

The remedy is to cultivate nosy neighbors if we don't want to be robbed. It's a wicked world. But there are even reservations to this, as we shall see.

Remedy: The Addict, p. 266; The Beaver, p. 278; The Dead Lucky, p. 290

The Prisoner (Itchy)

Suffer from a kind of paranoia because their security arrangements are so elaborate and sophisticated that they make an average medieval fortress look about as impregnable as a doll's house.

SIGNS AND SYMPTOMS

Wiring the home with a mass of electronic spaghetti connecting windows and door alarms, a sonic movement detector and a hidden "hold up" button to the control room of a security company: should one of the circuits now be broken by an intruder, a complex system of lights, buzzers and bells is activated on the company's panels identifying the house, to which a patrol car and police are despatched. . . . AND still looking under the bed before you go to sleep to see whether there is a man there.

CAUSES

Life in a well-protected city home, however safe and prosperous, has its disadvantages: segregation, claustrophobia and boredom. These are bred from the loneliness such security measures impose on us.

Various thoughts gnaw: supposing we lose our three keys so we can't get back in, or the police lock jams and we can't get out?

Small wonder various complexes grow depending on the number, size and quality of our barricades. We begin to suffer a form of jailer's syndrome.

Or there's the feeling that begins with a yawn, progresses to a fidget and finishes in depression. No one seems to know how to cure it, yet it can lead to wrecked homes, self-sabotage and even suicide.

All we know is that it is often caused by a sense of frustration and lack of fulfillment in our lives. Any person who has a monotonous, repetitive job is particularly prone to it.

ILLOGICAL BEHAVIOR

No tourist's guide tells you what to do if a prostitute knocks on the door of your hotel room and says, "Hi, sugar, do you want company?" If you say no, she threatens to scream "Rape." If you say yes, you are likely to be robbed—perhaps violently.

Nor does the convention itinerary mention the girl who may enter the elevator with you. What is the safest action when she says, "Okay, I'll be up after the banquet—just give me your room number"?

The lonely male often acts unwisely. Isolated in his hotel room or apartment he may have already decided to break out and find the action. And so it follows him back to his own doorstep.

The well-dressed male is vulnerable in any midtown hotel and street. The prostitutes who patrol the sidewalks and lobbies know the convention schedules better than hotel guards. They make their approaches here.

If you want to know why a prostitute had to bang on YOUR door, the answer could be you invited her to.

Few hookers will knock on just any door. Hotel rooms may house families, women on their own or groups of people. The prostitute who does knock on a man's door therefore often knows who is inside—because he has told her and probably shown her his room key as proof. Sometimes women at home also make themselves vulnerable to the prowling male.

There are women who will scream "Rape" at the slightest

provocation, whose hysterical imaginings can endanger reputa-
tions and even lives—theirs. The man who is an unknown quantity
might resort to any means to shut up a yelling woman. But did
she lead him on?

Let's ask HOW.

WHY did you leave your apartment or hotel room door ajar?
WHY do you lean from your window in only a bra? You should
also ask WHY when you leave the drapes undrawn, switch on a
light and walk naked or seminaked in front of it.

WHY do you answer the doorbell scantily dressed or with a
barely fastened robe or wrapper and let complete strangers into
the home?

No one can behave carelessly for long in the city.

**Remedy: The Noisy, p. 258; The Beaver, p. 213; The Dead Lucky,
p. 290; The Confused, p. 59; The Obsequious, p. 124; The
Fugitive, p. 202**

The Independent (Needy)

Cling stubbornly to a mode of *existence* rather than *life*. Although there are often sources of help nearby, they run scared
from them.

SIGNS AND SYMPTOMS

Doubling the amount of light during a brownout by placing
a mirror behind a candle/bulb/lamp about a foot away. Cooking
with medicinal paraffin instead of eggs (one spoonful per egg in
a cake). A smell of stew in your home. An onion in a tumbler of
water so you can grow green shoots for flavoring.

CAUSES

The elderly and destitute are always vulnerable in the city.
But it need not always be people suffering in rooms so damp
the wallpaper won't stay on the walls, where long flights of stairs

are a daily agony and where they must huddle in winter to keep warm.

The young and affluent can be as open to calamity when in the city for the first time and temporarily broke.

Stupidly independent pride can cause people of any age to refuse all chances of help from friends, relatives, institutions or city welfare organizations.

Such wincing sensitivity smacks of the grand old lady who would rather die than let neighbors know she's on welfare. It scorns sympathy and spurns charity.

Unlike THE LONER, THE INDEPENDENT may get on well with neighbors. But accept help from them? Oh no.

ILLOGICAL BEHAVIOR

Like THE UNASSUMING (p. 24), we conclude we don't have any valuables. Many a city villain has grown fat because of this belief.

Diamonds and antique silver are NOT the things that lure many burglars. They will be perfectly happy with your housekeeping money, with a savings or old checkbook, or your clothing, radio— or the television that old people living on social security cannot replace once it's been stolen.

Poorer areas have their thieves too.

These unskilled or semiskilled criminals are as capable of thieving from the apartment next door as of going through a house several streets away. They range in type from the kick-it-in man (see THE SMUG, p. 222) to the doorshakers who go through large apartment buildings (hotels too) between 9:30 A.M. and noon trying doors until they find one unlocked or ajar. They will steal from relatives and acquaintances when necessary.

THE INDEPENDENT person often has ineffective locks, doors and frames. He therefore falls foul of this type of criminal.

There are THUGS who always choose the afternoons for their raids. Their technique is to knock on the door, burst in, overpower their often aged victims and steal whatever they can find. These thieves show no mercy.

NARCOTIC ADDICTS will work away the door fastenings with a jimmy. They are looking for anything to steal for the smallest profit—so long as they can get rid of it to someone on the street. They fight when cornered, often work through the poorer districts, are often caught by the law and frequently go to jail. But more and more can now pick locks too.

CON MEN may bring a rougher approach, too. Three might come to mend the fence (see THE ACCOMMODATING, p. 213). Two of the men keep two old ladies chatting in the garden and the third takes their pension money and Christmas savings—and then asks them to change a $20 bill. This turns out to be a dud. There are also bogus priests, collecting for a fictitious church: "Christians, this concerns YOU. Souls saved. No place to worship. Need $5,000 urgently to purchase disused church. Please help. Please pray. Have you a gift for me, please say."

It is also the desperately independent who fall prey to the advertising sharks in city papers offering employment at home. Ripe for exploitation by unscrupulous employers are the poor and needy who work at home on behalf of a factory.

Exactly how many nifty-fingered persons are busy typing envelopes, assembling toys, painting samples, knitting babies' booties, stitching leather pieces for handbags in cities today is unknown, but the figure must run to millions.

In many instances the pay is ridiculous, perhaps 50 cents to $1 an hour's work. There are so many opportunities for the employer to work cruel tricks.

WHY, for instance, should a "registration" be payable to the manufacturer who advertises for women to stitch together panels for women's coats? Is the reason they offer good enough—"as proof of your sincerity that you will do the job"?

For if you do pay the fee and do work on the materials they send you, you will find yourself vulnerable. When you deliver the finished products, they can be turned down as "faulty on inspection." The firm says it has no alternative but to withhold payment. And there is no appeal: it is your word against the villains' if you protest that your work was perfect. (They've sold it.)

There are answers to the predicaments of THE INDEPEND-

ENT. We should look to these now—then turn to THE INSURED (below), where we cover such crises as fires, intense cold, falls and electrical and gas failures, which hit THE INDEPENDENT especially hard.

Remedy: All of Chapter 9.

The Insured (Sensationalist)

Base their life on a half-truth—you don't need any more insurance than insurance. But life insurance does not guarantee that you will have a better chance of living longer.

It is often the people who think they foresee *all* the risks who panic soonest when a real emergency happens.

SIGNS AND SYMPTOMS

Wearing a nightgown or pajamas in case of fire at night, but not checking that it is a non-inflammable one. Needing a gadget that makes a noise like an air-conditioner to ensure you can sleep on nights when the real air-conditioning isn't running.

CAUSES

Creatures of habit are the most likely individuals to panic and act in a suicidal fashion when faced with fire, flood, earthquake and all the other disasters which can hit the home.

Frequently we do the wrong things because we stick to fallacious survival remedies we have heard or read or seen in a movie many years ago—and even then we get it wrong.

Because the sensational aspects of disaster hit us enough to make us want to take out insurance, we stop there—once we have it. And are totally unaware of the factors needed for survival. When the real crunch, say a fire, comes, the basic step-by-step measures to ensure safety in a crisis must be known in advance.

It is no use relying on instinct. *Instinctive* actions can be fatally wrong in survival situations. We try to wriggle free when we should stay rooted, try to grab when we should punch, and jump for it when we should have waited.

Only thinking about and practicing survival training will give any real life insurance, the kind that gives us most chance of still being around to collect on the policy.

ILLOGICAL BEHAVIOR

At this very moment, somewhere in the world, a tall building is burning. It may be a high-rise block of apartments or a big hotel. It may be a short, sharp blaze that is over before the Fire Department arrives, or a long spectacular fire that makes headlines.

More and more people are living in high-rise buildings throughout the cities of the world, but few really understand the simple rules of survival when fire breaks out.

The most levelheaded tend to behave in a lemming-like fashion, as if death-wish-motivated all the way.

WE take elevators that stall halfway down and trap us—to choke or burn to death.

WE rush along corridors, leaving fire doors open in our panic. The blaze can then spread unimpeded.

WE scramble to the roof on the strength of a rumor that a helicopter is hovering above to pluck us to safety. But it is much more likely that firemen can get us down—even when we are several floors above the 100-foot level (the maximum a fire department turntable ladder can reach)—by using internal fire-resistant stairways to reach a hot point on a certain floor. Or, in some cases by adapting and using the elevator.

WE wrap ourselves in mattresses or lie on them and hurl ourselves from the 19th-floor windows in a vain attempt to cushion our landing—even when the flames are still several floors below.

WE snatch the door open on smelling smoke, even though the doorknob burns our hand—a sure sign that the fire is just outside and that if we do walk out of the room there is a strong chance it will be into a blast of flame.

WE spread panic by shouting "FIRE!" at the first whiff of

smoke, even though once a fire starts on the ground floor smoke can penetrate to other floors a safe distance away.

WE fail to find out where the fire exits or alternative stairways are.

Remedy: The Addict, p. 266; The Dead Lucky, p. 290; The Nervous, p. 52; The Obsequious, p. 124; The Fugitive, p. 202

The Defeatist (Blasé)

Go out of their way to make things difficult for the burglar— by leaving so many opportunities open to him that he's confused.

SIGNS AND SYMPTOMS

Indulging in cocktail party chatter about . . . burglars who are able to make a copy of any key by pressing it first in a piece of soap, then filing a blank key into this shape and calling back later when you are out (NO, they use cuttlefish in a small tin box, as cuttle is soft downward but hard and brittle across—it keeps its shape through all the filing and checking of the key blank) . . . burglar alarms that are ineffective, as witness the fact that their bells ring forlornly in stores on Sunday mornings and no one takes any notice (NO, the burglar not wanting to risk a stretch in jail *is taking notice.*)

CAUSES

The pessimist who acts on oh-hell-what's-the-use lines can be a most sensitive person at heart.

It is amazing how many of us fail to lock up properly when we are with other people who, we fear, will think us fussy (see THE CAVALIER, p. 86) if we stop to double-lock our front door.

City citizens seem too easily resigned to suffer burglaries—as an inescapable part of modern urban life, to be endured along with foul air and grubby streets.

We are content to trade burglary stories for cocktails and sympathy and continue our if-they-want-to-get-in-they'll-get-in attitude until we have been cleaned out once or twice or until we lose our insurance.

ILLOGICAL BEHAVIOR

Some fatalism is of course appropriate. Brute force will get a burglar into any apartment. However, many burglars like to avoid using this so long as there are plenty of easy pickings elsewhere.

By not locking our doors properly or not using proper locks (see p. 222) we are flattering ourselves they will *want* to get in. But they may only be trying our door in passing. If it opens easily, they are bound to clean out our place.

A crack burglar can comb quickly through an apartment building and go over perhaps ten apartments in less than an hour. He isn't noisy, leaves no obvious marks on the door and keeps his loot in his pockets. Pickmen once concentrated on prowling the corridors of top hotels; today they are a growing minority, as new members are coming from the lower-income areas with the added risk of violence as addicts and oddballs take up the skill.

We can never stop them unless we know *how* they breach locks (again, see p. 224 for more details about locks). Their methods are basically simple:

LOIDING is not so much picking a lock's mechanism as forcing the convenience latch open. Loids can be credit cards, plastic bank calendars for wallets, two playing cards glued together, airline SEAT OCCUPIED and hotel DO NOT DISTURB signs or just a plain strip of celluloid.

The loid is introduced between the door and the frame a few inches above the lock. It is brought down until it hits the sprung latch. Worked up and down, the wedge-shaped latch is pushed back and the door opens.

The burglar will have knocked or rung the door bell first. Only on getting no reply will he try the lock. Once inside he may throw his loids out of the window so as not to be charged with being in possession of burglars' tools.

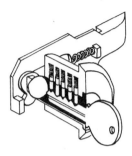

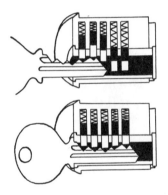

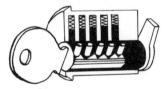

The tumblers are in two sections, whose lengths vary with each tumbler. The cylinder is free to turn when the right key raises the lower sections in line with the edge of the cylinder.

PICKING A LOCK is necessary when the mortise lock is double bolted. The metal bar of the dead bolt can only be slid back by using a key or using the lock picks which replace the key.

The diagram shows the lock cylinder and how the tumblers—usually five small pins—are arranged in the cylinder so that the hills and valleys notched into the key move the pins into the position that permits the core of the cylinder to turn and the lock to open. A good pickman can open a typical lock cylinder almost as easily as if he had the key—in a matter of seconds. Any key-operated lock is vulnerable.

With a small L-shaped steel hook (or tension bar) the burglar applies pressure on the lock cylinder from the inside as if he had put a key inside and was trying to turn it. Next, a thin piece of bent wire—the lock pick—is slipped into the keyhole through a hole in the tension bar. By probing inside the keyhole with the lock pick, the burglar pushes up the pin tumblers one by one. Because of the tension maintained by the steel hook, they stick as lifted. When all are up, the cylinder is free to turn and the lock is open.

SLIPPING A DOOR CHAIN depends on how the chain is fastened to the door. If the metal channel which houses the end of the chain is horizontal—as in most homes—the burglar can bypass it using a rubber band and a thumbtack.

He loids or picks the lock, slips a hand inside and presses the thumbtack into the door near the chain. Then he loops the rubber band from the thumbtack to the end of the chain (in the slide) and closes the door. The rubber band now pulls the slack of the chain to the end of the channel where it drops free under the pull of the band. The burglar opens the door and walks in.

This is not to say all locks are useless. Nor is it a waste of money to buy good ones. But the more obstacles you place in the path of the burglar, the better.

THE DEFEATIST, however, never considers that by *delaying* the burglar, he is forcing him to take longer on the job. And that there are consequently more chances of his giving up in disgust or being discovered before he can finish.

Remedy: The Guardian, p. 246; The Noisy, p. 258; The Addict, p. 266

The Blasted (Once-Hit)

DIFFER from THE DEFEATIST in that they have already been burglarized, but still show an alarming lack of caution in guarding their homes. Lightning doesn't strike twice, they say. The skylines of mountains are repeatedly hit by thunderbolts. And it is in cities, after all, that we find the high spots of crime.

SIGNS AND SYMPTOMS

Telling everyone you have been burglarized *after* the initial shock. Quickly lost interest when the questions you ask the locksmith are drowned by his turned-up-on-purpose emery wheel. Banking a check from your insurance company for a burglary claim that is a third more than the value of the possessions taken. Scratches on the cylinder face of your lock where YOU have tried to pick it to see how they did it. A slightly blemished mirror still bearing traces of the lipstick-written SORRY.

CAUSES

The greed which tempted us to inflate the claim for insurance on our first burglary tempts burglars, too.

Corrupt claims range from false claims for cameras/gems/paintings that did not exist, to $30,000 when only $18,000 was stolen. And burglars claim they cannot be conscience-stricken when certain people actually engage them to set up insurance fiddles.

It is blind stupidity that lets most of us down. By congratulating ourselves that the law of averages will save us from further intrusion, we don't bother to take any further steps to protect our homes.

We keep the same locks, alarms and manner of using them. This establishes a pattern of behavior—just as the criminal has his or her MO ("modus operandi" or method of working). And as the burglar's MO lets him down, so, too, will ours.

ILLOGICAL BEHAVIOR

We fail to put ourselves in the burglar's shoes. Why, for instance, shouldn't his motto be "If at first you *do* succeed, try, try and try again"?

Because this IS his practice—and he will.

It is not unique for a burglar to visit you twice. The second break-in may be a case of his returning to the scene of the crime because he is harboring a deep-seated wish to be caught. Or he may tell another burglar that the accommodation (YOURS) is easy—and point him at it.

By taking no extra precautions to block a second burglary, you push your reputation with the insurance companies. You say, "That's it, we're covered." THEY say, "It's the insurance companies who are the easiest marks of all. People look on burglary insurance as a form of divine right, but next time you get burglarized you may not get insured."

The city where you live now can be relatively crime-free compared with tougher conurbations, but the rise of crime is a general trend in all cities in the world. As a result the insurance companies are tightening up by chopping out the most accident-prone householders first.

Even in the gentler cities cover will often not be given unless certain steps are taken. The insurance companies either charge accordingly for homes they consider risky because of lack of burglary safeguards, or they simply refuse coverage in certain areas or under specific conditions.

It is more difficult, for example, to get insurance if you are a householder who is out at business all day and who leaves the home empty for long periods. Insurance companies prefer the wealthier homes to be linked to a central alarm system which rings in the nearest police or protective agency HQ. But this costs money.

In those areas of tough cities which suffer from a notoriously high crime rate, companies are canceling theft and fire insurance even when a householder has never made a claim. Insurance companies simply won't write high-risk districts any more.

But it isn't only the poorer areas that are hard hit. We can live on Park Avenue in a 20-room apartment with a doorman and an important job and still be refused coverage. The insurance company will tell us there is too much concentration of value.

Many insurance brokers have to advise their clients not to put in a claim—even when around $1,000 worth of possessions has been stolen. It is better, the broker's reasoning goes, to absorb it than to have your insurance canceled.

And we *still* leave ourselves vulnerable to that second burglary.

No amount of insurance, however, can cover the outrage and shock we feel when we find a truly ransacked home. In THE LONERS (p. 228) we saw how the thief searches for certain valuables—here he does wanton damage.

Dresses walked over. Underwear tried on. Shelves urinated on. Children's piggy banks, toys, etc. scattered and broken. Meals eaten, dirty plates left. Floors dirtied. Perfume splashed about and face powder spilled everywhere.

Often the cost of repairing a burglar's damage is greater than the value of the things stolen. The inevitable feelings of sickness and emptiness inside us are all the harder to bear when we realize this was NOT just a burglar—but someone of violently twisted nature.

Had we come back earlier and disturbed that person in the act of breaking up the furniture, pouring bathroom cleaning fluid into the television . . . there is no knowing what he might have done to US.

That we lose irreplaceable articles of sentimental value or that stolen goods are rarely recovered by the police is of secondary importance to the violence factor that can await us when a burglar-prowler crosses the threshold—a second, third or even fourth time.

Remedy: The Guardian, p. 246; The Noisy, p. 258; The Addict, p. 266; The Dead Lucky, p. 290

8

CITY DWELLINGS

WINNERS

It is far too easy to sink on to the bed after a tiring trip and imagine we are safe at last. Yet whether it is the bedroom of a large hotel, an apartment guarded by nightwatchmen behind double-armor plate glass doors or a quiet home in the suburbs, we are as lambs waiting to be snatched from the fold.

The delicious relief of shedding rumpled clothes, showering in warm water and slipping between clean sheets is a dangerous panacea to city stresses. It starts us on the wrong footing by injecting a false sense of security, so that even when we adjust to metropolitan life, we are still easy prey. Careless to the bitter end.

The Guardian (of the Keys)

Makes wherever he lives into a personal Fort Knox. Knowing NO lock is unpickable, *he* picks a choice of locks—not necessarily the most expensive—which take so long to force that the intruder looks elsewhere.

His question is "If I lose my key, can I get back inside easily?" Only a no will allow THE GUARDIAN to sleep in peace.

246

How to Sleep Soundly—and Overcome Jet Lag

Take a barbiturate one hour before retiring. Avoid excessive fluids in the last few hours before retiring (so you are not disturbed by need to urinate).

. . . Before You Sleep, Remember . . .

Home security (which includes home-for-the-night hotel rooms) starts with good locks. Ordinary locks are no obstacle to the professional burglar. Many locks, in fact, are only to keep honest people honest by removing temptation from the weak-willed.

However, the more deterrents you place in the way of the burglar, the more they delay him—so raising the chances he will be discovered before he completes his work or give it up as a bad job.

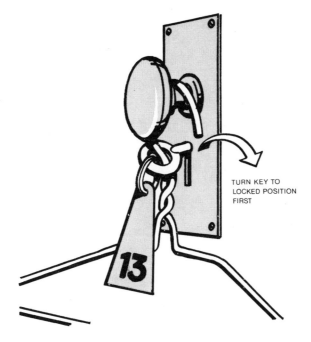

TURN KEY TO
LOCKED POSITION
FIRST

Secure hotel door by turning key to locked position and passing coat hanger through ring and over knob.

HOTEL ROOMS

1. DON'T LET ANYBODY SEE THE NUMBER OF YOUR ROOM KEY. Burglars/prostitutes/muggers who know the numbers of the single rooms mingle in busy lobbies—watching for those who collect these keys.
2. AVOID ORDERING EARLY MORNING CALL/TEA/NEWS-PAPER ON ARRIVAL (THIS ALSO ADVERTISES YOUR ROOM TO ANYONE WHO CARES TO CHECK).
3. LOCK THE BEDROOM DOOR WITH EVERYTHING PROVIDED. Turn the lock bolt on the inside of the door. Rotate key into locked position. Draw any other bolts. Secure door chain. Check Servidor (see THE SMUG, p. 222).
4. TAKE EXTRA PRECAUTIONS.
   A. Turn the door key as far as it will go in the locked position. Secure it with a coat hanger threaded through hole in key or key ring and hooked over the doorknob.
   WARNING: Never leave a key on the inside of a lock to prevent others from using a passkey as you sleep without this coathanger safeguard. There are simple instruments which can be pushed through and used to turn the key from the outside—or the key can be pushed out of the lock so that it falls onto a sheet of paper that has been slipped under the door and is now pulled back with the key on it.
   B. Twist the chain once or twice before securing to prevent the door opening more than an inch.
   C. Carry one of the portable locks shown in the diagram (not all hotel room doors have a keyhole on the inside). Use it.
   D. Tilt a chair with the backrest placed under doorknob when there is no keyhole/alarm/chain (see p. 251). Stop the legs from slipping by jamming into carpet. When there is no carpet, place the legs in shoes with rubber heels so the chair legs press over the heels—toes pointing toward door. A rubber bathmat will do just as well. Or use leather gloves.
   If there is no doorknob, slip a chair under the handle instead, so it is impossible for it to be turned down. Use a telephone directory as a wedge when the handle is at an awkward height.

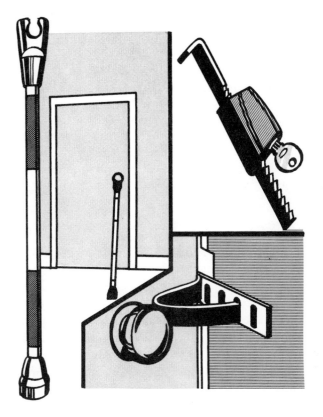

Portable locks

E. Make sure you hear what anyone who knocks on door says before opening up—especially when there is no chain provided. (Many people have the right to disturb you: maid, floor manager, desk personnel, maintenance crew, management, house detective and bell captain. *Anyone* can pose as one of these.)

IF YOU CANNOT HEAR, PLACE THE MOUTH OF A TUMBLER AGAINST THE DOOR. PRESS YOUR EAR TO THE OTHER END AND LISTEN. THIS HEARING AID WORKS AND IS SAFER THAN OPENING AN UN-CHAINED DOOR.

. . . When you wake up the next day . . .

5. CHECK VALUABLES: Your hotel is not responsible unless your money, travelers' checks, jewelry, business papers, etc. are secured in a safe-deposit box available in the lobby office.

6. SECURE YOUR DOOR WHEN GOING OUT (even for five minutes). Place the hooked chain across door from the *outside* to give the impression there is still someone inside (see p. 252). It blocks a burglar who sees you leave the building and who then asks the maid to open YOUR room with her passkey by pretending that it is his room and he has left his key downstairs.

Or if the room door opens out you can use a travel lock. (But if you stay out for several hours you may not get your room made up.)

APARTMENTS AND HOUSES

How to Choose a Locksmith

Locksmiths should be (1) licensed and/or (2) members of a professional association with membership credentials displayed on the premises and/or (3) recommended by the Better Business Bureau (or appropriate consumer organization). If in doubt of the standing of professional body, check with phone call to public library who will check for you—and give you the most authentic locksmithing source to contact for advice.

FRONT AND REAR DOORS

1 LOCK IS NOT ENOUGH.

2–3 LOCKS ARE NECESSARY.

4 OR MORE LOCKS = A FIRETRAP.

Choose (see also THE SMUG, p. 222) . . .

A good mortise lock incorporating a convenience latch + dead bolt

And

A vertical bolt auxiliary lock (also known as a jimmyproof deadlock or drop bolt)—possibly double-cylindered—and exchange the cylinder(s) for a good pick-resistant cylinder (this can be picked, but takes much longer than an ordinary lock). Protect a pick-resistant cylinder with a guard plate clamped in place with carriage bolts, again as advised by locksmith. But your door must not "give" or the plate can be jimmied. And a burglar can try to pound/wrench/pull the cylinder free rather than try picking it. (Exception: Keep the lock as it is when it already comes with a high-security cylinder, as advised by your locksmith.)

And

Buy a vertical-bolt auxiliary lock with a lock cylinder on the inside instead of a thumb turn when the lock is to be used in a glass-paneled door—so a burglar cannot smash the glass and

Jam door with a chair.

Twist a hook out of a short nail with a pair of pliers. Make the curves in a sharply bent S so that each end grips like a grappling hook. Use it to hold chain across door after leaving hotel room. Slip hook through chain link and place other end of hook through channel, so that when door is opened the lock holds, and the chain is pulled taut and the room appears occupied.

reach inside to turn it by hand. But hang the key in plain sight nearby out of arm's reach of the door. Then, in case of fire, nobody is trapped by being unable to open the door.

When the door has deteriorating or weak jambs . . .

Use a police lock (see THE SMUG, p. 222). Anyone who wants in will now have to break the door down, not just destroy the jamb.

WARNING: This type of lock is ineffective on glass- or thin-paneled doors, which can be broken. Any thief who can reach through the door will release the bar (even when lock is set so it cannot be opened from the inside, a burglar can still free it with expert use of an everyday tool).

Use a key chain (see p. 254) instead of the old-fashioned door chain lock. . . . On all exterior doors (and inside appropriate bedroom doors too).

If you use a combination lock (using push buttons instead of a keyhole) . . .

1. Don't let anyone standing nearby see which buttons you press.
2. Press all the combination buttons occasionally (as a burglar can tell which buttons are pushed regularly, although not the order of the combination number).
3. Never write your combination number down on a wall in case you forget. To remember, pick up any word with the same number of letters as there are digits in combination. First letter to appear in alphabetical order is No. 1, second letter is No. 2, etc. Example: MARY=2134 on your lock.

PATIO DOORS

Use the only safe way to protect this weakest point . . . change patio door glass to laminated glass and fit a proper patio lock (crossbar screwed onto door and key chain lock).

Forget about common method of using a broomstick set in sliding glass door channel after the doors are closed—burglars use force to wrench/twist/lever doors past this obstacle.

BASEMENT DOORS

SEE ALSO FRONT AND REAR DOORS.

OR USE HASP/STAPLE/PADLOCK. Buy only the best padlock, one that locks on both sides, has case-hardened case AND shackle, contains pick-resistant cylinder AND has very tough hasp with built-in locking bar which, when closed, covers the screws. These should be one-way screws that can only be turned in tightening direction. File off any code/symbol/marking so that no one can make a note of them and buy appropriate key at a hardware store. INSTALL NEAR TOP OR BOTTOM OF INTERIOR OF THE DOOR.

GARAGE DOORS

Consult your locksmith. The latch kind of lock set separate from the handle is favored more than a lock-incorporated-into-garage-handle on modern garages.

Use a strong padlock on older buildings.

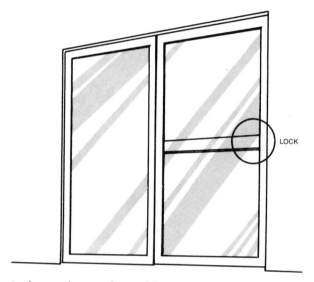

Protect patio doors with a crossbar and key chain lock.

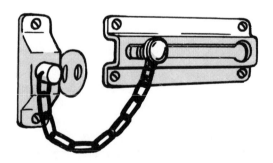

The key chain lock is secured from outside by snapping bolt into lock; for reentry unlocks with key from outside.

WINDOWS

No window is inaccessible to the determined burglar even though it is many stories from the street. Cat burglars—the most dangerous and possibly deranged type of thief—are often quite fearless and are prepared to enter your accommodation when you are at home.

PROTECT ALL WINDOWS

Best Tips

1. FIT ALL WINDOWS WITH LOCKS THAT CAN ONLY BE OPENED WITH A KEY (LIMIT OPENING TO 4 INCHES). THEY SHOULD LOCK WITHOUT THE KEY, BUT REQUIRE IT TO UNLOCK THEM (ONE KEY FOR ALL LOCKS).
WARNINGS: Have a key hanging in every room near the window and out of reach of small children, even though all keys are the same—in case of fire. Do not depend on twist-, wedge- or turn-style window locks which can be released from the outside with a thin-bladed tool or by breaking the glass and reaching in.
2. PROTECT A FIRE ESCAPE WINDOW WITH AN AP-PROVED FIRE GATE (ACCORDION GATE, EASY TO OPEN FROM THE INSIDE AND HARD TO JIMMY AS BASE OF GATE SLIDES IN A TRACK).
WARNING: Of all YOUR windows, be most careful of any window *near* a fire escape from which burglar may simply "step across." And remember to lock ladders up too.
3. PERMANENTLY BLOCK YOUR ATTIC AND BASEMENT WINDOWS WITH A STRONG METAL GRILL OR BARS SPACED NO MORE THAN 4 INCHES APART.
4. SWITCH FROM VULNERABLE ORDINARY WINDOW GLASS TO FAR TOUGHER LAMINATED GLASS (PLASTIC SANDWICHED BETWEEN TWO PANES OF GLASS). IT COSTS MORE, BUT SECURITY IS GREATER.

WHEN TO CHANGE LOCKS

When . . . a purse containing keys and your identification is stolen (change lock cylinder even if they *are* returned) . . . when a door has only a "spring latch" type of lock (opened easily with a credit/visiting/playing card) . . . when "skeleton" locks are used on basement doors (vulnerable to *any* skeleton key, paper clip or hairpin) . . . when apartment doors have keyhole-in-the-doorknob-type locks (even heavy-duty models can be wrecked by twisting) . . . when rear/side/basement door is secured with only hand shot bolts near top/bottom/middle (add a vertical bolt auxiliary lock too) . . . whenever moving into a new house . . . when moving to a new housing development (check new locks you buy are different in make from those in general use in the other houses) . . . when key to pintumbler lock has indentations or hills and dales of nearly equal depth (your lock could be picked with penknife blade/paper clip/hairpin YET when hills and dales are of unequal depth, as normal, there is one chance in 20,000,000 of anyone else having a key to fit given pin tumbler lock) . . . when you can wiggle your key in the keyway or open lock with key inserted only part way (new cylinder needed for lock).

HOW TO PROTECT LOCKS

When you go to buy locks on moving into new accommodation . . . tell your new neighbor and/or leave somebody at home until you return.

If You Live in a Private Apartment

1. CHANGE THE LOCKS ON MOVING IN. If the building superintendent or owner objects, place a duplicate key in thin cardboard, wrap Scotch tape around it and seal in an envelope. Sign your name across the joining of the flap and stick Scotch tape on top (not all superintendents are honest). Give to superintendent.
2. ADD A VERTICAL-BOLT AUXILIARY LOCK. Again, you must give a key of this lock to your superintendent or owner if your lease requires you to do so. (Be wary when door locks in a building are set to open to a master key kept by the superin-

tendent. He can gain access to your apartment in emergency, BUT if master key or duplicate falls into the wrong hands YOU are vulnerable; lock cylinders are often easier to pick in a mastered system.)

TAKE CARE OF KEYS

Never hide keys in "secret" hiding places (below doormat, in mailbox etc.). Leave a duplicate key with your neighbor to avoid the risk of being locked out.

Keep tabs on all keys (leave only car key when leaving car in parking lot or to be serviced—take your other keys with you).

Don't label your house keys with your name and address. Tag them with your business address (unless there are business keys on same ring or chain).

Keep keys on a chain.

Teach children to be careful with *all* keys too.

Avoid leaving keys in the pocket of a coat hanging in a public place—cloakrooms included. They can be copied and you never know until it is too late.

Fit all windows with locks.

The Noisy (Alarmed)

Arm their homes on sound principles.

From shriekers/klaxons/gong to "silent" (call-to-police) alarms
. . . from a radio playing in the bathroom to a barking Yorkshire
terrier (OR baying electronic dogs whose wires have been
tripped) . . .

Strong burglar deterrents each. Only, THE NOISY use them
in combination too for the most telling effect.

THINK OF BURGLAR ALARMS IN PAIRS, A AND B.
INTRUDERS OFTEN RELAX AFTER LOOKING FOR—AND
DISCOVERING—THE FIRST. BUT THE SECOND HITS
THEM WORSE. INTRUDERS HATE UNEXPECTED NOISES.

Locks with even indentations are easily picked.

HOTEL ROOMS

A burglar may have stayed in your hotel room previously and
made a copy of the key or doctored the lock by substituting
screws and springs with ineffective ones—so he can return whenever it is worth his while.

Or . . . the hotel's policy may be not to allow guests to lock
themselves in—no keyholes on insides of bedroom doors, locking
bolts on bedroom doors that can only be released by key from
the outside, etc.

Burglar alarms will safeguard your hotel room in all instances where locks are poor or nonexistent—both when you sleep and when you are absent.

Have the maid make up your room while you are there. When you leave, set your alarms.

USE . . .

ALARM A AND ALARM B

ON ARRIVAL:
PLACE "DO NOT DISTURB"
SIGN ON OUTSIDE OF DOOR
(simplest alarm of all). AND—

TAKE SMALL DRAWER FROM DRESSING TABLE, PLACE TWO GLASSES OF WATER INSIDE AND HANG ON CORNER OF DOOR FRAME WHEN DOOR OPENS AS SHOWN ON P. 262. OR—

PROP CHAIR WITH ONE CORNER OF ITS BACKREST AGAINST DOOR SO IT FALLS IF DOOR IS OPENED. AND—

HANG WIRE COAT HANGER FROM JUST-OPEN WINDOW WITH NOISE-MAKERS/KEYS/ HANGERS/SHOES ATTACHED SO THEY CRASH ONTO METAL PAPER BIN OR SOME OTHER SOUNDING BOARD IF WINDOW IS OPENED. OR—

HOOK COAT HANGER FROM TOP OF DOORFRAME WHEN DOOR OPENS IN SO THAT NOISE-MAKERS ATTACHED CASCADE ON TO EMPTY SUITCASE, ETC.

IF DOOR OPENS OUT, HOOK HANGER OVER DOOR KNOB OR FROM A MOLDING HIGH ON THE DOOR SO IF

ALARM A   AND   ALARM B

DOOR IS MOVED HANGER
AND NOISE-MAKERS ARE
BRUSHED OFF ON TO THE
SOUNDING BOARD BENEATH
AND—

KEEP AT THE READY
(1) WHISTLE
(2) AEROSOL HAND
ALARM
(3) A GOOD SCREAM

WHEN YOU GO OUT:
LEAVE TV OR ROOM RADIO
PLAYING SOFTLY OR PLACE
YOUR TRANSISTOR RADIO IN
BATHROOM, DOOR SLIGHT-
LY AJAR, SO SOUND IS JUST
HEARD FROM CORRIDOR (a
not-for-real alarm, but a noise
which can dissuade). AND—

PLAY PRERECORDED TAPE
(DURING BRIEF ABSENCES)
OF YOU . . .
TYPING, OR—
MAKING BED SQUEAK, OR
—COUGHING AT INTER-
VALS, OR—FLUSHING LAV-
ATORY, OR—ANSWERING
TELEPHONE WHICH
RINGS ON YOUR ACTUAL
RECORDING
WARNINGS: Only fresh tape
player batteries will reproduce a
credible noise; tape player should
NOT sound tinny (in which
case only TYPING and BED
SQUEAKS sound realistic); only
prerecord noises, as above, which
are staccato and have intervals of
silence in between.

ALARM A   AND   ALARM B

RETURN WITH AND (USE):
Any of these inexpensive portable
alarms sold by reputable stores
and locksmiths . . .

ALARM POWERED BY FLASH-
LIGHT BATTERY(IES) THAT
CLIPS / HOOKS / HANGS ON
DOORS OR WINDOWS—
WHEN EITHER IS OPENED
OR TOUCHED, A CONTACT IS
MADE AND TRIGGERS A
CLANGER. AND/OR—
POCKETBOOK ALARM
WHICH WORKS OFF BAT-
TERIES AND CAN BE RIGGED
TO LUGGAGE ON RACK/
SHELF/CHAIR. AND/OR—
DOORKNOB ELECTRIC
ALARM IS FIXED TO DOOR-
JAMB AND HUNG OVER
KNOB (FULLY PORTABLE).
AND/OR—
3-FLASHLIGHT-BATTERIES-
POWERED PHOTOCELL
ALARM THAT LOOKS LIKE A
TRANSISTOR RADIO. IT RE-
ACTS TO CHANGES IN LIGHT
LEVELS CAUSED BY AN IN-
TRUDER (WHEN LIGHT IS
REDUCED OR INTERRUPTED
IT GOES OFF). AND/OR—
SPECIAL SWITCH WHICH RE-
SPONDS TO NOISE AND
TURNS ON ANY APPLIANCE
UP TO 850 WATTS—
SWITCHES ON MUSIC FROM
TAPE PLAYER OR RADIO IN
BATHROOM AS INTRUDER
ENTERS YOUR BEDROOM

USE ANY OF ABOVE HOME-
GROWN *On Arrival* DEFENSES
IN COMBINATION WITH
NEWLY PURCHASED ALARM.
OR BUY TWO OF LISTED
ALARMS AND USE IN CON-
JUNCTION . . .
1 on door + 1 on window; or
1 on door + 1 in room; or
1 on door + 1 in room + 1 coat
hanger on window, etc.

A makeshift burglar alarm.

APARTMENTS AND HOUSES

Protect the whole apartment or house—all windows/all doors/ all floors so a burglar who checks your place cannot spot an obvious weakness in your alarm system.

Never let anyone outside the family into the secrets of your burglar alarm. A burglar who obtains good inside information on your alarm system has nothing to stop him.

GET ADVICE. Look in the telephone book under "Burglar Alarm Systems." Choose a reputable firm or individual who offers skilled installation of a complete variety of burglar alarms. Check to see whether it can give your alarms a regular checkup. Be sure you deal with an officed company (NOT just a salesman who is travelling on from town).

ADVERTISE AN ALARM'S PRESENCE. Use the THESE-PREMISES - ARE - PROTECTED - BY - ELECTRICAL-ALARM sticker. Avoid phony decals bought at novelty and hardware stores unless you have nothing else. Burglars can spot false stickers.

CHOOSE THE RIGHT ALARMS. Use an expert's help to pick triggering devices (sonics, wall vibrators, infrareds, mercury switches, heat and motion detectors, magnetic contacts, etc.) AND alarms (bells/horns/shriekers) according to the setup . . . safety of neighborhood, amount of time home is empty, valuables you are protecting and how much you can afford.

PAIR UP ALARMS. Look at all possibilities.

The ideal is

A LOCAL ALARM THAT MAKES NOISE AND MAY FLASH LIGHTS IN YOUR HOME—

PLUS

AN ALARM THAT NOTIFIES THE CENTRAL OFFICE OF A PROTECTION COMPANY TO SEND HELP. Stipulate in contract with security firm that they also call the city police whenever they receive an alarm from your home (a police car may be near when the alarm sounds). . . . THE MORE FAM-ILIES IN A BUILDING WHO SIGN UP FOR "AID"—"APART-MENT INTRUSION DETECTION"—THE CHEAPER THE INSTALLATION AND SUBSCRIPTION COSTS BECOME.

SETTLE FOR LESS (if you must). Good alarms need not be wired to Pinkerton/Holmes/Burns protection organizations. Example: a simple system costing under $50 has three sensor trig-gering devices (for one door and two windows), a control box, wiring and fire engine bell; buy it as a kit to be installed by you or your local security specialist.

AND use a preentry alarm lock (various prices), a sensitive unit that emits a warble as soon as anyone either starts tampering with the cylinder or begins putting pressure on the door.

PROTECT ALARM SWITCH. Never let anybody persuade

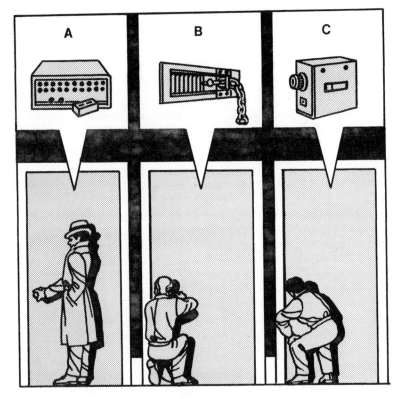

A. Alarm system fills the room with silent sound waves. When these are disturbed by fire or burglary, bells clang, horns blare and lights flash. Remote-control panic button enabled you to activate alarm when in a room away from the sound waves.

B. Lock alarm. Dead-bolt lock and chain coupled to an ultra-sensitive battery-powered electronic alarm. Picking and forcing attempts answered by audio signal.

C. Closed-circuit TV comprising camera, monitor and audio intercom.

you that it is best to place key control switch to a burglar alarm outside your apartment (so that you won't annoy neighbors when you come home and open the door). All alarms should have a time-delay mechanism which gives you 12–20 seconds to come inside and shut it off from *inside* your home.

REINFORCE POWER SUPPLY (when alarm is on house cur-

D. Hand alarm. Blasts 100 two-second shrieks per cartridge of compressed air.

E. Apartment Intrusion Detection (AID) which notifies neighborhood guard station of an intruder.

F. Alarm system of three elements and a master control—radar sensor, stress sensor and perimeter system. So sensitive the weight of a cup on a table is detectable.

G. Photoelectric beam safety alarm goes off as you step in front. Aimed at a well-placed mirror, it sets off a bell when disturbed.

rent). Have standby power supply to take over if burglars cut main supply (or during electrical breakdown). Battery alarms need batteries with shelf lives of at least 15 months. Change them every year, or every time they ring.

DOGS. Small dogs are the noisiest. Best is a two-dog team— one large, one small. Big dog scares the burglar after smaller dog has woken it up. But still fit an alarm system for when the dogs are away (say on holiday).

The Addict (Handyman)

Has a fixed thing to do: protect himself, his family and his home in all manner of ways that cost little, because he does it for himself.

Although a burglar knows how a certain shop-bought lock on a window can be forced, he will draw a blank at your homemade window lock which he has never seen before. . . .

FIX ALARM

Given good neighbors . . . fit simple electric bells in adjacent houses with one bell push in a bedroom and another at ground level. Arrange a reciprocal set of SOS signals . . . I am *being attacked/on fire/bedridden* . . . I can hear someone in the house, phone the police . . .

A local (and trustworthy) handyman can fix this. Check the bell pushers are out of reach of children. ONLY use them for the real thing.

FIX SCREWS

Don't leave screw heads exposed on door hinges/padlocks/ latches. They should be on inside of door. IF on outside . . . countersink by ½ inch. Drive well below wood or metal surface. Fill hole with wood filler/molten lead/solder that sets rock hard. Or file heads down. Nonretractable screws can be bought in hardware stores—they have special slots to take a screwdriver for screwing in, but the edges slope so you cannot unscrew them.

Check door-frame wood is not so rotten that screws holding

hinges can be yanked out easily (some carpenters use screws that are too short) . . . or a soft pine wood may be porous and absorb moisture . . . or a screw may be made from inferior metal which has rusted away. Unscrew random screws to check if they ARE long enough. And is the wood solid enough—like white oak?

Reject loose screws in sound wood. Replace with longer screws. Holes in hinge plates may have to be reamed out and countersunk to allow for thicker screws (take hinges and screws to automobile repair shop).

Fill old screw holes with hardwood pegs sawn off level with door surface (soak them first in wood glue). Drill new holes in hinge plates ¾ inch from old holes when wood below is solid enough to take new screws.

FIX LOCKS

Tools needed for modern pin tumbler lock installation = carpenter's drill or brace; 1¼-inch draw bit; screwdriver, hammer and wood chisels (if metalwork is to be recessed into wood). Good locks have clear directions.

INSTALLING POLICE LOCK WITH BRACE BAR (see THE SMUG, p. 222). . . . Easy to install: (1) Fix socket to floor according to lock instructions; (2) screw lock inside of door using self-tapping screws on metal doors (ten minutes' work). WARNING: Block the large keyhole on an old-fashioned door with concrete mixed with pebbles/grit/gravel. (Prevention against burglar threading wire through and slipping brace bar into unlocked position.) Or remove fittings of old lock and the inside doorknob. Cover hole with ¾-inch metal plate using nonretractable screws. Fix outside doorknob to door with long wood screw.

Check that NO locks can be removed from outside . . . if two small screws hold escutcheon plate to outside of door, as shown on p. 268, doorknob can be removed by unscrewing them AND exposed spindle can be pushed out the other side.

Camouflage your air-conditioners with plants. Air-conditioners can be stolen, leaving a hole in the wall. Use strong angle irons plus heavy nuts and bolts to secure them. Ask advice from firms who install them.

FIX LIGHTING

INTERIOR . . .

Screw a photoelectric adaptor into your outdoor fixture to turn light on automatically at dusk, off again at dawn. "Electric eye" timers are also available for indoor lamps and help premises look occupied when nobody is at home. AND set up electric 24-hour-cycling timer which turns interior lamps on or off at preset times when you are out.

This doorknob could be unscrewed from the outside and the spindle pushed through.

EXTERIOR . . .

Fit large light bulb into front door fixture. Cut away tree branches that stop light. Consider adding a light to opposite end of house to throw beam across normally dark side (or possibly two such lights as shown). Fix switch by bedside so they can be flipped on if you hear noise in the night. Regular lights or spotlights should brighten dark corners/walls/recesses, but watch floodlights which tend to blind you and not the burglar. Have all lights on or near house . . . AND place as many as possible light sources.

Go out at night with an extension cord. Try to work out the best lighting arrangement so NO dark places are left round your home.

FIX MAILBOX

Padlock your mailbox so a thief cannot inspect backlog of letters if you are away from home . . . or steal pension checks, family allowance checks, dividend checks or payroll checks mailed on certain days of month.

OR (best idea) make a mail slot in your front door. Letters should drop into a wire basket or cage screwed on inside of door.

FIX APARTMENT SECURITY CHECK

Walk from the street to the apartment door . . . is the front door always open? Are there tenants who will open the front door to anyone who buzzes their apartment? Is the doorman always there? How does the building superintendent organize duplicate keys (he could have 200 hanging from a rack in his basement office)? Are these keys listed by apartment numbers (DANGER)? or . . . by a code that only landlord/super/owner knows (SAFER).

Are there shadows on the steps? Dark corners/alleys/shrubbery near walkways? How well lit IS your building at night? Petition the management if necessary with other tenants for adequate lights in any area of the building that poses risk, including laundry rooms, storage rooms and garbage disposal areas AND hallways and stairwells when you must go up or down one flight of stairs to your apartment.

FIX BURGLAR'S CASING

Place yourself in a burglar's shoes.

Walk slowly to the end of the block and back again looking for weaknesses. Ponder easiest place to burglarize . . . chances of

Three delayed-action lights: Sky Watch, Moonlighter, Electric Eye.

detection . . . possibility of getting caught . . . amount of potential haul . . . net profit calculated against possible number of years in jail if caught.

Make your accommodation unattractive to a burglar from all points of view.

FIX FALLS

Fit nonslip mats, firmly fixed stair carpets (no rents/tears/holes), rubber mat in bath and a safety rail, good lighting on stairs, no trailing flex, nonslip floor polish, cupboards within easy reach . . . especially when about to retire.

The very young (under four) and the old are the most common victims of falls at home.

FIX FIRES

Fire prevention rules can never be complete, for each home has different circumstances.

BASICS are . . . NEVER fill oil heaters when lit . . . NOR near an open flame . . . ALWAYS have a fireguard to protect open fire or heater when you leave the room . . . A MUST = *fireguards* when children are about . . . DON'T leave matches or lights where children can reach . . . DON'T douse burning fat with water (instead use a damp cloth, lid or soil/sand/earth) . . . ALWAYS put out cigarettes and provide ashtrays even if you hate them . . . NEVER HAVE electric fires in the bathroom (electrocution risk) . . . NEVER use inflammable liquids (meths, turpentine, turp substitute, lighter fuel, paint stripper, varnishes, lacquers, paints, stains, etc.) near an open flame or when smoking . . . DO label them as inflammable . . . DON'T have mirrors above fireplace (setting-fire-to-clothes risk) . . . DON'T overload electric outlets . . . ONLY mend fuses with fuses of correct rating . . . ALWAYS have electrical repairs and alterations carried out by a qualified electrician . . . NEVER let garbage gather in attics/cupboards/under the stairs where hot pipes can trigger fires . . . KEEP attics and lofts cleared of inflammable materials . . . be FIRE-conscious all the time—prepared to fix/change/adapt the smallest household thing that constitutes a fire hazard.

FIX SURPRISES

NOT broken glass on windowsills. Spring guns. Trap doors. Deadfalls. Steel-jawed animal traps. Fishhooks/razor blades/barbed wire hung behind curtains. Broken bottles crowning garden wall. Snares. ALL are too dangerous. A thief could sue. Children can get hurt.

Make treadle mats instead (p. 272). Fit them under the carpet outside the front door and at points inside your home. Burglar presses mat as he stands on it, metal screens touch through holes in center layer of foam plastic and alarm is rung as circuit is completed. WARNING: Giveaway for burglar is when he steps off mat and alarm ends in midring. The answer is to connect mats to a good tape player (NOT a tinny sounding one) housing tape prerecorded with *second-long* sounds and short intervals in between . . . chink a cup and saucer, then a cough, then spoon dropped, then a curse, then window slid, then tap spurted etc. Potential intruder is bombarded with *brief* sounds and silences that can puzzle and sound real. And they happen in logical sequence as tape unwinds. It sounds as if somebody is in another room—often, the burglar does not want to find out.

FIX SAFES

Owners of important jewelery, negotiable securities or cash should keep them in a safe-deposit box at the bank. Unless a home safe weighs a ton, it can be easily wheeled out on a dolly.

For what you *do* keep in a safe, avoid hiding safes to one side of clothes closets, or behind pictures (unless the closet or picture is wired to an alarm). Burglars know.

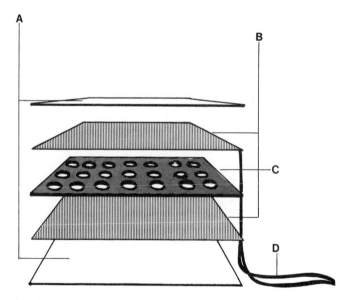

A. Thin floor mat   C. Foam plastic with holes
B. Metal mesh   D. Wires

Bolts of any bolted-down safe can be cut. Answer = protect bolts with a pipe set loosely over them so pipe spins round when sawing attempt is made—and leaves metal unscathed.

"Round door" safes embedded in concrete are best; they are made in thick laminated steel with tempered steel door and lead spindle inside to the dial. "Square door" safes are often only heavy and vulnerable fireboxes.

NEVER write down the combination number. Use mnemonic method as in combination door locks (see THE GUARDIAN, p. 246).

Beef Up Flimsy Doors . . .

FIX DOORS

Change glass-paneled fronts in doors to plastic—far harder to break. OR, best idea, change doors completely—see THE GUARDIAN (p. 246).

Change a door with hinge pins exposed on the outside.

Change two-piece Dutch doors often used for kitchens; they cannot be tightly locked at top/center/bottom.

Change metal to solid wooden door if possible; if not (because of fire regulations) . . . hire metalworker to clad outer surface of door with ⅛-inch toughened metal plate clamped to door with nonretractable screws. Look under "Locksmiths" in telephone book for companies who do reinforcement work.

Back up thin wood-paneled doors as shown on p. 275; there is no need to take the door down, but check that the hinges can take the extra weight . . .

1. Work from bottom by screwing ¾-inch planks across.
2. Cut ends flush with door edges.
3. Feed mixture of concrete/grit/pebbles down gap between planks and door panels as you work up.
4. Paint and stain to finish.
   THEN
5. Drill holes above and below lock through edge of the door.
6. Insert ¼-inch metal rods to foil drilling/sawing/hacking in these vulnerable areas from the outside.

MORE DOOR DO's

DO install a spyhole in your door—*thick* glass with wide-angle view (thin lenses can be broken by an ice pick or metal rod so that a wire can be inserted to tamper with certain locks and bolts from the inside).

DO install the strongest door chain. Door chain locks are best —they are locked from the outside with a special type of key— and can be locked when you are inside too.

But if you have only the old-fashioned chain lock, DO place the chain in CORRECT alignment. Mount the chain slide at 35-degree angle so that the chain is at full stretch when it drops into the end of the slot. The slide should also be placed slightly above the chain's anchor on door frame.

DO install chains on all outer doors—they need not all be door chain locks. Check list: screws securing chain should be 2 inches long or at least the longest length possible (NEVER just ¾ inches). And bite into *solid* wood. Buy chain with welded links, not links simply bent into place (motorcycle chain is ideal as it resists files/ hacksaws/tension wrench and can only be sheared by long-handled commercial bolt cutters); ask a large friend to charge at your door to test your handiwork.

When you leave, do lock an ordinary chain across the door by the method shown in THE GUARDIAN (p. 246) which, although insecure, gives the impression you are at home.

DO inspect where your door fits into its frame. Most outer doors receive the door's edge in a corner formed by a molding so that nothing can be inserted between door and jamb because of the 90-degree angle made by the molding. If not . . . use heavy hardwood molding to form a right angle. AND an angle iron screwed well home.

DO be careful about closing garage doors all the time. Automatic garage door operators help. AND add safety: you are able to turn on garage lights and open garage doors without leaving your car.

DO lock up garage doors over a long-term absence with extra padlock secured through extra holes drilled in overhead rails of garage doors.

FIX WINDOWS

IMPROVE . . .

EXISTING SPRING-LATCH CATCH (or any window catch that can be got at with a thin knife blade pushed up between sashes): Knock four or five finishing nails into the woodwork in front of the lock.

DOOR LOCK IN REACH-THROUGH GLASS DOOR:

Strengthen thin paneled doors.

Change ordinary glass for plastic glass (if you *must* have glass in a door). Safeguard lock with wrought-iron window guards which have all-welded *steel* construction so no hand can reach the lock.

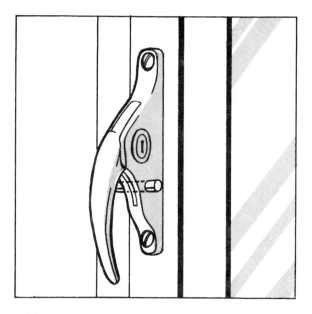

Secure metal-framed window.

OLD-STYLE DOUBLE-HUNG WINDOWS: Insert tenpenny nails in holes drilled through upper rail of bottom sash and lower rail of upper sash (one nail on either side can hold the window fast). Locking pins can also be made from broken drill bits. Metal ¼-inch rod bought in hardware stores is also effective. Cut ends flush and paint.

WINDOW CATCH FOR METAL-FRAMED WINDOW: Drill hole in catch as shown; insert ¼-inch metal pin to stop tongue moving. Ensure pin is easy to free with knife/magnet/ wire so it does not make a firetrap. Cut pin flush. Paint end to camouflage it from intruder.

VULNERABLE WINDOWS: (ground-floor windows, above-porch windows, near trellis/pipe/fire escape windows, just-below the roof windows, basement windows, accessible attics): Buy good window gates that fold and padlock in place with U-bolts— just fasten one side of the folding window grating to the wall and install lock receiver on the opposite wall. Grating should overlap beyond the window opening by at least 12 inches.

Test quality of steel in folding gates with a few strokes of hacksaw blade in store. Ideal = hard steel + metal strips close together + hard steel rivets. Large heavy-duty screws are necessary to support gate.

Don't buy wrought-iron gates (they are easy to saw).

CHECK that you have a way out in case of fire. Install a fire escape if necessary.

FIX HURRICANE PROTECTION

Heed radio/TV/newspaper warnings.

Have a supply of drinking water and ready-to-eat foods . . . have flashlight, fire extinguisher, transistor radio, first-aid kit . . . have all loose objects outside stored away (toys/tools/garbage cans) . . . have all windows boarded or taped up . . . have windows facing away from winds open to equalize pressure within your home . . . have your household ready for the main dangers: (1)fire; (2) injuries from flying objects . . . use phone only for emergencies like broken water pipes, sewer pipes or power lines.

FIX TORNADO PROTECTION

Heed the warning that tornadoes are fast and unpredictable.
RULE OF THUMB . . . try to place position of the "twister."

TO THE SOUTHWEST = DANGER—it is approaching.
TO THE WEST = POSSIBLE DANGER—it may be coming.
TO THE NORTHEAST = it will probably miss you.
TO THE NORTHWEST = it has already passed you.
TO THE NORTH = it will probably pass you.
TO THE SOUTH = it will probably pass you.

1. KEEP RADIO/TV TURNED ON FOR LATEST BULLETINS.
2. MOVE TO SAFETY OF CELLAR. Southwest corner of basement is usually safest area in the home. When NO basement . . . seek shelter under a heavy table/bed/work bench in center of room. Avoid outer walls. And watch your head when opening windows to equalize pressure—there is real danger of flying objects.
3. BE SURE WINDOW AND DOOR CAN BE OPENED ON SIDE FURTHEST AWAY FROM APPROACHING STORM.
4. STORE ALL LOOSE OBJECTS THAT CAN BE BLOWN IN THE AIR.
5. PROTECT YOUR HEAD AT ALL TIMES.
6. BE READY FOR FIRE. FILL BUCKETS/BASINS/BATH AS WATER PRESSURE WILL BE LOW IF "TWISTER" STRIKES.
7. AVOID DANGLING WIRES TORN DOWN IN STORM.
8. KEEP INSIDE UNTIL RADIO/TV BULLETINS SAY DANGER IS PAST.

The Beaver (Meager)

Doesn't have to be rich to make his home safe. Locks and burglar alarms are only the first stage in locking out the criminal. THE BEAVER gets his teeth into personal weaknesses and gnaws out deadwood.

Should so much as a chink penetrate the security screen by which he dams the current of city lawlessness, he stops it up.

ARRIVING

CELEBRATING (see also THE RELIEVED, p. 8) . . . be wary of massage ads in personal columns of city newspapers. They are often a cover for call girl services, who visit hotel guests.

MOVING. . . . Check firm is licensed AND/OR a member of the national furniture removals association. Shop around for estimates (some firms may move you more cheaply during the week). Get an estimate in writing BEFORE the movers start work (some deliberately underquote prices and add fresh charges).

Beware of firms prepared to give you a price by telephone without having checked your home or contents. Check estimates for: (a) does cost include packing? (b) does company supply packing cases and how much extra will they charge? (c) how are glassware and china protected? (d) what liability rests with movers for damage?

ACCOMMODATION-SEEKING . . .

Be prepared to be patient.

KNOW THAT permanent accommodation is hard to find in cities, despite the number of apartments advertised in metropolitan newspapers (some are nonexistent apartments, offered at bargain rents as bait by accommodation bureaus, who then offer their real accommodations at much higher fees). AND you must be ready to phone around in reply to apartment ads as soon as the ads appear . . . check with newspaper enquiries desk when the early edition is on sale. Ads in shop windows MAY be out of date—check the date in the corner of the card.

Phrase accommodation-wanted ads carefully; use a box number. Ads that are too bizarre are looked on by some as a respectable cover for prostitution. And you may be bothered with strange requests.

BLENDING

MAKE YOUR HOTEL BEDROOM, APARTMENT OR HOUSE LOOK OCCUPIED AT ALL TIMES . . . .

Keep lights on in your apartnment when the rest of block has most windows lit. Buy a timer or photoelectric cells. Two lights are more realistic than one. Draw shades or curtains just enough so that outsiders cannot tell if anyone is in. Time lights so that when one goes out for an interval, another stays on. Never depend on one small dim light. It won't fool anybody.

Use an electric timer to switch on the heater in the hallway when the house is empty. Burglars can smell there is no one living there otherwise.

Secure a wire cage below the mail slot (see THE ADDICT, p. 266) to stop a burglar seeing the accumulation of mail lying on the floor.

Ask a neighbor to empty your mailbox (and/or lobby mailbox). NEVER announce weddings or obituaries in newspapers. NOR contact society page journalists when they are likely to print a story on YOUR celebration/holiday/coup. Do it after the occasion is over.

Hire a telephone answering service. A continuously unanswered phone means that a burglar, who saw your nameplate on the door and who checked the telephone directory for your number, can dial the number and let it ring until he returns to the apartment. If it is still ringing, he knows that no one is at home. DO NOT temporarily disconnect your telephone—the telephone company's interrupt-message tells burglars there is no one at home.

Leave a radio on just loud enough to be heard by somebody at the front door, at a window or on the fire escape outside (see also THE NOISY, p. 258). Burglars know this is often a ploy, but it can still deter them.

Leave a car of secondary value in the driveway so it looks as if you are at home. Remove the distributor cap.

Load up the car in the garage when going for a Sunday picnic. Burglars drive round suburban areas at weekends looking for just those people who will be away for the day.

DON'T leave garage doors open when you go shopping. On return—drive straight in, close door and unload belongings out of sight.

Change your shopping habits. Don't keep to a strict daily routine. Even 45 minutes—if the burglar knows your schedule—is enough time for him to make his haul.

CANCEL milk/bread/newspaper deliveries if you are going to be away more than a day.

Leave the light on in the bathroom, door slightly ajar and cold tap running a trickle. A radio playing here adds effect.

Avoid parking your car in same spot two nights running. Know that residents' parking permits help burglars by advertising (1) who is a resident and (2) when they are not at home.

Be a good neighbor (so your neighbors help YOU). Call the police if you hear the apartment next door being ransacked (don't confront burglar); shove a piece of paper sticking from under neighbor's door out of sight (burglar's trick to see if paper is moved and anyone at home); collect their mail, cut their grass, sweep their leaves, shovel and make footprints in the snow in their drive as if they themselves were using it, adjust their heating in winter and air-conditioning in summer, readjust curtains . . . SO their premises always look occupied when they are away. And so they will do the same for you (see also THE ADVERTISER, p. 220 and THE LONER, p. 228).

Notify building superintendent/owner/landlord when you will be absent some time. Tell them how to reach you in an emergency.

Tell local police precinct you will be away so police can check at regular intervals.

In many communities police have a plan of protecting homes when owners are away, but in large cities such service is not available. Engage private guard or watchmen security on neighborhood or personal basis.

Advise those authorities you informed of your intended absence that your neighbor has WRITTEN permission to enter your house or apartment.

Ask an insurance agent for advice on theft and fire coverage during your absence.

ANSWERING

WHEN IT IS AN OBSCENE PHONE CALL . . .

IMMEDIATELY AND GENTLY HANG UP RECEIVER. Don't slam it down or you give the caller the attention he wants.

OR ACT AS THOUGH SOMEONE ELSE WERE WITH YOU IN THE ROOM and you were passing the phone over to them.

OR CLICK DOWN THE TELEPHONE RECEIVER BUTTON SEVERAL TIMES and say, "Officer, I want this call traced." Half shield the mouthpiece while talking.

OR TAP A RING OR PEN AGAINST THE MOUTHPIECE to make it sound as if you were connecting a wire or tape recorder to take down the caller's words.

CHANGE YOUR TELEPHONE NUMBER when it is a persistent caller who may know you and your habits.

REPORT COMPLAINTS TO POLICE AND TELEPHONE COMPANY. Don't be embarrassed. Authorities can help stop calls with new electronic equipment at no charge to customer.

REMEMBER: You may have an unlisted number but a random obscene phone call could still reach you . . . and be the start of a string of them if you let the person talk and obviously rattle you.

DOUBLE-CHECKING

DOMESTIC HELP: Be especially careful when hiring on a temporary basis. Check employment agency. Check references. Check employee actually lives at address given you.

WORKMEN: Check you don't expose anything of special value or beauty when strangers are working on/in/by your home (they may not take it immediately, but return later and burglarize you). Or tell.

NIGHT TOUR: Make a list of things to check before going to bed . . . windows/doors/skylights locked . . . chains secured on doors . . . ladders locked away . . . power tools secured *inside* (NOT in backyard) . . . AND *follow it every night.*

FIVE-MINUTE SHOPPING: Check windows and doors are locked before going to the shops or calling for coffee with a neighbor.

CURTAINS: Don't be smart middle-class and leave curtains undrawn at night so that anybody can see how you live when it gets dark.

FRONT DOOR KEY: Check that *no one* in your family dangles the key on a piece of string inside the mailbox when they go out, hides it on a ledge above the door or behind a loose brick or leaves note to the milkman saying they are away.

Make it a habit to double-lock your door AND engage the extra lock too every time you come inside. Check other family members.

TELEVISION: Check there is a light on in some other part of your home when watching TV (some burglars rely on your TV to keep the rest of the house clear).

GAS: Check taps are tight or—if small children live here—of the safety type; replace rubber tubing with metal connections; don't use a gas oven for heating kitchen; tell gas authorities immediately if you smell gas.

ELECTRICITY: Buy only goods conforming to government safety standards. Check for frayed wires. Use a reputable electrician for any repairs. Check that no one in your family EVER (1) touches switches with wet hands, (2) uses heaters designed to be put into baths to warm the water.

SUFFOCATION: Check hazards which can bring death to babies . . . Sleeping in the same bed as parents (you can roll over onto infant). Uninflated balloons (can be sucked down throats). Dolls' eyes (and other parts of toys that can be sucked/swallowed/stuck down tiny throats). Plastic bags (that can mold to faces). Angora woolens/Christmas decorations/feather pillows (all can suffocate).

POISONING: Check no poisonous substances like weed killer/paint stripper/disinfectant are poured from their original containers into lemonade bottles which children might drink from. Keep such substances in their original containers inside a high-level cupboard. AND lock away first aid kits and all medicine supplies.

TIPPING: Check your tips rise with the standard of city living so that you get best service where really needed. At home.

TAKING STOCK

Make a complete inventory of your possessions. Copy down registration or serial numbers of portable items: cameras, watches (watchmaker will tell you when you take it in for service), radios, televisions, stereos, typewriters, tape recorders, musical instruments, sporting equipment, power tools, etc.

Ask a jeweler to write an accurate description and appraisal of jewelery when you buy it for your records.

It is a good idea to lodge a copy of all this information at your bank.

Stick tiny name identifications inside radios, watches, etc. Or make secret marks (write them down in records so you don't forget).

Serial numbers are the best lead police can have in recovering your property.

Sometimes police catch a burglar for one theft and find his apartment full of other people's possessions—perhaps yours.

They could hang 20 burglaries on one person if only they had serial numbers. AND return the goods to people who lost them.

Check whether you have enough coverage under your insurance policy.

If not, boost the figure of your insurance to a more realistic amount. . . . AND don't wait until the policy falls due for renewal.

DOUBLE-CHECK DOUBLE CHECKS

Don't allow anyone into your home on the strength of identication he/she carries. Carry out this security check. . . .

1. KEEP YOUR CHAIN ON THE DOOR.
2. ACTUALLY TAKE HOLD OF CREDENTIALS AND INSPECT CLOSELY: Does printing/photograph/paper look authentic? Ask bearer to spell name as on the card; ask him to repeat details on ID card; ask for driver's license; double-check photograph (criminals often use photographs of other people). Credentials should give . . . individual's name, clear photograph, physical dimensions, physical characteristics, signature, serial number, name and address of employer.
3. CLOSE DOOR WHILE YOU CHECK WITH SUPERIORS.
4. CALL PHONE NUMBER GIVEN AS CONFIRMATION: Check it is not a private number with an accomplice waiting at the other end—check phone number bearer gives you is the same as the phone number of firm or call Information if in doubt).

When in doubt, keep them out—by making things as difficult as this, you are persuading any criminal that it is best to leave you

alone and move on to laxer victims. Be polite while being obstructive.

KEEP THINGS HIDDEN

WALLET/HANDBAG/CHECKBOOK: Hide everyday valuables on your person (see THE CANNY, p. 40) rather than leave
them in hotel rooms inside shoes/third drawer of linen closet/
clothes hamper *unless you locked and alarmed room efficiently*
(see THE GUARDIAN, p. 246 and THE NOISY, p. 258). DON'T
keep credit cards/savings bank passbook/keys near open door/
window of your home where a sneak thief could snatch them.

DO keep cash reserve/jewelry/business papers in hotel or
bank safe deposit box.

To hide valuables overnight in a hotel while you sleep . . . tape
money/checkbook/traveler's checks to underside of dressing table
or bureau drawer—NEVER inside a locked drawer.

PERSONAL MOVEMENTS: Keep secret everything concerning your personal life. If a caller asks, "Is that 379–1234?" and
your number is not, simply say so (do NOT volunteer your own
number). . . . Report repeated wrong numbers or silent calls to
phone company. If your phone number is listed supply only your
initials, NEVER full name. Give negative answer to "researchers"
or "salesmen" who want to know (1) value of personal property,
(2) if you are going on vacation soon, (3) what nights you watch
TV/go out/etc. . . .

IT IS VERY EASY TO GIVE DETAILS QUITE UNWIT-
TINGLY OVER THE PHONE THAT HELP BURGLARS ROB
YOU.

WARNING: Brief small children carefully to keep closed about
family affairs when answering the phone; tell them to ask the
caller to call back later.

TELEPHONE NUMBERS are best unlisted. List last name and
first initial only when you choose to have phone number in the
directory. On a mailbox . . . single women should add name of a
made-up roommate (again, initials only). Use box number when

advertising for job/room/roommate. When phone caller asks to speak to your husband, don't say he is out of town or that you are not married; say husband is busy and will call back if caller leaves a number.

TIME-KEEPING

Be conscious of TIME of day/week/year when you are more vulnerable. And do something about it.

CHRISTMAS: Burglaries increase (buy Christmas present for your home by fitting locks to all doors and windows lacking required security); suicides increase because Christmas does accentuate the sense of apartness and loneliness through the *pressure* to feel good which can cause agony and distress; threat of fire increases because homes are full of inflammable paper decorations; letter bomb dangers increase because of the vast amount of mail handled in this period. . . .

HOW TO TELL A LETTER BOMB (also to be expected during any wave of terrorist activity in city): Book-sized parcels (rather than large ones) . . . anything from unusual sources . . . items addressed in foreign or unknown style of writing . . . springiness in top/bottom/sides of parcel . . . lopsided feel to letter or parcel . . . wires sticking through paper . . . smell of almonds or marzipan . . . greasy marks from explosive sweating . . . rattling sound like a loose safety pin inside when shaken gently . . . cardboard or metallic stiffening inside envelope . . . more than usual number of stamps on envelope . . . unusual thickness for a letter . . . additional envelope inside addressed personally to somebody (possibly tied with string or tape).

IF YOU RECEIVE SUCH AN ENVELOPE/PARCEL/PACKET, PUT IT DOWN IMMEDIATELY AND CALL THE POLICE. DO NOT START TO SLIT ENVELOPE; DO NOT ATTEMPT TO DEFUSE SUSPECTED PACKAGE BY PUTTING IT IN WATER/SAND.

STRIKES: Gas/electricity/garbage strikes = risk of con men entering homes of old people in order to "check for leaks, wiring, hygiene, etc." AND steal pensions and life savings. They often work in twos (one keeps the householder talking while the other one steals). See DOUBLE-CHECKING (p. 282).

MONDAY/TUESDAY/WEDNESDAY: Women at home leave front door "on the latch" while going out with garbage or to pick up mail from the lobby downstairs. WHEN YOU GO OUT, ALWAYS TAKE YOUR KEYS WITH YOU AND DOUBLE-LOCK DOOR.

THURSDAY/FRIDAY: Payday prowler aims to hit a large number of small homes or apartments.

SATURDAY: Daytime burglar strikes under cover of NOISE from automatic washers, vacuum cleaner, lawn mower or hedge clipper. LOCK ALL DOORS BEFORE CHORES.

SUNDAYS: Burglars drive around suburbs to check people loading cars for picnics/church/excursions.

See BLENDING (p. 279).

ASCENDING/DESCENDING/TRAVERSING

Regard stairways/elevators/corridors in apartment buildings as places accessible to the public. Expect the worst.

Carry a hand alarm or whistle (see THE NERVOUS, p. 52; THE FUGITIVE, p. 202).

Staircases can be safer for those able-bodied enough to run and who would be helpless attacked inside an elevator. On a stairway you can run into a corridor and buzz apartments and/or whistle/shriek/yell (call "Fire!").

ELEVATORS (when you must take self-service elevators, as most must) . . .

1. LOOK INTO THE ELEVATOR BEFORE YOU ENTER (fisheye convex mirror fixed high up in corner opposite door gives view of interior without your having to step inside).
2. DO NOT ENTER ELEVATOR IF A SUSPICIOUS PERSON IS IN IT (i.e. virtually any single stranger WHEN you are alone). WAIT FOR THE NEXT TRIP.
3. WHEN A STRANGER ENTERS THE ELEVATOR AFTER YOU, STAND BY CONTROL PANEL READY TO PRESS— AND KEEP PRESSING—ALARM BUTTON BY HAVING

HAND CUPPED OVER IT BEHIND YOUR BACK. PRESS
BUTTON FOR THE NEXT FLOOR AND GET OUT IF YOU
SENSE TROUBLE.
4. IF ALONE AT NIGHT, DON'T DELAY IN LOBBY (collecting
mail, fumbling for keys, etc.). USE ELEVATOR AT ONCE
AND GET TO APARTMENT QUICKLY—KEY IN HAND.

BUT NEVER . . .
GET INTO ELEVATOR WHEN IT IS BOUND FOR BASE-
MENT IF YOU ARE GOING UP. REGARD BASEMENTS
AS DANGEROUS.

And in unguarded buildings which make you nervous:

1. Reach into elevator, press "B" button and let the elevator descend
to the basement without you, then bring it up again so you know
elevator is NOT going immediately down again.
2. Get out on ground floor if you find elevator is going down to
the basement.
3. Make it a general rule to hold elevator door back with shoe when
alone and about to press button for your floor—only take foot
away when lighted arrow shows car is bound for UP. If DOWN
signal shines as you press your button, get out; it could be a
mugger in the basement attempting to bring you down to him.

WARNING: Try to persuade the landlord of an unguarded
building to put locks on the basement elevator door so it can be
secured down there after dark.

REJECTING

NEVER LET A STRANGER INTO YOUR HOTEL ROOM/
APARTMENT/HOUSE WITHOUT A THOROUGH CHECK.
ALWAYS:

1. KEEP CHAIN ON ALL OUTER DOORS.
2. NEVER OPEN DOOR UNLESS FULLY DRESSED.
3. USE THE PEEPHOLE.
4. DO NOT RELEASE DOOR CHAIN UNTIL YOU HAVE
DOUBLE-CHECKED ON CALLER.
5. BE READY TO SLAM DOOR SHUT WHILE IT IS STILL
ON THE CHAIN.

6. NEVER GO FOR A PURSE AND LEAVE THE DOOR OPEN.
7. RESIST SALESMEN WITH INCREDIBLE BARGAINS.
8. TURN AWAY CALLER WHOSE CAR "HAS BROKEN DOWN"—AND SAY YOUR PHONE IS OUT OF ORDER TOO.
9. SUSPECT CALLER WHO PROTESTS AT YOUR REQUEST TO SEE IDENTIFICATION AND WHO ARGUES WITH YOUR DECISION TO CHECK WITH SUPERIORS (genuine callers won't mind).
10. YELL/SCREAM/SHOUT IF A STRANGER PUSHES INTO YOUR HOME.

TURN THEM DOWN:

DOOR-TO-DOOR SALESMEN: Use a reputable dealer if considering house repairs. Don't let door-to-door callers begin their pitch. Be polite and close the door. If you do buy goods at the door . . . unwrap and inspect them before paying.

STRANGER USING INTERCOM SYSTEM: Don't "buzz" main building door open when he asks you to admit him on some excuse (like having to leave flowers in the lobby, say).

FREE GIFTS (FROM PACKETS OF WASHING POWDER TO BIG FIGHT TICKETS): Say no, thank you. Remember: thief steals a car and returns it with note saying "Thanks." And leaves two tickets to opera/movie/play—only to burglarize home when householders use those tickets.

SHOP/BANK/POLICE OFFICIAL ASKING YOU TO COME AND COLLECT THE WALLET OR HANDBAG YOU LOST: Say it is inconvenient at the moment. Can you call back? Then telephone back to confirm the number they gave does exist, check your security arrangements when you go.

BEARER OF BAD NEWS SUCH AS DEATH OR HOSPITALIZATION OF RELATIVE OR FRIEND. Before you leave home phone relative or friend's home to check.

BE ALERT ABOVE EVERYTHING ELSE. TREAT STRANGERS WITH SUSPICION AND DEMAND IDENTIFICATION AND TELEPHONE NUMBERS WHICH YOU CAN CHECK BEFORE TAKING THE CHAIN FROM THE DOOR.

AND IF YOU WEAKEN AND ADMIT A SALESMAN WHO HAS YOU SAYING YES AGAINST YOUR BETTER JUDG-MENT, USE LAST-MINUTE SAFEGUARDS:

1. SAY YOU ARE UNEMPLOYED WHEN ASKED YOUR OCCUPATION.
2. CHECK THAT YOU ARE ENTITLED TO CANCEL AN AGREEMENT WITHIN SO MANY DAYS.

TURN DOWN JOBS

Beware of fantastic jobs for women advertised in newspapers (can be an excuse to obtain your name/address/telephone number) . . . be chary of applying for nude modeling—"'all work according to existing law" (this phrase has no meaning in countries where prostitution is legal anyway; work is likely to involve prostitution and modeling for pornographic films) . . . also watch how you phrase ads for spare-time work.

SUSPECT THOSE ADS REQUIRING SPARE-TIME WORK-ERS AT HOME . . . AND WHICH REQUEST MONEY IN ADVANCE TO COVER LOSS OF MATERIALS OR EVI-DENCE OF YOUR GOOD FAITH. Genuine suppliers of assembly work usually advertise only in their own area of the city, arrange delivery and collection of materials and work on normal employer and employee terms.

The Dead Lucky

Survive by being in the right frame of mind during crisis. And so their dreams of staying alive come true as a result—NOT because they ought to, but because they caused them to.

That they escape is a result of previously figuring on what to do IF. . . .

GETTING HELP

See also THE NERVOUS (p. 52) and THE FUGITIVE (p. 202).

LEARN HOW TO DIAL POLICE/AMBULANCE/FIRE DEPARTMENT IN THE DARK. Know emergency number in YOUR city (like 911 in New York).

Phone police if you see someone being attacked or breaking into a house or robbing a shop—and call them if you see someone loitering around a neighbor's side door or trying car doors. The police prefer a false call to a theft/rape/killing.

CALLING POLICE . . .

1. GIVE LOCATION WHERE IT IS HAPPENING.
2. EXPLAIN WHAT IS HAPPENING: Number of people involved, description of suspects, description of scene, license numbers of vehicles.
3. STAY ON TELEPHONE UNTIL TOLD WHAT TO DO.

If you don't know telephone number for emergency services, dial "0" and say "POLICE/FIRE/AMBULANCE DEPARTMENT—EMERGENCY" (whichever you require). Look for directions on what to do in an emergency in phone booths. You may not need a coin in some cities. If you have no coin and DO require one, try the telephone . . . someone may have left a coin in the machine.

YELL YOUR HEAD OFF IF AN INTRUDER FORCES HIS WAY INTO YOUR HOME. SHOUT "FIRE!" TO ENSURE SOMEONE COMES OR TELEPHONES FOR ASSISTANCE.

WHEN STRUGGLING WITH AN INTRUDER . . . have your wife/husband/children run to a window to call for help. Smash the glass when window is locked and there is no time to use the key.

NEVER allow anyone—unless he has a knife or gun—to tie you up without a struggle. *Do not believe him when he says if you let him tie you up he will not hurt you.*

USE ANY METHOD OF GETTING HELP OR ALERTING PASSERSBY OR NEIGHBORS THAT IS AVAILABLE WHEN YOU ARE TRAPPED: Throw paper dart bearing message from a window . . . tuck distress note under dog's collar and let it out

. . . write HELP! backward (!PLEH) in window dirt/steam/frost
. . . set off electric alarm which flashes "HELP—PLEASE CON-
TACT POLICE" (such warning units fitted with internal emergency cords can be attached to the outside walls of houses or
apartments—ideal for old people who live alone).

WHEN LIFE GETS TOO MUCH . . .

DIAL SAMARITANS, SAVE A LIFE LEAGUE OR OTHER
SUCH LIFESAVING SERVICE MANNED BY VOLUNTEERS.
Or operator, who will connect you with them.

The Samaritans are staffed by people who are sympathetic, un-
shockable and caring—from all walks of life, of any religion (or
none) AND who help the troubled with humanity, common sense
and personal concern.

WARNING: BE PREPARED FOR BUSY SIGNAL. BUT DO
NOT GIVE UP. KEEP TRYING. DON'T LOOK ON A BUSY
TONE AS AN ACT OF FATE.

FINDING PROWLER

PROWLER OUTSIDE WHEN YOU ARE INSIDE. . . .

1. Check all doors and windows are locked.
2. Telephone police.
3. If, too late, you find he is already trying to enter the house
   through a window, let him stick his head through then bring the
   bottom sash down to trap his head and shoulders.

WARNING: Don't keep a gun in the home unless there are
special circumstances. Odds are on a professional criminal's side
when using firearms. There is always a risk of accidents with a
gun in the home. And it can be turned on you (see THE BEL-
LIGERENT, p. 160).

PROWLER INSIDE WHEN YOU ARE OUTSIDE. . . .

1. Never go in and tackle criminal when you see a window or door
   has been tampered with.
2. Go to a neighbor's house and call the police.

WARNING: If you should return home at any time and notice prowlers on turning into the driveway, stop. Back out. Head for nearest phone. Call police. Intruders then may think you were just a car turning in the driveway—and so be caught red-handed.

DOUBLE WARNING: If you think somebody is inside, never charge at the door. A bullet fired from the inside at the door is almost guaranteed to pass through and hit you.

FINDING BURGLAR

WHEN YOU WAKE UP IN THE NIGHT AND DISCOVER A BURGLAR. . . .

IF IN BED. . . .

1. Pretend to be asleep.
2. Dial for police in the dark.

IF HE WAKES YOU. . . .

1. Find out what he wants—if it's money or property, better let him take it.
2. Don't provoke him. Keep quiet.
3. Try to remember what he looks like.
4. Phone police when he goes.

IF YOU SURPRISE A BURGLAR. . . .

1. Don't attack unless you are capable. It is safer for most people to pretend to faint.

IF YOU ONLY SUSPECT SOMEONE IS IN YOUR HOME. . . .

1. Never turn on lights. This gives burglar an advantage—he can hide and then jump out on you.
2. Phone police immediately.

Burglars often have an accurate knowledge of YOU/family/ habits. Priority for burglar on entering premises is to check his exit. Give him a chance and probably he will use it rather than attack you.

WARNING: CAT BURGLARS ARE OFTEN ADDICTS OR UNBALANCED AND DANGEROUS CRIMINALS STRONG

AND WIRY ENOUGH TO SCALE NERVE-RACKING HEIGHTS. THEY ARE THE MOST LIKELY BURGLAR TO HARM YOU IF YOU RESIST. THEY WORK BETWEEN 1 A.M. AND 6 A.M.

ONLY FIGHT BACK WHEN THREATENED WITH BODILY HARM AND YOU CANNOT STOP YOUR INCLINATIONS . . . AND THEN TRY EVERY DIRTY TRICK.

USE a member of your family as a decoy to distract approaching burglar. Hide behind a door or round a corner. Wield poker/baseball bat/vase on intruder's head. Call Police.

WHIP rug/mat/carpet he is standing on from under his shoes if he comes for you (but is not carrying a gun). Wife/daughter/mother-in-law can distract him as you bend down. Club him with a heavy object as his feet go out from under him.

CUT house lights or main switch (or throw room switch). Keep moving away in the dark—using knowledge of room's layout. Throw things at intruder. Don't use a flashlight (you give your position away).

TOPPLE heavy furniture down the staircase if you know an intruder is coming upstairs. Wardrobe/dresser/bureau will do. Take a running jump—feet first. Use handrail to guide your charge.

BEING TIED UP

Tense your arm and leg muscles as they are bound. Slightly bend your joints. Try to pump your muscles up to their maximum size. Kink rope if you possibly can. Take a deep/deep/deep breath. Tense against the bonds.

THEN . . . (when alone) relax completely. Just the ½ inch of slack rope so won is enough to help you wriggle free (if rope is wet hold it to heater/fire/sun).

BURGLARIZED

Don't touch anything on returning to find your home has been ripped off. Telephone police.

HARD TIMES

Survive hardship. Whether from gas or electricity strike that paralyzes the city or firings/layoffs at work that suddenly leave you unemployed. . . . Improvise.

It is the same when holed up in a cheap room with scant funds and—for the moment—no place else to go.

FOOD: The only necessities are a mug, spoon/knife/fork, plate and small immersion coil to boil tea/soup/stew in the mug OR a hot plate. If you have no electricity or gas to cook with . . . use candles.

Examples: cook stew of scrag ends until electricity power is cut in a strike, then place half-cooked stew in a cardboard box lined with hay (bought from pet stores). The hay's heat will keep the stew cooking (also works with nearly boiling kettle) . . . make substitute for bananas from boiled turnips; mash up outer layer then sprinkle with sugar and banana essence . . . produce jam from finely chopped cooked beets and melted-down strawberry jelly . . . slice potatoes and onions, place in alternate layers on a TV dinner tray, cover with gravy and cook on moderate heat for an hour . . . hardboil egg in mug with immersion heater inserted in the water. . . .

LIGHT AND POWER: THERE ARE MANY IMPROVISATIONS . . .

BUY a modern (or secondhand) oil lamp which gives out heat as well as very pleasant light.

KEEP food hot when electricity is off in a large Thermos bought at drugstore. Or heat over two night lights which burn for eight hours.

BRIGHTEN dim candlelight by placing a mirror a foot away behind candle.

MAKE a candle from a cup containing margarine; place a pipe cleaner or length of string which has been soaked in margarine in the cup—leaving ½ inch above the surface—and light.

OR pour 3–4 inches of water into a cup, carefully add 1 inch of salad oil on top; smear some of oil on pipe cleaner or piece of string; tie nail as ballast for bottom of the wick, thrust top end of wick through a bit of cork or cardboard which will float on the surface. Now pull ½ inch of wick through this, lower into cup and light.

TAKE GREAT CARE USING MAKESHIFT OR PROPER CANDLES. MATERIALS USED ARE INFLAMMABLE; THEY CAN BLAZE OUT OF CONTROL IF YOU ARE NOT CAREFUL.

ALWAYS PLACE CANDLES IN HOLDERS WITH WIDE/ FIRM/HEAVY BASE. WEIGHT DOWN CUPS OR JAM JARS WITH SAND OR SOIL. ADD WATER/SAND/SOIL IN BOTTLES WHEN USING THEM AS CANDLEHOLDERS.

COOK with candles by placing them inside an empty soup can with holes punched in the sides. Place a larger can of soup/stew/ baked beans over them, but open the can first. One candle will give 10–15 minutes cooking time.

USE butane gas cooker for clean/simple/cheap family cooking. With one gas cartridge it can be kept at full pressure for two hours.

SWITCH OFF decorative lighting. But don't take risks; keep stairway properly lit, especially for children and older people.

DRAW CURTAINS to keep out drafts.

KEEP MOVING when heat goes off in winter. Loosen tight clothes. Reinforce clothing with layers of newspaper round the body. Keep limbs moving. Warm hands inside clothing or beneath the armpits. Eat something warm each day.

LIGHTNING

Stay inside. Keep away from sinks. Don't use the tub. Avoid windows and open doors near high trees. And freezers, cookers, washing machines, pianos. Switch off and unplug appliances like TV/hair driers/electric razors.

FALLING ELEVATOR

Try to get your feet off the floor. Jump up to reach for any ledge just below the roof. Hang on.

If there is no handrail (or you are too old/short/frail) . . . jump up and down in the hope you are in the air when elevator car overshoots terminal floor to strike the shock-absorbers below.

JAMMED ELEVATOR

FIGHT PANIC.
Try NOT to take elevators when there is a high risk of power cuts . . . when too many people jam inside . . . when the building is on fire . . . when one particular elevator has shown signs of faltering for some time . . . just after an earthquake tremor.

WARNING: Don't be overcasual about the chances of being rescued quickly . . . elevator may break down, its alarm bell fails to ring and they hang an "out of order" sign on the door. It is some time before the engineer arrives. SO . . .

1. DON'T YELL YOURSELF HOARSE: You may need to give voice later when you hear people in a neighboring elevator shaft.
2. DON'T BEAT ON THE DOORS OR WALLS: This encourages panic.
3. KEEP PRESSING THE ALARM BUTTON: You may not hear it even when it is working.

LOCKED OUT

Don't climb ivy/drain pipe/bricks to open upper floor window. Call police.

FALLS

1. Try to relax. Many fall victims have walked away unhurt, especially children, drunks or suicides—in all cases people who fell without tension and with slack muscles. Some have fallen up to 275 feet and at speeds approaching 90 mph.
2. Attempt to land on well-padded parts of body (buttocks/shoulders/thighs).
3. Let bent arms hit ground just before main impact to lessen the shock.
4. Try to roll with fall, tucking head well forward.

5. If you do land feet first . . . bend knees and give as you land with your main aim being to "run" forward.

WHEN you have a choice of *where* to fall, pick the softest landing . . . roof of a car . . . grass lawn that slopes . . . gravel driveway . . . compost heap . . . patch of earth . . . or mattress/cushions/pillows thrown down ahead of you.

Never, never leap from a burning building when higher than the second floor unless flames have actually reached you—and you cannot back away from them any further.

Exception: when you are on the second floor and within reasonable distance of the ground (and can jump onto a lower roof or soft landing). . . . Lower yourself to full arm's stretch from the window ledge to shorten drop by approximately 8 feet. Turn out as you jump.

EXPLOSIONS

THE BOMB: Put out fires after blast wave has passed. Do whatever repairs are needed in next 30 minutes. Nail planks across windows to dam back fallout. Check you have enough food in your shelter. Stay inside until TV/radio/police instruct that it is safe to go out. Stay inside as long as you can if there are no instructions. If you could be contaminated by fallout take off outer clothing and leave it outside, well away from refuge room; wash/scrub/rinse head, neck and hands; brush under nails, bathe eyes, rinse out mouth with salt and water, cough and blow nose hard.

EARTHQUAKES: UNLIKE BOMBS/HURRICANES/TOR-NADOES, EARTHQUAKES GIVE NO PRELIMINARY WARN-ING. Motion is not constant; there may be several seconds between tremors.

1. STAY WHERE YOU ARE.
2. DO NOT RUN OUTSIDE.
3. USE DOORWAYS FOR THEIR OVERHEAD SUPPORT. Crouch beneath desk/table/bed if possible—the doorway is simply best minimal support if you can find nothing else.
4. AVOID MASONRY/CHIMNEY/VENTS/LARGE WINDOWS.

Tell children to stay where they are when an earthquake occurs. Most injuries happen as people enter or leave buildings. ONLY if the walls of a building are crashing straight down on you should you run to where it is safe.

IF in doorway below a toppling wall, stay there. Let it fall. Try to jump on top of the settling debris. OR run to another side of interior of building watching for the best chance to reach safety outside.

Apparent dangers of an earthquake are more devastating than the actual tremors. Don't panic and commit rash actions. There is usually time to take shelter. (Remember: earthquakes are not explosive enough to hurl objects off shelves, but will usually only shift them around . . . so you must stand a chance.)

BURIED ALIVE

It is possible for a large person to squeeze through a small space. Only the bony structure of hips and chest present obstacles and even these measurements take in flesh—which gives—too.

DO NOT PANIC. (Signs: Respiration quickens; heart pounds loudly then starts to hammer; head aches; sweat pours.) Fear can cause bodies to swell and stick fast in apparently roomy enough spaces to wriggle through. Try to breathe less deeply and less frequently.

We use far less oxygen when stunned or lying unconscious in a small space than when conscious and struggling to escape. Try to keep the mind at rest. KNOW you can survive.

Know that . . . where your head and an arm will pass through, so will your body. And a relaxed person of average build can worm through a space no wider than the spread of the fingers on one hand if he or she is not wearing bulky clothing, belts with large buckles or more than one layer of garments. But of all these qualifications, the most important is to be relaxed.

KNOW . . . people who are stuck can be "talked" through tiny spaces . . . a reassuring hand on ankle or wrist helps the trapped relax . . . NEVER, if you go to help, squirm down an incline, both arms ahead—it is impossible to retreat unaided.

THE BEST WAY TO FREE SOMEBODY WHO IS
TRAPPED. . . .

1. PASS VICTIM A LINE (POSSIBLY MADE FROM TIED
   BELTS/SHIRTS/OLD ROPE) WITH LOOP KNOTTED AT
   END.
2. IF POSSIBLE HELP VICTIM TO SLIDE A SHOE IN THE
   LOOP.
3. GET VICTIM TO BEND THAT LEG AT THE KNEE.
4. NOW TAKE IN THE LINE AND ANCHOR IT.
5. VICTIM SHOULD NOW STRAIGHTEN HIS LEG PRO-
   PELLING HIMSELF FORWARD UNDER ITS POWER . . .
6. AND FLEX HIS KNEE AGAIN.
7. PULL IN SLACK LINE, REANCHOR AND REPEAT.

WARNING: Avoid trying to heave someone out of a tight spot
by giving him a handline and telling him to hang on. This makes
his arm and shoulder muscles tense encouraging his body to jam.
Hauling on a line tied around victim's waist also has the same bad
effect.

FIRE

Be aware of danger of fire transcending effects of earthquake/
tornado/hurricane which started the flames in the first place.

Keep cool and never jump from a burning building when you
are above the second floor—unless the flames are touching and
you can get no further away.

REMEMBER . . . in most countries tall buildings are constructed on one of two fire-resistant designs: (1) there is more
than one stairway, separated by fire-resistant glass screens SO that
if one staircase is blocked by a blaze, the other is always free OR
(2) the building has only one stairway in the center, but this has
fire-resistant walls and doors to isolate it.

By law, the door of each room must be a maximum distance of
15 feet from a lobby adjoining the staircase to each floor. This
ensures lobbies are ventilated, can suck out any smoke and be
reached from any room.

PLAN OF ACTION FOR EVERY FAMILY IN CASE OF
FIRE . . . .

1. BRING EVERYONE IN THE HOME TO THE GROUND FLOOR.
2. CHECK THAT THE FIRE DEPARTMENT IS CALLED AT ONCE (DON'T THINK THAT SOMEBODY HAS ALREADY DONE SO AND LEAVE IT AT THAT).
3. SEE EVERYBODY IS SAFE.
4. DO ALL YOU CAN TO ELIMINATE DRAFTS WHICH MAY FAN THE FIRE. CLOSE DOORS AND WINDOWS EVEN IN ROOMS AWAY FROM THE FIRE.

IF CLOTHING CATCHES FIRE. . . .
Lie down on the floor. Roll over in rugs/curtains/blankets. If another person is on fire—throw him down. Carry out same action.
IF A TELEVISION CATCHES FIRE. . . .
Smother set with a blanket. Call fire department. (Never just switch off TV set at night—pull the plug out.)
FOR MOST FIRES water is best (except for burning fat which MUST be smothered with lid/towel/cloth). However, never throw water on electrical appliances unless you have switched off current by pulling plug or throwing main switch . . . stand well back when throwing water on oil heaters . . . call fire department at once if a chimney catches fire.
IF CUT OFF BY FIRE. . . .

1. TOUCH DOORKNOB WITH BACK OF HAND IF YOU SMELL SMOKE IN THE NIGHT. If too hot to touch, it means flames are outside the door. If doorknob is cool enough to touch, you are still far enough from the flames to reach safety by the stairway, which is clear of smoke. Always know the alternate route to safety in your building. BUT if this is blocked . . . go back to your room and close the door.
2. KEEP DOOR CLOSED; it will take 30 minutes to burn down.
3. PACK NEWSPAPER/TOWELS/RAGS INTO CRACKS AROUND DOOR TO STOP SMOKE.
4. STAND BY A WINDOW AND ATTRACT ATTENTION. LEAN OUT AND WAVE IF NO SMOKE OR FLAMES ON THIS SIDE.
5. WAIT FOR THE FIRE DEPARTMENT.

6. IF SMOKE BECOMES TOO DENSE, LIE ON THE FLOOR AND BREATHE CLEAR AIR IN 2-INCH LAYER NEXT TO THE CARPET.

7. HAVE SHEETS/CURTAINS/BLANKETS KNOTTED TOGETHER TO MAKE A ROPE IN CASE THE FLAMES DO REACH YOU. One end should be tied to a heavy table or wardrobe and the other end lowered outside. But you will rarely need to slide down it; firemen will rescue you first.

BURNS AND SCALDS

1. GET THE AFFECTED AREA INTO COLD WATER; do it at once and keep immersed for seven minutes.

2. WRAP PATIENT SUFFERING FROM EXTENSIVE BURNS IN SHEET SOAKED IN COLD WATER.

3. NEVER REMOVE ANY CLOTHING.

4. DO NOT USE BUTTER/LARD/SOAP.

5. DON'T BREAK BLISTERS. For a hand injury try to get jewelry off before the fingers swell; remove boots and shoes from injured feet if possible.

6. REASSURE/COMFORT/KEEP WARM TO HELP LESSEN DELAYED SHOCK WHICH, IN ITSELF, CAN KILL AN ELDERLY OR WEAK PERSON.

GASSING

1. GO OUTSIDE THE ROOM AND TAKE A DEEP BREATH OF FRESH AIR.

2. DRAG THE VICTIM INTO FRESH AIR.

3. GIVE THE KISS OF LIFE. AND . . .

4. YELL FOR HELP.

SUFFOCATION AND CHOKING

INFANTS:—If obstruction is still in the windpipe, hold up by the legs and smack three or four times between shoulders.

CHILDREN:—Lay them head down over your thigh; smack between shoulders.

ADULTS:—Ditto; with three or four sharp blows.

ELECTROCUTION

1. MAKE SURE YOU DO NOT GET ELECTROCUTED TOO.
2. SWITCH OFF CURRENT, RIP PLUG OUT OR TEAR CABLE FREE.
3. IF IMPOSSIBLE TO DO THIS WITHOUT ENDANGERING YOURSELF STAND ON A PILE OF DRY NEWSPAPERS, RUBBER MAT, OR WOODEN TABLE (for normal household current, NEVER high-voltage cables) AND . . .
4. KNOCK VICTIM FREE WITH WOODEN BROOMSTICK, TREE BRANCH OR CHAIR (NEVER WITH YOUR BARE HANDS OR ANYTHING THAT CONTAINS ANY METAL).
5. TREAT WITH ARTIFICIAL RESPIRATION AND/OR TREAT FOR BURNS.

POISONING

DON'T PANIC: Signs of poisoning . . . rapid breathing, breath smells peculiar, burns around the mouth, stomach pains, sleepiness.

WHEN VICTIM IS UNCONSCIOUS AND NOT BREATHING . . .

1. IMMEDIATELY CARRY OUT THE KISS OF LIFE AND POSSIBLY—
2. HEART MASSAGE TOO (see THE COLD-BLOODED, p. 187).

WHEN VICTIM IS UNCONSCIOUS BUT BREATHING . . .

1. CLEAN OUT VICTIM'S MOUTH.
2. ROLL ONTO SIDE SO TONGUE FALLS FORWARD AND SALIVA CAN FLOW FROM THE MOUTH.
3. DON'T GIVE AN EMETIC OR ANYTHING TO DRINK (RISK OF IMMEDIATE DEATH OR PNEUMONIA).

IF VICTIM IS CONSCIOUS . . .

1. MAKE HIM VOMIT IF HE IS NOT ALMOST ASLEEP OR IF THE POISON WAS CORROSIVE. An efficient emetic is 2 tablespoons of salt in tumbled of warm water OR a teaspoon of mustard in half a tumbler of warm water.

2. ENSURE PATIENT IS LYING FACE DOWN (TO STOP VOMIT BEING SUCKED BACK).
3. USE WATER TO DILUTE ANY POISON LEFT IN STOMACH.

ALWAYS CALL AN AMBULANCE—even if, say with an infant, you are not sure he/she has actually swallowed poison.

NOTE: Know right dose of medicine for whatever the age (but don't administer medicine to babies without a doctor's advice). Adult dose should be multiplied by the child's age then divided by the age of the child PLUS 12. Example: adult dose = 2 tablets. Then if you have a six-year-old: $2 \times 6 = 12$, $6 + 12$ (= 18). So 12/18 — two-thirds of a tablet — is the child's dose.

Part Five

CITY BUSINESSES

Shops, Banks and Offices

9

CITY BUSINESSES

LOSERS

WHATEVER OUR business in the business and shopping centers of the city, we can't bank on personal safety. Shoppers and storekeepers, customers and bank clerks, callers and officeworkers—all are wide open to urban violence.

Assembled in the business areas is wealth of all shapes and sizes vast enough to attract violence for both gain and malice. And God help us if we get in the way. Bank raids, smash-and-grab heists, payroll snatches, sports-fans-on-the-rampage, the bomb on the 17th floor. . . .

We just don't expect such mayhem. But when it seems just bad luck that crisis strikes downtown, we should think again. Often it was simply bad management of our inner selves.

The Defiant (Suddenly)

Act on the spur of the moment so that when out shopping they could be accused of shoplifting—even they have no intention of stealing.

If you don't believe that innocent people get accused, think again—and always before you go shopping.

SIGNS AND SYMPTOMS

A raised voice at the salesclerk who doesn't know if the fabric she is selling is washable. Receipts for the six pairs of shoes you don't need. Flirting with other customers or sales people in the hope of a pickup. Walking around counters aimlessly. Checking at mirrors to see how you look. Carelessly holding only one handle of two-handled shopping bag.

CAUSES

Accidental or deliberate shoplifting when we can afford to pay often springs from love problems.

The root of the trouble could be a broken marriage or a quarrel or a romance that has gone stale. Whichever it is, it has often been demonstrated that a person with the money who shoplifts craves attention and affection.

When a person is depressed for a long time (see also THE TENSE, p. 73), tension builds to a danger point, and we hover on the edge of a nervous breakdown. It is found that this is a likely time for a person to steal.

Wishing to make the cause of his depression aware of what he is doing, a person like this often makes no attempt to hide his theft.

People also shoplift because they are bored or simply want some kicks. Like kleptomania (a morbid tendency to steal for its own sake), these instances are more rare.

But many of us end up in court because it looked temptingly easy to take something for nothing off store shelves when we felt unwanted and unloved.

ILLOGICAL BEHAVIOR

We have all been guilty at some time or other of misleading behavior in supermarkets or department stores:

OF PICKING UP AN ARTICLE and handing the right money to the clerk. But she is busy and doesn't notice or ring up the money. We don't wait for a receipt or for the article to be wrapped . . . and could be challenged outside the store to prove we have paid for it.

OF BUYING AN ITEM and after a few days taking it back to the store to match it with something else—a set of china, say. Only we have lost the receipt, the labels have been washed off and we are found with both items, only one of which has been paid for.

OF BROWSING and examining many pieces of merchandise and—afraid of being lulled by soft music and splendid counters into absentminded stupidity—looking over your shoulder and glancing furtively around, at once drawing attention to yourself. Especially at Christmas, when store detectives know many shoplifters infiltrate their precinct, they are watching for ANY giveaway signs.

OF WANTING A BETTER LOOK at some article in daylight and carrying it to a window. Because we hold the item in a normal manner—as opposed to holding it high in full view—our manner is described as "furtive" by a floorwalker and we could be charged with removing goods from their proper place with criminal intent.

Supermarkets and department stores spotlight their shoplifting precautions. As hundreds of millions of dollars worth of merchandise are stolen a year from supermarkets, and the average large city department store loses at least 3 per cent of its gross sales to shoplifters, the shopkeepers are telling their store detectives to pounce whenever they see anyone acting suspiciously.

We can never be too careful in the large store where we are encouraged to walk around and buy whatever we can be tempted to buy. Yet so often we are not careful enough; people DO forget items placed in their own shopping bags. Only too often has a supermarket proved "a temptation to the needy, a paradise for the pilferer and a trap for the innocent."

To claim we are unaware of the extent of shoplifting and how it can affect us adversely is naive. We have only to use our eyes —most stores know it pays to publicize their antithieving precautions.

Sensitized tags are attached to goods, which when taken through an electronic beam set bells ringing and lights flashing (the tags can be removed only by a clerk using a special implement) . . . small plastic detectors saying DO NOT REMOVE electronically trigger an alarm if you do . . . store detectives look much like other shoppers (apart from their eyes, which they have to avert on the pretext of looking at merchandise because they are never still) . . . there are peepholes for unseen security staff . . . closed-circuit TV cameras . . . one-way and two-way mirrors . . . convex mirrors that see around corners . . . more electronic wafers stapled in the folds of garments . . . and tiny invisible electronic dots on price tags and labels which can activate alarms.

Such aids are universal, and to get by safely we must learn to automatically follow a sequence of rules that becomes a habit. There is such a one.

Remedy: The Hard One, p. 360; The Nervous, p. 52; The Comforted, p. 179

The Awed (Timid)

Are intimidated by the prosperity of highly polished shops with gleaming merchandise. Their very size bludgeons our senses when we are nervous.

SIGNS AND SYMPTOMS

Stuck holding open the shop door for everyone else after your companion has already gone through. Straightening your tie in the bank counter glass screen for the benefit of the cashier. Not buying a suit after the sales woman has said: "A suit, madam? People aren't wearing suits these days." Saying "Thank you" to the salesclerk for selling you something you don't really want. Passing several shops before entering the first one. Not looking to see if you have been shortchanged because you don't want to make a fuss.

CAUSES

We all fail occasionally to complain when we have had just cause from the person on the side of the counter. One reason is natural politeness; another, downright fright.

By the same token, we are too easily intimidated.

How else can we explain our willingness to be bullied into trying on something we don't want, our insistence on being made to feel uncomfortable as we are hounded by aggressive salespeople from the moment we set foot through the door?

And stores *know* that shoppers are nervous.

Customers are no longer necessarily right. When a complaint is made against a salesperson in a busy department store, the supervisor has often to be careful not to alienate him—it can cost more to replace a clerk than a customer. The result is that the staff bands together against the shopper.

Salespeople are on their feet seven or eight hours a day and walk six or seven miles, accumulating a "fatigue load" at the end of the day which exceeds that of the average docker. This doesn't help.

WE, growing more and more abject, fall prey not only in the bartering but in more serious ways too.

ILLOGICAL BEHAVIOR

Why is the salesclerk handing us a bunch of soiled bills as change in such a high-class store? Is it possibly to pass on bogus money he has been saddled with? We never ask.

THE AWED feel it will look impertinent if they examine their change in front of the salesperson. We take change on trust all the time.

Millions of counterfeit bills of various denominations are in public circulation all over the world. They are passed on by people whose attitude is "If I don't know I've got phony money, I don't mind passing it on to someone else."

But each bogus bill is a silent thief. The law requires that forged money be handed over to the police and the loss is ours. It is an offense to pass a counterfeit bill on to someone else in order to avoid this loss.

Many forgeries are bad. But we let them pass and put ourselves at risk. Of:

POSSESSING bills made from a good engraving printing press,

camera, special paper, inks, etc. (Most of the equipment is stolen —three men can break into a printing plant and walk out with a litho.) The plates are made by photographing a genuine note through color filters and under colored light. Each photo is printed onto a sensitized steel plate, and the lines are hand-etched. The paper must be the right quality with a watermark and a metal or plastic strip, and each bill must be engraved with each plate in exactly matching register so that there is no overlapping of lines and edges. And *still* the note feels wrongly textured, has a scarcely discernible watermark, shows a badly printed number with certain letters out of register. And may even be the wrong size.

AWED characters, however, would no more question a bill given as change by lifting it up to the light to examine the metal strip running through it in front of a sophisticated salesperson than they would verify the dimes and quarters of their loose change by biting them.

We are also prone to writing checks that can be "kited" by anyone—i.e., someone else with a few deft strokes of a pen changes the payee on our check from a company to an individual's name. They also raise the amount to be paid to a higher figure— then they cash it.

Check forgers make over $100 million a year in the United States because of our carelessness with checks. We don't want to appear suspicious of the salespeople. So we often write our checks for merchandise casually on purpose.

And if we don't fill in every line and space tightly with words, numbers or lines-drawn-straight-through, other figures and letters can be added. Our actual numerals and letters are often so careless that they can be altered too.

DAVIS INC. can become David Inch. THE DEN can become T. Henden. SAMUELS CO. can become Samuel S. Coxon. Forgers are separating honest people from $2,000 every minute.

Remedy: The Speculator, p. 332; The Grocer, p. 341; The Leery, p. 47; The Nervous, p. 52

The Hunter (Bargains)

Is usually a woman. Intent on tracking down the best buys, her personal habits, rather than goods at knocked-down prices, become the giveaway.

SIGNS

Hacked shins, sore elbows, aching joints, bruised ribs, battered calves, jumping heart, scuffed shoes. Clothes you feel wrong in, shoes that hurt and hats that don't fit. Always taking bread and buns from the back of a shelf to ensure they are fresh—unaware yesterday's buns go here to fool us.

CAUSES

Everyone shops for bargains to such an extent that regular customers are a vanishing breed. Both buyers and sellers are strangers —personal service no longer an essential.

When every penny counts, daily shopping represents immediate survival. But the universal compulsion (see THE WISE GUY, p. 22) to purchase anything so long as it is being sold for considerably less than it is worth is—greed.

When it becomes an obsession to hunt for bargains, there may be deeper reasons than you would expect. It is a form of warding off mounting internal pressure. Various forms of sexual maladjustment, boredom, aging, and the fear of death manifest themselves in eternal shopping trips.

Whatever it is, it can make us prone to disaster.

ILLOGICAL BEHAVIOR

Our distraction is complete in crowded shops and stores, everyone looking for bargains; it is totally illogical on our part because it is so favorable for pickpockets and purse snatchers.

The purse or handbag taken because we leave it on a shelf to go to the fitting room . . . the purse stolen from the top of the shopping cart (as you step over for some items so does the thief) . . . the credit card left on the charge plate of the machine . . . the handbag opened by a "hanger binger" (hanger = shoulder bag; bing = to steal) as it rests on the counter while its owner is engrossed in the merchandise—the thief matter-of-factly opens it and takes out the wallet. . . .

Any of these can happen to the most careful individual when he sights the bargain of a lifetime. But all are small fry compared with having a baby stolen as you shop.

How often do we ask:

WHY do I take my baby shopping?

WHAT stops me from taking the child inside the supermarket?

WHERE is it safe to leave the carriage and child?

HOW can I safeguard the baby as I shop?

WHO would steal my child anyway?

These are the queries we ignore when it is bargains-galore. Yet we can't afford to.

So often the mother will leave the child outside because she will only be five minutes—but ONE minute is too long.

The only foolproof way of avoiding the risk is to leave the baby at home in the care of someone trustworthy. But every busy mother—possibly with two or three small children—knows that this is not always possible. Where Mother goes, the baby goes too —when Mother goes.

Could that be too often?

Most supermarkets and chain stores will not allow carriages inside, particularly on busy days like Fridays and Saturdays when 10,000 people will cram through the doors in one ten-hour period. Nor will many stores take the responsibility of looking after babies. Even the simple idea of paying a pensioner to watch carriages outside is fraught with legal snags which stores aren't prepared to take risks over.

And while a toddler can ride in the cart as a mother does her shopping, the tiny baby has to be left unattended outside.

Baby snatchers are often young unmarried women who want

to mother a child and have no intention of harming it. They act on impulse, dominated by an overwhelming love and tenderness for a helpless baby.

Lonely, possibly unable to have children of their own, such women do exist among the numbers mingling both inside and outside city supermarkets. Any unattended child could be taken —and play an unwitting part in one of the most baffling and pathetic crimes the police are expected to solve.

Remedy: The Hard One, p. 360

The Cozy (Paid Up)

Bask in the glow which follows a successful shopping trip, a bright day in a nice office or a worthwhile journey to the bank. Though not exactly euphoric, they are pleasantly vulnerable.

SIGNS AND SYMPTOMS

Soapy-smelling hands because handling money brings contact with germs. Opening packages on the coffee shop seat to look at purchases. Leafing through a checkbook over coffee and a dough-nut. Changing a typewriter ribbon the correct way: (1) pressing the shift key (2) changing the color key from BLACK to RED (3) jamming four keys together . . . all of which raise the ribbon carrier to its highest point and make threading the ribbon through it easier. Shopping after lunch because you have read a psychological study proving that customers who go to supermarkets after a meal spend less.

CAUSES

People like shops. Open or shut, in January sales or on a wet Saturday. Many of us would sooner trek along a row of closed-up stores lit with orange/yellow/red lights than across a slope of snowflakes.

There is nothing like a department store to make us glow when we are feeling low. It also makes the shabby feel it—and all the more ready to spend cash in an effort to smarten up.

Now back at the coffee counter or desk, we count the cost and find—because it really is what we wanted—the cost WAS worthwhile. And we get a charge through our systems which makes us oblivious to all else for several minutes' sheer bliss.

The hot coffee revives, the seat renews the strength in our legs and the support in our feet and we feel convinced that it is our day.

Just shops? Offices with warmth, light and the proximity of others will also bring the stomach-glowing heat—on days when we have extra cause to feel good, whether we are in love, getting richer or have heard bad news about someone we dislike.

ILLOGICAL BEHAVIOR

Both consumers and merchants are vulnerable under a general feeling of well-being in every department of city business centers —*especially TO people who do nothing to disturb their equanimity,* like . . .

THE SUIT-WEARERS: But why so smart, with only a driver's license or library card as identification—easily obtained and completely worthless as IDs?

THE NAME-DROPPERS: Have never seen us before, but repeat our names several times in as many minutes. Is it because they *want* something from us—like a phony check cashed? People like to be called by their names. Nameplates, name tags and names on coveralls and shirts are a boon to bad check criminals. We forget about *how* they know our name in our pleasure at being so addressed. He could as easily have asked another employee our name when name labels are not visible.

THE BIG SPENDERS: Flash large-denomination bills but make small purchases—a $20 bill for a pack of cigarettes, say. Could they be "dropping" a forged bill? And might not the person who telephones to request the delivery of a COD order and who also asks that the delivery boy bring change for a $10 or $20 bill also have the same motive?—to tender a bogus bill or bad check?

THE SPOKEN-FOR: May seem good as far as their *identifica-*

tion goes. But is a check 100 per cent safe when we don't know them? COULDN'T their credit cards have been stolen? Their Social Security or Selective Service cards have been forged? Their bank passbook obtained for identification by depositing a phony check? (The book shows the deposit, but not that the check bounced a few days later.) Their very checks stolen?

THE SEX KITTEN: Rivets men behind shop counters, but why *so* sexy? Is it because it is easier to pass bad money—like $20 bills—when the shopkeeper is too busy looking at her? Or could it be that the goo-goo eyes are trying to clinch the store-keeper into taking a fraudulent check by first distracting him and then offering the check with the top line blank? "You can stamp this with the name of your shop, can't you?" asks the girl—knowing that once the storekeeper does, that makes the check HIS and no longer hers. A psychological trick.

THE MOANERS: Gain our sympathy. Is THIS why they are *so* miserable when they visit our pleasingly bright and modern office? Are these disgruntled telephone repairmen, typewriter mechanics, window cleaners and even executives, or are they thieves looking for purses left on desks as we step out to the water cooler or typewriters en masse? They could well be. A team of burglars have only to enter an office building in well-used overalls and with pockets full of screwdrivers—and constantly grumble to allay the doorman's suspicions. Everything has gone wrong today. So the doorman helps them when they ask which offices have television sets. They return to the front door with the best TV in the building and moan again. Somebody has to sign their ticket or they do not lift a finger. The doorman signs—and it makes the removal of the TV so official that no one thinks any more about it for a week or so.

THE BROW-WIPER: Looks harassed as he follows us from the bank, but why perspiring so in November? Might he be setting us up? He has been watching the teller's counter while pretending to make out a deposit slip. To kill time he crumples up one slip after another—until he sees us draw out a thick wad of bills. He follows us through the door, mopping his brow as he goes, and tucking his handkerchief into the pocket which corresponds with the one where we stashed our money. This is a signal for the pickpockets waiting outside who now know where the money is and that it is worth taking. A favorite spot to take it is in the revolving door of an office or store . . . as we step through it a pickpocket gets into the same compartment. In the squash he steals the money while another accomplice in another compartment of the door jams it and pretends it won't move.

And many a con man is clever enough to get his bogus check cashed even when the notice above the counter states NO CHECKS CASHED. And, moreover, when the honest person with a good check will not be allowed to cash it.

Remedy: The Speculator, p. 332; The Grocer, p. 341; The Hard One, p. 360; The Cold-Blooded, p. 187

The Starstruck (Dazzled)

React to everything that glitters, from fool's gold to a sparkling sales pitch—and get sold down the river every time.

SIGNS AND SYMPTOMS

Sipping the clear water on a hot day from the tumbler on the jeweler's counter—placed there to test diamonds (genuine ones keep their brilliance when submerged). Buying a "gold-washed" or "gold-flashed" article because it sounds good (though actually it has the least amount of gold). Avoiding opal, unique among gems, because it is unlucky (NO, only to burglars). Rubbing a zircon on your teeth to test its authenticity (WRONG—this is the test for a pearl, which feels like a rusty nail, while a fake slides like silk).

CAUSES

IGNORANCE is the main cause.

Not one in a thousand people has any knowledge of precious stones or metals. Not one in 10,000 can call himself an expert.

We are fooled by the glitter, which scatters entrancing points of light before our eyes.

But we may lose much more than the money spent on worthless gems/rings/watches as a result of becoming STARSTRUCK.

ILLOGICAL BEHAVIOR

We don't really question whether what we are buying is authentic.

TICKING soon stops because of inferior mechanism in sidewalk-sold watches. These bear forged Swiss names and have glittering gold cases (mostly brass with a gossamer-thin wafer of gold on top). "Want to buy a watch cheap?" is the usual approach. It is said to be smuggled, and so it is—but not to evade import duty, for duty on Swiss watches to certain countries was abolished in 1966. The reason is that the "18-carat gold case" has no hallmark and is illegal.

SCENTS fade rapidly when we buy perfume from street traders. The scent they gave us to try was real. The bottles are authentic. The cartons expensive-looking. Selling outside large department stores, the peddler hints they have been stolen and come through the back door of that store. He even has a copy of *Vogue* showing a full page ad proclaiming the perfume at four times his price—but it's a phony page.

GRINS (suppressed) on your own face in a jeweler's mirror soon change to chagrin. You were offered a gold ring said to be worth $500 for $200 by a stranger on the street who said he needed the money. "Take it and check its value with any jewel dealer in the city," he suggested. You did. And three separate dealers all agreed the ring was worth at least $1,000. You hurried back and paid the $200 . . . only to find the seller had palmed and switched the ring as he took your money; the one you are left with is worthless.

Unfair and dishonest dealers will always be found in city business districts. They may deal in *bait advertising* (advertising articles at alluring bargain prices with no intention of selling them) or use *fictitious list prices* (using a fictitious price as a basis of comparison with their sales price) or a number of other illegal practices. But they are harmless compared with the jeweler who is a "fingerman"—*who sets you up for burglary.*

IS it logical for your jeweler to know if you have a safe; the safe's combination if you have; your movements to and from the city; your unlisted telephone number; how much jewelery you have; the number of people in your family; the kind of burglar alarm system you own?

Yet jewelers are often given these details in the course of conversation with their customers. With a little prompting, any unscrupulous jewel dealer can soon find it all out.

Dishonest jewelers *do* work with burglars. Sometimes they buy back from the burglar jewelry which they made (and evaluated for insurance cover) in the first place.

And so the burglar knows the exact amount of wealth we have in our possession at a particular time.

There are ways, however, in which we can thwart him . . . and save ourselves from being dazzled in other dangerous ways too.

Remedy: The Speculator, p. 332; The Illogical, p. 354; The Confused, 59

The Slicker (City)

Invests in insensitivity to the implications of sudden events and situations in the city center. The crash comes from a totally unexpected direction—having nothing at all to do with stocks and shares—and he is among the first to collapse because he didn't speculate enough.

SIGNS AND SYMPTOMS

Blue-chipped fingernails from stacking piles of new silver coins. Gilt-edged hands (and green/brown/black too) by 5 p.m. after sorting bills daily. Counting bills the fastest (Scottish bank clerk's) way: holding the wad in one hand and tapping them flush, then curving the fist so the notes form a U shape—and counting them off by thumb as they spring back straight. YOUR earprint on the one telephone in the street nearby which works, fingerprints on the buttons of the swiftest elevator in the building, toothmarks on the post office counter ballpoint that writes best. A wallet containing seven credit cards, photograph of Mom, three life insurance policies and 230 embossed business cards.

CAUSES

Familiarity breeds indifference when the city is our parish. Not only are survival instincts dulled, but we sometimes shade them on purpose because of a strong parochial pride.

Especially when we mix with visitors to our neck of the asphalt woods, the nerve center of metropolitan life. By avoiding at all costs the appearance of being impressed, whatever the happening or view that is riveting others, we consciously mark ourselves out as city residents. We've seen it all before, hence our world-weary expression.

Behavior can consequently become bucolic even though we sport pin-stripe/umbrella/single-breasted lightweight mac, button-down collar shirt, well-polished shoes and square black briefcase.

Lethargically pointing the way, offensively pushing past the person standing on the left-hand side of the moving stairway (city protocol sometimes demands we keep to the right unless passing) or deliberately barging the sightseer uncertain where to go next are typical ways in which we establish WE are on home ground.

In putting on this no-go show to show we are Big City, we exorcise insecurities and frustrations. But the good feeling we may experience can so quickly melt into sudden fear.

ILLOGICAL BEHAVIOR

Even when we are aware of the hazards which, local to a particular city, exist in city business centers, we rarely *look into them*. The stranger in a crisis-stricken area should never rely on the advice of residents, who may not even know how to protect themselves.

WE FAIL to get out of the way when sports fans terrorize a

city center in a pregame spree of senseless violence. They batter
office windows, wreck stores, petrify shoppers; we, however, stay
put on the sidewalk we usually walk. These hooligans, as psy-
chiatry shows, are stuck in the nine- or ten-year-old stage of
development, the "tribal war" period. This is the time when
children form gangs and imitate war, often with quite violent
mock battles. The emotionally backward troublemaker at football
games is doing the same thing. His team goes to war with the
enemy. When he goes on the rampage and smashes up property
he is acting out the part of the pillagers and looters who follow
victorious armies.

WE FAIL to change our normal route between the counters
when fire bells shrill through a department store. Because no one
else takes any notice—shoppers or staff—we assume it's just a
routine test. So long as the clerks keep on serving, customers will
keep on selecting . . . and when it begins to dawn on 2,000 people
in the store that this is for real, and a cloud of black smoke bil-
lows up the stairway, we are panic-stricken *and* the furthest of
any from the exit.

WE FAIL to prevent our teenage boys waving cap pistols (for
use as party noisemakers) in the street and it is only a policeman's
split-second decision NOT to shoot that saves their lives . . .
though they later appear in court on a charge of causing a public
nuisance.

WE FAIL to consider that giving children pocket money in
public, no matter how small the amount, IS flashing cash. Just
one dollar bill is a threat *against them.* No place, for example,
is less safe than the museum cafeteria. All the time other
youngsters are watching. They follow our offspring and get to
quiet stairs or behind a display cabinet in a lonely gallery and
rob them. If the young victims don't hand over the money, they
are attacked. After they have snatched the cash, the thieves run
away via the maze of galleries/doors/stairs.

WE FAIL to change our schedule when caught in a hurricane
whose lull lures us outside the office building. But this is the
eye of the hurricane and we are caught by vicious winds racing
in the opposite direction. There is no excuse. We are given a pos-

sible 24 hours' advance warning by radio and television—with instructions on what to do—when a hurricane is headed for the city. These storms are among the most powerful the atmosphere can produce: one hour of hurricane energy is equivalent to all the electric power the United States can produce in a year. Devastating an area 100 miles in diameter with winds approaching 80 mph, they can also blast a tract 400 miles in diameter with gale-force winds of 40 mph. And THE SLICKER will still ignore the warnings and may lose his life.

Remedy: The Speculator, p. 332; The Illogiical, p. 354; The Hard One, 360; The Researcher, p. 90; The Obsequious, p. 124; The Dead Lucky, p. 290

The Zealous (Heroic)

Hurl themselves into affairs most definitely not theirs. Newspaper headlines term them have-a-go-people. Newspaper obituary columns have their fill of them too.

SIGNS AND SYMPTOMS

A red neck under long hair after standing in the "speed" line of a bank for 30 minutes, being told you will have to see an official and then having to get back into line again. A soiled newspaper clipping in your wallet advertising a correspondence course and claiming, "We don't care how depressed you may be, or how sick of being one-of-the-crowd doing a dull routine job for third-rate pay—we promise we can start you on the high road to success." A palm that itches to push the policeman in the small of the back as he leans over the railings of the plaza fountain pool.

CAUSES

We all, at some time or other, dream the sensational, hair-raising gesture of bold defiance that will spotlight attention on us. The opportunity to tackle bank robbers can be such a chance.

The old soldier, made bitter by what he regards as the treason-able behavior of the youth of today, may, in an I'll-show-them mood, plunge into the heart of such action taking place next to him.

The henpecked husband, the laid-off workman, the grand-mother who feels passed over by most of life's opportunities, will on occasion be only too eager to grasp the chance of glory— and not consider the risk.

The longing to be St. George and have a go becomes irresistible.

ILLOGICAL BEHAVIOR

The odds of the uninformed, untrained and unfit citizen bet-tering tough, desperate and armed killers are long ones. We simply don't stand a chance. Now and then, of course, the have-a-go individual will foil desperadoes, but the exception only proves the rule.

Quite simply, THE ZEALOUS are bound to fail because they are not quick enough, strong enough or knowledgeable enough. The spurt adrenalin shoots around our system is our only hope— and a slender one at that against a bullet or bomb.

For these are the two most likely challenges THE ZEALOUS will take on when everyone else stands trembling: the guns in the bank/office/store or the bomb in the building.

Anyone who feels duty-bound to snatch a suspected bomb and dump it through a window simply doesn't know how ef-fectively the modern bomber packs his explosives. They work with murderous simplicity. . . .

The bomb or Molotov cocktail, for instance, with its milk bottle full of gasoline and soapflakes and a tampon for a wick. And the pocket incendiary bomb where the gunpowder is placed in a tin can or paper box on the windowsill and a magnifying glass in the lid uses the sun's rays to detonate the charge. There are incendiaries of household weed killer/sugar/cigarette packs, all made up with an extra item—a prophylactic filled with acid which eats through the rubber so that the cigarette pack explodes.

Also deadly is the length of lead piping plugged at both ends and packed tight with matchstick heads, while an empty soft drink can be filled with a stick of gelignite, 3-inch nails slotted into the holes in corrugated paper and topped with nuts and bolts to make a nail bomb.

Suitcase (or briefcase) bombs crammed with 40 to 50 pounds of gelignite can shatter glass and wreck masonry: a cheap alarm clock acts as timing device. Or it may be a clothespin that is used as the timer, the jaws kept open by binding thin wire around the far end—this eventually snaps under the strain, the jaws close and contact is made.

Bomb demolition experts today never treat identical-looking bombs alike—not when urban guerrillas and terrorists vary their ingredients and even incorporate failed fuses in bombs to conceal the active ones.

Similar principles apply to tackling an armed bank bandit. The thought "it's now or never" is dangerous in the extreme when facing a man with a sawed-off shotgun.

When your tactics fail, it is too late to ask, "What the hell am I doing, me with a wife and baby?"

It is desperately dangerous to try to wrest the gun from a holdup man. It is not at all like going for an empty pistol or toy revolver in practice or when play-acting, then a simple-seeming procedure. Here is facing a situation where to escape you will have to remove your whole body—while the other person has only to move a finger a fraction of an inch.

Let's consider how the soldier, law enforcement officer, secret policeman or ranger can deal with a homicidal gun-pulling criminal. Could WE do the same? Like. . . .

DIVING sideways at the experienced gunman's feet—he is standing a good 5 feet in front of us—to roll into him with the speed of a barrel speeding downhill. This after first distracting him by snapping our fingers as we raise the arms to his command (to make him glance up).

Or KNIFING DOWN AN ARM from the hands-up position to catch the gunman holding a pistol on you on his gun wrist.

And then wading in, punching. Distraction? We first raised the arms fairly quickly but punched one higher in the air at the end to pull his attention upwards.

Or even WHIRLING AROUND AND CHOPPING DOWN AN ARM in much the same way on the gunman prodding his weapon into the small of our back. To distract him before spinning round we say over a shoulder, "Sure, I'm no hero. . . . I'm not stupid. . . . Anything you say." This gives him the idea we have given in completely. Only we flourish one of our raised hands to make him look up and divert his attention.

Any normal, scared, unnerved person trying such tactics will be gunned down without a second chance. The average person does not have the essential lightning reactions.

When it is a case of life or death and we are going to end up shot anyway, then we must take chances. But in a bank robbery our only hope is to lie low when they say so—down on the floor as the raiders motion us to with their gun barrels.

Remedy: The Illogical, p. 354; The Hard One, p. 360; The Obsequious, p. 124

The Fireproof (Safe)

Imagine a SAFE will be safe for their valuables.

Small businessmen, especially neighborhood merchants who run their stores with few employees and meager funds for buying security, are wide open to robbery when that craggy chunk of hardware—their SAFE—stands as a symbol of security.

SIGNS AND SYMPTOMS

Jotting down the safe's combination number on a wall. Standing sideways to give you more light when opening a safe. Feeling extrasafe when a safe is fire-resistant. Choosing a combination number to match the numerals in your telephone number/license plates/birthday (say 12/21/33) as a mnemonic. Or a combination number with digits 5 or 10 in a row—5 10 15 20 or 10 20

30 40, for example. Not making a point of spinning the combination dial several times after each use. Keeping the same combination number after an employee leaves.

CAUSES

OBVIOUSNESS = selecting a combination lock number from a set of numerals already in use. Thieves look first in the paperclip box on the desk. Here they find the key to the desk drawers. They open these and scan the desk diary for birthday dates, telephone numbers, etc., which often lead straight to the combination number.

APATHY = writing combination numbers on walls/windowsills/bookshelves. Burglars know these places. APATHY too in leaving a combination number the same when someone leaves your employment and could sell the number to a burglar.

SHORTSIGHTEDNESS (MENTAL) = standing to one side so the light will shine on the lock we are opening. A passing thief in the guise of shopper/priest/workman can easily watch. Some use a 30X rifleman's spotting scope on a tripod from a window across the street when the safe is visible from one of your windows.

LAZINESS (SPIRITUAL) = believing any safe IS safe, a "steel god." Safes intended solely for fire protection are by no means always burglar-resistant. Many safes are 60 years old. Although still as strong as the day they were first delivered, they are no match for safecrackers who have learned a lot since then. Many safes, in fact, offer as much protection as an old baked bean can.

LAZINESS (PHYSICAL) = not turning the combination dial after each use several times. This leaves the safe on a "day comb" (you give the combination dial only half a turn after closing the safe door so that you have moved the combination only a few digits from the final, single number it takes to reopen the safe—and there is no longer the bother of having to redial the whole combination each time). BUT although the handle won't turn when the combination is only half-rotated, the safe is NOT secure (as burglars know). It can be opened by turning the dial slowly *and* pressing on the safe's handle. As the last digit in the combination is struck, the handle gives.

People who consider themselves THE FIREPROOF on the basis of such faulty reasoning show themselves vulnerable on a far wider scale too.

ILLOGICAL BEHAVIOR

For every fallible aspect of the safe in our shop/store/office there will be more weaknesses in other sections of our premises which we overlook . . . caused by the same safe-inside-a-safe philosophy which accounts for OUR illogical lack of proper safeguards.

A SAFE is vulnerable to X-ray equipment; criminals carry a mobile X-ray machine which can "read" the combination numbers of certain types of lock widely used on safes. AND—

Thieves can see with virtual X-ray eyes the contents of our briefcase or bag carried to the bank at certain times each week. When the routes, times, departure and arrival points of such trips are never varied, how can they miss?

A SAFE can be PUNCHED—sometimes. Hammer off the numbered dial, and the spindle shaft can then be beaten backward to break off the lock nuts which secure the door. AND—

By the same token, a temporary office employee can give the businessman a HAMMERING by diverting checks from the incoming mail into his own bank account; by acquiring a key to let himself in because he is doing such a good job and returning one weekend with an accomplice who cleans out everything of value on the premises; by passing on the contents of the safe and its combination number to burglars; by stealing the check-writer and blank checks, also books of sales, receipts, delivery forms, shipping tickets and other forms carrying the firm's name—all of which can be used to criminal advantage. These "temps," invariably professional thieves and con men, work with gangs of crooks. They work hard at several offices beforehand so that they can produce excellent genuine references.

A SAFE may be PULLED when the spindle is made from lead instead of steel. Punching it with a hammer will now cause the softer metal shaft to mushroom and spread out instead of going backward and through the gut box (diagram p. 330). So now a pulley and vice can be used to grip and drag the spindle shaft out of the safe in an effort to sheer the lock nuts.

We also fail to PULL attention when WE, the small storekeeper, are being victimized by thieves in our own store . . . because we have crammed the windows so full of goods/decorations/signs no one can see into the interior from outside and fetch possible help or raise the alarm.

A SAFE is open to DRILLING. The burglar makes his hole in a certain place near the combination dial and inserts a punch which has to hit and snap the lock rod in two (as shown). This frees the drop dog, the vertical locking rod, which fastens the safe door.

A display window, too, can be DRILLED by the sharp point of an ice pick to make the glass shatter (display windows ARE valuable). If, as many merchants do, you object to metal bars/gates/grills because they obscure displays of merchandise, watch out for smash-and-grab raids. Many special glasses which will resist hammer blows and brick throws will give way to an ice pick (and criminals have other methods too).

A SAFE can be PEELED. Sledge hammers and cold chisels or drills are used to spring open or make a hole in the top left hand corner of the door. Then, working down from the opening with a crowbar, the layers of steel are peeled down like a can of sardines without a key. When the burglar can slip a hand inside he can reach the safe's contents.

By the same token, bright orange decals advertising a burglar alarm system and placed prominently on our front door or window can discourage some thieves. But not backed up by a proper alarm system, THE FIREPROOF storeowner can find the psychology behind the decal doesn't always work. The store may be entered and the safe broken into as easily as the decal is peeled away from the glass.

A SAFE will sometimes submit to an AX. Square-door safes

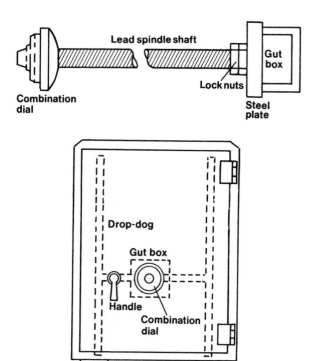

are vulnerable underneath. So the burglar turns them upside down and hacks his way through.

Our valuables, too can be AXED when we leave a solitary glass skylight unguarded (no closely spaced metal bars or mesh of iron or steel placed beneath the skylight and solidly fixed). And we are burglarized from above.

A SAFE will always open to THERMAL BURNING—in time. The most pull-, punch- or peelproof safe will still yield to an acetylene torch which gouges a hole in the center of the safe door to destroy the lock dog—and leave the handle free to turn.

By the same token, any storefront with a recessed entryway— i.e., with the door sent back between two opposing window displays—will hide the FLASH of a burglar's flashlight as efficiently as if he is standing in a tunnel. True, there may be accordian-style folding metal gates protecting and set flush with all the windows.

BUT as long as there is no folding gate or gates across the entrance to this mini-alley, we are vulnerable to lockpick and safecracker.

THE FIREPROOF, however, prefer to think on changing-the-system-is-too-much-trouble lines. They do not realize that the most important changes can be made quickly, easily and reasonably inexpensively.

Remedy: The Speculator, p. 332; The Grocer, p. 341

10

CITY BUSINESSES

WINNERS

No MATTER how refreshed we feel after our first sleep in town following an exhausting trip, we should resist any eagerness to plunge into the marketplace.

Such care is AWARE. Not just of details such as . . . new bills stick together (so be careful when shopping) . . . or the corpses of informers against organized crime are embedded in the concrete of new office buildings (short of tearing down buildings on suspicion they can never be found) . . . but of how our own character changes color in the crucible of offices/banks/shops.

The Speculator (Intuitive)

Follows signals. And uses his sixth sense to spot red lights ahead of most people still at the green/amber stage of awareness. Pondered conjecture and reflective thought—done fast, as most people can with practice—save us in the city.

HONE INTUITION

Awaken your sixth sense by constantly . . .

Guessing the time before glancing at your wristwatch or a

clock; registering the mood of the company you are in; checking if your first impression of a stranger *was* correct; deciding in advance the type of businesses around a street intersection still blocks ahead (shops? banks? offices?); calculating how long it takes to cover the distance from bank B to shop A (and does it?).

(*Intuition* is the ability to add up series of tiny impressions into an immediate and vivid picture of situations/events/people. Faster than logical argument or reasoned deduction, it is usually discounted because an intuitive decision seems to spring from nowhere. And you can only say "a feeling" flashed the signal when intuition was right. *Yet intuition makes unconscious use of all the faculties most people—not just women—possess. These can be trained to become even sharper, the vital sixth sense which helped our ancient ancestors to survive.*)

HUNCHES

Have a hunch whenever offered large-denomination bills. Especially when the purchase is of the pack-of-cigarettes-for-$20-bill variety (and the possible forged bill distributor is attractive enough for you to focus attention on him or her instead of on the money.)

Check large bills, whether they are offered as payment or tendered among change. Too many traders neglect to examine bills.

And remember it is an offense to pass counterfeit money on to someone else in order to avoid the loss.

Look for (as shown):

1. Texture of paper slightly thicker than that of a real bill. It doesn't feel crisp when rubbed between thumb and finger. It *should* "crackle."
2. Watermark faint and, sometimes, not discernible.
3. Numbers obviously badly printed—some are different sized, others out of register.
4. The background design is sharper and more distinct on genuine bills than on counterfeits. Part of the design may be missing or too faint.

5. Genuine notes have a metal line running through—only seen by holding the note up to the light. In a forged bill the line is plainly visible to the eye.
6. A forged bill may be fractionally smaller (or larger).
7. The portrait of sovereign/president/etc. on a genuine bill is composed of a screen of fine lines which are clear, distinct and unbroken. Forgeries have blurry, broken and indistinct lines which give the face a strained appearance.
8. Look for planchets. Certain bills (depending on the country) contain small discs of green/blue/gray paper (planchetes) embedded into the paper. These can be picked out of a genuine bill with a pinpoint leaving recess in the paper. Forgers sometimes copy planchetes by printing dots of appropriate color on the note (or by sticking circular paper dots on counterfeit notes).
9. Best test: Compare a real note with the suspected fake.

ALSO: Be wary of postal orders for large amounts of money when there are extra postage stamps (people who sniff suspiciously at a £5 postal order in Britain seldom question a fake postal order with genuine stamps on it).

Bad paper/poor design/funny feel are WARNING SIGNALS. Compare it with a real postal order.

FUNNY FEELINGS

Feel funny about the man in crowded shops/stores/banks who glances a lot at women's coats (especially when he is holding a folded newspaper).

Let him remind you there are others you never notice. Pickpockets who steal from the pockets of a woman's coat slip the purse into the folds of the newspaper, ready to be thrown away if they are challenged (see also THE LONG SUFFERING, p. 71).

Always hold your purse in a clenched fist. Don't ever put it down when it contains valuables (credit cards/keys/checks).

Women carrying a considerable sum of money should wear a tight-fitting coat (loose-fitting coats are preferred by thieves as their hands then don't touch the victims' bodies).

LITTLE BIRD TOLD YOU

Listen to the little-bird-tells-me feeling when you are offered a genuine $50 bill for a small item AND then are asked to give smaller change for the $20 you have just given back as part of the change for the $50 bill.

That $20 may not be the same bill as the one you handed over (a forger's accomplice could have palmed a counterfeit $20 bill).

Warning signals: The store is busy at the time (e.g., Christmas); the suspect pretends to count his change from the $50 bill while a line forms behind; then he asks you to split the $20 bill—while other shoppers become impatient.

AND LET YOUR INSTINCTS warn you off city business centers when visiting sports fans are running amok INSIDE stores as well as on the street . . . stealing sheath knives from sports shops/smashing glass shelves in department stores/stone-throwing in arcades.

Move away from trouble before it starts. But if you *are* trapped: (1) remember the colors of the vandals' scarves/hats/favors; (2) get anything of the same color or colors and wave/display/wear it to avoid being victimized.

The more elderly or very young you are the more likely you are to be victimized by teenage hooligans who form such pillaging gangs.

Warning signals: headlines in morning newspaper quoting big match odds; sound of horns/rattles/fireworks; chanting as gangs approach; running feet; breaking glass; police activity.

PREMONITION

Be on alert to any premonition of somebody carrying disguised weapons openly in business areas of the town. Potential muggers all.

Watch out for anybody who is carrying what legitimately could be called "a tool" yet which could prove a deadly weapon. Thugs do this to avoid being picked up by the police for carrying concealed weapons. . . . Warning signals: TOOLBOXES or WORK-

MAN'S TOOLS carried on a shoulder in vicinity of Con Ed crew ripping up sidewalks; a HACKSAW/WOODSAW/BUCKSAW held in one hand on the street beneath construction work on new skyscraper; PICK or AX gripped in the gloved fist of a worker in coveralls; CROWBAR, HAMMER, WRENCH or LENGTH OF RUBBER HOSE (mugging weapons first class); PIECE OF FURNITURE (CHAIR/STOOL/TABLE) being toted on pretense of apartment removal—chair leg is removed to be thwacked on YOUR cranium; BEER/CORDIAL BOTTLE (carried in or out of a paper bag—and deadly if they break); TWO-BY-FOUR PLANK or any similar pole/branch/stanchion which can batter a victim to pulp; HOUSE BRICKS (or HALF BRICKS) which, in the hand of an attacker, can kill or maim; BROOM/MOP/ SPADE handle ditto.

SECOND SIGHT

Look twice when faced with ANY proposition to sell you something for much less than it is worth in city business areas: watches/perfume/Christmas crackers.

Don't buy ANYthing on city sidewalks, even though it is represented as being a fantastic saving in value. There is always a catch. *Often goods are said to be stolen*—hence the saving to YOU—*but they seldom are.*

FELT IN ONE'S BONES

Feel it in your bones when drawing money from the bank or department store or supermarket check-cashing desk . . . *that you are being watched* (see also THE COZY, p. 315).

IS there somebody filling in deposit slips at a nearby counter who, having had the opportunity to see the amount of money you withdraw, follows you outside? Does anyone appear to trail you on leaving the bank?

The bones-itching person should shake off possible pursuers (see THE FUGITIVE, p. 202) *before* entering another building through a revolving door, moving at half-step on busy streets, or descending subway steps (likely places for pickpockets).

JUST KNOW

Be able to say you *just knew*.

When YOU are a cashier and somebody asks you to change 20 single dollar bills for a $20 bill ("It's for a birthday present," he says placing the $20 into an envelope and sealing it) . . . see a red light. Especially when you discover they have handed you only $19—one dollar bill missing.

They hand you the envelope, ask you to keep it in the cash register until they return with the missing note, take the 19 singles and vanish—for good. They palmed the $20 instead of placing it in the envelope (which contains a single slip of blank paper or a forged $20 bill).

SUSPICIONS

Suspect lunchtime callers to offices and small stores who have documents for signature. Because it is noon the supervisor in charge is at lunch so they try to press a junior staff member to sign.

This fact alone should make you *just know*. Refuse. Tell them to come back later (no matter how attractive their chat/style/smile).

(See also THE COZY, p. 315.)

SMELL A RAT

Sniff something wrong when purchaser buys a slip, say, with $50 bill as shops close. Warning signals: profuse apologies of purchaser/late hour/big bill. And attractive personality, looks, etc.

Don't cooperate next morning when "police" call and show photograph of the purchaser, wanted for dropping counterfeit $50 bills. Stall when the "policeman" asks did such a person trade a bill the day before?

Telephone the police department to check, because he may well be a colleague who will give you a signed receipt for the

$50, confirm you will hear from the Treasury Department—and disappear with the $50.

INSPIRATION

Use informed inspiration to spot faked checks. There are usually four kinds: (1) a genuine check that has been raised by altering it to show increased amount (see THE AWED, p. 310); (2) a genuine check that has been stolen and is signed with a forged endorsement; (3) a false check drawn on a non-existing account; (4) a genuine check drawn on an existing account which has insufficient funds.

Use warning signals:

1. Nervousness of the endorser at delays which you contrive. Such as—

Insisting on the endorser signing the check in your presence. (If check has been previously endorsed compare the signature). A potential forger can be balked by being slowed down. Some forgers can only preforge a signature by turning the original signature upside down, starting at the end and working toward the first letter of the signature.

Watch for faulty forging common when a forger is under surveillance . . . Concentrating too hard instead of relaxing. Keeping a slack wrist and rigid fingers. Trying to copy the general "wave" of signature—ups and downs—rather than crossing T's and dotting the I's correctly.

If still not satisfied ask endorser to endorse it a third time.

Check with payer on telephone as to authenticity before cashing check.

Explain that endorser must be identified by a known and trusted customer of your business (or bank) establishment.

Ask questions about the check and its passer. (This alone can make a suspect stranger nervous enough to leave.)

SIMPLEST TEST: Offer stranger an ink pad and ask him to put a thumbprint on back of check (most criminals dread fingerprints).

2. See the red light when innocuous identification—fishing li-

cense/library ticket/driving permit—is all the endorser can produce. Such ID is meaningless (as is any a criminal is likely to produce).

3. An endorser trying to rush you is often a sure sign there is something wrong with the check.

GOLDEN RULES: KNOW YOUR ENDORSER . . . AND don't cash checks that show signs of alteration; be sure a check is drawn by a individual concern or individual at an actual bank; never endorse a check for anyone you don't know to be reliable; be wary of certified checks or cashiers checks (they could still be bogus); don't cash checks for juveniles (not legally responsible and they may be runners for a forgery setup); beware of a stranger who offers a check for more than the amount of his or her purchase (see THE COZY, p. 315).

SIXTH SENSE

Let your sixth sense rule when a temporary secretary may not be what she seems (is she using shorthand as a shortcut to robbery of not-so-petty cash? or stealing trade secrets?).

TEMPS agencies big or small can't check everyone 100 per cent. The failure rate among the thousands of temps supplied by agencies IS small, but there are always exceptions. Make sure you don't lose out.

Warning signals: Temp seems too good to be true; works hard/ efficiently/enjoyably; early to work, late to leave; qualifies for bonus with sheer effort; excellent genuine references (see also THE FIREPROOF, p. 326).

Double-check on temp (and agency that supplied her; a few don't ask too many questions about temp's past). Read the references *yourself*; a trustworthy person won't object to providing credentials or telling you where to turn for reference.

If reading between lines of reference is difficult because it is written in noncommittal terms, phone. Or pay a call. A lot can be said in conversation than can't be written down.

But don't treat this personal check as top security clearance, or be too obviously suspicious. Let a new employee break herself in. (Employers most likely to be gypped by temps and new staff are usually owners of small or medium-sized businesses and shops. Big businesses tend to screen new staff more efficiently.) Never fall for "she-looks-up-to-the-job" line of thinking when short of staff.

Resist giving a key to a temp so that she can let herself in when she arrives before other staff . . . letting her handle mail/petty cash/confidential matters concerning deliveries, contracts or cash routine . . . allowing HIM to drive a delivery van with thousands of dollars' worth of goods in his care . . . asking him (or her) to bank a large check etc.

Remember too: security experts feel bugging devices are often old hat when an attentive ear in the right spot picks up more information than a tiny radio transmitter in matchbox/sugar cube/hat ever will.

And temps can walk into the relevant room at 5:31 P.M., slip a confidential file under a coat and wander off with the last of staff.

Always remember: a temp may have been bribed to betray you.

SNIFF A FIRE

IF your own store/office/shop catches fire . . . lead everyone outside quickly and calmly. Then cut the draft fanning flames by closing all windows—if possible—and doors. If an electrical appliance is ablaze, switch off current before dousing flames (never fling water on burning oil—it spreads flames). Last resort: Even if flames force you out of window high off ground, there will often be a ledge/balcony/pillar to cling to until help comes. If quite near the street and you *have* to jump, see THE ADDICT (p. 266).

While getting people to safety, forget salvage of office files/store invoices/key papers. People come first.

Let nothing distract you from calling the fire department immediately. If you can't, get somebody else trustworthy to do it. Check that he has. (People fail to raise fire fighters because they are mistakenly convinced someone else has done so.)

Don't try to put the fire out unless you are certain you can do so without risk to yourself.

NEVER enter a burning building by yourself. This is a calculated risk for firemen, certain danger for YOU.

Don't do any do-it-yourself fire fighting when NOT sure what materials are on fire: nitric acid and hydrochloric acid = poisonous fumes; cyanides form prussic acid gas if hit with water; magnesium sometimes explodes when doused.

Avoid throwing stones through windows to let in air—drafts fan flames fast.

Only open window to call for help, if trapped, when door is firmly shut; otherwise the draft created sucks fire *into* the room.

FIRE PREVENTION in small commercial or industrial premises is best based on advice from the fire-prevention officer of the nearest fire department or the fire surveyor from your insurance company. Advice is free, accurate and vital. Only the specialist fire fighter knows the dangers of new materials/chemicals/ products a small businessman may be harboring in fire-prone conditions as well as 1,001 other fire-risks that go unnoticed daily.

The Grocer (Prudent)

Pays attention to detail.

His watchword is DON'T LET THEM GET AWAY WITH IT —the criminals who do their late-night shopping after the store is shut. Or any other lawbreaker.

Security is THE key.

CHECKS

See also THE SPECULATOR, p. 332, and THE AWED, p. 310.

Let grip on pen (never a pencil) remind YOU of mental grip to take when writing checks in the city. Don't be careless.

Tightly fill every line and space on the check so nothing can be added later. Begin writing at extreme left of every line. Fill in blank spaces, as at end of printed lines, by drawing several lines through them.

ALSO slant the word "and" after the dollar total to make it difficult to incorporate it into another word.

Bad hands at writing should make checks legible by printing.

Checks intended for business concerns should have full business name spelled out. Words like "Company"/"Corporation"/ "Incorporated" can be changed too easily from their shortened form. (A forger who steals checks made out to a company will generally try to alter a check so it looks as if made payable to an individual—then he forges the necessary personal identification to back up a fraudulent transaction.)

Go over your bank statements to make sure checks haven't been meddled with.

You are guilty in law of negligence if you fail to notify your bank of a fraud "within a reasonable time." And are therefore responsible for covering such losses.

Guard canceled checks and deposit slips. Check artists know the value of such documents as models in making fraudulent checks and as copies for signatures. Keep them under lock and key; forgers hire burglars to steal these vital aids from offices/ shops/stores.

Lock up company checks and check writers for same reason.

Pensions/dividend/payroll checks are a target for a criminal using forged credentials (see also THE COZY, p. 315).

SHOPBREAKING

Contact police. Ask local crime-prevention officer to inspect premises. Or request insurance company to send burglary surveyor (whose services are also free). They will advise on how to make your premises safe.

All kinds of shops and stores are vulnerable. Although tobacconists/radio dealers/liquor sellers and jewelers are favorite targets (stock is valuable and easily fenced), any business premises not properly safeguarded is likely to be hit by burglars.

Yet most shopbreaking can easily be prevented. Much is

spontaneous, disorganized theft committed by unskilled thieves. The following straightforward precautions will persuade such criminals to leave your property alone and look elsewhere. (Many of these safeguards cost nothing; others are comparatively inexpensive. All are within range of the most modest-sized store owner.)

MAIL SLOTS

Flap on door requires a spring + strong wire cage on inside of door to prevent errant fingers reaching for the lock or bolts. Cage must be bottomless so that no one can steal mail from outside.

DOORS

Sixteen-gauge steel sheet well screwed-in will beef up hollow-cored or thin wood-paneled doors on the inside. Stout wood or metal doors ARE vital (see also THE ADDICT, p. 266).

Glass-paneled doors need (1) georgian wire glass (it doesn't shatter like toughened glass) and (2) backing up on the inside with iron or steel grills or with flat steel bars spaced 4 inches apart.

Don't have back or side doors glazed; solid 2-inch-thick timber is safer.

DOOR HINGES

Outside hinges must have unremovable hinge pins. Hinges need nonretractable screws.

DOOR FRAMES

If it is impossible to replace or buttress the frame, use brace or bar locks so that the efficiency of the lock does not depend on a weak door frame.

Mail slots should be well sprung. Inside cage should be bottomless.

BACKYARD DOOR AND SURROUNDS

Solid doors in walls or fences require locking bars secured by STRONG close shackle padlocks with hardened steel cases (which are highly pick-resistant). File away coded identification numbers before using.

Fit inspection panel to door so police can enter.

Grill gates are best in a solid backyard wall; check they can't be lifted off their hinges.

Chain link fences rimmed with barbed wire are more burglar-proof than walls—they are difficult to climb and, like grill gates, are see-through.

NEVER, if you can possibly avoid it, have back (and back-yard) door as the one you leave premises by.

Overhead roll-down doors are best secured with electric power OR inside slide bolts on the bottom bar and then fixed with pick-resistant cylinder locks.

Accordion/sliding/swinging garage doors can be electrically operated or locked from inside by tough bolt, side bar, cross bar or rod with strong cylinder lock.

Use a powerful padlock (see earlier) or jimmy-and-pick-resistant lock if such a door is the only way IN and OUT of premises.

DOOR LIGHTING

Backyard and recessed doorways must be well lit. So should doors in alleyways.

Ensure switches are hidden. Wires are protected. Lighting fixtures are placed high. And dud bulbs are replaced.

DOOR LOCKS

NECESSITIES . . . *jimmy-resistant locks with pick-resisting cylinders* (see THE GUARDIAN, p. 246): spring latches used MUST incorporate dead bolts; front door needs two mortise locks, one at top and one at base if door isn't designed to take a central lock; THAT central lock, when applicable, should be double-cylinder deadlock keyed from outside and operated inside by turn knob; double doors are safest when NOT used as final exit door (when they are have two bolts fitted flush to edge of the door that shuts first); WHEN jimmyproof Segal or bar lock is unusable on single door, use best vertical dead-bolt lock you can afford; IF glass panes are near lock . . . double-cylinder deadlock IS a must (this means lock needs key for opening from inside as well as from the outside). INTERIOR DOOR LOCKS: fit them bottom and top with 10-inch bolts—mortise bolts, as shown, are best.

WHEN YOU CLOSE THE SHOP/STORE/OFFICE DON'T

ONLY CHECK ALL DOORS AND WINDOWS ARE SE-
CURELY LOCKED AND BOLTED, BUT ALSO THAT NO-
BODY IS HIDING—IN LAVATORY/BASEMENT/BROOM
CUPBOARD ETC.

BASEMENTS

Bolt and padlock flaps over hatchways from inside. If on weedy
side, strengthen with 16-gauge sheet steel well screwed home.
Padlock gratings with toughest chains.

Local fire laws dictate certain precautions: slide bars, barrel
bolts, padlocks, crossbars, etc. Check.

Lock and bolt basement doors. Test for strength.

ROOFS

Axle grease/barbed wire/spikes or anticlimb paint on drain-
pipes. ALL (especially a combination) = strong deterrent to prevent thief from gaining roof *in first instance*. Lock ladders away
with chain and padlock as well as inside a locked door.

Stripe skylights with ¾-inch mild steel bars 4 inches apart, cross
tied every 2 feet and, where possible, cemented to brickwork on
inside rather than simply screwed to the window frame.

WINDOWS

Check accessibility of all windows other than display windows.
Too near ground? Within reach of ledges? Near some other takeoff point (tree/wall/roof)? Leading on to fire escape (most vulnerable of all)?

If answer is YES: stripe accessible windows—except display
windows and fire-escape-adjoining windows—as for fanlights and
rooflights with metal bars.

Don't have more back windows than are needed for ventilation
and light (new shops should have back and side windows too high
up to look into, too narrow to squeeze through and/or made of
glass bricks). Brick up all unnecessary windows. Never rely on
ordinary window fasteners; fit window locks, preferably key-

operated. Or use mesh/folding gates/bars or heavy shutters. (If installed on outside, securings must = dome-headed flush bolts; and windows hinged from outside.

WINDOWS ADJOINING FIRE ESCAPE: Fasten with key-operated inside lock (see THE GUARDIAN, p. 246).

DISPLAY WINDOWS: Take valuable merchandise out of windows overnight. Swap with dummies. Mesh steel grill is necessary when goods are left in windows and showcases. Link display windows with burglar alarm system. Check with crime-prevention officer which protective glass is most likely to withstand hammering/chipping/splintering with heavy implements, Molotov cocktails, etc. (glass technology constantly makes improvements). Important notes:

1. Let police see in. Don't draw blinds. Don't stack merchandise too tightly/high/far.

2. Slide folding metal gates across front of store windows (and even already locked doors) and along top and bottom slide tracks, lockable with at least one powerful padlock.

3. Protect windows (and doors) inside recessed entryways with a folding gate or gate that runs straight across entryway so nobody can gain cover there.

With all three points, see also THE FIREPROOF (p. 326).

NEIGHBORING PREMISES

Check shopbreaker can't steal in from next door (at any level from basement to roof).

BURGLAR ALARMS

Buy the best you can afford (insurance companies insist on them and will advise). Properly installed burglar alarm will secure your property for the 16 hours out of 24 when it is closed—and most vulnerable.

Ensure arrangements are made by contract to keep it maintained in efficient condition. And regularly serviced and tested by manufacturers.

BEST TYPE: Silent alarm that calls for aid from central station, whether robbery *or* burglary. All entry points (doors/windows/transoms, etc.) are wired so they can be tripped by an intruder AND alarm bars/mats/buttons are positioned for storekeeper to press during armed hold-up. (Danger of local alarm that triggers siren/bell/shrieker *on* premises: NOISE + PANIC = GUNMAN SHOOTING before help arrives at your store/office/shop.)

Silent central station alarm systems are costly.

Alternative: Use existing alarms that raise the alarm on premises and improvise improvements.

But these are only efficient when you are clued-up to possible deficiencies.

There are two kinds in particular, that go together.

1. Stick decal inside window by door warning store IS alarm protected. Back it up with loud alarm—Freon-powered hooter, say. Burglar who has now had two warnings will run rather than risk possibility of store *also* being linked to central station. Note: Burglar must not be able to see the alarm (for obvious reasons). AND—

2. Rig silent alarm on buddy principle . . . neighboring merchant has quiet buzzer activated by buttons you have in premises and/or on person. You do the same for him by housing his alarm buzzer. Alarm is silent on scene of emergency as button is pressed AND neighbor has time to scan crisis from street and raise help (as well as remember car license plates, descriptions of villains, etc.).

PERSONNEL (AND PERSONAL) PROTECTION

Devise secret code whereby first employee to arrive in morning signals that all is well within—by raising or lowering a blind, say.

Stagger arrival times.

Caution employees never to discuss money shipments or payrolls in public places.

Have special section in cash drawer to hold package of "bait money" of which serial numbers have been recorded. Main purpose, however, is to have *something* to hand to hold-up man if cash register has just been emptied (gunman may shoot out of spite).

Observe loiterers outside—they may be casing your premises. Call the police. (Criminals CAN act furtively, hanging about until streets and stores are empty . . . a man who is keen to escape notice will often swivel his eyes from side to side, and try harder to look unconcerned when somebody passes by.)

Make it a rule *never* to reopen a shop or store after closing time, NOT even when that afternoon you found a handbag on the shop floor put it in a safe place in case the owner returned to claim it. Danger of a con trick followed by a mugging if you open up to the late-arriving handbag "owner."

Give gentle hints when an employer works YOU late and doesn't provide transport home. *Any* female is vulnerable returning home late from work in city centers.

SAFETY EQUIPMENT

Bolt down valuable office/store/shop equipment—electric typewriters, adding machines, dictating machines, TV sets, cash registers, vending machines, Xerox copiers, etc.—with bolt-and-lock combinations sold at locksmiths (seven-inch tumbler cylinder has matching cylinder-shaped key which secures piece of moveable equipment).

PERSONAL PROPERTY

Choose a responsible member of staff to see employees DON'T leave purses on desks even if it is just to step out to the water cooler; DON'T leave desks unlocked on going to lunch; DON'T leave coats on chair backs when out of room (and wallets remain inside pockets); AND to ask strangers their business (petty thieves with assurance and good excuse move freely in many business premises—until questioned).

Repairmen are common sights around offices. Nobody pays much attention to a competent-looking visitor carrying a toolkit and a sheaf of orders.

Telephone repairmen, typewriter mechanics, window cleaners,

executives are all cover for thieves who regard city office blocks as great for daylight robbery.

When theft happens: cut suspicion of each other among staff by giving it's-possible-it's-an-outsider-theory as possibility.

KEY SECURITY

Only hand keys to responsible members of staff. Never allow keys kept on the premises to be hung in an unlocked cabinet or left inside locks during the working day. Risk—that a rogue employee might "borrow" or copy the key with robbery in view.

Individuals should NOT be allowed to carry store/shop/company key on personal key ring. NOR tag them with personal or company's identification.

Skip master-keyed systems when, for example, you occupy an office in a master-keyed building. Hand the management sealed key of your own lock. Organize own cleaning scheme. IF you comply with master-keying, bolt down all moveable equipment (see above) and lock up all materials, goods, etc.

If an important key vanishes (or doubtful employee leaves), change the relevant lock cylinders.

ACCOUNTING ACCOUNTS

Don't leave one employee in charge of any one book; the more people there are accounting, the less chance of embezzlement.

PROTECTIVE SCREENS

Use toughened glass screen on receptionist area/shop counter/ etc. where possibility (high crime-rate area of city) of ammonia raid hold-up exists. (Commercial ammonia, squirted from plastic liquid bottle has 30-foot range and ability to strip desk varnish/ wall paint/eyesight—*unless washed out immediately.*)

RECEIPT OF GOODS

Ensure staff is as careful as you when (1) checking goods on delivery; (2) rechecking in storeroom; (3) making spot checks yourself; (4) NEVER allowing visitors from outside into stock-room or receiving bay without good reason and never alone; (5) locking up stockroom and bay when not in use.

SHOPLIFTING

Vulnerable times are mealtimes, coffee breaks, holiday times when full staff is not on duty. And just before closing time when staff is concentrating on going home.

Broadcast deterrents: observation apertures, fisheye mirrors, decals warning of TV cameras/electronic tags/store detectives (even when they don't exist). DO adjust mirrors, remote control TV cameras, etc. whenever displays are moved, counters shifted and boxes stacked in aisles.

Stick valuable/portable/desirable merchandise out of reach. Or have efficient staff watch over it. Or, best of all, do both.

Lastly: Never leave unused checkout aisles open; don't keep small expensive items in the open or near a door where thief can run out; use hard-to-snap plastic string and tough-to-tear plastic tags on all merchandise.

PAYROLL PROTECTION

Pay staff by check/credit transfer. Sell staff idea that this is safest measure—they must agree before you do it.

Seek advice on payment from bank.

BANKING

YOUR BANK = safest place for cash. NEVER make it a habit to stash cash in a shop. Experienced criminals know all the hiding places.

Best way to bank cash . . . employ specialist security firm: many offer reasonably priced cash-ferrying services. Delivery is guar-anteed; risks of worry/injury/death cut.

Make frequent daily bank deposits when business (and cash intake) is thriving.

If you HAVE to move cash yourself, wonder. What will happen if YOU are hit on the head/maimed/murdered on your way to the bank? What will you tell the family of employee(s) who become victims?

Foil would-be cash grabbers by thwarting them in the TWO things they rely on.

1. SURPRISE: expect thieves to snatch takings when it seems least likely; don't feel self-conscious about scanning people/cars/ Santas with suspicion; be on guard, suspicious-to-the-end. NEVER believe that, because you are on home ground, you are safe; if you have any reason for suspicion, inform police in advance; vary route/times/cash-carrier constantly, never announcing your intention of moving cash to the bank beforehand. (DON'T be cute: stowing greenbacks and coins in pockets while carrying empty cash bag you plan to hand to cash-snatchers— possible reprisal when they find it empty. Pack bills in pockets— see THE CANNY, p. 40, and THE LEERY, p. 47—and put cash in ordinary suitcase. Or in thief-resistant waistcoat or specially designed bag approved by your insurers. Don't use carrier bags/brown paper parcels/shopping baskets; they attract sneak thieves.)

2. SPEED: Delay urgency with which cash raiders inject the GO/ GO/GO that helps them. Lock all doors on premises when counting large sums of money; don't take cash due for bank deposit from safe unless carrier and escort(s) are present; see sidewalk and street are clear before carrying cash to car from shop AND ensure a strongbox or container is clamped to floor or trunk of car; SEND TWO RELIABLE/FIT/WARY MEN WHEN CASH HAS TO BE WALKED TO THE BANK; send third person when extra large sums are toted—to walk 15 yards behind and keep eyes open; ALWAYS have cash carriers met by another party (phone call ensures this is done); be extra careful over the first and last 100 yards when NOT met; when met, middle yardage covered needs extra caution; avoid quiet streets; face oncoming traffic (see THE PLODDING, p. 170) to avoid attack from car pulling in behind; don't bank at night unless essential (the bank's night deposit safe, however, is more secure than your own premises).

SAFES

FAIL-SAFE STANDBYS:

1. SCRAP OLD/CHEAP/TINNY SAFES. They pinpoint cash/ securities/records, but are easily cracked; they tempt you to hide cash elsewhere because you know the safe will draw attention of burglar, but this means he takes revenge on finding safe is cashless by tossing in a match and burning your records AND/ OR still finds cash you hid in bucket/cistern/file.

2. BUY COMMERCIAL MONEY SAFE or FIRE-RESISTANT-SAFE-WITH-MONEY-CHEST-BOLTED-INSIDE for daytime use. Limit nighttime use to protection of company records from fire AND guarding minimum amount of cash needed to open up business the following morning. Good sales these days are made from EDR (explosive and drill-resisting) and TDR (torch and drill-resisting) alloys. These are nonferrous metal compounds full of diamond-tough chunks. And the locks can be incredible. The safecracker tries to drill and smashes a pane of glass inside the lock that activates a cord that retriggers the locks. Similar things happen if an explosive is detonated.

   (Clamp less-than-a-ton-weight safe to floor. Display in full view through front window. Illuminate at night to spotlight attempted theft. Don't locate against back or side wall when burying it into concrete—it is easy to chop through the wall from the next building without tripping burglar alarms.)

3. SAFE WITH COMBINATION AS WELL AS KEY LOCK IS A SOUND PLAN: Key and code can then be given to different members of staff. ALSO consider safe employing locking device that neither store owner nor employee can open alone—it needs both present together (the chances are a holdup man discovering this will rake the loose change from the cash register instead).

   Drop-depository-safe-with-baffled-slot-on-top (it is sunk into concrete) is excellent deterrent. Cash is dropped through slot as received. Only away-from-premises owner or security guard can open the safe. Display a notice stating that none of the available staff can open the safe to warn-off a potential hold-up robber.

4. SAFEGUARD KEYS AND COMBINATIONS. . . . Watch people who know combinations and change combination numbers IMMEDIATELY when anybody leaves your employ; seal duplicate

safe key in envelope and deposit at your bank; never leave safe
combination on day comb AND—don't leave safe key on the
premises in a drawer/paperclip box/"safe place"; don't write
down safe combination *anywhere* on business premises or make
up a safe's combination number from any notation based on a
sequence of numerals to be found written down on the premises
. . . birthday date, private telephone number, license plate number, etc. Keep the combination number in your head. (EXCEP-
TION: Write it on a card and put in bank safe-deposit box in
case of death, loss of memory, etc.)

5. KEEP ON YOUR TOES. . . . Change combination number occasionally when safe's combination dial has multispins (constant
use means the dial tightens as you reach each combination number); ALWAYS stand facing safe's combination dial, never sideways—you can be spied on easier.

CASH REGISTERS

Transfer contents of your till into the safe before too much
cash accumulates. Only hold enough money in cash register for
current transactions at any one time—no more than $50, say.

Keep till locked unless in use (electric cash registers can be
controlled by a floor mat which keeps them locked unless you
stand on it).

Bolt down cash registers.

INSURANCE

Insure premises BEFORE you open up a new city business.

Burglars watch out for small—and medium-sized stores/shops/
offices about to open up.

Workmen, delivery men, new staff are strangers. There is no
regular routine. The resulting chaos is an ideal time for a burglar
to strike before opening day.

The Illogical (Logical)

Don't fall for solutions which the majority of us cling to when
in trouble. Consequently, because instinct—as opposed to practiced intuition (see THE SPECULATOR, p. 332)—is only too

often wrong in survival situations, they fare better than those who follow the norm.

In this context the ILLOGICAL are LOGICAL. Apparently eccentric behavior is not always wrong simply because it is different from standard practice (for WHOSE standard do we follow when in danger?).

HANGOVER

WHEN you are suffering from a throbbing hangover and have to face *essential* business confrontation/interview/task. . . .
USUAL REACTION = cup of black coffee (not enough to do benefit); Alka-Seltzer (aspirin contained harms empty stomach); more alcohol (postpones final reckoning; creates confusion; can smell).
SURVIVAL LOGIC:

1. DRINK SEVERAL CUPS OF COFFEE/TEA/FRUIT JUICE AND SWEETEN PREFERENCE WITH SUGAR (NOT SACCHARIN) EVEN WHEN YOU USUALLY GO WITHOUT.
2. EAT HONEY. THE SUGAR HELPS BURN AWAY ALCOHOL CAUSING PAIN AND STRAIN IN BRAIN (ALCOHOL SENDS AN ABNORMALLY HIGH FLOW OF BLOOD THROUGH THE BRAIN, SWELLING BLOOD VESSELS).
3. TRY ASPIRIN.
4. KEEP DRINKING (WELL-SALTED BEEF BROTH ALSO HELPS DEHYDRATION).

BOMBED

But WARNED (by telephone).
USUAL REACTION: Office switchboard operator screams and runs for the door when she gets a call that a bomb is about to go off.
SURVIVAL LOGIC: Ask what time the bomb is due to explode (NOT a daft question as caller may give some indication). When no answer, get everyone outside the building.
Ask these questions when there IS time:
WHERE IS THE BOMB LOCATED?

HOW BIG IS THE BOMB?
WHAT TYPE OF TRIGGERING DEVICE DOES IT HAVE?
IS IT A BLACK POWDER OR A NITROGLYCERIN BOMB?
WHY BOMB US?
Jot down replies. Note time/sex/stutter-or-lisp-etc. of caller's
voice.
Telephone police. Stay on line for their briefing.

BOMBED

NO WARNING.
USUAL REACTION: Stupid mistakes on first sight of the
bomb, which could be anything from a length of lead pipe
plugged at both ends to a brown paper parcel ticking/humming/
plugged-into-power-point. Typical reactions . . . picking up bomb
what-the-hell's-this-?-style . . . bolting for door . . . copying TV-
film where bomb is chilled with mixture of CO_2 fire extinguisher
foam plus director's whisky bottle alcohol (resulting icy slush
freezes battery so no spark) YET this wouldn't prevent mercury
or acid-timed device exploding.
SURVIVAL LOGIC:
1. TAKE LONG/LONG/LONG LOOK TO SEE IF OBJECT YOU
   SUSPECT IS BOMB (at least a minute).
2. THINK (any extremist bomb attacks lately in skyscraper office
   blocks? on whom? do you qualify?).
3. DON'T TOUCH (may be designed to go off then).
4. DON'T PANIC (people imagine bombs everywhere once one is
   suspected).
5. GO CLOSER TO LOOK AND LISTEN (is object really out of
   place? is it in place where it shouldn't be, say by a costly computer? does it go tick tock or is it in the path of a light beam
   which, if broken, triggers bang?).
IF YOU DO DECIDE OBJECT IS DEFINITELY WEIRD . . .
1. OPEN WINDOWS AND DOORS OF ROOM (to dampen ex-
   plosion's force: blast is efficient only when triggered in close con-
   finement—tea can be brewed on a block of TNT when it is NOT
   confined).

2. GET EVERYONE IN OFFICE (AND NEXT DOOR) OUT-SIDE (don't create a big disturbance in the building—bomb damage is not as extensive as people think).

3. CALL POLICE FROM OUTSIDE PHONE (while evacuating office turn tables on their sides to act as blast-baffles, or, if the object is very small, cover it with a thick mat as a blast-sup-pressor).

4. KEEP GUARD AT END OF CORRIDOR UNTIL POLICE ARRIVE (don't broadcast why).

5. DRAW MENTAL PICTURE OF WHAT "BOMB" LOOKED LIKE (position, any wires, dial with pointers, if crudely made type of container—bottle/box/tube, etc. . . . ALL help).

PUMPED

Greenbacks taped beneath dressing table drawers? Gems in safe behind the oil painting? Holiday abroad? Evenings at the theater? Weekend beach parties on Fire Island?

USUAL REACTION: Telling of material possessions worth telling—*and* personal routine when exotic enough—to hairdresser, jeweler, beauty shop owner or regular shopping acquaintances who may then trade confidences (oneupmanship is involved).

SURVIVAL LOGIC: Never tell anyone anything which can help a burglar. The burglar's problem is NOT to break into a house, but to choose which house has the most valuables; NOT to crack a safe, but to decide which safe is going to be worth-while; NOT to ransack just any duplex apartment, but to find one with nobody at home . . . Tell people such vital details and you may tell a burglar (he may even overhear).

JOSTLED

Pack of shoppers barge in as you inspect best china/expensive necklace/crystal goblet by the counter in a busy department store.

USUAL REACTION: Holding on two-handed so you don't drop the goods; remonstrating on Who-do-you-think-you're-shov-ing lines to people nearest you . . . who could be members of pickpocket outfit.

SURVIVAL LOGIC: Watch your wallet; expect jostling especially in central shopping areas on Thursday/Friday evenings when pay day comes and shops stay open longer for the thousands with weekly pay packets; *THINK pockets.*

BLACKMAILED

Few people have nothing to hide.
USUAL REACTION: Pay up rather than face disgrace/music/comeuppance.
SURVIVAL LOGIC:

1. REFUSE TO PAY
2. GO STRAIGHT TO POLICE
3. DON'T WEAKEN

It's the only way to beat a blackmailer, who banks on your fear. Pay up now and you will always be paying.

ROUGH SHADOWED

A frightener used by the blackmailer to clinch the victim's fear.
USUAL REACTION: Submitting to blackmail when everywhere you go a stranger-in-dark-glasses goes too . . . brushing past you in different streets; nudging your elbow in a department store and, ten minutes later, waving at you from a car stopped at traffic lights; standing ahead of you in line at the bank and, later that day, sitting in the barber's chair before you.
SURVIVAL LOGIC: NOT giving in to this menacing persecutor. Go to the police.

ROBBED

If your wallet is stolen from your pocket, or purse vanishes from top of shopping basket/top of supermarket trolley/top of counter when you went to fitting room in clothing store. . . .
USUAL REACTION: Relief AND willingness to comply when

telephoned by stranger who says wallet/purse has been found. SURVIVAL LOGIC: Be suspicious.

Don't allow the phone call to stop you from (1) informing loss control office of credit card company(ies) of loss of credit card(s) or if in town hotfooting it there with written notification that credit card has been stolen; (2) informing bank of loss of checks; (3) changing locks of doors at home.

(Thief will phone to say he has found your wallet and has given it to the store or supermarket manager who is sending it on—a ruse to delay your informing the credit card company so the criminal can use your card carte blanche. OR the thief poses as store employee phoning to say your handbag has been found, will you come now and collect. Then he ransacks your home while you go to the store; your address and front door key were in the bag. Victims are so relieved to hear their property has been recovered they never even question how the caller knew an unlisted number.)

HELD UP

At gunpoint in bank or supermarket . . .
USUAL REACTION: *Panic.*
SURVIVAL LOGIC:

1. DO EXACTLY AS TOLD.
2. DO EXACTLY AS TOLD.
3. DO EXACTLY AS TOLD.

WHEN TERRIFIED: *Act* (by noting description of hold-up man): keep calm (excitement makes you forget): remember the 4 W's—WHO/WHAT/WHERE/WHEN (forget WHY, which is police task); remember any scars or distinguishing marks (better than describing clothing, which can be changed); picture small details—bank-robber-spits-on-mezzanine, etc.—when impossible to see all that is happening; pinpoint mannerisms (heister gnaws inside of little finger); take note of any attempt at disguise . . . *write down the details as soon as possible after the raid* (draw a diagram to help police identikit artist).

The Hard One

Never look it. Hardness, not to be confused with muscle, is a strength chained in the brain. And goes unnoticed until the chips are down. It also helps stop them falling.

HARD ONES are calculating and ruthless. They let nothing stand in their way when once convinced that what is right is right —for them.

Like a misleading appearance.

CRYBABY

Be tearful (you can't help it when unhappy), but be extra sharp under that pipe-smoking/gum-chewing/handkerchief-clenching exterior, *because such habits do help you to think straight when tearstained.*

REMEMBER:

1. Do anything which helps you concentrate when, perhaps in a long period of unhappiness, you are vulnerable in business areas.
2. Count a miserable love life as WARNING of direct inducement to shoplifting, even though you have adequate funds.
3. Steel yourself *beforehand* to concentrate on decisions to be made shortly in shops/banks/offices . . . especially when unhappy.

Concentration aid. . . . Don't eat a heavy meal before decision-making (shopping/banking/wheel-'n'-dealing); blood is diverted to the stomach and digestive organs making the brain sluggish. Eat a light meal before shopping—a partly full stomach cuts down spending.

BABY-FACED

Be cherubic/beaming/beatific (happy nature will always show through facially), but inject titanium into your soul when headed for busy commercial and financial centers of cities.

Carry a mental scowl. Take a brass face mask. Anticipate rudeness, bullying, impersonality-to-the-point-of-insult from employees in banks/offices/shops.

Be ready to give as good as you get. Some kind of reply, no matter how feeble, will give at least SOME satisfaction in large department stores where monstrously bad service can rankle and upset you all day.

Not everyone can copy a swagger suggesting a chauffeur-driven limousine doubleparked round the corner, but TRY not to be bullied for the sake of your own morale.

TIMID AS A MOUSE

Go gingerly (you can't do otherwise when genuinely scared of big cities, so don't try), but nurse a lion's roar for when YOUR rights are questioned by department store staff. Know them.

1. DO YOUR SUPERMARKET SHOPPING BEFORE VISITING OTHER SHOPS SO YOUR SHOPPING BAG IS SEEN TO BE EMPTY WHEN YOU PAY AT THE CHECKOUT.
2. NEVER PUT ANYTHING FROM THE SHELVES STRAIGHT INTO YOUR OWN SHOPPING BAG.
3. ALWAYS KEEP RECEIPTS SO THAT IF YOU SHOP AT ANOTHER SUPERMARKET AND ARE ASKED WHERE YOU GOT THE PURCHASES IN YOUR BAG YOU WILL BE ABLE TO PROVE YOU BOUGHT THEM ELSEWHERE.
4. IF YOU WANT TO GET A BETTER LOOK AT GOODS NEARER DAYLIGHT, GET PERMISSION TO GO TO THE WINDOW BEFORE MOVING. IF NO ONE TO ASK, LEAVE GOODS EXACTLY WHERE THEY ARE.
5. REMIND YOURSELF THE LITTLE OLD LADY OR YOUNG MAN IN LEVIS STANDING BY YOU IS PROBABLY A STORE DETECTIVE.
6. INSIST YOU HAVE ALL GOODS WRAPPED.
7. DON'T PANIC IF YOU ARE STOPPED BY STORE DETECTIVE. SAY THAT YOU ARE INNOCENT AND GIVE YOUR EXPLANATION. THEN DEMAND THAT IT BE WRITTEN DOWN AND SIGN IT.
8. IF DESPITE THIS, YOU END UP BEING CHARGED, GO TO A LAWYER. AND DEFEND YOUR NAME BEFORE

JUDGE AND JURY. Do not plead guilty to something you did not do. It can never be worth it to save you bother.

WALLFLOWER

Fight shy in public (the natural shrinking violet always will), but fight dirty in private self-analysis concerning how you shop in department stores too.

WORK AT AN HONEST SHOPPER PROFILE EVEN THOUGH YOU HAVE INTEGRITY. BE RUTHLESS IN EXAMINING YOUR BEHAVIOR.

Pass store detectives' appraisal. They are everywhere, zealous and on the watch.

OBSERVE PROFILE:

TOO QUICK? Floorwalkers pay more than a passing glance to quick-stepping shoppers, who may only *seem* to be in a hurry. Honest shoppers saunter in a fairly aimless way in their search among showcases/aisles/counters. Experienced shoplifters tend to be more confident in movement.

TOO FAT? Shoplifters favor loose garments and often look fatter going out than they did coming in. They may wear stolen blouses/shirts/coats beneath a topcoat after a visit to the fitting room. And/or carry special pockets sewn into rainwear that allow many items to be stashed away—especially at Christmas or in bad weather when people bundle bodies into warm clothing.

TOO LADEN? Large zipped bags (may have a zip along the bottom too, through which to shoplift goods on a counter). Lunch boxes. Big purses. Musical instrument cases. Thick books (hollow). Loaded baby carriages. Suitcases or attaché cases (with false sides and bottoms). Gift-wrapped boxes (with a bow on top, but no base so they can be plonked on top of whatever goods are to be stolen). Your own shopping bag held by one handle only (so it gapes and scooped-up items could be dropped in). . . . ALL will focus a floor walker's attention on you.

TOO CANNY? Constant alterations to a shopping list with felt-tipped open could be a cover for the swindler who changes the amount on store price tags with the same type felt pen.

TOO VAIN? Paying too much attention to how you look in convex mirrors of department stores (they can see round corners) can mean you are casing counters for easy thefts—especially on busy Fridays and Saturdays.

Check on all these things, or a floor walker will notice YOU and follow your progress shopping.

CHICKEN

Act yellow (when born to save your own skin you have no other choice), but be red-blooded enough NOT to fear getting your clothing dirty when emergency strikes. NEVER be a victim because your immediate instinct for self-preservation was blocked by images of scratched suede/ripped threads/scuffed buttons.

Do anything to get safe when buildings topple/bullets fly/ flames lick. Dive into the gutter. Wriggle under a car on your elbows and kneecaps. Lie in slush/mud/debris. Fling your body into snow. Press up against oil/soot/excrement-smeared wall. Squeeze between rusting pipes. Crawl over old nails.

DO it immediately in that second where a moment's hesitation makes the difference between life and death. Never think more of your new clothes than you do of what's inside them.

ACID TEST OF THE HARD ONES: THEY NEVER JUS-TIFY SOFT-SOUNDING ACTIONS—THEY KNOW THEIR STRENGTH INSIDE AND HAVE NO NEED TO PROVE IT TO ANYONE ELSE.

Part Six

CITY LUNGS

Parks and Stadiums

11

CITY LUNGS

LOSERS

THERE IS NO escape in the city—not even in the park, zoo, botanic gardens, racetrack or football/baseball/basketball/boxing/ice hockey/boxing/bullfight arenas.

We are as vulnerable in the park as in a laughing, singing, pushing, scrambling tide of sports fans flooding the stadium for the big game. Degenerates who molest children and women lurk in city greenery along with rapists/perverts/muggers. There are sneak thieves everywhere.

Help is never near at hand. Distance separates us from others in the park; proximity to others in a stadium blocks assistance too. Utterly alone and unable to move, we should have looked earlier at the *reasons* why we needed to escape to CITY LUNGS in the first place.

The Chauvinist (Fan)

Need not necessarily bellow his encouragement to make it obvious where he stands in a huge sporting crowd.

The most docile person is still vulnerable when deep inside he roots like hell for his side and breathes defiance and damnation at the enemy.

SIGNS AND SYMPTOMS

Buying chocolate/candy/mints after the game when YOUR team has lost; cigars when they win. Displaying favors with the colors of YOUR team. NEVER going home relatively content if your side loses, even though it was a superb, hard-fought game. Particles of wax on your teeth from the paper cup bitten in the heat of the moment. Yelling "KILLIM KILLIM" when either prizefighter is in truly desperate straits.

CAUSES

Part of every large sports crowd are the brow-beaten and frustrated who can't help taking an eager, vicarious pleasure in being in on the final, soul-destroying blow as a deadly giant (the opposition) is brought crashing down by THEIR team. They hope.

Like the henpecked husband who goes to the ballgame each week just to yell at the referee—because the referee can't shout back—we find in this a safety valve for our emotions.

The aggression which is satisfied in sexual achievement by the potent can be sublimated in the stadium by the impotent. Whether or not this is true of YOU (US), the general crowd fever can still make us victims *when we have also been drinking.*

ILLOGICAL BEHAVIOR

Occasional chauvinists—the at-times-bellicosely-patriotic—who are normally quiet can suddenly show their true feelings at the wrong moments when watching THEIR team/fighter/athlete.

Such excessive patriotism and fierce loyalty can produce talking too much, rowdyism, ultranationalism, brashness, insolence and arrogance in *any* spectator.

The sneer at a stranger who says, "Don't give me that stuff, he's not in the same league as Smith" . . . a wild cheer when your favorite star scores a touchdown . . . an I-told-you-NO laugh as the enemy pass receiver drops the ball . . . a quick shove on the man in front as your team scores again. . . . All are human enough.

By showing our support for one side or the other, however, we draw attention to ourselves. And so fall prey to the madman-fan who is capable of great aggression against ANYbody cheering for the other side.

The ordinary fan doesn't mean to be offensive when he tries to get crowd sympathy for the heroes he glorifies but simply hopes that everyone will yell his team on to victory. But when he says, "Aren't they the greatest?" to the man at his side as his team scores a winning goal, he may get himself into trouble.

It makes little difference if the stadiums in our own city are safe with little record of crowd violence. We have only to visit an "enemy" stadium, possibly in another country, to find the situation completely different.

Our stadiums may be fitted with seats throughout, and crowd behavior *is* infinitely better-mannered when everyone sits. The stadium in a distant city, however, could be largely standing room, and there could be violence everywhere. Look at the police segregation of the fans standing on concrete terraces, the barbed wire fence and deep ditch moating the field of play from spectators.

Nor do we always realize how visiting supporters of an *away* team can run riot in our stadium—so many of them unwashed/unshaven/unsober after a long trip to see their side win.

These are the chauvinists whose week from Sunday to Friday is made or marred by what their team does on Saturday. We can be caught in the middle of their dangerous scuffles. And they *are* dangerous.

Remedy: The Amused, p. 394; The Sleeper, p. 399; The Obsequious, p. 124

The Strolling (Dog-Walkers)

Yearn for company. They accept offers of conversation from strangers in the hope of a little companionship. Good judgment goes by the board until it is too late, both on the open grasslands and among the jumble of rocks/trees/pools in a city park.

SIGNS AND SYMPTOMS

Frequent and erratic interest in a tree/leaf/flower which makes you break stride and pause. Perhaps then walking off in the opposite direction. Letting a dog off the leash as another person approaches. Sometimes walking rapidly, sometimes slowly. Turning back to pick a dandelion, examine an acorn, nibble on a piece of grass . . . having purple lips and not liking blackberries. Sitting at the end of park benches, never in the middle.

CAUSES

City parks give ample opportunity for the lonely. There are so many different people drawn here, and we have a great many excuses for conversation with strangers in the open air.

It is easier for the introverted and shy to start a conversation when watching kites blown/frisbees thrown/grass mown—or ducks on the pond (breadcrumbs flying). There is, too, a communicative atmosphere in a winding path through undulating landscape which suggests a leisurely, contemplative feeling—unlike the direct getting-somewhere-fast sidewalks of the city.

There is more room to move and maneuver into the company of others without making it obvious. The choice of routes is plentiful: paths at upper and lower levels, arches and tunnels between them, steps to all levels and terraces and ramps too. These enable us to reach that attractive and solitary person over there by a way which looks normal.

It all seems safe. The color and scents of the trees, shrubs, and flowers inject a sense of well-being and desert island escapism. In these poetic settings, it is hard to imagine that the person we are about to meet may have VD or serious antisocial problems.

ILLOGICAL BEHAVIOR

By giving others every chance to talk to us in the park, on the common or by the heath we are not in the strongest mental position.

THE MAN AHEAD: WHY is he slowing down by the edge of such a dense patch of secluded underbrush? Especially as he has been matching our stride across the grass even though in front of us. Was he concealing a palmed piece of mirror in the hand he kept wiping his brow with? Is he plotting to drag us into cover and club us with a heavy rock or log?

THE WOMAN WAITING among the dark shady creepered rocks and twisted boughs: Might she accost us? Why is she here when everyone else is out in the sun? Why her fur coat, semblance of good looks and torn tennis shoes? Is she an aging alcoholic hooker who might turn on us if we snub her proposition?

THE BOY IMPLORING for a hand-up to pull him over the top of the large rock he is climbing (which is below the level of our footpath): Could he mug us by tugging hard on our outstretched hand so WE lose balance and crash over the edge? With his companions waiting out of sight just below, he can then rob us at leisure. WHY does he reject our butcher's grip (fingers to fingers) and insist on grabbing our wrist? Is it because it will give him the best pulling advantage? Why is he scrambling on rocks at his age? Why did he ask for our hand so urgently when he is near enough the ground to jump down? People have been robbed in this way. Some have been killed by the fall.

THE MAN FOLLOWING us into the park toilet: Is he a pervert? Why does he take the lavatory compartment next to ours when there are eight other cubicles all vacant?

THE GIRLS RUNNING toward us over the ornamental footbridge: Are they muggers zoning in? Why are they wearing coats on such a hot day—to conceal weapons? Why don't they carry bags themselves? Because they are planning to take ours? Why run over such a narrow bridge? To trap us in this cul-de-sac in time? Why US? Is it because our expensive outfit and large handbag made us a target from afar?

Human flotsam—derelicts, drug users, prostitutes, muggers, rapists—have always sought refuge in the secluded parts of city parks. On benches, under deck chairs and in park shelters, social outcasts sleep rough because they have no place else to go.

There is such effective cover for the abnormal, criminal and mentally deranged. Trees and shrubs are grown densely to absorb the noise from the streets and the heat from tall buildings in summer. But they also give the city wolves a screen ideal for prowling, peering and pouncing.

And we still journey along blissfully forgetful that we are now in a jungle within a jungle.

Remedy: All Chapter 12.

The Determined (Intent)

Have eyes for nothing but the ball/fists/hooves at that moment. The only good-and-evil existing is out there on the pitch/ring/ track; it absorbs them completely. Yet the stadium can be a cauldron of fury, its crowd whipped into a baying mob.

SIGNS AND SYMPTOMS

Keeping your own secret code name, APPLEJACK, in your head; it is electronically programmed into the Off Track Betting (OTB) computer when you place a bet over the telephone (your plastic card carries only your name, account number and the phone number of your OTB telephone operator at home) . . . AND, while 2,000 miles away at the races, spotting dirty racing tactics from afar through binoculars: a jockey SHOUTING, "Get back you bastard," in the last two furlongs of the race to make a young horse challenging him fall back; a jockey LEANING (he squeezes both legs together and leans his body slightly over to barge a rival horse); a jockey WHIPPING another horse's head as if by accident while pretending to strike his own horse's rump; two jockeys SQUEEZING out a third and intended victim by blocking his horse's path.

CAUSES

Horse racing, football, boxing, bullfighting . . . all grip the true aficionado's attention even when he has no money on the result. The fact that he is watching his own thing is enough; it could just as easily be the pop music fan at the concert in the park.

Determination makes us vulnerable: it is the state of mind which allows long-sought desires to overrule good judgment.

Anybody whose desire to reach THE big fight, say—regardless of setbacks, distance from home, difficult hours or even danger to life is likely to be a Loser.

THE DETERMNED use every ounce of energy to reach the event, every fraction of concentration once they do arrive to extract every morsel of enjoyment as they watch and listen— leaving none to sustain the powers of self-preservation.

ILLOGICAL BEHAVIOR

Determination "to do or die" often pushes sportsmen into sub-jecting themselves to the most hazardous pressures to reach and view an event.

Look at how we fail to respond logically to certain pressures in a sporting crowd.

THE BALL GOES BETWEEN THE GOALPOSTS: So WHY, instead of cheering, do we wheel around to face the man standing behind and pat a hand to our wallet? Because we had felt fingers—his?—touch the pocket. But he simply stares past and we leave it at that. Or he answers our unspoken accusation with a look of outraged innocence.

Pickpockets know that they can stand behind a Loser (or even sit) and by resting their arm lightly across his shoulders, quite possible in a tightly packed crowd, feel if his own back muscles tense as they fan his pockets. This gives them time to pull the hand away. Usually an accusatory stare and a check that the wallet is still there will satisfy the Loser.

Another way the pickpocket judges the best time is by watching the red blush creeping up the Loser's neck over the collar and around the ears. A goal scored is the time to try.

THE BALL GOES BETWEEN THE GOALPOSTS AGAIN: And still we don't cheer, but half-turn this time toward the man behind. But WHY only half-turn? And WHY don't we feel for our wallet this time either?

Pickpockets know this will be our illogical reaction the second time they try (and actually take the wallet). Almost every Loser is more afraid of appearing too suspicious by grasping for the wallet a second time than he is of being robbed.

Not that this is by any means the limit of THE DETER-MINED's eccentricity. He will, for example:

BARTER for a ticket and pay twenty times its face value (and even more in street corner "auctions") outside the stadium. And the ticket is found to be forged. The risk of forgeries when buying from a tout is high. So many people are now involved in printing, photography or working with reproduction machinery that they produce the most blatant forgeries—from photocopies of an original ticket with new dates printed on it to inferior reproductions.

Again, THE DETERMINED are not beyond:

A DESPERATE BET at the races to recover the money they have lost. It is as we lose everything that someone takes us aside and asks do we have any insured valuables. If we do have several thousand dollars' worth, it is suggested a burglar—for around $1,000—will provide the evidence of a break-in. By going through our home himself, the police will know that a professional's been there and the insurance company pays. WE, who own the insured goods, are told to hide them somewhere well away from our home and the burglar will put us in touch with a fence to dispose of them for us for an agreed fee (we have to sell, we are advised, the wife would be suspicious if the goods turned up). Yet to tell the enemy that if he attacks you will surrender without resistance—which is what we are doing—is to invite him to attack again and again. And possibly with blackmail too.

Still at the racetrack THE DETERMINED are likely to:

CARRY their money in a buttoned waistband pocket where pickpockets can't find it. But stash their take from a BIG WIN momentarily in their inner jacket breast pocket. And fail to ask in the flush of victory:

WHY the gypsy is so eager to pin a flower on our lapel? Is she a pickpocket who, as she pins with one hand, steals our winnings with the other? Or—

HOW come at the finish of the next race our wristwatch is level with our chin? Is it because pickpockets saw us collect the winnings and followed us? They know someone intent on watching the finish of a horse race can be made to lift his own arm to get it out of the way by the experienced "wire"; a slight pressure will start it and the victim automatically moves it wherever the thief wants him to.

What hope is there for THE DETERMINED when their own momentum sweeps them on to catastrophe? And yet we have only to lift a finger to save ourselves in time.

Remedy: The Adhocist, p. 386; The Sleeper, p. 399; The Canny, p. 40; The Leery, p. 47

The Sunny (Natured)

Flock to the park with their children and dogs because the sun is shining down. But while the sun is the poor man's blanket, it can be a bludgeon which assails the Loser too.

SIGNS AND SYMPTOMS

Knowing which grasses give the juiciest-tasting bottom half inch of stem. A whistle in the pocket made from the hairy stem of beaked parsley (you nick the hollow stem near the end and blow it after placing a finger over the other end). Speaking pond language: "SPLAT" = a fish jumping, "SPLISH" = a kingfisher fishing, "PLOP" = the noise an acorn makes dropping into water. Your footprints always pointing into the sun.

CAUSES

A day of hot sunshine after a week of storms or high winds will draw us to the park as much as the lure of any hot summer Sunday.

A windy city, for example, has been found to cause a great many people to feel uncomfortable, nervous, fidgety and quarrelsome. Strong winds preceding cold fronts or thundery conditions DO slow our reactions and create mild inner tension. Doctors put it down to a form of hypertension of the sympathetic nervous system.

Then out comes the sun . . . and thousands of us to whom sudden contrasts of weather can lift or dash spirits head parkward to relax, cares shelved.

Unrestrained in thinner clothing, we are reborn on grassy swards and leafy slopes. But this gives subdivisions of our character already shown to be potentially harmful in city situations a chance to strike again as the sun goes to our heads.

ILLOGICAL BEHAVIOR

We emerge from the caves of our rooms to stroll, sit or lie in the open air, as did our ancestors. But those ancestors never relaxed their vigilance over what was happening around them. And we do. Our emotions warmed in the sun readily take over.

ULTRABUOYANT (ELATED): We disregard the warning signs of ice on a park pool. It is splitting into sundial-like rays. There are empty moats ringing rocks previously thrown on to the ice and frozen into position. An insulating rug of snow on the ice has blanketed it from the toughening effect of the cold. And running water below has eroded it into a thin shell. Now the snow has melted under the sun and the bare ice's own quality of magnification is boosting the sunlight toward overthaw temperatures. So the ice caves in under our weight. AND the one sign we did see but chose to ignore—*the high fence around the water*—disappears overhead. Yet it showed the main danger: that the water was deep.

BLUE (DESPAIRING): We give way to the sun's warmth and fall asleep on the grass. The result is that our bicycle is stolen. Yet we should have known that when going through a rocky period of home life this can happen: the desire to sleep-and-sleep to escape the bleak reality of marital/financial/career problems that seem insuperable. These will still catch up with us despite the beauty of the park. Sunny months moreover can even increase melancholy. May, for instance, has been found to be the most miserable time of year for many people, despite the uplift ascribed to the advent of spring. This is the peak time for suicides and the type of accident described here.

SUPERHOLY (SELF-RIGHTEOUS): We do not question the preacher in the park.

WHY does he fail to react when the drunk rushes up and punches him hard?

WHY does he go to town on trying to reform the miscreant who is so obviously beyond redemption? WHY should he pass round the hat on behalf of the drunkard when he will immediately drink the proceeds away no matter how much he has promised to tread the straight and narrow? Or are we being too cynical when we suspect them of being in league?

We may lose our wallet to a pickpocket, but only after contributing $5 to the "unfortunate's" welfare.

FREEWHEELING (CASUAL): We spin through the park on a bicycle inviting danger from the bicyclized rapist/mugger/adventurer who draws level with us on a path, knocks us to the ground and drags us into the bushes. Or simply jumps us from the undergrowth, pulls us off the bike, then steals the machine. And we get hurt. Wheels which make us mobile can draw us into trouble more effectively than we can pedal away from it—a fact we forget in the sun.

OVERFRIENDLINESS (PALSY): We are too late in realizing that the dog approaching is savage. We forgot the simple rule: Never touch a strange dog. A large, dangerous dog will always sense fear on our part. He will also sense confidence—which leaks out to him. (Laid out flat, the whole smelling area inside a dog's nose will cover a handkerchief; a man's, a postage stamp.) Alsatians/Dobermans/Rottweilers are all dangerous dogs with a history of park attacks. But Labradors and terriers have bitten strangers too. (It is NOT only postmen who are bitten—because unlike milkmen and delivery men they are not seen to be accepted by the dog's owners.) Even the dog's owner can be savaged. And WE still think, "It can't happen to me, I have a way with animals."

EXHIBITIONISM (SHOWING OFF): We keep well away from the side of the lake in the park because the sloping footpath round the edge is muddy—as we are parading our best clothing and footwear in the sun. Our small child falls in the water (through the railings) and we can't swim. Instead of doing something we stand frozen. Quick thinking can enable even nonswimmers to save lives in the water, but not when they have been too full of thoughts about themselves even to consider the possibility of danger.

There are many more subdivisions of our characters which will lead us toward accidents in the park. No one likes to think about catastrophe while relaxing in the sunshine. But be ready: Intelligent anticipation can save life.

Remedy: All Chapter 12. See also The Cold-Blooded, p. 187; The Obsequious, p. 124; The Fugitive, p. 202

The Tarzan (Active)

Are the Peter Pans who, young or old, must play in the park. Whatever their activity, the more feverishly they indulge it, the higher the chance they can be caught out by the city pirates.

SIGNS AND SYMPTOMS

Good shoes muddy from a spontaneous game of soccer. Softball bruises. Scratched wedding ring/wristwatch crystal/fingernails from scaling rock outcrops. Red-ringed finger from kite flying. Bramble-whipped shins. Newly chipped tooth and splintered toboggan. Bruising on the neck where your head stuck through the oval part of a Barbara Hepworth sculpture. Racing, pushing, sprawling, running, giggling, laughing, crying, shouting, shrieking over swings/seesaws/slides in playgrounds. Dizziness after flying a control line model aircraft round and round on wires.

CAUSES

Parks are the one area where the active and energetic can show off their flair. Anything requiring agility and/or skill in the open air, normally denied us in the grey ravines of the city, can be practiced here.

By doing our own thing in front of a ready audience, we stand out. That's how we want it to be. In a society which has so much uniformity and lack of color, the frustrated extrovert can give a public performance with all the power of a maestro when his hobby/pastime/interest needs a skill, nerve, dexterity or energy lacking in most people.

The older person engaged in his game is as engrossed as tiny children in adventure playgrounds. We become immersed in the action, yet are pleased when people stop to look, no matter how diffident we may try to appear.

But the rotten-most realities of the park are still there.

And indeed may now have drawn that much closer to us, whereas before they might never have singled us out.

ILLOGICAL BEHAVIOR

Tragedy doubles up on us when our behavior shows we can imagine *nothing* sinister nearby.

The mountaineer practicing rock climbing in the park (or one of its monuments, it being the only thing resembling a mountain face within city limits) is flattered to see onlookers watching as he hand-jams his way up a vertical 20-foot crack and forgets his expensive ten-speed bicycle left locked to a tree. It is stolen by a thief who picks the lock while the owner's back is turned a bare 20 yards away.

The newcomer to the city who craves a game of soccer will stand by the park game in progress, kicking back the balls which go out of play. And praying he will be invited to play—which he is. In his delight he overlooks the fact that his coat now goes on top of the goal posts made up of discarded clothing; his wallet is taken—cash/credit cards/ID and all—by one of the spectators whose presence not only spurred him on, but all the other players too.

The senior citizen who competes each Sunday on the park checker tables—a TARZAN in his own mind as he swings through a forest of branch moves—is oblivious to all as his opponent threatens with his king; before he can develop his play he is the one crowned—over the skull by an empty bottle clutched in the hand of the violent derelict who had come lurching up behind.

But SINISTER?

Nothing is more so than the observer of young children on the skating rink/play areas/park paths. And at any time of year, although school vacations are the worst occasions.

Such men haunt wherever the very young gather—and they need NOT be the obvious nasty old men known to park attendants/police/custodians. They can be complete strangers. Well-dressed. Young.

To the child he eventually approaches, the man may be nice-looking. In a youngster's mind what can possibly be evil about a smiling stranger who asks help in finding his lost dog—and offers candy while they go looking? It is practically impossible to convince a child that certain men are bad with the admonition, "Don't speak to strange men."

Yet we rarely consider what we should tell our children that WILL deter them from wandering off and accepting various forms of sick overtures without making them overfrightened.

For it is certain that unless we encapsulate them indoors or accompany them every minute of the day, they will meet not one but several incidents of unnatural and disturbing adult behavior in the city. True, these may be mostly of the mainly harmless forms of exhibitionism or accosting, but the outcome is still unpredictable.

The hair fetishist, for example, who is gripped by an overwhelming desire to touch little girls' hair, can let his obsession run away. He must get some hair. To escape risk of arrest he waits in the greenery of parks, watching children play. And trails one appealing little girl who talks to him. He encourages her to let him unbraid the hair which has had his fantasies throbbing. No sooner has he untied the blond tresses, however, than he produces a pair of scissors to chop off lengths. When the girl begins to cry and cry, he bundles her into the shrubbery and strangles her in his panic.

It is a common experience for many parents in the park to become aware—suddenly—of a stranger's gaze on their four-year-old girl (or boy for that matter). Hearts beat faster when they notice just how sinister that gaze is. We feel color rising in our face too when a small daughter returns from the park with an apple a "nice man" has given her.

It is not only children from large, poor families or disturbed children or educationally subnormal children who prove victims. Nor is it necessarily the nine-year-old girl from a split-up family who misses her father and is resultingly flirtatious with grown-up males.

It can be the little boy with the above-average intelligence who loves to ride the carousel or the appealing twins—also from a loving home atmosphere—who always draw an audience with their parrotry. Both have the outgoing approach and charisma which pull the pervert.

And we still don't search our own selves first as parents in case the cause of a little one's potential assault/rape/death could lie in us. Logically it is surely wise to explore our own senses in this age when respectable and well-adjusted fathers themselves may joke among themselves about the neighbor's "sexy little daughter" (who is of prepubescent age) who occasionally wanders downstairs into her parents' bar without a stitch when she has suddenly wakened around midnight . . . .

Do WE suffer from a tribal fear of misfits? If we, like most people, harbor a dread of strange behavior, it could affect our children. When we can't bring ourselves to speak about the danger of strange men except in roundabout, misleading euphemisms, it can be because of our own fear.

Remedy: The Adhocist, p. 386; The Sleeper, p. 399; The Canny, p. 40; The Nervous, p. 52; The Pessimistic, p. 99

The Romantic (Tribal)

Dread the worst before it happens. An all-too-vivid imagination helps precipitate them helter-skelter over the brink of panic at the first suggestion of crisis.

SIGNS AND SYMPTOMS

Trembling bottom lip as an object flashes in on a high trajectory, catching the gleam of the floodlights, to bounce off the goalkeeper's head—an empty paper cup. Rushing back UP a stairway when you have almost left the stadium five minutes before the final whistle when the crowd-howl says YOUR team is now one goal UP. A Bible with a page corner turned down at 1 SAM. 17:4 ("And there went out a champion out of the camp of the Philistines, named Goliath . . .")—your favorite fight story. Fervently believing in a system at the racetrack. Appreciating rustling leaves and rippling water and sighing wind through branches and splashing fountains which camouflage the sounds of town.

CAUSES

Sports lovers are a romantic and imaginative tribe—as shown by the takings in the bars around a stadium after a small-time team knocks a giant team out. The tills rattle up four times as much as the usual takings after a David-Goliath giant slaying.

Race-goers, too, manifest their unquenchable hope of making a fortune every time they place their bets. It shows in their belief that the professional gambler must win with a mysterious, immensely complicated system where the odds-on horses are backed for huge sums—whereas, in fact, the professional simply never bets unless *everything* about a horse is right.

Dreamy lightheadedness will affect the great outdoors lover who sees mystery in the vistas of a great park; a cameo wilderness set among the jagged spires and pinnacles of a wild mountain skyline—city buildings.

Here is a sense of magic, the park never revealing its secrets at once. The flowing shape of a lake is interrupted visually by thickly wooded islands which mask the true end of the water from wherever we look and make it seem to extend to infinity . . . a curve conceals what happens at the end of a path . . . or we reach the edge of a terrace and now see a flight of steps leading down to an amphitheater ringed by trees—a surprise each time we see it.

City residents tend to live on the edge of panic. Always half-expecting some major catastrophe, their imagination sees it already happening when certain signs threaten.

Without stopping to think, we get "lost." Yet a twisted person soon lets his imagination run away. He imagines what can happen instead of what actually IS. Given enough moonlight/pine trees/shrill cries he can see wolves on the park snow when there are no wolves for thousands of miles.

ILLOGICAL BEHAVIOR

A mist has only to rise from a packed section of fans at a ball game and other areas of the crowd can panic. People scream FIRE! and there is a stampede for the exits. That the fog was caused by body heat warming damp men's trousers shows how easily we leap to the wrong conclusions.

"RACE FANS PANIC AT TRACK AS MACHINES HISS!" Headlines are full of similar tragedies. Broken bones/heart attacks/concussions have all resulted when soft drink machines occasionally spring a leak in their CO_2 system (stored in tanks inside to give the drinks their fizz) and the loud hiss sounds as if they are going to explode. Everyone surges away.

It is this kind of terror that causes massive tragedies with scores of fatalities. As when the crush barriers buckle under the immense pressure in a crowded stadium and the crowd avalanches.

Yet the initial force that triggers such a human landslide is small and insignificant—were it not for the chain reaction it sets up among spectators.

FANS coming in late, for example. While there is plenty of room at the front of the stadium, they are pressed in too tightly at the rear. A few fans begin misbehaving by tumbling down through the crowd. Because there is enough room below they gather speed, the momentum spreads and spectators beneath, thinking the whole crowd is moving, sway and surge . . . and the pressure causes crush barriers to collapse fast, one after another.

Prepared for such an emergency, there are ways in which the individual can survive in a panicking crowd. Even then, the *sudden* effect of deafening noise/violent movement/intense light can still unhinge THE ROMANTIC, although they know safety measures.

A FLASH of lightning so close that we hear the thunder almost simultaneously and smell ozone (similar to weak chlorine)— always the signs of a near-miss—will, for example, invariably send most people in the park sprinting for any available cover. But poor shelter is worse than none; studies by insurance companies show that at least a quarter of the victims of lightning sought protection under isolated trees. It is well-known that this kind of shelter IS dangerous, yet people take no notice when their imagination tells them to get out of the rain at all costs.

We are also vulnerable to lightning at open-air sporting occasions and pop music festivals. One flash of lightning at a racetrack —and spectators can fall like bowling pins. The current of warm air rising from massed bodies is a good conductor of electricity, but THE ROMANTIC also offer themselves for sacrifice through their own mistakes.

Holding steel-tipped umbrellas in heavy rain at the golf championship, standing next to iron railings which make a satisfying row as we bang them to spur our team on, or standing tall on a wooden box so we have the best view . . . all draw lightning just that much better to *us*.

UFO's—unidentified flying objects—will produce similar characteristics in THE ROMANTIC: things in the sky, flying saucers, a flock of flying lights, shadows, even weird-looking flying machines sitting in a lonely belt of park have caused heart attacks, mass hysteria, car accidents and groups of people fighting to get through gates in their effort to flee.

Seeing UFO's can be a most nerve-wracking experience. The

fact remains, however, that no one has yet found a *real* UFO. And there are many explanations which can account for our sightings both on and off the ground: hallucinations, satellites in orbit, weather balloons and ball lightning (which can hover, change color, move unpredictably and even wink out suddenly or just be bright-colored balls of light dropping from the clouds).

Rather than reason that there are tens of thousands of unidentified flying objects, but that no one has yet identified any as a flying saucer *for certain*, THE ROMANTIC fail to realize that there is NO scientific evidence of aliens in the neighborhood of the earth.

As spaceship hulls are proof against meteors traveling at hundreds of miles a second, such measures smack of futile panic fired by imagination. There would seem to be no hope for us. To the contrary, however, there are ways by which we can put a fertile imagination to good use.

Remedy: The Amused, p. 394; The Sleeper, p. 399; The Dead Lucky, p. 290

12

CITY LUNGS

WINNERS

A TRIP to the park may be the result of a sudden impulse, while a 5,780-mile charter flight to the big fight may have been planned for months. But both serve the same purpose: a mental unwinding and escape from city pressure in a section of town that is different—the grass among the concrete, the ferment among the flab.

Bottled up until the great outdoors or king of sports (whichever our fancy) takes ourselves out of ourselves, our innermost urges show themselves honestly when we are so stimulated. From picnics in the botanical garden to the boos/V-signs/cheers at the ballgame, we can too easily be caught on the hop when unaware just how our real selves are on display.

The Adhocist (Improviser)

Makes do with whatever is available to help out a problem, whether it is four paper cups and two pocket mirrors to fix an instant periscope to see over the heads of other sports fans, or a frisbee used as a soup plate by the park fountain.

Use the same principles of improvisation in dangerously serious situations too.

AVOID KIDNAPPING

Use fluids to keep you awake when out with a carriage. Know the danger of falling asleep if troubled/tired/hot on warm grass; your infant could be stolen (possibly by other children). Splash the undersides of your wrists under a fountain or water cooler to revive you. Dip your bare feet in water where handy. Sit on a balustrade/plinth/bench rather than on the grass (less conducive to dozing).

UNTWIST YOURSELF

Use a twig to trace on the ground the path you have traveled when lost in the park. Try to fit the pieces together. Often such thinking back makes the difference between getting out of the park where you entered and exiting a mile or two away—perhaps in a dangerous neighborhood.

It is easy for strangers to lose direction. The surrounding city skyline looks much the same in all directions. There aren't always people about to ask. Trees/rocks/water can make direction-finding difficult when you are trying to retrace the route you took.

DON'T PANIC

Sit down for 15 minutes and think where you have been. Try to backtrack—the lakes you passed, bridges crossed and trees negotiated. Draw your map.

Don't let your imagination get loose. Don't run. Don't ask the first person you see unless he looks all right. Beware of park weirdos/freaks/derelicts.

If you still think you're lost, walk toward that part of the skyline that you THINK you came from. There are usually plenty of police about to ask if you are timid about getting directions from just anybody.

Next time: *Pinpoint on entering the park a tall building that is noticeable by shape etc.; so that you can take bearings from it.*

SLEEP SAFELY

(Only when you *have* to: sleeping overnight in city parks is often illegal—and can be dangerous.)

USE thick bushes/trees/undergrowth *by a fence* for the overnight site. Look around during the day for the right place. Climb back over the fence after dark. Bed down quickly without disturbing flower beds, ducks, foliage.

Avoid sleeping on benches in the open at night. Police will wake you up. You are also a target for seamy characters.

You want an overnight sleeping site bordering a safe area of the city—not a dubious crime/ghetto/riot-stricken zone where night prowlers are common.

SPOT FORGED PASSES

Use somebody else's ticket (or pass) to a stadium to check the ticket (or pass) YOU buy is genuine.

Go early to the stadium when you haven't been able to obtain a ticket so far for a big-time sporting event—and hope to pick up a black market ticket on sale in the street (perhaps at as much as 20 times its value). Or go the evening before.

Make friends with early-bird fans. Ask a bunch of them to show you a ticket (a group is more likely to oblige than a single fan who may be suspicious of your motives). Note down the color (though colors of passes may vary according to different areas inside the stadium) and the paper it is printed on.

Jot down these main points. Memorize them before looking for tickets sold at street corner "auctions."

Be resigned you may not get in the stadium after all.

PROTECT BICYCLE

Use bicycle chain itself (the power transmission) to chain machine to park rails/tree/fence when you must leave bike unguarded. Riders of rented mounts usually lack proper bicycle locks and chains.

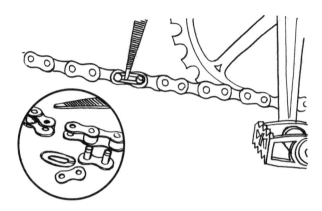

Warning: When replacing clip, place open end of clip so it travels last as chain goes round.

Bicycles are worthy targets for city thieves. Unclip/clip/unclip/clip the spring link of the main chain with a nail file point or fingernail as shown. Wrapped around the frame and something solid, it will often deter a bike thief.

(To protect your fingernails dig them into a bar of soap before pedaling away.)

STOP A THIEF

Use a thin tree to bind a captive when you have no cord, shoelaces, etc. (group catches a lawbreaker and needs to hold him ready for the law). Force him against the tree. Make him put his arms and legs around it as if he were going to climb. Right leg crosses the left leg and the toe of the *right foot is pushed behind the post*. Now push the victim down to a sitting position—and he can't rise without help (toe of left shoe binds right leg; toe of right shoe binds the tree and arms can only be used to hold on with). The prisoner is immobile until taken by his arms and lifted.

EASE BEE/WASP STINGS

Use either fingernail or needle (or pin) sterilized in a cigarette lighter flame to take out a bee sting (wasps don't leave stings behind). Don't try to squeeze it out as this could spread the poison. (Wasps can be more toxic, more liable to cause injury, and stings are more serious when they hit a blood vessel or the back of the throat or YOU are allergic to them.)

Do not panic. You are far less likely to be stung if you keep calm and move slowly. Marauding wasps, especially, sting when you panic them.

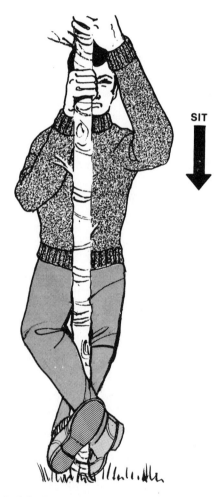

SIT

Immobilize a thief. Toes lock body captive.

Keep your mouth shut. Gasping with fright could suck the attacker in—and a sting at the back of the mouth can choke you to death (if you *do* get a sting in the mouth *rush* to the nearest park cafe for some ice to help keep the swelling down).

Keep some antihistamine pills. These help to combat the effects if you are stung.

(If allergic to stings carry a decoy in hot weather for the park. Half fill a small glass jar with a mixture of beer, honey and Formalin solution. Tie on a paper cover and punch a hole in it with a pencil. Now screw the lid back on and use for picnics—the enemy will be more interested in it than in you and will be drowned inside.)

If a stung person chokes or faints, get medical help fast.

SURVIVE BROKEN ICE

1. USE edge of ice that still hasn't collapsed as a handrail when the ice on a park lake suddenly cracks. The ice will keep on breaking —so keep reaching. Give a big breaststroke-style kick to try and bob you high out of the water before clothes get wet. Keep kicking. Keep trying to slide out on top when the water is too deep for you to wade. Don't stop. Keep reaching for the chance of some solid ice to hold onto. Extend your arms over the ice to spread the load. If really cold, sleeves will freeze to ice giving extra grip. Even brittle ice can be a partial support so long as you keep buoyant kicking. As you reach stronger ice bring your body as horizontal as possible, arms outstretched, legs swimming; get one leg over and roll on to the ice.

2. USE long branches, fence posts, planks, rods, cables, life belts, clothing tied together with reef knots (and slid out across the ice by being tied to a rock/bicycle/pair of skates) WHEN SOME-BODY ELSE HAS GONE IN. Or, risky but effective, get several helpers lying prone on the ice, each grasping the pair of ankles in front of him until the first person can hand the person in the water a looped scarf or belt. Once the person has gripped whatever you have managed to reach him with, instruct him to hold on and keep kicking with his legs. This way you can pull him to safety.

Don't go out on the ice near a person struggling in the water. It will let you down. Shout that you are going to get help. Tell him to keep holding on to the ice and to keep kicking when there is nothing immediately at hand to skim across the ice.

Most ponds/lakes/lagoons *in* parks are shallow. This is not always true, however. Sometimes there is a fence—if the water forms a reservoir, say, and there are warning notices—but even if you climb over or disregard the warnings, your life is still threatened if the ice gives.

What looked like a tough, thick covering—and has held you well at first—suddenly creaks (along with squeaks, a DANGER sound of cracking), collapses and plunges you into icy water . . . .

Heed the warning first.

SAVE A DROWNING CHILD

Use anything buoyant to reach out with or throw to a child who has fallen into deep water (and you can't swim). *If the water is shallow, you can wade. But you may not know its depth and be frozen with fear. Many people with a fear of water are. And shallow water to an adult can still be too deep for a child.*

Inability to swim is no excuse for doing nothing. There is plenty of unexpected lifesaving equipment about in city parks.

Here are examples of objects which can save the life of anyone struggling in deep water.

A spare wheel or empty gasoline can from the trunk of a car. (Despite its steel rim and hub, a spare wheel will float reasonably well; little effort is needed to roll it into the water, and YOU can get into the water, hang on to the wheel and swim out under its support.)

A long branch can hook a small child to safety or aid the drowner who is old enough to cling to it. Bind the ends with string/tape/tie to make it easy to grasp in the water.

Inflatable rafts/beach balls/foam-rubber mats—ALL float. Deck chairs float; they also let you reach out with them to someone out of your depth.

Lie on the bank and reach out with a stick when you can't grab the victim.

Get into the water, hold onto the bank and reach out with a hand when the victim is within reach and you can't swim. Planks/boxes/poles/fencing/wooden bench—ALL float. Towel/shirt/coat should be taken in whether you go in with or without a float —as a tow. It lengthens your reach and prevents the victim striking or pulling you under in panic.

Form a human chain. Face in opposite direction holding each other's wrists.

Grab and paddle/row/propel pleasure boat out to drowner fast. Don't come in broadside on reaching him or gunwhale is pulled under. Approach with stern or bow, tell him to hang on and tow him back to the side.

Let the person know (when old enough) that you are coming to the rescue when you have to cast further afield for objects to reach out with or to throw. Important: *Never let the victims think you are deserting them or they give in too soon.*

(When rescuing a child and you CAN swim, travel on your back holding the child's head, one hand on either side of the face. Support the child on your forearms and chest to keep his or her face clear of the water.)

OVERCOME SQUEAMISHNESS

Use a handkerchief over a stranger's mouth when you can't bear the thought of any kind of kiss—and the kiss of life is needed (see THE COLD-BLOODED, p. 187).

Or rip away a section of shirt/blouse/dress and use that. It still works.

SAVE A DOG-ATTACKED CHILD

Use your coat. Throw yourself on the dog, wrapping your coat around its head. Hold on tight to prevent its biting you as it releases the child. Then lean your weight on the dog's body. (You can choke the dog with a stranglehold around the neck or crush the wind out of it with your body.)

Or hit the dog on the nose with a shoe (or stick). Two or three such blows will break any dog.

Other tactics: Kick it hard in the groin just under the ribs; grab and twist at the dog's testicles; grab its tail, swing hind legs off the ground and spin the dog in circles (sudden, sharp pain will make the dog lose its grip).

SIGNAL SOS IN A CROWD

USE . . . white handkerchief when someone collapses. This SOS will be taken up by others nearby. Patch of fluttering white signals among mass of color—instant attention from ambulance men.

Do as advised. Either wait until they reach you in the crowd OR pass invalid over heads with others' help as instructed by the first-aiders below.

HELP CHILD STUCK IN RAILINGS (by head)

Use another person to help you (no need to call the fire department to chop through the rails).

The child gets stuck because the ears flatten as he puts his head in, but refuse to do so as he tries to pull his head out.

One person must stand on each side of the railings and gently turn the child over so that he is facing up instead of down. His head can then be eased out forward as easily as it went in.

Sheer fright can make the head and neck swell. Calm the child. Quell panic.

The Amused (Straight-faced)

See the funny side of a heart-stopping emergency which, although serious, is then brought into a perspective that prevents panic. This begins to calm others.

Often survival measures do seem humorous at a distance. The

person who remembers the comedy angle is often found to cope best.

ATTACKED BY SAVAGE DOG

STAND STILL, DROOP A LITTLE, TURN YOUR BACK.
By staying submissive and cowardly you may get the dog to leave you. Only then should you move away slowly, always with your back to the dog. Avoid looking into its eyes (sign of aggression to a dog).
Don't run for it until there is a perfect avenue of escape.
Remember: *Dogs sense tension in a person and it worries them. Aim to be perfectly relaxed. And friendly. Stand still.*
PRESENT YOUR ARM FOR DOG TO BITE.
It is safer to be bitten on your arm than at your throat. You will have to stand the pain of the dog's jaws, but fight the impulse to react violently when it is obvious the dog is going to spring.
Note: Some dogs will respond if you stand perfectly still and shout LEAVE.
When even this fails . . . TALK TO THE DOG.
Say "GOOD BOY, GOOD BOY," until it releases you. Talk quietly and when it lets go, keep talking and slowly backing away, avoiding staring at the animal.
If you turn and run or make any sudden movement the dog will attack again.
Note: All dogs behave differently. Some dogs get their teeth into you and hang on; others attack with a chopping motion of the jaws.
GIVE THE DOG MORE ARM.
Push your arm toward the animal's throat when it bites. The further toward the back of the arm you can push your arm, the more likely the dog is to let go. At the same time you can gradually push the animal backward and steer it toward some avenue of escape for you.
Standing still while being bitten means you will have a clean wound rather than a torn bite. Wash the bite in running water. Go to hospital for an anti-tetanus injection.

ATTACKED BY ANGRY SWAN

SPLASH LIGHTLY WITH WATER.

Docile enough to be kept in parks, swans can still be dangerous (especially when there is a nest or brood of cygnets any time between March and October).

They glide along silently. Dogs can make them angry. Their danger; breaking a bone with their wings or upsetting a child into the water with their beaks.

TRAPPED BY HORSE (standing on your foot)

PUSH BACK. Do this hard to make the animal shift its weight.

Be wary of horses if you walk park bridle paths. They can do great damage, sometimes proving untrustworthy and aggressive (even when with their rider). Warning sign: horse lays its ears back. Stay well clear of horses, especially their back legs. Don't turn your back on a frisky animal.

CONFRONTED BY FLYING SAUCER (landed in park)

CALL AIR FORCE. Get to a telephone as fast as you can!

ENDANGERED BY LIGHTNING

FLING YOURSELF FLAT.

Lie on your face on any bare ground (which parkland mainly is). You will get wet, but you will live to catch cold. Jettison any metal objects (even medallions).

Lightning *doesn't* always kill. It may just bombard the ground around. Or make golf clubs sing/hair rise/eyebrows sizzle. But anybody standing upright in the open risks being struck down and killed with heart/brain/nerve damage.

Know the warning signs: hot weather, dark clouds, heavy static crackle on transistor radios, blobs of rain and bad light. To tell how far you are from the lightning strike, divide by five the number of seconds between the flash and the thunderclap. When you see the flash and hear thunder almost at the same time and smell ozone—see THE ROMANTIC, p. 382—the strike was very close.

AVOID being in a boat, on horseback, on a hill, in a cave, under isolated trees, by a metal fence, in water swimming, below overhead wires, on a bike (it is a fallacy that the tires protect you; cars are only safe because a lightning charge spreads over the surface of the metal and goes to earth—sometimes the tires exploding), beneath overhanging rocks (the lightning spark makes an arc from rock to ground like a spark plug arc with *you* fried in between), in a crowd in the open (the current of warm air rising from bodies is a good conductor of electricity), below walls (see rock overhangs), under metal-tipped umbrellas.

The safest places (besides lying down in the open) are in a building (park comfort station/cafe/kiosk) or in the middle of thick woodland (lightning is unlikely to strike more than one tree, which will probably not be yours).

When somebody is hit by lightning, REMEMBER the flash can be anything up to 100 miles long and pack a punch 100 times more powerful than all the USA's power stations put together, yet a casualty could still be apparently unmarked—only his or her clothing scorched.

Treat for shock and fractures (see THE COLD-BLOODED, p. 187), burns (see THE DEAD LUCKY, p. 290), stoppage of breath (see THE COLD-BLOODED, p. 187) . . . whichever is needed.

SQUEEZED IN RIOT (in stadium)

TAKE A DEEP BREATH (*important in ALL crises.*)

Take your hands out of your pockets. Move away, if possible, from any solid pillar/wall/barrier you may be pressed against. Avoid linking the fingers of each hand in front of you, but brace your arms in front of your body, each held in front of you and tensed against the pressure of people on all sides. Don't let your shoes be trampled on; instead, stand on other people's shoes. Try to get an inch or two off the ground so that, with the deep breath you keep taking, you are in a stronger, more buoyant position. Keep moving when possible.

The safest place to stand on stadium terracing is near the sides (though not against barriers) and at the rear. While the crowd is not moving (in equilibrium) it is safe enough at the front. But a drastic swaying crowd movement makes the mass of people unstable (in flux) and can precipitate a forward human avalanche.

Feedback of information is slow. The front of the crowd doesn't know what is happening at the back until too late.

If the stadium crash barriers buckle, DON'T GO UNDER. Climb up on top of the other people in front. Keep scrambling UP to keep on the crest of the human wave toppling down the stadium terracing. (Crash barriers are designed to withstand crowd stress pressure of more than the maximum number of people it is possible to stand behind each barrier—say 340 pounds of pressure for 88 people, whereas there is only room for 44, but the most violent crowd surge where people are piled *on top* of other people can still buckle the metal).

DANGER SIGNALS: latecomers bursting down through the crowd standing on terraces to less densely populated rows below (see THE ROMANTIC, p. 382) . . . ANY steps leading *down* to exits rather than up to the street (fans leave the stadium before end of play then run back up the steps at the sound of crowd pandemonium telling of another score, someone slips and those fans at the top who are coming down fall on to those coming up) . . . intense feeling between supporters of participating teams (perhaps on a sectarian/racial/ethnic basis instead of a sporting one) . . . droves of police . . . pop concert guards skirmishing with sudden and selective overkill strikes against troublemakers . . . ALL wrestling fans (too drunk or high to care and willing to fight anybody) . . . barbaric incidents on field of play . . . no score until dying seconds of ball game . . . more terracing where fans must stand than seats . . . referee who is fat, restless, robust, active and otherwise endowed with masculine qualities (sociologists tell us that such a referee—who also often has too many sisters—is more likely to cause a riot with controversial decisions than the one who is tall, conformist, formal, and graced with feminine traits like patience, moderation and perserverance).

(Not fatuous: Remember, THE AMUSED foresee possible

trouble by their whimsical appraisal of a situation more somber citizens don't notice. It is the principle that is important.)

The Sleeper (Underestimated)

Wins by using horse-racing strategy, THE SLEEPER being the nag that is held back for the right race and which, until that particular event, competes in races by merely running down the course.

Comes the test, and he amazes everybody. His main strength, however, is not so much coming on strong when he needs to *as remaining unnoticed and blending with the scenery for so long previously.*

WALK UNSEEN

Walk where there are people. Don't split away from others and take shortcuts across the grass—especially when shrubs or trees border your path.

Remember being near other people does not give you complete protection—everybody may just mind his own business. But at least you will be harder to pick out for any potential assailant who, if he is going to rape/rob/kill, is more likely to go for the person on his own and away from other people—the reason he noticed the victim in the first place.

Steer clear of inviting steps or paths leading away from the main park paths—they could lead to zones marked out (tacitly) for freaks (drugged)/derelicts (drunk)/queers (menacing).

Watch where you walk. Thick wooded areas, and even their edges, should be skipped by the nervous. Keep to those main thoroughfares of the park where most other people go.

Beware of walking along bridle and bicyclepaths—they can take you further from help than you need to travel.

Keep an eye on others from a distance when your long hair/legs/boots stand out. Watch for surreptitious shortcuts made by strangers who may be planning to intercept or follow you across the grass.

IF FOLLOWED see THE FUGITIVE (p. 202).

IF ATTACKED see THE FUGITIVE (p. 202) and THE NERVOUS (p. 52).

JOG BLENDINGLY

Early-morning athletes are safer in the park. Watch the temptation to urinate into bushes, however (because there is nobody about). Vagrants/derelicts/addicts have all used such occasions to attack the unsuspecting.

IF ATTACKED, put your running to the test. Know where park police station, parked patrol cars and the safest streets adjacent to the park are.

CYCLE SOFTLY

Avoid too sexy attire when bike riding in a park (see THE PROVOCATIVE, p. 68).

Pedal along main park paths. Avoid cutting-across-grass detours to woody/busy/shrubbery areas. Never consider yourself danger-proof because you are on wheels (an attitude which shows when you bicycle in front of cars/taxis/horse carriages on park roads).

If harassed by bicycle pest, stop. Wait for others to catch up. Or ride back toward one-way oncoming traffic. Don't attempt to outspeed or outmaneuver (and excite) him.

Remember, if you catch your front wheel on his rear wheel tire you fall.

IF ATTACKED: Get help (see THE NERVOUS, p. 52 and THE FUGITIVE, p. 202). Use your bike tire pump to fend off the attacker—stab it forward in two hands like a bayonet at his stomach. OR use your bike itself to parry off an attack from some park nut (hold cross bar and saddle stem to keep machine between you and thug).

NAP UNNOTICED

(See also THE LEERY, p. 47.)

Sit on a bench by a busy path (not in a secluded area of the park). Use body language to show you want to be alone: sit on center of bench/shift body away/cross furthest leg from newcomer over top of other leg.

If lying on grass, do it where there are plenty of people around, NOT on shady slopes alone near trees or by lonely edges of lakes.

IF ATTACKED: Call/whistle/scream help (see THE NERVOUS, p. 52, and THE FUGITIVE, p. 202). But block the attack too—even when you are lying down and at their mercy (or so it seems) . . . come up on one knee, reach down, get a firm grasp on the cuffs of attacker's trousers, then suddenly stand up and pull hard (he'll topple like an axed pine); come up on a knee, clasp your hands together into a double-wristed fist and swing it up into his groin; OR do any of these lying-on-the-grass kicks . . . bend up on one knee and drive the bottom of your heel against his shinbone/kneecap/genitals; pretend to push up off the grass by shoving down with both hands on it and let fly with one foot backward into the tormentor's stomach (the agile/fit/athletic can kick *both* feet high as if doing a handstand—right into the opponent's face); suddenly hook your right foot behind your assailant's right ankle as you lie flat on your back and hammer your left shoe at his right knee (to knock him down or cause dislocation); draw both legs up to your chest then let go with a double-barreled kick on your side with both shoes into his shin as the attacker comes in to kick you; duck your face out of the way when the attacker launches a kick at it and grab the foot, twisting it— then (at the same time) lash a foot at the ankle of the leg he is standing on to bring him down.

REST INVISIBLY

Don't *look* for company in parks where smooth-talking rapists and killers among flower beds/duck ponds/tinkling fountains move in on attractive girls sitting on the grass.

Sit within speaking distance of others sprawled nearby.

Alert suspicions. What was that flashing over there? WAS it from the glass of the binoculars now hanging around the neck of the stranger who has just sat down close by?

Avoid direct eye contact.

Get up and walk away if the stranger begins to shorten the distance across the grass between you by pretending to lie down, sit up, lie down, etc.—and so caterpillar toward you. IF ATTACKED, see NAP UNNOTICED (above).

PLAY INCONSPICUOUSLY (Children)

Let them play as children will always play, BUT brief them every day with a warning *given as often as a goodnight kiss* (whether going to park carousel/play area/boating pond or not).

HAVE NOTHING TO DO WITH STRANGERS WHATSOEVER

(Warnings given only sporadically are listened to by children with half-opened ears—and quickly forgotten in their single-minded aim to go into the park and play.)

Discuss the dangers of men in parks frankly. Be informative. And unemotional.

If your child asks or you feel he or she is mature enough, be explicit about what to expect from the twisted male (possible child-slayer or sexual pervert) who watches/trails/approaches anybody of the age between five and 14 in the park. IMPORTANT: Stress that these people are unhappily sick and in need of help.

To say that they are evil can terrify a child too much. A child rooted to the spot with terror is an obvious victim, much more easily elbowed/bundled/side-tracked into bushes.

Play it down. Explain that incidents likely to happen in the park will be comparatively harmless; that when a stranger asks a child to go under his umbrella out of the rain, he probably does not intend physical harm but don't be surprised if he tries to touch a hand or brush back some hair . . . actions that are so pathetic they should engender a wry sympathy rather than absolute revulsion (revolting as it actually is).

All the more reason to tell your children . . .

1. HAVE NOTHING TO DO WITH STRANGERS.

2. HAVE NOTHING TO DO WITH STRANGERS.
3. HAVE NOTHING TO DO WITH STRANGERS.

Ask them—without making it obvious—if they ever do. "Who did you see in the park today?". . . . "Many people watching you play?". . . . "Does anybody walk with you to school?". . . . "Who gave you that candy—does anyone ever?"

Encourage children to keep in groups. And to watch out for each other (the presence of group of children being hostile to the pest who approaches one of them is an excellent deterrent).

Children should be clocked in. Make a deadline for their return. If the child is late, give one more hour—and then if there is no possible explanation for the delay—report as missing to the police. (Don't wait too long hoping there is an innocent explanation and for fear of making a fool of yourself; too many wasted hours can make the task of tracing the child impossible.)

PARK PLAYGROUNDS: Inspect the slides carefully before children toboggan down in Levis/knickers/rompers. Get them to look too . . . for honed points of sheath knives, nails or tin tacks hammered up through the metal by vandals—and intended to rip tiny genitals apart.

IF ATTACKED: Give a child a whistle. Tell him or her to blow it and run. Don't give weapons. An attacker could take the weapon and attack the child.

PLAY INCONSPICUOUSLY (ANYBODY)

ICE-SKATING: Be alert when leaving the park rink and you have been the most eye-catching girl skater on blades. Leave with a group if you are not WITH anybody and it is getting dark (you have been in the spotlight for anyone who cared to watch and harbor strange dreams). See also THE PROVOCATIVE, p. 68.

BALL GAMES (casual): Watch coats used as goalposts/bases (and depositories for valuables like money, wristwatches, etc). Also cast-off shoes (when possessions are stuffed inside). Keep your gear with everybody else's, but remember which is YOURS. And notice anybody strolling in that direction.

WARNING: If a participant in a pick-up game insists that his big dog should run about too—in football, say—don't, in the heat of moment, tackle that player hard—(see THE AMUSED, p. 394).

TENNIS (on park courts): See ICE-SKATING (above).

TOBOGANNING/SKIING: Beware of slopes running among or near to woodland. Stick with other buffs on popular park slopes rather than search for virgin snow in more secluded parts of the park.

BOATING: Don't land on isolated shores of a big park lake (especially when it is fringed by a thick screen of trees)—row where people and other craft are near. (Attacks do happen when lone voyagers put in at secluded park bays—it can be two lovers, for example; the man is knocked out, the woman raped.)

CHECKERS/CHESS: Watch anybody watching you, especially when you are elderly and a regular at park checker tables, a soft touch for the mugger who knows your habits. Travel through parks with companion enthusiasts.

MOUNTAINEERING: Rock outcrops are irresistible scrambling grounds for children; warn them of the dangers of leather-soled shoes (rubber soles grip best), broken glass on ledges and the slippery paint used by the parks department. Also of holding a toy in one hand as they play (a child stuck on a rock is a godsend to the child-molester rescuer).

WATCH UNWATCHED

When you don't know the score at a stadium—say at a bullfight arena—find out how the land lies from an aficionado in a nearby bar or cafe (go early before the happening to find sober informants) . . . see also THE RESEARCHER (p. 90).

Check just what kind of stadium it is. Is there standing room only, or are there seats? What may prove standing accommodation on terraces in one country may be sitting-room-only in another where the custom is to sit down on cold concrete rows. If so, take an extra sweater.

Ask the police outside where it is safest to head for in a foreign stadium when you are following a team—and when you don't already have a pass into some sector of the ground.

Avoid those sections of the stadium where only the most partisan go. They are breeding grounds for violence, and the view is poor (often scarves are brandished banner-fashion obscuring the field of play for spectators).

Button buttons (and zip zippers) on mingling with a half-step crowd approaching the stadium—especially the top buttons of coats and overcoats. Secure your wallet and valuables in different areas of your person (see THE CANNY, p. 40).

Black-market tickets bought on the street pose an extra risk (see also THE ADHOCIST, p. 386). Pickpockets pull your attention by offering a genuine ticket for sale. At the last moment (as you take your wallet out) another member of the pickpocketing troupe pretends to snatch the ticket and run. He is stopped, but in the ensuing scuffle your wallet is stolen after you put it back in a pocket. . . .

Keep such money in your hand. Only part with it when you have a firm grasp on ticket/pass/etc. offered.

Don't sport partisan buttons and pennants either at home or away games; there will always be a rampaging element of fans supporting the other team ready to take you apart. Blend best in any stadium by being inconspicuous.

Why force your own support of a team onto a small child? Look into your own psyche. And be extra careful when taking a youngster to a large stadium anywhere. *Keep with him all the time.*

Should your child wear a cap/button/badge displaying team allegiance, play safe. Pin lightly anything that has to be pinned to a coat—so that if it is torn away by passing hooligan/vandal/teenage fans it doesn't cause harm.

Don't allow a scarf to be worn round the neck. A sudden violent tug could throttle or terrify a small child. A scarf should be held doubled in a hand or threaded through coat belt so it will slide out at sudden pull (brutal scarf stealing does happen).

Forget about retaliating or remonstrating if a pennant is snatched by a mad-hat element—especially if it's just to look big in eyes of a young companion. Let it go.

Once among any gathering—stadium, park bowl, racetrack, exposition/fair/exhibition—watch your wallet when you are inside and have undone the buttons of your outer garments.

(Buttons/hooks/zippers are no guarantee a pickpocket can't still rob you, but they do make you rather safer. By fingering fastened buttons you are reminded of any valuables on you.)

If you feel fingers (or think you do) at a pocket, *turn round sharply* (see also THE DETERMINED, p. 372) when *standing in crowd. Shortly afterward look round again. And then look round a third time to deter the potential thief trying again.* Don't be too embarrassed to whip round ANY time you think your pocket is being robbed—don't just think about doing it, *do it.*

Watch out when you are collecting winnings at the racetrack. If it is crowded hang back. Know you are probably safe from being passed counterfeit money (too many plainclothes police and quick-eyed bookies who soon spot fakes). But pickpockets —no.

Anyone with serious problems at home/work/play should be careful about behavior in stadiums. Play down urges to shout, chant and cheer as your team gains ascendancy; it can prove a dangerous time.

Don't try to get crowd sympathy for your team. Listen to the fans around you before showing YOUR allegiance.

Remember tough nuts who infiltrate pockets of crowd in ones and twos—armed, all they look for is some soft-touch supporters of the other side to stab/punch/kick into oblivion. Look out of eye corners at those who squeeze in by, or just behind you, during play.

Stadiums vary too. Some have supporters of both sides mixed throughout the ground. In others, the most fervent fans are segregated in particular zones by walls/barricades/police. Some accommodate fans divided equally into opposing camps: from the halfway line of the football game along one side, round the end of the stadium and then back along the opposite side as far as halfway line are to be found the collective fans of one side; supporters of the opposing team form the other U of stadium.

Find out which is the setup in your stadium. If unsure—and you can—move from where you are until you reach a nucleus of fans obviously supporting the same players as yourself.

Don't provoke crowd anger by obstructing others' view to gain a better view yourself—say by climbing up pillar/girder/ stanchion. If fans in a sector behind abuse you—put aside your pride (and the fact they can't get at you because of a barrier) and step down. Missiles showered at you can hit the neighboring crowd whose anger will then be aimed at you.

Carry a pocket-sized bottle of whisky/vodka/etc. before leaving home to offer crowd-neighbors—if the situation warrants it.

Watch your personal behavior at AWAY contests. Certain city police—especially abroad—will not tolerate fans who invade field/bowl/arena (as is the custom in some cities) at the end of a game or fight. Scramble onto the area of play in a foreign stadium and YOU might face baton-charging police (even though at home fans are allowed to stand before the grandstand for presentation of cups, etc.).

Do as HOME spectators do in a foreign stadium. Copy them and forget the etiquette of fans from your home city.

Button up again before leaving the stadium—peak time for pickpockets.

Warm weather can be a curse. Pickpockets' fingers are more supple, and the victims are wearing less clothing than in winter, which means easier pickings. Also, there are more tourists carrying valuables—traveler's checks, for instance.

In a sudden violent squash while leaving the stadium look beyond the imminent squeezers—those around you—to check if the crowd movement is local or caused by mass movement.

Beware of any *local* pressing; it could be a ring of pickpockets putting pressure on you in attempt to distract you while they go through all your pockets.

In this situation, keep your hands on vital pockets rather than tensing them in front of your body—the best position if a crowd avalanches (see THE AMUSED, p. 394).

Also shrug off any attempt by a stranger to help push you through a jam-packed crowd to an exit—the skilled thief goes through your pockets on the way as he tugs you here, pulls you there.

BET SYSTEMATICALLY

This does NOT mean use a *system*.

Don't plunge at races when the reason for your betting is a matter of life and death and more hangs on your success than a grand day's sport . . . but possibly your neck if you fail.

To fail is better than to dive even deeper into debt, whatever you may think now.

NO betting system can be trusted (though many come frustratingly close).

A cruel tilt of the odds will murder any system supposed to guarantee quick winnings. None can. It's too easy to misread the law of averages where you see winning and losing as rhythms; when you're winning you think you'll ride the hot streak and jump off before the icy patch follows.

But ANYTHING could happen; odds are calculated on infinity. And infinity means endless possibilities.

Because of UPS and DOWNS, systems depend on betting over a lengthy period to flatten out the peaks and valleys of winning and losing . . . much longer time is needed than allowed in a mere day at the races. Or two. Or three.

Also those systems that, in principle, mean you double up on losing bets until you eventually win—and most systems *are* based on this theory—overlook the fact that a race may be dishonest. And none take into reckoning the track percentage that goes to the state and the track.

Even if all races were honest, systems based on the tidal flow of luck theory would still be fallible.

An example is "the martingale" system, which consists of betting with a certain unit (whatever amount you choose) while winning and stashing the winnings. On losing, however, you double the bet so that when the hot streak returns you have regained your losses.

Here is an example. You begin with these numbers (it's a system which originated at the Ascot racetrack): 3, 6, 9, 12, 20, 25, 45, 50, 75, 125, 200.

The middle number is 25, and so you make that the first bet $25. Lose, and the next down the scale is 20 ($20). Lose that too and you come down to 12 ($12). Now a win. Go back to 20. Win two more and you're on 50. And so on (the theory is that you boost your bets when Lady Luck smiles, then cut your losses as Fate turns).

If, however, most of your horses are losers on that day, then you still can't make the system work and you end up being a Loser yourself. There's no way the system can work when this is the case.

Professional gamblers leave strictly alone the immensely complex and maze-like systems—much more intricate than the Ascot, but still basically the same—where odds-on horses are backed for massive sums. They know systems are for victims.

They only back a horse heavily when price is the right. And never bet unless everything about a horse is right. This means hard work. There are no shortcuts.

Their Bible is the racing form. They know something about most horses in training and EVERYTHING about those they back. They spend hours of homework on next day's card with record books that tell: weights, draw, distance, track and going, gallop times and stable records. And only then do they eliminate no-hopers, slim out those remaining and consider the handful left that look in with more than a chance. (And even then form is checked with contacts: they telephone owners/trainers/jockeys —on retainer payroll—for those oddments of information which help decide on certain horses.)

You, the average bettor, will fall short of such dedicated research. But at least you can still follow certain rules:

1. NEVER BET MORE THAN YOU CAN AFFORD.
2. FOLLOW FORM AND NEVER FANCY.

3. DON'T BET WHEN DRUNK.
4. STICK WITH ONE WIN (THE MORE YOU BET THE GREATER YOUR CHANCES OF LOSING).
5. NEVER CHASE YOUR LOSSES; CUT THEM.

And even if you do get a tip straight from the horse's mouth, don't be tempted to raise your stakes as even the best tipster's assurances will cancel out in the end.

Part Seven

CITY BRIGHT LIGHTS

Bars, Diners, Theaters, Clubs

13

CITY BRIGHT LIGHTS

LOSERS

BRIGHT LIGHT districts distract. Glittering neon, cheap boutiques, pinball machines, sandwich counters and bars/restaurants/theaters will transfix the ordinary visitor as surely as the wolf does the lamb.

Ready to let our hair down, we can be shorn, clipped and fleeced. Eating out in a famous restaurant, we may be made the meal of. Going to the theater or movies, we might have the wool pulled over our eyes. For while the entertainment centers of cities are mostly safe, they too have their menaces, from robbery with violence to VD, from a drug overdose to food poisoning.

Our instincts tell us to be careful. But those kaleidoscoping city BRIGHT LIGHTS spotlight our vulnerabilities all too brilliantly when we don't know what to hide.

The Winner (Celebrating)

Is obvious to everybody in his desire to be happy. But oblivious to danger.

Fueled with alcohol, he is foolhardy long before he reaches the fatal tottering-drunk stage.

SIGNS AND SYMPTOMS

Money scattered in every pocket. Wishing all a Mewwy Chthmsth. Calling "Takshi." Sabotaging balloons floating down at the end of a dance with a cunning to put James Bond to shame. Considering the girl at the end of the bar ugly at first, beautiful later. Being hit by certain neon words: SCANDALOUS/ FLESHY/NAUGHTY.

CAUSES

Alcohol alone can make us feel Winners. But the Winners who Lose are those of us who are feeling fantastic before we set out drinking.

Mix euphoria (see THE RELIEVED, p. 8) with determination (see THE DETERMINED, p. 372) to have a ball, and we speed vulnerable instincts forward. Our attitude is to forget all— throw restraint to the winds.

Times for celebration consequently bring casualties. Christmas, for example, is the season when more people get bumped on the head (getting their jaws broken and losing teeth) than at any other time of year. Frivolity and punch bring out the violence in all of us.

ILLOGICAL BEHAVIOR

Drunken behavior will always attract sex, violence and robbery. Of the three, violence could be the least harmful.

Happy drunks, unlike the angry drunk or fighting mad, make no effort to save themselves until it is too late. By relaxing, not realizing and going with the blows instead of resisting, they generally suffer less physical harm than the more aggressive.

Happy drunks wanting sex, however, face more hazard. They have only one thing in mind and make every effort to get it.

Six times out of ten we avoid danger in entertainment centers. It is in the interests of those who organize crime and prostitution that BRIGHT LIGHTS districts should have a reputation for safety, otherwise potential victims would keep away. But there are always free-lance "mustangs" and out-of-towners—girls who look on prostitution more as an escapade than a professional chore.

So unless we do question the motives behind propositions put to us in the theater district, the most solid and respectable citizens—when drunk—can be taken.

Why, for instance, does the girl escorting us from the bar by holding us upright with an arm beneath our armpit swap sides at an intersection? Is it because she has gone through all our right-hand pockets and is now starting on the left?

Why should the stranger who says he will get a girl for us and who is patently none too honest, return with our money (he had taken it to show the girl) when we had given him up for good? Could it be that he needs to convince us he is honest because he most definitely isn't? He first put our money in an envelope, stuck down the flap and disappeared into a hotel—only to return with an envelope stuffed with blank paper. But we don't open it to check; that would show we didn't trust him. And we let him lead us to a door where he instructs us to wait, knock twice then hand the girl the envelope. Only there is no girl and he vanishes before we realize it.

Where is the prostitute really going when she walks out of the door after persuading us to get into bed first in the hotel? Is it really to get a bottle of whiskey? Or is it to go below and rifle the pockets of our clothes? We don't find out until too late. Similarly, WHY should the prostitute insist we first have a shower in the hotel/apartment/house bathroom? We had washed, shaved and put on our best clothing before hitting the BRIGHT LIGHTS. So why is she so particular? Could it be so that she can lock us in the bathroom, rob us and leave?

The gambler who has been drinking and goes looking for company is a sure-fire bet—to be played along and relieved at the earliest opportunity of the green stuff he is so happily celebrating with.

Remedy: All of Chapter 12.

The Sagittarian (Arien)

Or Scorpion/Capricornian/Piscean . . . or anybody who bases his day-to-day life on the misguided belief that everything is preordained by fate and that he has no say in his affairs, is a likely Loser.

SIGNS AND SYMPTOMS

Considering this an unlucky chapter without having to refer back to its number. Acute depression when the horoscope of your far-distant beloved forecasts that the Eleventh House of his or her solar chart is accented in a happy way with a new romance starred. (Or NOT reading your partner's forecast in case of such a prediction.) Not wearing a wig in case you meet a phrenologist. Tea bags out; tea leaves only for your teapot. Reading events from the way froth hangs on the side of an empty beer glass. Skipping calcium intake for a week or two so that lines on your palm are etched in white before you visit your palmist.

CAUSES

The most intelligent and well-adjusted individuals can prove as susceptible as these signs show. There will never be a scarcity of otherwise solid citizens who allow themselves to get mixed up in such romantic follies whose outcome spells risk.

Such fantasies are harmless UNTIL the occasion when we relinquish all hope of finding happiness—like the young woman who despairs each time a love affair comes to an end. And we then turn to fate in making decisions rather than trust our own judgment.

ILLOGICAL BEHAVIOR

Astrology is always a useful pickup line. "You look like a Cancer-or-whatever" is a socially acceptable way of conversing in CITY BRIGHT LIGHTS. To give anticipated fate as directed by stars/moon/planets every chance, however, is often a case *of making a prediction (astrological or otherwise) come true.*

Our fantasies play into the hands of crooks who sniff out our weakness and loneliness.

Quite sober, we deliberately submerge any doubts we may have —based on our usual nonbelief in being lucky enough to meet someone attractive who is single—and justify the situation as being in the control of Jupiter/Mars/Venus.

The result is that, as if we were drunk, we fail to question suspicious events.

Like: WE ARE SMALL, HE IS MEDIUM-TALL: Why then does he not sit in the cinema seat directly behind us but in the one next to it? The seat next to us is empty, true. But a large person could take it and spoil his view. If he sat right behind us, however, he would have a clear view of the screen guaranteed.

Note: It isn't only in bars that danger exists for THE SAGIT-TARIAN.

Or don't we notice because we are too absorbed in the play or film? Or in the other man who has sat next to us on the other side? He is pressing a foot against our shoe (*and our stars did say we would find romance today*). Yet this male on our left could be a partner of the man behind on the right. As the one by our side draws our attention, the one behind gently tips the seat on the other side so that our handbag drops in front of him. He takes the purse/wallet/keys and returns the bag unnoticed by our side.

Millions of imponderable permutations of behavior exist when we pin his faith on astrological predictions.

Remedy: The Relaxed, p. 436; The Impervious, p. 449; The Canny, p. 40; The Obsequious, p. 124; The Fugitive, p. 202; The Sleeper, p. 399

The Too Friendly (Sycophants)

Are *so* anxious to please. Yet it can cost them dearly to try to fawn their way into unknown company. Hunting companionship, if only for a drink or two, can be fatal.

SIGNS AND SYMPTOMS

By the bar alone: men speaking to anyone who goes to buy drinks, half-listening to others' conversation; women clutching purse and sipping a drink. Patting dogs you don't like. Looking through the door into the bar, not liking the look of it but still going in for one drink because you had made the move of opening the door. Staying in a bar longer than necessary because you think others will notice if you leave too quickly. Sympathizing attentively with the drinker complaining of slipped disk/bad weather/unequal leg lengths, when really bored to tears.

CAUSES

Sycophants crave to mix because they are a mixture of:

LONELINESS: We don't have to be new to the city to be lonely, but just a part of the city. Our need for company becomes obvious in a strange bar.

SENSITIVITY: By showing we are approachable and pose no threat, we hope strangers will accept rather than reject us—our secret dread.

HAPPINESS that makes us want to talk to others; to be part of the communal life in this unknown fragment of the city. Perhaps inspired by a good telephone call from the bar.

NERVOUSNESS and fear of the city, because we are visitors. Friendliness helps bolster feelings of insecurity.

TREPIDATION when slumming: Trying to ingratiate ourselves into honky tonk bars and dives is a sure sign.

CHRISTIANITY: We sincerely wish to get on with our fellows and will meet them more than half-way in attempts at friendship.

PARSIMONY: The intention is not only to buy as few drinks as possible, but to have others buy them for us because we are broke, miserly or perpetual scroungers.

ILLOGICAL BEHAVIOR

Imagine you are wearing an expensive wristwatch which draws comment wherever you go—an instant conversation piece in any bar.

In fact, you find yourself holding drinks in your left hand (although you are right-handed) to draw attention to your left wrist piece.

This is an attitude as logical as counting money with the left hand while holding it in the right when you are right-handed. Because it is your right hand that is the business hand—used for counting money/winding watches/cutting food. This is why people hold bank notes in their left hand and count each one with the right, the *safe* hand.

The result of your trying to pull attention is that you lose the watch from your wrist while still sober and without your knowledge . . . to a con man who perpetrates the WRISTWATCH STEAL. There are many versions.

Basically, our new-found friend at the bar gains our confidence over a few drinks—a *few*, note; drunks are too observant in unpredictable ways. He then performs a trick. It may be to make a coin which he holds in his fist vanish and reappear in a handkerchief which we have been gripping. Or he may tell us to clench our fists tightly. He takes cigarette ash from an ashtray, dabs it on the back of one of our hands and blows it away. And we find the ash has penetrated through to the palm of that hand (a simple trick made unbelievable with good patter—he had previously touched the palm of that hand with a finger carrying cigarette ash).

Whatever the illusion the effect is the same. He has accomplished the psychological part of stealing our watch. And when he says he can now make a coin fly invisibly from our left fist to our right we really believe he will perform a miracle even more imposing than the last one. Our full attention is taken.

As he makes the challenge, he turns our left palm up (that is, if the watch is worn on that wrist). And places the coin in it, at the same time grasping our left wrist with his right hand. He

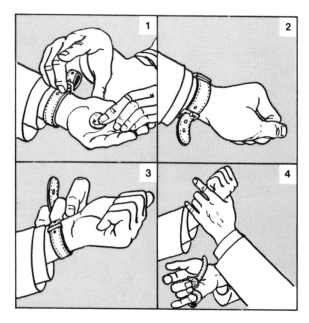

The con man steals your watch.

brings the tip of his second finger to the end of the wristwatch strap and pushes it so that it distorts (as shown in the diagram where the first finger is lifted to show the movement of the second finger). The second finger presses the tip of the strap in the direction shown.

He now closes our left fist and as he turns it over, kicks the strap loose (as shown). "Can you feel the coin?" he asks, taking his hand away and stepping back. Of course, we can.

His right hand grasps our left wrist again, simultaneously clipping the strap between his second and third fingers (as shown) with his thumb pressing on the watch glass. He tells us to hold on tightly to the coin and now turns our fist over so that it points up, at the same time slipping the strap from the metal catch.

"Are you left- or right-handed?" he asks, and his left hand grips our right hand and lifts it to the same position as his left hand, fist toward the ceiling. But his right second finger also pushes the catch over so that it can't flip back into one of the holes in the strap. Whatever we answer, he instructs us to open the left hand.

His left hand now takes the coin and places it in our right hand—so fixing our attention *there*. And, with his left hand grasping our left fist, he orders, "Hold tight." As we do so, he presses slightly with his right thumb on the face of the watch and raises our left fist in a quick movement while the right hand steals the watch (as shown).

He lets go of the hand and asks, "Can you guess if the coin is a head or a tail?" And he concludes with glib chatter and leaves, before we notice our loss. (If we *had* noticed, he would have said, "I was wondering when you were going to ask me.")

Because we wish to make friends we cooperate with the con man and our interest gradually grows *until we are totally distracted*.

Think of the countless other ways we can become Losers in CITY BRIGHT LIGHTS when we try to win friends by appearing to let others influence us. And we finish in their power.

Remedy: The Relaxed, p. 436; The Baby-Faced, p. 458; The Canny, p. 40; The Cold-Blooded, p. 187

The Joker (Impractical)

One of the more engaging Losers, he can still end up rolling in the aisle or falling about . . . kicked/whipped/beaten as the result of misplaced humor.

SIGNS AND SYMPTOMS

We complain of a cracked glass, the barman says, "Don't bleed on the bar then, Mac" and we grin. Winding our watch in a restaurant having previously palmed a metal-spring-and-cogwheel novelty which creaks rustily as we wind. Laying a toy silver pistol on the card table and joking, "I'll use this on anybody I catch cheating."

CAUSES

A desire to be one of the boys will encourage humor from the gifted or semidrunk. It urges us to integrate ourselves rather than ingratiate ourselves (see THE TOO FRIENDLY, p. 417) into attractive company.

Perhaps we inherited a sense of humor from our parents or our environment.

In some company we can feel superior. If we consider others beneath ourselves, it is easy to act the fool as an escape from boredom.

An inferiority complex can make us THE JOKER too. The reason? That if people are going to laugh because of us (our secret dread), it is better they laugh with us than at us.

ILLOGICAL BEHAVIOR

Humor doesn't travel well. This is not only true internationally, but nationally too—from city to city within one country where local humor may differ.

At home we know where we stand, more or less. But even at a Christmas office party a badly placed joke can see us scanning the ads for a new job. Misplaced laughter-power can have explosive effects. It can cost us the best of friends—and be dangerous too.

We should study the humor of a city wherever possible in advance (see THE RESEARCHER, p. 90). But we never do.

And we forget that laughter we may create in the city could stem from hostility toward us.

It is not simply that jokes are a manifestation of what we secretly feel and that by raising laughter over the matter, whether sexual/racial/religious, we proclaim the real WE. We can go too far and insult a stranger whose feelings are strong and directly opposite to ours.

Minority jokes, for instance, go down well with a majority audience. But who are we to gauge the outcome when we tell minority jokes in a strange bar where the regulars may be of that minority—or have their sympathies?

Or a jealous man could think we were getting too much attention from his girlfriend and start a nasty fight.

Millions of people have hang-ups of one kind or another. And we, caught up with our own wit, forget that as little as a beer knocked over can incite a stranger to violence. The person who has severe problems, doubts, fears, depression or is ill may lash out at *us*—both the trigger and target.

And we still believe nobody can upset us. If anyone insults us we just laugh with them and make fun back. We try to turn everything into a joke and start fooling around. And that's when trouble starts . . .

When—

—We pour beer over the head of the person who first poured beer over us. This is out of order, however, as this is the *second* time our beer goes over them (the first tit-for-tat pouring was allowable). Now we have gone too far and are blocked in the eye by the drinker whose thinning hair is sensitive to chilled liquor.

—We wager a bar table can be lifted with a beer glass. We set fire to a pile of match heads on a soggy beer mat which has been pressed hard on the table to make it stick. The empty glass is now turned upside down on the blaze. As the air pressure is reduced inside, the glass is clamped to the mat. The glass can then be lifted—taking the table with it. Only sometimes the table falls on to someone's shoes, and scattered match heads burn clothing . . . and, you've guessed, the joker gets a punch in the head when all he wanted was laughter.

No one is more vulnerable than THE JOKER who is expecting hilarity, but who gets hurt instead. It doesn't matter who or where we are in CITY BRIGHT LIGHTS—our guard is non-existent.

And alcohol has no respect for people or places. Bar fights that result in maiming or death occur in the most respectable establishments selling liquor. Often the cause is misplaced humor, whether gentle or boisterous.

Remedy: The Relaxed, p. 436; The Loser, p. 465; The Researcher, p. 90

The Sensitive (Egotistical or Front Runner)

Try to shine in public. But by overshadowing others, they find that their best behavior can draw as much unwelcome attention as if they were eccentric or boorish. They are the natural enemy of anyone padding behind.

SIGNS AND SYMPTOMS

Feeling like weighing yourself in the restroom of a diner, stripping off your coat and placing it over the dial, putting your head underneath like a photographer and sliding a coin in the slot to read the figures on the dial in private. Not looking around when a glass is dropped in the restaurant and everyone else turns to look. Being able to touch an eyeball with the rim of a cocktail glass without flinching because, for once, you are not wearing contact lenses (which toughen the eyeball).

CAUSES

Anybody who is inwardly unsure of himself and who dreads looking ridiculous in front of others is vulnerable through vanity.

It can be the most surprising person. Outwardly secure and confident, he privately dislikes himself to such a degree that he can't think of himself as worth loving for himself alone:

The conservative man who is a president of a business (or who owns one), a doctor, lawyer, judge or crook who has never been out with a girl he didn't have to pay. Such a man may not be much to look at, but he has forgotten what it is like to be poor.

The young man yearning to impress his beautiful girlfriend in the exotic restaurant, who warms to the waiter for using a napkin to sweep the tablecloth even though there isn't a breadcrumb or speck of dust in sight.

The Mr. Universe muscleman who strives for a perfect complexion to go with his perfect body; he pats shampoo lather on his face and rinses it off with warm water rather than risk using soap and water.

So often we envy a person's sophistication, wealth, youth, physique or other attribute and fail to realize that he himself has his envies. Perhaps, in some way, he envies us.

And we rise too easily to the fear of being put down/found out/rejected in public, often going out of our way to establish an image we feel is all-important. By force.

ILLOGICAL BEHAVIOR

Vanity surfaces whenever CITY BRIGHT LIGHTS give us that floating feeling. Then, after a drink or two, there is nothing like the power of anti-endorsement to make us behave irrationally.

Anti-endorsement is an egotistical motivation which works in various ways—all of them dangerous.

A group's consensus in a restaurant is "Money, you either love it or you hate it—we hate it." You either love this opinionated group or you don't, and THE SENSITIVE who doesn't can yield to the temptation to flash a wallet full of money in front of them.

These people may be acquaintances and their friends. But we overlook the fact that even honest people with a few drinks inside them will get ideas when they see someone foolish enough to wave his money around.

Or we may take our best girlfriend to some two-bit dive in a raunchy part of town. We do this not only for kicks, but also because her friends are big spenders who appreciate everything money stands for. We can't stand them. And show it with dangerous slumming trips by which we endorse our own disregard for the things that money will buy—and run immediate risks.

The average person is well-behaved in notorious underworld areas. We don't blend. Anyone who takes a girl slumming asks for trouble. There are always local toughs just waiting for some victim to show up with a nice girl. They may attack us, knock us out or even kill. What they do to our attractive girlfriend can be worse.

Anyone with a contempt for homosexuals can make known his feelings when the person next to him in a bar puckers up his lips and makes a kissing noise. He turns his back—a risky move. The fellow could be after our wallet. Pickpockets signal with various chirping sounds and a kissing sound means they have discovered where we keep our wallet. Not realizing, we get caught up in a distractingly animated conversation with the stranger on the other side—and are robbed by the "hook" who was guided by the sound.

Hatred of a city itself can be enough reason to delay getting treatment for venereal disease which we have caught in a BRIGHT LIGHTS area, probably from someone young and perhaps promiscuous. Because, above all else regarding social stigma and THE SENSITIVE, VD *is* at present the source of much unnecessary guilt and fear, and the ego-conscious person will use any excuse to put off seeking medical advice and help. He may even act on the ludicrous tip he overheard: No need to go to a doctor or clinic; just offer to give blood—if they take it, you're clean.

Suppose we *think* we are infected. City authorities warn that VD symptoms are not always obvious; that VD is now second only to measles as the most widespread infectious disease, but that, unlike measles, untreated VD can make us sterile, insane, crippled or blind. *BUT because the city endorses seeking early treatment, we—with our this-city-stinks attitude—can use anticity feelings as an excuse to put off going to the doctor or clinic.*

We'll hang on at all costs rather than seek treatment in THIS city, even though it is important to get treatment quickly for diseases such as syphilis, gonorrhea, thrush, trichomoniasis and urethritis.

Remedy: The Impervious, p. 449; The Loser, p. 465; The Canny, p. 40; The Obsequious, p. 124; The Fugitive, p. 202

The Obvious (Non-natives)

Present a target for the regulars in bars/restaurants/clubs just by sounding different and acting a little different from everybody else (see also THE AMERICAN, p. 65).

SIGNS AND SYMPTOMS

Relishing hot dogs that locals know will give us a hot-dog headache (supposedly caused by sodium nitrate used to dye the meat red). Searching a European city for a 42nd Street Special/Edible Submarine/Blintzes. Dialing a city telephone number from a bar and starting with the superfluous city prefix (212 in New York, 01 in London, for example). Asking to have regular-ese translated: Sin Loose Carnals which means St. Louis Cardinals baseball team in a Webster Groves bar; Lantabraze which means the Atlanta Braves in a Decatur diner.

CAUSES

It takes only a little alcohol or headiness produced by CITY BRIGHT LIGHTS to feed our egos and help us establish ourselves as non-natives and proud of it.

As with THE AMERICAN, we may then come to grief from the sober citizen-regular who is nevertheless not quite sober. Or with the local who is sobriety itself but who suffers from an attack of xenophobia as a result of our behavior and sees that we suffer too.

We need not even be strangers from another city, but just from another district of this one. We can still be too conspicuous.

For example, we may be quite well-off compared with the average worker in this section of the metropolis, able to spend more. Nor will the soldier who sticks out like a sore thumb endear the regulars when his hair is shorter and his accent and general bearing are different.

It is not because we don't subscribe to the adage "When in

Rome . . ."; it's just that we don't yet know what it is the Romans do do. And our own non-nativeness makes us rather too casual about finding out.

ILLOGICAL BEHAVIOR

THE OBVIOUS is a blanket personality electric with vulnerabilities. There are four characteristic ways in which an unwary stranger can spark a crisis.

THE VULGAR (OSTENTATIOUS) throw their weight around. *Sign:* Ordering the wine waiter to dispense with the wicker basket and tasting bit and to stand the bottles upright in front of you so that you can pour it yourself, disorient him and reduce his tip. *Cause:* See THE OBVIOUS (above), but this is also a case of the unfamiliar paradoxically breeding nervousness, fear and damp brows as waiters hover. *Consequence:* Probable subtle victimization possibly resulting in food poisoning which can cause agony for days or kill. We are given the food or drink known to be potentially risky on purpose by needled irresponsible restaurant or bar staff. . . . WE are given the ice cubes made from local water to cool the Perrier water we have brought along as a precaution against unpurified water; WE are served the stew with moldy meat, the underdone fish or raw shellfish on a hot day from a dirty kitchen (or the dirty part of an otherwise clean kitchen), the dangerous frozen-defrosted frozen food covered with a rare sauce; WE get the draft beer overspill which has run down the sides of glasses into the drip tray and has picked up disease germs; We also get the soggiest, oldest hot dog which the seller has kept bubbling all day (food hygiene regulations tell us these are ideal cultures for nourishing food poisoning bacteria).

THE MEDDLING (INTERFERING) crash in where angels fear for their heads. *Sign:* Going into a bookstore to read on in the paperback thriller you have already bought but left at home. *Cause:* An impatience for action where the action is; impetuosity mixed with (do) goodliness. *Consequence:* A broken head from trying to separate the scrappers in a bar or helping another drinker through when the people at the bar are blocking his way. Unknown to us, this is a piece of daily horseplay by the regulars who turn a mock battle into a real one when one of them in particular gets cut up and nasty at the outsider who doesn't understand and who becomes serious—US. Many regulars' ploys (like shouting "Don't take that man's money—he's a forger" as a local enters the bar) can initiate trouble when the foreigner butts in thinking it's for real.

THE BRILLIANT (FASTEST GUN) face unnecessary show-downs. *Sign:* Being able to see the dust on top of things that smaller people don't know is there. *Cause:* Being tall/well-dressed/happy—a threat? *Consequence:* Bigheadedly befriending the friendly girl (known to others in the bar who steer clear) who keeps urging us to drink more and more. She either invites us back to her room and gives us knock-out drops or drops a Mickey Finn into our drink on the bar, takes our wallet and splits. Or she may flatter us into talking of the piece of ice we have just brought the wife, the string of pearls that cost $15,000; either she gives our address to a burglar or a listener follows us.

THE IRREVERENT (KNOCKER) has similarities with THE VULGAR, THE JOKER (p. 421) and THE WINNER (p. 413). *Sign:* Banging a fork on the table and telling the waiter you expect more than ham sandwiches, cheese and onion sticks, pineapple and cheese sticks and cheap white wine when the menu says salmon, prawns in aspic, vol-au-vent, smoked trout, roast turkey, galantine of ox, a variety of salads and cheeses and half a bottle of champagne. *Cause:* Ignorance and/or an inferiority complex. Self-made success from lowly beginnings. Liquor taken. *Consequence:* Potential food poisoning when in a restaurant or a coat stolen because the staff have turned a blind eye to *our* possessions; potential trouble in a bar because of similar behavior. We are suckers for the argumentative person who may deliberately set us up for a going-over. By provoking us, he will goad us into talking back and then invite us down an alley. Often he will act drunk until he gets us alone. He might also have colleagues waiting to give him a hand in working us over.

There are other personality defects which can cripple under CITY BRIGHT LIGHTS. We must learn to short-circuit them fast.

Remedy: All of Chapter 14.

The Worried (Haunted)

Go down drugged—permanent targets for those denizens of CITY BRIGHT LIGHTS areas alert to the pitfalls they hope the addicted will fall into.

SIGNS AND SYMPTOMS

Jaundice (from grubby needles). Minty breath before breakfast to swamp the smell of just-drunk whiskey. Home-rolled cigarettes and a sharp-sour odor. Excitable behavior. Needing a drink before facing anything requiring just a small amount of nerve. Ascorbic acid (Vitamin C) in pockets (to reduce bad LSD trips). Children underfed. Multiple dents/abrasions/tears on car body. Time lost from work. An increasing disinclination to open mail from your bank. Family disruption. Lonesome drinking which can produce TOO-FRIENDLY signs.

CAUSES

Alcohol drugs the central nervous system. We use it as a social beverage. And abuse it to the extent that it is the major drug problem in many countries. Look at the record of the average American drinker.

He consumes the alcoholic equivalent of nine gallons of whiskey a year—or 12 bottles of whiskey, 15 bottles of sherry, 30 bottles of wine and 380 bottles of beer. Nine million Americans are alcoholics—nearly 10 per cent of the labor force.

Addiction to alcohol—as to hard drugs like heroin or cocaine, both *peddled among CITY BRIGHT LIGHTS*—IS caused by problems. No one is immune who is worried stiff—perhaps subconsciously.

Yet many potential addicts never realize. They just think they like a drink, for example, and that it eases the tension of competitive city life. But take it away from them and they experience withdrawal symptoms.

Alcoholism is as likely to hit highly paid executives or their lonely, bored wives as those with lowlier jobs unfortunate enough to have to buy their own drinks (they don't have expense accounts).

And drugs . . . ? The teenager with severe personality problems can easily graduate from marijuana to hard drugs. And the older person with a strong anti-establishment philosophy can deliberately base his life-style on the believed nonaddictive (but killer-potential) LSD or acid, which deprives him of his judgment and lands him in real danger. He might jump out of a high window thinking, under the influence of LSD, that he could fly.

Young or old, the end result is ruin. And for sick reasons.

ILLOGICAL BEHAVIOR

Generally speaking, the mature and well-balanced run little or no risk of suffering damage by drinking alcohol or smoking pot. They know when to stop, unlike the addict who is sick as a result of human deprivation, weakness and personality maladjustment.

Many people smoke. Untold thousands of middle-class couples offer after-dinner pot with coffee, where once it was port or brandy. It is not only lawyers, doctors, teachers, social workers and young professionals; marijuana is used by miners, butchers and garage mechanics too.

Pot is not, as many people suppose, the monopoly of the dropout any more than brandy and vodka are that of the executive. It is the freaky types, however, who are just the ones to get caught, although they represent only about one per cent of the people who use cannabis.

Our illogicality, though, is in taking too much drink too often— or using harder drugs—and doing nothing about it when we would like to, because city pressures direct otherwise:

When drinking imperceptibly becomes habitual, as when we have to take business people out to lunch and to dinner. We find that between business lunches and social dinners we are going through two bottles of wine plus five or six other drinks a day. Or we may have to accompany the boss all the time; he likes to drink and we feel we can't very well say no (though we'd like to).

When we feel better after a drink and feel we can cope, although in more sober moments we know this is the exact opposite of the truth.

When we are highly conscious of the self-awareness that cannabis has given us and can *see* our route to ruin—we shall lose our jobs, suffer illness and possibly die, turn to stealing, prostitution and go to prison, have infants born already addicted, lose our friends and our associates will become other addicts—and STILL we are prepared to experiment with lysergic acid (LSD) or heroin.

When we are always full of ideas, but hardly ever come round to translating them into constructive action for we discover our pleasure (cannabis-smoking) in such an effortless and simple way that we all too easily give way to the temptation to sidestep tasks requiring long-term effort/dedication/perseverance.

When we consequently lose invaluable opportunities to grow steadily in emotional maturity by having to face reality and having to cope with everyday difficulties and challenges. And we realize we are in a habit which makes us do so.

When we secretly wonder if pot-smoking is *really* affecting us as the scientists say, causing severe loss of brain protein and the cell component, RNA, which is vital to brain function. For we seem to have all the signs—that initial sense of tranquillity leading to sluggish mental and physical responses, some emotional instability, irritability, irrational aggression, loss of weight, mental confusion and impaired memory.

And yet we don't seek medical aid or get religious help, which is available in the city, whatever habit is growing . . . alcohol, marijuana (*psychologically* addictive), hallucinogens, amphetamines or barbiturates mixed with drink.

No addiction is hopeless when it is discovered and diagnosed in the *early* stages. It can be ended long before we become fixed on hard drugs or the well-disguised bottle and change into hopeless junkies or alcoholics.

But it is in CITY BRIGHT LIGHTS where we can first become hooked. And perpetuate the habit aided by drug pushers. For illegal drugs are contagious. Their users seek the company of other users. They are the focal point of infection, offering the first heroin shot/cigarette/saturated sugar cube/pills to the uninitiated.

Remedy: The Impervious, p. 449

The Cheap (Scroungers)

End these odd-numbered chapters of accidents (on Losers in the city) by being first in tightfistedness, the Even-Stevens who must never finish under par but who overdo it.

SIGNS AND SYMPTOMS

Seeing our family holds fast to its mutual funds and long-term growth stocks and, in addition, adding to the real estate holdings, easing off slightly on capital investment and dumping a few short-hauls . . . AND having the nickname Harry the Swerver (because of our skill in never buying drinks); always buying the first round when a drinking school promises to expand later but always buying last when the school will not increase, as then you will be a drink or two up on the others by the time you all finish; refusing a drink and when asked why emptying your pockets to show they have nothing inside—but eventually accepting the drink when pushed.

CAUSES

Many characteristics beget cheapness. Some, in fact, have been covered before in previous chapters. There are so many it would take a booklet to list them, but here are some of the more glaring:

THE TOO-FRIENDLY (p. 417) who may only be so to scrounge as many drinks as possible—the rapt listener, nodding approvingly to whatever old rubbish we are saying. THE CONFORMIST (p. 164) too who (like THE JOKER, p. 421) feels the company is undergrade, and that buying drinks here is throwing pearls before pigs. THE NARCISSISTIC (p. 155) can only think of themselves and have no intention of spending money on anyone else other than, perhaps, the one person they are transcendentally zonking. THE ADVERTISER (p. 220) who like many rich men can be the richest man in the bar and still be dead mean; he likes to see how long he can go before buying a round of drinks. THE VULGAR or IRREVERENT (p. 429) or THE WISE GUY (p. 22) may actively admit they *won't* buy drinks, but still have people offering to buy them liquor and get away with it by posing as "characters." There is no end to the CITY BRIGHT LIGHTS scroungers, ranging from the bluff, hearty fellow with the booming laugh who seems the finest fellow in the bar (and who is not short of cash either) to the mild/meek/gentle character who enters a bar and never says a word. And WE, however generous and popular we usually are, can still resort, at some time or other, to their ploys when we don't have the price of a drink in our pockets and feel oncoming panic as we are trapped in a group of hard-drinking drinkers.

ILLOGICAL BEHAVIOR

No one likes being taken for a ride in CITY BRIGHT LIGHTS, least of all US. Yet a display of meanness here can leave us sitting ducks.

If we decide to venture into CITY BRIGHT LIGHTS, we must expect a shady side and be ready to take the consequences no matter how unimportant-but-unpleasant. . . . They can escalate.

Watch your attitude, a state of mind which states nobody is going to sting us among the blinding neon. Out of this outlook arise emergencies.

ANY time when it crosses our mind to quibble about what are relatively small-time stakes in the CITY BRIGHT LIGHTS, we risk a host of trouble, some of which can be disastrous to our families, career, life-style or even life.

REMEDY: It takes more than a booklet to cope with such vulnerabilities. The final Loser, literally, should turn to *all* even-numbered chapters again—starting at Chapter 14.

14

CITY BRIGHT LIGHTS

WINNERS

THOSE OF US about to leave the city after a business trip or vacation now come full circle. City theaterland is the logical end point with the final evening's—or day's—farewell drink/meal/show. For regulars who live in the metropolis, CITY BRIGHT LIGHTS can emblazon the end of yet another day.

Having survived our stay or day so far, we can relax. There is nothing to be won from being too tightly wound or too expectant of disaster crashing down among the Soho/Times Square/Hollywood-and-Vine branches of asphalt forests. Such behavior will make us blend all the better into the city throng—when backed by that subconscious vigilance that marks the final four Winners.

The Relaxed (Bar Cloth)

Mop up unprovoked insult and embarrassment the way a bartender's rag wipes spilled drinks because they primed themselves in preparation for such incidents—by wringing themselves dry of prejudice/unworldliness/naïveté.

Shocks come as no surprise, the element which makes for 100,000,001 victims. And by forestalling traumas, THE RELAXED prevent more serious crises.

Unhappy. Tense. Lonely. Cold sober. No previous experience of large cities whatsoever. It is still possible to relax among neon waterfalls when you know what to expect.

KNOW RELAXANTS

Find peace of mind. Know where to go after midnight. Find out first (see THE RESEARCHER, p. 90) or ask a policeman or taxi driver for late-night lavatories, medical treatment, drug-stores, places to eat, money-changing facilities (air terminals, big hotels, bank vending machines, certain post offices), places to sleep if locked out.

COMPOSE INQUIRIES

Keep calm when asking favors. Make your inquiries easy to understand. Don't take NO for an answer. EXAMPLE: A news-paper kiosk notice says, "No Change Given for Telephones". . . . *DON'T tap a coin on the counter.* Wait. Explain how your need to telephone is so urgent—short of life and death. And how you only have this coin. . . . Remember, it's the approach that counts.

SOAK UP SHORT CHANGE

Don't make a fuss if bartender/cashier/hat check girl holds back some loose change while counting it out. Blow hot and YOU look in the wrong because . . . change-giver says, "Sure they're yours," and gives you the coins.

SWALLOW INSULTS

Insults may be THE attraction of a particular bar/restaurant/ show where clients *go to be ribbed.* Take it in great part when a Chinese waiter rides YOU throughout the meal (even when it isn't fun).

ABSORB NAMES

Get others on your side. Remember their names (or nick-names)—the most pleasant sound to anyone. *Listen* to rather

than look at a stranger during an introduction. If you forget the
name (or never knew it) . . . take a coaster and ball point pen to
show how a forger copies a signature by turning the original
autograph upside down and starting from the last letter (see
THE SPECULATOR, p. 332). Ask strangers to write down
names so you can demonstrate.

TOLERATE TRANSVESTITES

NEVER get uptight when you discover your companion is of
the same sex as you. Heterosexuals—pass it off. Don't recoil in
horror or become violent when not normally given to scrapping.

Transvestites can be vicious—they have fewer inhibitions than
normal men and rejection antagonizes them for they think they
are beautiful; they also keep together and gang up. So be careful if you encounter any.

DON'T TURN A HAIR

Say you saw nothing when witnesses are questioned by police/
heavies/priest over a BRIGHT LIGHTS incident. Don't get involved (you never know what IS involved). Dissolve your facial
expression so that it hides your feelings and knowledge.

To act know-nothing is safest.

TAKE REJECTION QUIETLY

Leave a bar/restaurant/etc. whose management disapproves
of your long hair/jeans/tee shirt. You can't win. OR when obvious
regulars are anti. Exit too from head/freak/dropout establishment when you are wearing a suit and tie (no matter how inexpensive your threads).

ACCEPT HOMOSEXUALS

Anticipate homosexuals in BRIGHT LIGHTS areas. Especially
in dimly lit gay bars which can take the unaware by surprise
(YOU just wandered in). If a homosexual asks you to dance, re-

fuse *politely* (unless you are interested in the invitation). No violence, please, or you suffer (outnumbered and outfought). Leave scenes NOT yours when you realize. Don't go into these places for kicks when you are straight.

REST EASY

Don't be uptight about being conned. The more you are, the more likely you are to become a victim.

Be ALERT below the casual facade you should always assume under BRIGHT LIGHTS.

POCKET AFFRONT

Shell out when threatened by buy-me-a-beer-or-else muscle. Drink up. And go. (It's not only in the most shady areas that this can happen.)

STICK WITH A DRINK

Don't get drunk when alone in foreign territory (only in bars where you are regular/accepted/friendly). Being one-third intoxicated is the maximum allowable. Over this borderline, you ARE vulnerable.

Know your own drink threshold (people differ greatly). You are within the safety limit when you remember to slip your wristwatch off and reverse it on your wrist so it will remind you of some fact just noted while drinking AND still remember why the pointers are the wrong way around next morning.

SMOTHER SECRETS

Toss wet cloth on public chat concerning private movements, possessions, details. Be wary of expansive moods in bars "with the boys." Don't try to top others' tales about business or impress them with your ingenuity/acumen/verve.

NEVER discuss money earned, takings taken, valuables purchased, even when dropping into your local bar after a day's work, or during lunch).

Loudmouths always interest . . . waiters, waitresses, bartenders, plainclothesmen, income tax informers who like to collect a store of personal details. Gamblers are also quick to pass YOU on as a hot tip to a burglar if you advertise you are making book, handling large sums of cash, winning at racetrack/crap games/card games.

Switch on a remote look if pressed. Reply when spoken to, but let the eyes glaze over. Be more occupied with NOT giving secrets away than with your interrogator. Close your "windows."

Be bugging conscious. A Chinese restaurant is often the safest place to talk confidentially in public.

Foil potential bugs (perhaps a tiny radio transmitter with 1,000-foot range hidden in a sugar cube or a tape player in somebody's breast pocket). Discuss top-secret information over a running tap in the toilet; beneath flickering neon light in a bar; inside a car with the windshield wipers working (make an excuse about washing the glass) ALL of these will interfere with recordings.

TURN OTHER CHEEK

Be the first to drop your gaze in eyeball-to-eyeball confrontation with strangers.

Don't lock stares with strangers in bar/club/discotheque. Remember a beer mug hitting YOU can mean you lose one of the eyes which triggered trouble (psychopaths are paranoid about a stranger's stare).

Don't turn round to look when it is suggested you should observe somebody behind. Sneak a glance, if you must, a little later on the pretext of turning to talk to someone else.

Don't comment about a stranger to an attractive female companion so that SHE turns and looks. Try not to glance across the woman at a solo stranger (even accidentally) and make an innocent comment when there is hilarity between you. The ensuing laughter can trigger a paranoid's temper.

A stranger may seem to stare you out only because he is wearing contact lenses, which can when new be a source of severe discomfort.

If confronted by a stranger with squint/glass eye/lazy eye . . . look at the nose. Don't try to spot the good eye and respond to that one. You may be wrong.

ACT UNCONCERNED

Avoid panic when late for film/show/act. Haste along crowded sidewalks makes you vulnerable (see THE DEPENDABLE, p. 80).

THINK: *How many times have I been late before and by the final curtain REALLY regretted missing the start (and forgotten that original panic too)?*

STAND TOUCHING

Move away in time when YOU have a strong aversion to being grabbed, patted, stroked, mauled in busy bars.

Watch it in foreign cities; erogenous zones vary from one country to another. A stranger's hand on a strange part of the anatomy in a strange city can shock/unhinge/throw ultrasensitive or ticklish characters.

Keep both hands to yourself too. Don't pat/pet/push strangers (who may detest contact—and retaliate when drunk/uptight/mad enough).

To make your way through a crowd, use firm, gentle and obvious hand movements on shoulders/hips/waists of people blocking the way. Brush gently, then press. Or vice versa. Apologize with "Scuse me's" rather than shoulder-barging through.

HANDSHAKE DRUNKS

Sidetrack intoxicated pests by shaking hands. And split.

But disappear on a jukebox-playing/toilet-going/must-see-friend-over-there pretext—NOT straight out through the door into the street.

Be patient in your evasive maneuvers.

Beware of the handshake maniac who offers you his hand. And attempts to squeeze it to pulp (yell out about your broken finger he's pressing on). Or he may offer you a steel hook/artificial limb/fingerless stump—a handicapped drunk's grisly humor.

Don't show revulsion. Expect incidents like this to happen sooner or later.

KEEP YOUR HAIR ON

DO count spilling a stranger's beer/accidentally treading on a shoe/chance remark to which stranger objects as serious in any BRIGHT LIGHTS establishment.

It's not enough to say sorry. Or to offer to make good the damage (buying replacement drinks, paying the cleaner's bill or footing the shoeshine fee). Though you must offer.

IMAGINE the spilling-victim received a horrifying injury from a samurai sword which almost severed him in two and since then has been looked on as a soft target; spilled beer is THE last straw.

BE READY TO DUCK; watch his fists (NOT his eyes) and wrists (if his wristwatch is worn on the right arm, expect a possible left-hand punch to arrive first).

If attacked, see THE FUGITIVE (p. 202).

When beer is spilled on YOU, be cool. If it was purposely poured over your head—and if nothing will stop you—drench the original pourer too. Don't get out of step and trickle the third glass of the fray over the person who threw drink No. 1. This now makes you 2–1 up—and invites a punch from the shower bath originator.

Intoxication is the usual cause of bravado/pride/low jinks. Be the first to break the tension barrier by stepping down when face to face with a barroom scuffle. It is a relief to most potential assailants who are often only posturing mad NOT fighting mad.

If you DO get the first blow in—usually the winning punch—AND the Loser you beat reappears at a later date, mention the scrap (just in case he's looking for another). Once men talk of violence, it rarely happens.

TAKE JOKES ON THE CHIN

Laugh when ribbed. Play yourself down. NEVER feel you have to justify yourself against laughter aimed at you. Laugh with THEM laughing at YOU. See your own ridiculous side.

Back down from barroom arguments—common ground for fist/knife/bottle fights. Realize the danger in time.

ACCEPT DELAY

Be resigned to waiting in line for restaurant table/movie show/ Saturday night singles bar.

Do anything to aid patience: chew gum, work coins in fists, look in mirrors—a proven line sedative (often provided for this purpose by the theater management), eat chocolate/raisins/nuts (especially when hungry). Pull out of line and go another evening (or matinee) NOT on a weekend.

Be ready to scrap your evening's plans when the crowd crush is too much.

CUT CLIP-JOINT LOSSES

Lone males hunting sex are inevitable victims of the clip joint —found in every city (see also THE WINNER, p. 413).

On realizing the nature of the club you have entered . . .

MAKE AN EXCUSE AND LEAVE.

(Be quite firm. Say you have no money left *before* they wrest it away by trickery. Walk out courteously but with purpose. Don't let inviting girls prevent you from leaving.)

HOW TO TELL IT IS A CLIP JOINT: Apparent reluctance of the management to let you in, while the girl you met outside or who beckons you from inside insists she will sign in; membership book to be signed by you; cozy layout and, except for the stage, much darker than a real night club; strippers who, between acts, persuade customers to buy watered drinks (they get a cut each drink); a girl always on the spot where you are seated (who peeks into your wallet to see how much you are worth);

girl(s) prepared to sit with you even if you object; speedy service ferrying drinks you never requested; a girl suggests a date for the evening (but to square the management you need to buy a bottle of champagne)—she tries to con you into buying another bottle and disappears when your funds run out OR she may start to walk out with you but be stopped at the door by the manager who says she must finish her time in the show (and apologizes to you).

Go as soon as the truth dawns. Don't let pride stop you from abandoning a girl who promises sex (you are in for a disappointment). NEVER kick up a fuss. Never stay and sulk.

Cut your losses fast. Clear out.

WINK AT BRIGHT LIGHTS

Explore theater/topless/go-go areas by day when they take on a different identity. See life as it is lived by the natives of theater districts. And get your bearings from neon signs/movie ads/skin flicks pix advertising the show within.

GRIN AND BEAR BODY EXCHANGES

Body exchanges/single bars/pickup places—ALL are bars catering to single people only which sell liquor and reasonably priced meals. They are packed from Friday to Sunday evenings, often quiet on Tuesdays or Thursdays.

Know where to find them when you are lonely. Just *any* bar will not do. Read ads/ask people/phone visitors' bureau (see also THE RESEARCHER, p. 90). The bars could be along a strip or scattered throughout part of the financial district. Or both.

Arrive just before 5 P.M. to get a seat at the bar (action happens from 5 P.M. to 9 P.M.—OR from 9 P.M.-ish on in singles bars belonging to apartment-block areas rather than Wall Street ones). In 5 P.M. establishments there is free food to go with the drink you buy (some give a plate for holding food-on-a-stick tidbits).

Where there is a washroom attendant (coat brushes/cologne/talc available at wash basin), DO leave a tip in the saucer.

Everyone knows singles bars are there so people can meet. It is a mistake to think you have it made, however. There are inevitable cliques. Creeps. Hard-to-get-to-know phonies. And uptight, tense people spoiling for arguments.

Don't expect miracles. Secretly question the people you meet as they will doubt you; it IS the safest way in these bars.

Prostitutes often infiltrate certain 5 P.M. bars.

Don't scorn a prostitute when, drunk, she insults you. Paranoid hookers can cause trouble in a crowded bar. Be polite rather than smart. A humane answer is the one most likely to get you off the hook.

NEVER flirt from one prostitute to another *striking bargains* which you forget as you see another hooker you fancy even more. Their jungle telegraph may see to it that you are set up for a street attack later.

If you are determined to go with a prostitute, the rule is abide by any agreement you make. If you change your mind tell her. BUT don't approach others in the meanwhile. Business IS business.

KEEP YOUR SHIRT ON DANCING

Don't get rattled—or rattle others—on a crowded dance floor when a spinning couple knock into you, a balloon-pricking maniac bursts your balloon, your partner abandons you or a stranger accuses you of treading on his shoes.

Follow the dance style of the particular establishment. Don't dance differently for the sake of being different. Fast/angular/jerky movements with your limbs flying will not make you popular on a small floor among regulars shuffling around in a relaxed and quiet style.

Watch the habits of your partner . . . straightening your tie . . . smoothing down your lapels . . . slipping her hands around your waist beneath your coat; pickpockets have these habits too.

LOWER YOURSELF

Loneliness is more obvious among BRIGHT LIGHTS areas than in any other part of the city. Are YOU a sad figure likely to be—even on your last night in town—watching while others have fun/sitting alone in a cinema/eating at a table for one in a restaurant?

Friends are there for the making in ordinary city bars— but you need to make the effort. And shun the transparently smooth cocktail-type bars where your feeling of isolation will increase.

Use smaller "local" bars frequented by off-duty theater staff, hotel workers, waitresses, writers, actors and actresses and possibly even off-duty con men/burglars/pickpockets too (don't flash money or money talk and you will be left alone).

These places lack glitter. But you will have company. And you will be safer.

BE ALL THINGS

—to ALL men.

Despite suspicious/leery/canny instincts essential to city survival . . . NEVER be a snob. The attitude makes you vulnerable as well as lonely.

DO UNTO OTHERS AS YOU WOULD HAVE THEM DO UNTO YOU—ONLY DO IT FIRST

Corny as it sounds TAKE YOUR TIME:

1. Be patient. Don't yearn to talk to *some*body so much you approach *any*body in a friendly "regulars" bar. That these regulars are friendly does NOT mean they are well-disposed to YOU— yet.
2. Buying the bartender a drink too soon brands you as a Loser. Don't be too eager to splash money around. Don't press drinks on a group of people; buy one particular person a drink first. Then, if it does come to buying rounds, *never* miss your turn.
3. Casual behavior is more attractive. Don't catch a woman's eye too often when she is with a liable-to-be-jealous escort—drinkers have been stabbed or shot for less.

4. Suspect the friendly girl sitting alone at the bar who grows on you the more you drink. Don't rush. If she is so amenable, why aren't more of the regulars talking to her? Even if she says it's her first time here, doubt her . . . especially if she urges you to drink more, suggests you can go back to her room and you have, in course of buying drinks, opened your wallet.

5. Make it obvious you ARE a stranger rather than try to hide it. AND that you enjoy *this* city as the greatest. Regulars who disagree will still feel local pride even if they don't admit it. Contacts made in "local" city bars are sources for THE RESEARCHER (p. 90)—willing helpers, once you are accepted.

    Show ignorance to get city drinkers to like you better. If asked how you found The Block/Bay/Biscuit don't say OK when you don't know what The Biscuit/Bay/Block is.

6. Don't be a crawler/toady/sycophant. Assess fellow-drinkers at bar. And always when homesick. Don't be all over a person from your "home" town/country/city. He may hate the place and be anti-YOU; he could be a con man just pretending to hail from way back to build up the trust that will make you a victim.

7. Watch it watching TV sport from a bar stool. Continued drinking makes you vulnerable to violent arguments/fighting fans/pickpockets, etc.

8. Turn down offers to settle an argument "outside"; it may be a way of setting you up for a going-over NOT just from the character needling you but from his accomplices waiting outside.

9. Avoid a belligerent blowhard looking for a fight. This type picks on a person he knows he can beat up and is often backed up by sycophants. Sadists love hurting others. They usually work in gangs so as not to suffer harm themselves.

10. AVOID *rushing into any venture in strange bar no matter how harmless it may seem when you don't know all it involves. At the first hint of trouble—move on.*

STOMACH NEW FOOD

Be appreciative. And easily pleased when city's food is served before you. Forget the food back home—how can it be the same? There are bound to be differences in preparation.

NEVER make a fuss because food looks or tastes different from what you expected (incorporating more butter and cream/spicier or cooked in oil perhaps).

Take out health insurance before a city holiday.

Scrimp on exotic or different (ethnic) food at first to give your stomach a chance to acclimatize. Indulge two/three days later. *You should be able to eat or drink anything in larger hotels and restaurants, used to catering to foreign visitors.*

Ask taxi drivers where THEY eat when looking for cheap meals; their choices will be the best value if less salubrious.

Carry a supply of antisickness pills. And water-sterilizing tablets too when you are fastidious-and-can't-help-it. (If you are unsure whether the local water supply is contaminated because of city strikes/droughts/bombings, drink only boiled water, bottled-water-with-your-purifying-tablet-added or mineral water—and use this for washing teeth too. Avoid ice cubes and salads.)

SAFETY RULES (keep them to yourself) . . . fresh and golden french fries are a good sign for the rest of the food too (anemic/greasy/limp potatoes mean low standards in the kitchen); skip shellfish and salads on a hot day in a dirty-looking restaurant; avoid food that could be frozen-unfrosted-refrozen (dangerous); stick to food that has been well cooked and recently cooked rather than uncooked food; *make it your rule not to eat underdone meat/raw shellfish/little-cooked fish.*

Check restaurants big and small before selecting for regular meals OR a big-deal meal. By eating there.

Do this before taking a girl to an expensive restaurant for the first time. Then you know what to expect.

CHECK: *Whereabouts* of bar/cloakrooms/tables (you can then ask for a certain table when phoning your reservation for two); *who* is head waiter/wine waiter/roast carver (and who is tipped separately from the bill?); *how*, when you are unsure, to carry out the wine-tasting ritual, checking the bill, etc. . . . by watching others (a waiter may inflate your bill when you are with a girl, but will quickly correct it when you query the amount *without fuss*).

WELCOME MASHERS

Fight jealousy when you are with a woman in BRIGHT LIGHT districts. Play it cool if a womanizer horns in on your date. Women prefer you this way. Don't blow your top or you may lose the female.

Don't turn your back on the intruder; this is antagonistic body language and leaves you vulnerable to attack (and you *are* subconsciously daring him to make a move).

If grabbed round the body and arms . . . either

STEP BACKWARD—and drive a shoe heel down on his instep as hard as possible. Or

SIT DOWN—lift both legs off the ground and sit down heavily while shooting both arms up. Slip out of his grasp.

Tactic for the able-bodied: Throw both arms up and back to lock them round his neck . . . bend forward, pulling down on both hands . . . jerk up hips and buttocks . . . and toss the attacker over your head so he lands in front of you.

The Impervious (Bolshie)

Still appear relaxed, but go their own sweet way in BRIGHT LIGHTS areas. And damn-well-please-themselves.

They *know* that (1) it is impossible to please everybody, (2) if they are told something they don't want to hear, it's best not to listen, (3) once they make a decision no amount of discouragement or persuasion will normally make them give way.

Hot water rolls off the back of THE IMPERVIOUS in matters of . . .

EXTORTION

(See also THE BEWILDERED, p. 20, and THE ILLOGICAL, p. 354).

Beware of strangers offering easy ways of sexual pleasure . . . coffee shop/singles bar friendships that result in immediate offers of marriage . . . marriage agency questionnaires requiring strange information plus photograph in bathing suit . . . newspaper ads for couples interested in "pair skating" (group sex).

ALL *can place you under a blackmailer's pressure.*

WOMEN: Find out about the would-be husband first (fortune hunter out to avoid the actual marriage ceremony?); quiz him with direct questions and pin him down to concrete replies; check his answers—make a discreet phone call to the firm where he claims to be the accountant, say, and ask for the accountant's name.

MEN: Be as wary of overtures from females. Check: *Did* the girl have sudden abortion as she said, or is her story of a moonlight operation because of a suspicious husband a frightener fabricated to make you pay? Ask AND pin down answers; ARE you being set-up for blackmail by a married woman whose husband (in league) is rigging your affair?

Be your own private detective: double check. Or employ a private eye.

EXERCISING RIGHTS

YOUR basic legal right in a restaurant is to be served wholesome food. You can sue if the food is off and gives you food poisoning.

SPILLED FOOD: The restaurant is not automatically liable—only if there has been negligence (lack of reasonable care or skill one would be entitled to expect). Most restaurant managements will pay the cleaner's bill if they think a customer has a reasonable complaint.

INEDIBLE FOOD: You can complain about food not fit to eat or "not of the substance or nature demanded" to the public health department. A portion of glass/string/bug in the food, say.

STOLEN COAT: Restaurants are only liable for loss of a customer's hat or coat if a member of the staff took your property and hung it on a hook for you. Disclaimer notices by coat and hat stands *used by you* have no legal effect as, in this case, the restaurant is not liable anyway.

BONE IN THROAT: You can sue if injury from eating fileted meat or fish is serious enough (fileted means boneless).

ALCOHOL

Are YOU one of the city millions who, legally, should not have driven a car for years (because of your daily intake of alcohol)?

When it is impossible for you to say NO, know: *In America 4.2 per cent of executives swallow 35 or more drinks a week—an amount said to be definitely harmful. And many more men die of cirrhosis of the liver in the professional-executive class than in any other social group.*

IF YOU HAVE TO DRINK, the best time is at the end of the business day before dinner.

Drink a pint of milk before drinking alcohol to help reduce the level of alcohol in the bloodstream.

Eat protein food *before* drinking. After is too late. Kaolin mixture (used for stomach upsets) slows up the absorption of alcohol. Mashed potato is good, too.

Eat honey while drinking when you don't want a hangover; sugar burns up alcohol fast (see also THE ILLOGICAL, p. 354).

Drink slowly. The average person needs to make a small whiskey/gin/sherry last an hour for the safest effect. But *talking* helps.

Avoid the worst hangovers by drinking vodka or gin instead of beer/brandy/bourbon.

ROBBERIES

Watch for companions' destructive attitudes. It is no use securing your wallet inside your inner coat pocket with a safety pin (see THE CANNY, p. 40) if you are going to relax the need to pin up the pocket *because of their a-safety-pin-so-what shoulder-shrugging* during the evening. Pay no attention.

SEX

It is NOT easier to find sex in honkytonk bars used by derelicts/tramps/addicts. Stick to the CITY BRIGHT LIGHTS of theater districts for your excitement.

ARRESTED

ASK WHY: The police can arrest you without proof, but they have to give a reason (remember what it is); GO QUIETLY when picked up on sidewalk/bar stool/dance floor—don't protest innocence (just *say* you are); BE POLITE but firm—give your name and address and ask for legal aid; REQUEST A TELEPHONE CALL—as entitled—to call your lawyer or a responsible friend who will find you a lawyer; SAY NO MORE—or as little as possible (the least thing, *and* some things you may not have said, can be repeated and misconstrued in court); MAKE A STATEMENT only when advised to by a lawyer; ASK FOR WRITING MATERIALS, another entitlement, and note down the gist of interviews at the time (or soonest afterward); BRIBES —never try them or follow police advice that to cooperate will mean a lighter sentence/better treatment/bail (it works to their advantage); KEEP CLOSED—even to the sympathetic policeman who is trying to persuade you to help him *with the police case against you.*

HANDSHAKE SADIST

When your hand is squeezed deliberately in an iron grip (1) make your left hand into a fist and corkscrew your middle knuckle hand into the back of THE JOKERS's (p. 421) right hand so he has to let go OR (2) grab hold of the little finger on his right hand and bend it backward.

VENEREAL DISEASE

IF YOU THINK YOU HAVE CAUGHT VD:

1. KNOW THE SYMPTOMS.
2. GO TO A CLINIC IF YOU FEEL AT ALL WORRIED YOU MIGHT HAVE SOMETHING.
3. NEVER WAIT IN THE HOPE THAT IT WILL CLEAR UP.
4. BE SURE TO TELL ANYBODY YOU MAY HAVE INFECTED THROUGH INTERCOURSE OR GENITAL CONTACT.

ks harder producing increased angina risk because (a)
tempts to constrict blood vessels and (b) drinking tries
em.

ES, HYPNOTICS, SLEEPERS, GOOFBALLS +
= FATAL INTERACTION.

s produce an abnormal feeling of well-being, are ad-
can kill quicker when mixed with drink than a massive

RESSANT PILLS + ALCOHOL = DANGER.
iness is instant result. Certain wines interact riskily
antidepressants.

+ PEP PILLS/AMPHETAMINES/SPEED =
EFFECT.

ally addictive, they excite, energize and give a "speed"
cheaply in CITY BRIGHT LIGHTS teenage disco-
bs/coffee houses; easily produce hallucinations and
g which reckless acts may be committed.

ALCOHOL MAKE EACH OTHER WORSE.
(see also THE WORRIED, p. 430).

: Both the leaf and the resin of cannabis or the
are used by drug takers . . . LEAF (called pot/
like dried grass clippings or herbal tobacco which
cigarette paper, rolled into a crude cigarette (a
nd passed round from hand to hand so each per-
s . . . RESIN, or the solid extract (called hash),
in climates not suited to marijuana-growing and
ll crumbly black/brown/yellow bouillon cube;
han grass unless it has been adulterated with
ish/wax and can be smoked in a joint when
ong ordinary tobacco OR baked in a cake—and
ith a cup of tea—when beaten in with the flour

acid diethylamide): A mind-expanding drug
dropped) in pill form, some pinhead-size pills
id); it can also be dropped on sugar cubes or
ND has strongest effect of all the drugs. LSD
—a colorless, odorless, tasteless liquid. ASCOR-
AMIN C) BOUGHT FROM DRUG STORES

When in doubt, find out.

Telephone the local hospital. Ask where the clinic is and exactly how it is labeled—to avoid having to ask embarrassing questions later.

Don't feel furtive. Over half of those who visit clinics find they are not infected with VD. Treatment cures completely. When treatment is prompt, it is short/easy/painless. And totally confidential (no need for a letter from your doctor). There is no atmosphere of criticism or reproach, no notifying the police (it is not a crime) nor are you duty-bound to say whom you caught it from.

The doctor will question you about recent sex life; he needs correct answers to make an accurate diagnosis. If you do have

SIGNS

WOMEN	MEN
	Gonorrhea
Hard to detect; often either NO symptoms or very slight ones—	Almost always noticeable with immediate symptoms—
—light vaginal discharge	—yellow discharge from penis
—need to urinate frequently	—itch to urinate frequently
—burning sensation when you do	—sensation of passing bits of broken glass
—upset periods (may develop almost at once or perhaps take several weeks; but delay in display of symptoms causes spread of gonorrhea as woman can be carrier unaware because of no symptoms)	
Later . . . low abdominal pain/sickness/fever could mean consequent complications like blocking of fallopian tubes; results in infertility, total sterility or permanent pain in pelvis	Disease leads to sterility in males if left untreated
Incubation period: 2–21 days	Incubation period: the same as for women

WOMEN	MEN

Syphilis

(30 times rarer than gonorrhea, as easily cured, but far more deadly if NOT treated)

WOMEN	MEN
FIRST SIGN: Painless ulcer which may be internal and go unnoticed (ulcer can be around sex organs or inside mouth)	FIRST SIGN: Painless ulcer on penis which feels like squeaker button on toy Teddy bear. It can ooze or crust over, then disappear (sex organs/mouth/anus can be ulcer site instead)
ULCER DISAPPEARS IF LEFT UNTREATED (start of *second stage*); again, vague symptoms—	
—painless coppery skin rash	Symptoms during *second and third stage* are same as for females
—aches and pains	UNTREATED THIRD-STAGE YEARS LATER CAN CAUSE MADNESS/BLINDNESS/ HEART DISEASE FOR MEN AND WOMEN—AND BE FATAL
—run-down feeling, etc. (disease is highly infectious at this stage; symptoms can vary erratically over years without treatment, then disappear)	
If allowed to pass into *third stage* disease lies low until you are ill/ injured/weak and strike fatally	
A woman who feels no symptoms can pass syphilis on to her child	

Incubation period for women/men usually three weeks but can be up to 90 days

---

VD or any sexually transmitted disease, follow medical advice and abstain from liquor and sex for the stated period.

TELL THE OTHER PERSON

A girl may be totally unaware she is infected possibly until years later. An affected male can pass on VD during the seven–ten days between infection and the appearance of symptoms—if he is promiscuous—to even more females.

OTHER SEXUALLY PASSED INFECTIONS (common diseases transmitted by sexual contact):

NONSPECIFIC URI
tract with symptoms sir
infection of vagina w
THRUSH: irritation wh
course—itchy-with-disc
rhea; VENEREAL SCA
WARTS: growth aroun
infesting pubic hair see
benzyl benzoate emulsi

OBNOXIOUSLY DRUNK

There are two ways to
know what he is doing
can absorb three knocko
EITHER

1. Push the drunk's head
   legs, grip the wrist o
   is helpless AND prop
   him going, keep up n
   OR
2. Grasp the seat of his
   forward on his neck; l
   him forward. Keep hi

DRUGS

Don't be smug. Liquo
—from cups of coffee to
they may develop a cravi
alcohol.
*Take extra care when
in entertainment centers*
WATCH THESE DRUG

1. BLACK COFFEE +
   No proof you will sc
   should work too; both
2. TOBACCO + ALCO

Heart w
smoking
to dilate
3. SEDAT
   ALCOH
   Barbitur
   dictive a
   dose alo
4. ANTID
   Great s
   with so
5. ALCOH
   REVER
   Psychol
   high; s
   theques
   terror o

MARIJUAN
DON'T DR
MARIJU.
marijuana
tea/grass)
is poured i
reefer or jo
son has 2–
is more co
looks like
it is stron
incense/sh
crumbled i
washed do
and eggs.
LSD (l
usually ta
(called m
blotting p
looks like
BIC ACI

WITHOUT A PRESCRIPTION WILL REDUCE A TERRIFY-
ING LSD EXPERIENCE (500 mg. is the amount needed).

HEROIN: White tablets or powder which have to be dissolved
in hot water before injecting (called fixing). THE major drug
problem . . . although in the early stages few would-be addicts
feel they will be hooked. However, the skin-popper soon becomes
a mainliner, fixing his or her habit into the blood vessels. Over
90 per cent of drug addiction is heroin. The addict craves for
increasing amounts to gain the same effect.

OTHER ILLEGAL DRUGS include:

OPIUM (looks like soft black hash made from poppyseed sap
and is usually smoked in a pipe).

PHYSEPTONE (addict's substitute for heroin, because it is
cheaper).

COCAINE (expensive white powder which addicts take like
snuff).

DRUG OVERDOSES . . . see THE COLD-BLOODED
(p. 187).

THE IMPERVIOUS *are NOT swayed by the opinion of others
when they don't REALLY want to try experimenting with drugs.
SO THEY DON'T.*

NOR ARE THEY EASILY LED FURTHER AGAINST
THEIR WILL WHEN—IF THEY DID WEAKEN—THEY
WANT OUT. THEY DAMN WELL DO AS THEY PLEASE
. . . AND STOP IN TIME.

REMEMBER . . . *reliance on drugs can mean you wake up
at 30 and find ten years of YOUR life missing with nothing to
show. Not even friends. Your ASSOCIATES are other users.*

OF THE DRUGS . . .

MARIJUANA makes you susceptible to suggestion; the initiate
can be persuaded under its influence to try harder drugs.

LSD is so potent that a single dose may cause irreparable
damage to brain cells, psychotic behavior, suicidal tendencies and
damage to the genes.

HEROIN induces loss of interest in school/job/sex; fits of excitement, outbursts of anger, periods of depression AND a loneliness in which the user refuses to eat. The craving increases with

the need for the drug and, with it, the need to commit violence. WHEN AFRAID DRUGS ARE GETTING HOLD (you can't ignore the signs by then):
KNOW...

1. ADDICTION *CAN* BE ENDED.
2. EARLY DISCOVERY AND DIAGNOSIS ARE VITAL.
3. PARENTS/FRIENDS SHOULD LOOK FOR SIGNS OF CONTAMINATION WHEN THEY SUSPECT.
4. IMMEDIATE HELP TO THE VICTIM IS NECESSARY.
5. HELP IS AVAILABLE FOR EVERYBODY TODAY. CONSULT YOUR DOCTOR. MAKE USE OF RELIGIOUS HELP. AVAIL YOURSELF OF SYMPATHETIC FAMILY/FRIENDS.

Parents can help youngsters. Explain that drug addicts work hard to collect new victims—to ease their own loneliness. Don't begrudge gifts of food and money to offspring who have left home for the city—even if you get no thanks for them. Encourage your youngster(s) to share an apartment with friends—cheaper/safer/companionable.

The Baby-faced (Trouble-shooter)

Is a contradiction in terms—the cliché from 1,002 films and TV plays who is never what he or she appears to be. And who, in fact, is much less susceptible than he or she may look.

Things are never what they seem, so why should we be? This is why THE BABY-FACED—already starring in THE HARD ONE—practices firing holes in arguments as Billy The Kid riddled bean cans/silver dollars/spent bullets from 32½ paces when in training.

Only people don't expect it from sweet-looking YOU. . . . YOUR very strength *when those virginal/naive/innocent looks make you a victim-target of the unscrupulous in the first place.*

TAKE POTSHOTS

If you suspect your drink is spiked (or you are being liquor-plied while your partner stays sober) . . . (1) put *his* hand around your glass, (2) place YOUR hand on his glass, (3) explain the ritual whereby two people toast each other by linking arms, each swallowing the other's drink, (4) crook your arm round his elbow, still holding the drink, (5) see if he balks as you sip.

COCK AN EYE

Watch out for transvestites (see THE RELAXED, p. 436) in women's restrooms.

Male thieves dressed as women look for victims in lavatories (they pretend to be fixing their makeup, snatch property while the victim is engaged and mingle with drinkers/dancers/clubbers outside).

Watch handbags/coat pockets/luggage.

Do NOT leave rings or watches beside the washbasin when washing.

COCK BOTH EARS

. . . at a chirping or hissing sound nearby in a CITY BRIGHT LIGHTS throng whose source is not obvious.

Rub the back of your neck to feel your wallet with the inside of opposite elbow. Don't relax if it is still in place. That sound is a pickpockets' signal (see THE LONG-SUFFERING, p. 71).

MAKE GUNPLAY

The crudest forgeries go undetected in intimately lit clubs/bars/discotheques, favorite places for passing them on to the unsuspecting.

Always *feel* your change. Don't just count it.

Form your right hand into a gun when receiving large bills as change; the forefinger is the barrel. Slot it down the U of a folded note and feel both sides of the U with a thumb-and-middle-finger motion. Does it "crackle"?

Don't just use thumb-and-forefinger motion while nipping the U of a folded note in between; obvious forgeries can escape this way.

Make a point of fingering notes given as change so you question it at once if you FEEL you have been tendered bad paper.

Practice the test even on $1 bills to make the motion unobtrusive.

FIRE OFF

Remind a friend to watch his wallet during an evening out in CITY BRIGHT LIGHTS when he is showing you the town, *especially when he warns you first that villains here will steal even your pockets.* That companion is just the type to have his pocket picked as a result.

Watch wallets (and do YOURself a favor).

HOLD FIRE

Is a girl a prostitute? Avoid fantasies brought on by candle/moon/strobe lighting.

Not all working girls are obvious. Don't jump the gun.

It is impossible to tell by dress/appearance/posture. Average CITY BRIGHT LIGHTS streetwalks are better dressed than many tourists. Inside entertainment center bars/ballroom/clubs, often the only way to be sure is to wait for girls to approach you.

Prostitutes who ask you straight if you are looking for "company"/"nice time"/"business" are often straight-shooting themselves. They will make their approach soon after meeting and won't try to double-cross the john.

THINK!—if this is NOT the case. BEWARE OF THE GIRL YOU FEEL SURE IS A PROSTITUTE BUT WHO SEEMS CONTENT TO SPEND TIME WITH YOU AND DOES NOT MENTION MONEY.
DANGER SIGNS:

Asking you to buy her—and her friends—a string of drinks; *asking* you to buy her meal/cigarettes/gift; leading remarks; going back to her place where she may cut your hair/watch TV with you/make you coffee, but . . . no sex.

Many victims go along with the belief that she may be a pros-

titute but that she wants them for themselves—that this is their lucky night. And so they fail to mention money in case this should risk destroying their fantasies. Result: They are often robbed and get no sex.

The safest way to find a prostitute (although by now you should know better) is through a well-tipped hotel room service clerk/bellhop/bell captain . . . bartenders . . . cab driver . . .

KILL THE LIGHT

Suddenly switch off the light in a room which may contain a two-way mirror . . . with its attendant risk of blackmail should you be filmed in compromising positions. (A two-way mirror is an ordinary sheet of transparent glass with a thin deposit of silver or copper zinc applied on one side. So long as the light in YOUR room is kept at two and a half times the light in the room on the other side of the glass, it appears as a mirror on your side and as a window in the darker room. If you switch off the light before the people behind the glass have time to do the same, their light shines through.)

Don't say you are going to switch off the light. Just do it.

SHOOT ACROSS

Pick off the least busy aisle/stairway/ramp during a movie or show intermission when you leave your seat—even though it may mean stepping past people still seated. Avoid packed gangways.

Busy aisles, etc. are a favorite haunt of pickpockets, who have had the opportunity to scan the audience from the theater rear before the lights went down. They jostle the victim as he or she steps into the crush.

Wait until things quiet down if everywhere is busy AND you are carrying a lot of money.

DRAW A BEAD

Carefully aim to turn off the too-friendly stranger in a bar who you suspect may be a con man.

SOME TIP-OFFS:

IF he calls himself "doctor" (a better ploy even than "broker"/
"lawyer"/"sportsman" to win trust); IF he tells a joke and a
nearby stranger overhears and finishes off the punch line (then
the pair of them work on you); IF he shows you a "miracle" which
really does amaze (pills that turn water into beer/fatal fascination
tablets that work/palm reading that tells of a secret in your past).
    Say "Oh."
    Repeat as many times as necessary.
    Don't try to be smart. City con men can tie a victim in knots
in a battle of words/wills/wiles.
    "Oh" is the standard confidence trickster's answer when playing
along a victim.
    Avoid committing yourself *before* the subject of money is raised.
Expect a con when buttonholed in any CITY BRIGHT LIGHTS
area.
    Other noncommittal phrases are:
    "Really?"
    "Is that so?"
    "I wonder!"
    "Lay it on me, dude."
    Play dumb when it is suggested you should in some way, part
with hard cash NOW (as loan/investment/sign of good faith).

GET THE DROP—1

Anticipate the pickpocket who admires your suit in a bar. He
looks inside for the tailor's name, feeling the cloth between one
hand on the outside and the other which remains on the inner
lining (and steals the wallet).

GET THE DROP—2

Beware of tipsy neighbor at the bar who, while engaging you in
conversation casually holds cigarette so burning tip is in vicinity
of your trouser's seat.

Auto-suggestion distracts (you imagine you begin to feel red-hot pinprick scorching through cloth). And the wire/hook/mechanic *on your other side* empties contents of nearest pockets as you look to see if cigarette has burned through (and tipsy "neighbor" apologizes, brushing nonexistent bits of ash away).

GUN DOWN

Kill suggestions to kill time with friendly games for low stakes (see THE WISE GUY, p. 22). (ANY game can be rigged; even when you are good at pool/dice/cards there is always somebody better—and all hustlers are good. The victim always has more money than ability; watch out especially when you have recently won on horses or collected a bonus.)

TIP-OFFS:

WHEN the idea of a game is put to you; WHEN you win several small amounts in opening games; WHEN the opponent acts embarrassed at losing; WHEN he says, "My friend over there will give you a bit more opposition"; WHEN the second player loses narrowly too; WHEN he suggests raising the pot with a look of desperation; WHEN he narrowly beats you and suggests a final game.

NEVER PLAY WITH STRANGERS. *Only play—if you must —in reputable clubs where everyone is known.*

STOP IN TRACKS

Stop dead any attempt by a stranger to bet with you on the result of games between other strangers (hustlers triple their take by laying side bets with spectators on the result of games).

Recognize the signs (see also THE WISE GUY, p. 22).

EXAMPLE: You meet hustler A (braggart) in a bar with pool table; he asks if you know any girls and flashes a wallet full of money as he buys drinks. Hustler B (friendly) apparently overhears, says he knows some and goes to phone. Hustler B returns to say the girls will be over in a couple of hours—how about him and hustler A shooting pool to kill time. Obnoxious hustler A begins to lose heavily; hustler B manages to suggest at an opportune moment that you should go to the bank, draw some money and bet on him because he's going to whip objectionable hustler A. The victim who does this finds that in the end hustler A's game suddenly improves and he wins by a couple of points. Victim is then hurried away in a supposed police raid, hustlers disappearing with his money.

LEVEL AT BARGAINS

Hand back supposedly stolen goods going cheaply in bar/club/ dance hall. Turn the merchandise down politely. Say you already have "one like this." Or you are out of work—broke.

Don't underestimate the plausibility of a barroom trader. Nor the toughness of his breed (the reason why you should be polite).

SHOTS IN THE DARK

Unholster your suspicions in a movie theater so that events— other than on screen—don't take you by surprise.

Question your own motivations. WHY are you sitting in this particular seat, wearing this outfit or behaving in that way?

MAKE YOUR MOVE:

1. SHIFT TO A DISTANT SEAT when a man sits next to you despite rows of empty seats nearby AND you have blond tresses/ phosphorescent blouse/psychedelic earrings which glow in the dark.

2. GO TO ANOTHER SEAT when most are occupied but a neighboring male presses against your arms/shins/shoes with his biceps/legs/feet. OR he may reach for your hand when he thinks you have returned the pressure to his shoe (and he had unknowingly been pressing on the seat support in front with his foot).

3. MOVE YOUR HANDBAG/CAMERA/PURSE TO YOUR LAP and keep hold throughout the film. Avoid the temptation to place your possessions on adjacent vacant seat. Example: drunk/ derelict/unpleasant person makes his way along YOUR row of

seats. To prevent his sitting in the next seat, you place a handbag by your side to indicate that the seat is spoken for—and you forget to take it back on your lap, so making it an easy target for the seat-tipper (see also THE SYBARITE, p. 76).

4. PUSH REVERENCE ASIDE . . . seat-tipping thefts happen during opening nights/gala performances/grand opera.

Keep alert when you look forward to being entertained. And find you are.

The Loser (Apparent) or Crazy Brave

Knows how to handle himself but, of all the Winners, he is the one who needs to most of all because—despite all warnings—he still ignores his weaknesses and deliberately heads toward danger.

Yet it is THE LOSERS who, when they find the trouble which they seem to go out of their way to seek, actually stand a chance of getting away with it. And when they fail, perhaps that was what they subconsciously wanted anyway.

These apparently foolhardy and seemingly irresponsible people —in spite of their own self-destructive efforts—succeed in surviving where the normal self-preservationist fails.

BADGERED

When you *would* go with a girl from a bad part of town . . . PAY UP when "surprised" by her male accomplice who is armed and catches you both in bed (see THE BORED, p. 11, and THE WINNER, p. 413).

If you are attacked because you don't have enough money, or argue or throw a punch . . . your assailant may use a knife (see THE FUGITIVE, p. 202).

A chair in the room is his other favorite weapon:

1. DUCK OUT OF HIS WAY AS HE GRASPS THE CHAIR. (Forget about pulling on pants or buttoning shirt.)
2. BLOCK HIS BLOW WITH ANOTHER CHAIR OR SOME HANDY OBJECT.

3. OR STEP IN AND . . . FLASH A HAND FOR HIS FACE as if tossing something into his eyes. As he closes them for a split second, stride forward with your right foot, THEN step back on your left foot. Duck low below the uplifted chair. Grasp his left ankle with your left hand and, *as you yank up,* smash your right forearm just over his kneecap. Apply more pressure on this powerful lever as he falls on his back and drops the chair.

VICTIMIZED

When nothing will stop you from exploring honky-tonk and waterfront bars in rough districts, try to blend. Present a low profile.

Take your bottom teeth out. Do not "look over company" (i.e., stare at strangers). DANGER SIGN: When a drinker stares at you hard and rubs the side of his nose with a finger, he is indicating you are being too nosy.

Undo your tie and take it off. Unbutton the top buttons of your shirt. Let your eyes glaze a little. Rumple your hair more than usual. Look at no one other than within passing stare that swings from side to side. Let your shirt hang over your waist. Pull your socks down so that, sitting at a bar cross-legged, you expose white shins. Dot tattoo marks around with a ballpoint pen. Your fingers should be grubby. Pick up discarded newspaper on the bar but read only the horse-racing pages; figure out betting selections—even when you don't gamble—with a stub of pencil in a slow drunken scrawl; don't flinch from an aggressive drunk who annoys you; shake your head as if you are drunk, no focus to the eyes; don't complain if your drink is stolen or your change lying on the bar disappears. Look as though you have a right to be here *because you are down on your luck,* NEVER as if you are slumming for kicks.

ROLLED

You have had a ball in CITY BRIGHT LIGHTS bars. Foil those about to take advantage.

UPEND assailant who tries to give you the bum's rush (see

also THE IMPERVIOUS, p. 449) down flight of stairs/toward dark alley/into strange car. . . . As he grasps the scruff of your neck and tries to force your head down with his right hand, step backward suddenly to place your left foot behind his right shoe; fling your left arm up across the front of his body AND reach your right hand behind his right knee as fast as possible; force back with left arm, lift with right hand AND straighten your knees to throw him on his back.

Beware of the friendly stranger who guides you along the sidewalk. When too drunk to avoid him, however, avoid violence if you feel his fingers in your pockets. Sacrifice the loose change kept there so long as you secured the rest of your money previously (see THE CANNY, p. 40, and THE LEERY, p. 47).

Shrug him off. Act stupid. Walk away alone.

Submit when cornered by several thugs. Let the small change scattered through your pockets go. You may lose the money in your socks too, but you knew it *could* happen if you got into this state.

UNSATISFIED

You ask for trouble with a prostitute when you ignore these DANGERS . . . trying to kiss her when she says "no" (VD risk is one reason); persisting in trying to make love when drink/guilt/drugs have made you impotent; arguing when she turns you down because she discovers you have crabs/VD/dirty body and insisting she should return the money you paid; attempting to prolong love-making when you paid only for a "short time"; going to her (or hotel) room knowing you don't have the amount of money you promised to pay and hoping she will take a lesser amount; not expecting her to ask you for the cost of the hotel room as an extra when you had already agreed the cost of her services.

Don't start arguments. And never ask for your money back. You won't get it. Cut your losses and leave.

Do hand over some cash for her trouble (to save trouble) when you have wasted her time—like changing your mind at the room door.

If you were prepared to enter into business transactions in the first place, be prepared to abide by her code too. Pay up. Look a gentleman.

DON'T let a prostitute kiss you while she kneels on the floor and you lie on the bed (this leaves both her hands free to run through your jacket and trouser pockets which she has previously kicked underneath).

STEERED

If you know you shouldn't, but you DO (allow a stranger to take you to "girls" or a "live sex show" on his say-so) DON'T . . . (1) sort money furtively from one pocket to another as you walk with him so that when it comes to paying you will be able to pull out the minimum money and not your whole wallet (he will still see you); (2) NEVER hand over money until you are *with* the girls or inside the door of the "club." (The risk is NOT that he will vanish if you advance him money to "show the management as proof that you are bona fide"—he *will* return. The risk is when he next asks for your wallet on some pretext and now you trust him. . . .)

ROOKED

You still play cards with strangers (see also THE BORED, p. 11). You suspect they are cheating and letting you win . . . .

It is worse still when you think that they think you have been cheating.

1. BE PREPARED BEFORE YOU PLAY TO LOSE ONLY A PREDETERMINED SUM OF MONEY. You require from 30–50 times the limit of the game as the amount you are ready to lose —and after that you stop. Anything from $30 to $50, for example, when the limit is $1.
2. STATE THE AMOUNT OF CASH YOU HAVE TO STAKE BEFORE PLAYING. AND THE TIME YOU INTEND TO FINISH.
3. DON'T BE PERSUADED BY JEERS/TAUNTS/JIBES FROM

STICKING TO YOUR INTENTIONS (DON'T TAKE OFFERS OF LOANS).

Secure the money you have in reserve on other parts of your person (see THE CANNY, p. 40). Don't dip into this after losing your original stake. Just go.

DON'T . . . sit with your back to the wall (and hidden mirror or spyhole) . . . OR trust two players who appear enemies (and may be setting you up with a system of signals) . . . OR play long in games where the same players consistently win small amounts (know their cheating will soon bring large winnings too) . . . OR discount the possibility of three straight players ganging up (all they need do is keep raising to force you out; YOUR resources fail to compete against a three-combined-as-one stake).

DO . . . ensure hands from previous play are well shuffled into the deck when YOU deal . . . check that hands tossed into discard are properly separated so no winning combinations are bunched together (beware of the dealer who casually picks them up and slaps them on the end of the pack) . . . cut AWAY from the dealer when he taps the pack suggesting you cut toward him . . . when it is your turn cut high or low rather than in the center . . . be alert for a "crimp" (a card bent slightly so the deck cuts naturally at that point); overcrimping can cause an obvious bridge in the deck—point it out without accusing anybody and call a misdeal.

REMEMBER THE RISKS OF PLAYING CARDS AND DRINKING.

ALCOHOL AFFECTS YOUR BETTING/JUDGMENT/MEMORY AND WILL CANCEL OUT GOOD INTENTIONS REGARDING POINTS 1–3.

ATTACKED

Bottle/fists/chair are usual barroom weapons to expect when the fighting drunk is enraged just because you are there.

The attacker will often aim for your face or head. ACT FAST on receiving the danger signals.

"SPLASH" (a glass of liquor is flung at your eyes):

1. BOUNCE STRAIGHT BACK AT SPLASHER.
2. HANG ON TO HIM UNTIL YOU CAN SEE AGAIN.
3. PUNCH HARD IN STOMACH/GROIN/CHIN. (Liquor-thrower counts on you clearing both eyes to give him time; your quick rebound takes him by surprise.)

"CLICK" (switchblade knife pulled . . . see THE FUGITIVE, p. 202).

"CRACK" (bottom is broken off a bottle AND the attacker cuts at you with it):

1. GRAB FOR SHIELD LIKE TRAY/STOOL/TABLE.
2. TRY TO SMASH BROKEN BOTTLE WITH HARD OBJECT LIKE ANOTHER BOTTLE OR SOLID ASHTRAY.

When there is nothing like this in reach EITHER throw the nearest drink into *his* eyes as a distraction (see THE FUGITIVE, p. 202) and hurl a glass in his face or crack it on his head OR . . . run at him, jump up with both feet, ram both shoes into his stomach (you will both go flying, but you will be safe for the moment and he will let go of the bottle).

"THONK" (about to happen if an attacker brings down a heavy bottle on your skull);

1. RAISE LEFT ARM HIGH IN FRONT OF YOU.
2. STEP IN CLOSE TO FEND OFF AS "BOTTLE" ARM DE-SCENDS.
3. WRAP LEFT ARM DOWN AND ROUND UPPER PART OF HIS RIGHT ("BOTTLE") ARM.
4. PULL IT IN TIGHTLY TO YOUR SIDE.
5. HIT HIM WITH RIGHT FIST AS BOTTLE MISSES.

"THWACK" (result of a chair wielded by a drunk smacking your head unless you act) . . .

1. CROSS BOTH ARMS QUICKLY IN FRONT OF FACE.
2. SAG AT KNEES AS YOU CATCH THE BLOW.
3. KICK AT HIS GROIN/SHIN/INSTEP . . .
      OR
A. LEAN BACK SUDDENLY AS CHAIR DESCENDS.
B. RAISE ARMS ABOVE YOU, AND AS IT MISSES—

C. HELP CHAIR ON ITS WAY PAST RIGHT INTO HIS OWN
ANKLES/SHINS/FEET.
OR
HURL YOUR BODY AT HIS FEET SO THE CHAIR MISSES
AND YOUR MOMENTUM ROLLS HIM OFF HIS FEET.

"WHOOSH" (antagonist lets go a roundhouse blow):

1. WATCH FOR WILD/SWINGING/SUPER HAYMAKERS.
2. LEAN TO THE RIGHT SO IT PASSES OVER LEFT
SHOULDER.
3. LOCK BOTH ARMS OVER AND NEAR HIS ELBOW.
4. PULL DOWN ON AND AGAINST THE JOINT TO KEEP
IT LOCKED.
5. TWIST TO YOUR RIGHT . . . and keep pulling down; your
assailant will have to bend over forward under pressure which
could break his arm or dislocate his shoulder or elbow.

"CRACK" (heads collide as an assailant butts you in the face):

1. KNOW THE DANGER WHEN LAPELS ARE GRABBED OR
YOUR HEADS ARE CLOSE TOGETHER.
2. LOWER HEAD SO BROW ANGLES FOR TOP OF HIS NOSE.
3. SMASH FOREHEAD ON TO BRIDGE OF HIS NOSE HARD
BEFORE HE MAKES HEAD-BUTTING MOVE.

"SMACK" (YOUR fist catches troublemaker first, BUT):

1. WATCH OUT IF HE HAS A THICK NECK AND ISN'T FAT.
2. IF HE DOESN'T FALL DOWN—RUN.

(To make the first punch good, *aim for the BACK of his head so
you have to go through his face to get there.* To make your punch
effective when outclassed, first slip a ring on to your right-hand
finger and place a broken matchstick between ring and finger so
the sharp end reinforces your punch.)

TAKEN FOR A SUCKER

*The same risks apply to rolling dice AND drinking as to play-
ing cards.*

CHECK HANDS:

1. SAY "Let's go—stop wasting time" when you suspect a player is switching crooked dice in and out of games.
2. SMARTLY TAP the back of his throwing hand which *looks cramped* AND any about-to-be-switched-dice illegally palmed will fall on the table.

TEST DICE:

MAGNETIZE (if you carry a magnet) . . . dice secretly controlled by hidden magnets will stick to your pocket one.

TOUCH with your fingers to feel for rough little burrs on certain numbers (they can cause the dice to tumble on to a smooth side when thrown on a baize-like surface).

COUNT to check that both dice DO total seven on opposite sides (misspotted dice go unnoticed in fast/confused/alcoholic barroom games).

SCRAPE your fingernail across the dice to feel if any edge is raised in a tiny ridge which can affect the tumble.

PRESS the dice between thumb and finger to feel if one side has been scooped slightly concave—done to ensure dice tumbles a certain way.

BALANCE different sides of both dice on top of each other; when the upper one wobbles, it has been beveled into slight belly shape (so it will flip over from this side on to a flat side).

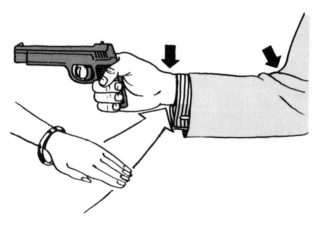

Disarm a gunman with a chop on a joint.

TEAM UP two dice on a flat surface to check all sides are square and NOT shaved/polished/sanded into out-of-true "shapes."

DIG your thumbnail into dice; if it leaves a mark, that side may have been chamfered away and replaced with a layer or cap of bouncy substance which affects the tumble of the dice.

RUB two dice together; BOTH "burred" and "capped" dice tend to stick together.

KNEAD the corners of transparent dice—when rounded, look closer to check if the dots of certain numbers have been drilled a little deeper to accommodate "loads."

PIVOT dice between thumb and finger lightly and spin to see if rotation always stops at the same numbers (because of an inner load).

DUNK dice in beer/water/lager to check if favorite numbers always settle in same position—because dice is loaded. OR, if dice has been hollowed on one *side,* dice will float favorite side up.

IGNITE dice accidentally-on-purpose with your cigarette lighter and the dice will burn away to reveal any load that is inside.

FLICK with a fingernail first, then pivot or dunk in liquid to check if dice has been loaded with mercury (this only moves to favorite position inside the dice when tapped first).

SUSPECT a thrower who manipulates honest dice . . . BY rattling only one dice in the cup while holding the other back in his throwing hand—to be slid out favorite number uppermost as the dice in the cup is released . . . BY applying "side spin" when the dice are shot by hand so that favorite numbers stay on top while dice rotate (watch for throwing hand flipped back quickly as middle fingers impart spin) . . . BY shooting dice from relaxed grip between first and little finger on to a cloth-covered surface so that both dice roll end over end only and the numbers on the sides never come up tops (a "blanket roll") . . . BY holding one dice above the other in his throwing hand so that the top dice is flicked off by third/fourth fingers while the bottom dice is slipped along polished surface—selected number on top.

GUNNED DOWN

When nothing will stop you NOT only exploring bad areas of a city where the risk of a shooting is high, *but also trying to disarm a gunman single-handed* (a gamble nothing short of suicidal) . . . the fastest way to disarm a pistol attacker is:

1. KNOW A REAL GUN CAN LOOK LIKE A PLASTIC COPY.
2. NEVER TAKE EYES FROM GUN.
3. MAKE A DISTRACTING MOVE (see THE ZEALOUS, p. 323).
4. FOLLOW UP INSTANTANEOUSLY WITH . . .
5. CHOP ON GUNMAN'S WRIST OR ELBOW JOINT WITH EDGE OF YOUR HAND AS HARD AS YOU CAN (AS SHOWN).

Such action is justified when you face cold-blooded execution from a gunman you recognize or who is demented/violent/frightened. Otherwise you chance your arm against a flick of his finger on the trigger as you make this *fatal* move . . . .

Postscript

PERHAPS YOU SHUNNED SURVIVAL ANYWAY THROUGH THAT SUBCONSCIOUS DESIRE WHICH, IF CERTAIN CAB DRIVERS/POLICEMEN/BANK CASHIERS REALLY DO CHOOSE OCCUPATIONS IN WHICH THEY CAN GET SHOT (AND IT HAS BEEN FOUND THAT SOME DO) BECAUSE OF THEIR HIDDEN URGE TO BECOME VICTIMS—THEN YOU HAVE FINALLY FULFILLED YOURSELF. WHEN NOTHING WILL CURB YOUR INBORN DEATH WISH, THERE IS NO EXPLANATION FOR SUCH FOOLHARDINESS OTHER THAN IT GAVE A STRANGE HAPPINESS AS YOU PRECIPITATED THE PURPLE FLASH . . . NOT QUITE THE LOSER YOU APPEAR TO BE TO THE VERY END.

INDEX